THE SITE'S ARCHITECTURE, ITS FIRST SIX HUNDRED YEARS OF DEVELOPMENT

Breyek Attiyeh el-Jiteily, Controller of Antiquities for Eastern Cyrenaica 1970-1988

University Museum Monograph 76

THE EXTRAMURAL SANCTUARY OF
DEMETER AND PERSEPHONE AT CYRENE, LIBYA
FINAL REPORTS
Donald White, Series Editor
VOLUME V

THE SITE'S ARCHITECTURE, ITS FIRST SIX HUNDRED YEARS OF DEVELOPMENT

Donald White

Published by

THE UNIVERSITY MUSEUM
The University of Pennsylvania
Philadelphia 1993

For
THE LIBYAN DEPARTMENT OF ANTIQUITIES
As-Saray Al-Hamra
Tripoli
People's Socialist Libyan Arab Jamahiriya

Design, editing, production
    Publications Department
    The University Museum

Printing
    Science Press
    Ephrata, Pennsylvania

Library of Congress Cataloging-in-Publication Data
(Revised for vol. 5)

The Extramural Sanctuary of Demeter and Persephone at Cyrene, Libya.

   (University Museum monograph ; 52,   )
   Arabic and English
   Spine title: Cyrene final reports.
   Excavations conducted by the University of Pennsylvania, Philadelphia and the Department of Antiquities of the People's Socialist Libyan Arab Jamahiriya.
   Two folded plans in pocket, v. 1.
   Includes bibliographical references and indexes.
   Contents: v. 1. Background and introduction to the excavations / Donald White –[etc.]– v. 3. The Site's architecture, its first six hundred years of development / Donald White –   – v. 5. The Site's architecture: its first six hundred years of development / Donald White.
   1. Sanctuary of Demeter and Persephone (Cyrene) 2. Cyrene (Extinct city) 3. Demeter (Greek deity)–Cult. 4. Persephone (Greek deity)–Cult. 5. Excavations (Archaeology–Libya. 6. Libya–Antiquities. I. White, Donald, 1935-   . II. University of Pennsylvania. University Museum. III. Libya. Maslahat al-Athar. IV. Cyrene final reports. V. Series: University Museum monograph ; 52, etc.
DT239.C9E98 1984   939'.75   83-19866
ISBN 0-934718-50-4 (set)
ISBN 0-934718-51-2 (v. 1)

Copyright © 1993
The University Museum
University of Pennsylvania
Philadelphia
All rights reserved
Printed in the United States of America

To Joan and Arthur for all those years in Cyrene.

In memory of Sandro Stucchi.

Contents

Figures...xi
Plates..xv
Minor Abbreviations xix
Bibliographical Abbreviations xxi
Preface..xxv
I   Introduction 1
II The Earliest Walled Remains Ca. 620-500 B.C. 5
      Recovery..5
      The Earliest Peribolos 7
          Peribolos South Wall 7
              Wall P3...7
              Wall P2...7
              Wall P13...7
              Wall P12...9
              Wall P11...11
          Context and Date of the Peribolos South Wall 11
              Wall P3...11
              Wall P2...14
              Wall P13...14
              Wall P12...14
              Wall P11...15
          Summary of the Dating Evidence for the Peribolos South Wall 16
          Peribolos Southeast Corner..18
          Context and Date of the Peribolos Southeast Corner 19
          Peribolos North Wall 20
          Context and Date of the Peribolos North Wall..24
          Peribolos West Wall...24
          Context and Date of the Peribolos West Wall 25
      The Earliest Peribolos, Some Final Observations 25
      Temenos Interior 26
          Wall P3A...26
          Wall P1 27
      Wall Features South of the Peribolos 29
          Walls P2, P4, P5, and P6..29
          Context and Date of Walls P2, P4, P5, P6..29
          Original Appearance of Walls P2, P4, P5, P6 30
      Early Wall Remains at the Level of the Upper Sanctuary 31
          Walled Structure P14 31
          Context and Date of Walled Structure P14...33
          Wall P15 33
          Context and Date of Wall P15 35
      Commentary..35
          Hillside Setting..37
          Peribolos Enclosure 38
          Dual Temene..39
          Building Techniques..41
III The Later Archaic, Early Classical Sanctuary Ca. 500-440 B.C. 43
      The Later Archaic Peribolos...44
          Recovery...44
          Appearance..44

  Peribolos South Wall...45
   Wall T1 45
   Wall T7 49
   Wall T6 49
  Context and Date of the Peribolos South Wall 50
   Wall T1 50
   Wall T7 53
   Wall T6 53
  Peribolos West Wall 53
   Wall T5 55
  Context and Date of the Peribolos West Wall 55
  Peribolos North Wall 56
   Wall T4 56
   Wall T3 56
  Context and Date of the Peribolos North Wall 56
   Wall T4 56
   Wall T3 57
  Peribolos East Wall 57
  Context and Date of the Peribolos East Wall 57
  Southern Extension of the Peribolos 57
Summary: Date and Layout of the Later Archaic Peribolos 57
Commentary 58
  Peribolos Plan 58
  Pseudoisodomic Masonry 58
   Second Artemisium 60
  Block Proportions 63
Later Archaic, Early Classical Structures south of the Peribolos 71
  S3 Ashlar Structure 71
  Context and Date of the S3 Ashlar Structure 72
  S4 Ashlar Structure 73
   North Wall 73
   West Wall 76
   East-West Partition Wall 76
  Context and Date of the S4 Ashlar Structure 77
  Commentary 78
Pseudoisodomic Bislab Walls South of the Peribolos 79
  S2 Building 79
   East Wall 80
   West Wall 80
  Context and Date of S2 Building 81
   East Wall 81
   West Wall 81
  Commentary 82
  Wall W30 82
  Context and Date of Wall W30 82
  S19 Structure 82
Interior of the Walled Temenos 83
  S1 Sacred House 83
  Context and Date of the S1 Sacred House 85
  S5 Sacred House 86
   Building Interior 86
   West Wall 86
   South Wall 87
   East Wall 88
   North Wall 88
   Superstructure 88
   Associated Sculpture 91
  Context and Date of the S5 Sacred House 93
  Sacred House S6 94
   Building Interior 94

South Wall	94
West Wall	94
Door	95
Context and Date of the S6 Sacred House	95
Wall W38	98
Commentary	98
Building Type	98
Cult Bench	104
Masonry	106
IV The Later Classical Sanctuary Ca. 440-330 B.C.	**107**
Southeast Corner of the Peribolos: Wall W2	109
Context and Date of Wall W2	113
Western Extension of the T1 South Peribolos: Wall T8	113
Context and Date of Wall T8	114
Retaining Wall W1	115
Context and Date of Wall W1	116
Water Channel F3	116
Context and Date of Water Channel F3	117
V The Hellenistic, Early Roman Sanctuary Ca. 330-31 B.C.	**119**
The Hellenistic Replacements to the Peribolos	121
Recovery	121
East Wall of the Peribolos: Wall T9	121
Context and Date of Wall T9	122
Southeast Corner of the Peribolos: Wall T9A	122
Context and Date of Wall T9A	123
Northwest Corner of the Peribolos	123
West Wall of the Peribolos: Wall T14	124
Context and Date of Wall T14	124
Southwest Corner of the Peribolos: Wall T15	125
Date of Wall T15	126
Extension South of the Peribolos?: Wall T17	126
Context and Date of Wall T17	127
Commentary	127
Peribolos Plan	127
Peribolos Wall Masonry	130
Earliest Version of the Upper Sanctuary Propylaeum?	132
Context and Date of Wall W3	133
Courtyard Entrance?	137
Context and Date of the G1 Threshold	138
Upper Sanctuary Fountain Complex and Drain	138
Context and Date of the F2 Podium and Wall W29	140
Context and Date of the F4 Conduit	140
Commentary	140
F1 Fountain and R3 Steps	141
Context and Date of the F1 Fountain and R3 Steps	142
Commentary	144
Middle Sanctuary Steps	147
R1 Steps	147
Context and Date of R1 Steps	148
R3 Steps	148
R4 Steps	148
Context and Date of R4 Steps	148
Middle Sanctuary Access to Upper Sanctuary	149
R2 Steps, G5 Doorway, and S31 Structure	149
Context and Date of the S31 Structure, R2 Steps, and G5 Doorway	150
S7 Sacred House	151
Wall Foundation Trench	152
Stone	153
West Wall	153
East Wall	155

South Wall	158
North Wall	158
Building Interior	158
Painted Decoration	159
Context and Date of the S7 Sacred House	160
Commentary	160
Painted Interior	160
House Contents	162
Restoration of the S7 Sacred House	163
Comparative Structures	167
S11 Storage Chamber	170
North and East Walls	170
West and South Walls	171
Roof	171
Context, Date, and Function of the S11 Storage Chamber	171
S12 Chamber	172
South Wall: W10	172
North Wall	172
East Wall	172
Roof and Late Modifications	174
Context, Date, and Function of the S12 Chamber	174
Commentary	175
VI Conclusion	177
Appendix I	
Dates of Archaeological Contexts Organized by Area, Trench, Stratum, and Classes of Objects	187
Appendix II	
Block Height-to-Length Ratios	197
Index	199
Arabic Summary by Jamal el-Harami	213–201

Figures

1	Trans-site section I	follows page 6
2	Trans-site section II	follows page 6
3	Trans-site section III	follows page 6
4	Trans-site sections IV and IVa	follows page 6
5	Trans-site section V	follows page 6
6	Trans-site section VI	follows page 6
7	Trans-site section VII	follows page 6
8	Trans-site section VIII	follows page 6
9	Trans-site section IX	follows page 6
10	Trans-site section X	follows page 6
11	Trans-site section XI	follows page 6
12	Plan of site's Areas and Trenches	follows page 6
13	Plan of southeast quarter of sanctuary periboloi	8
14	Plan of S6 Sacred House	12
15	Section of D15/16, 1 fill	13
16	Section of D12/13, A	16
17	Section of fill in D12/E12, D	17
18	Section of fill in E10/11 (Area 1) 1	20
19	Section of fill of D11/E11 balk	21
20	Section from P3 peribolos wall	21
21	Section of fill in E10 balk	22
22	Section of F14/G14 fill	23
23	Section of fill associated with peribolos walls P8 and P9	25
24	Section of fill between P9 and its T4 replacement	27
25	Section of fill covering P10 wall	28
26	Section of fill over P3 wall and at west end of D12/13, A	33
27	Section of fill between S15 Colonnade Vestibule and S17 Southwest Building	34
28	Plan of southwest corner of Sanctuary (C15/16, 1)	36
29	Perspective drawing of southeast corner of peribolos	48
30	Reconstruction of wall T1	49
31	Section of fill covering T1	51
32	Section of fills in D11/12, A, E11, 3, (Area 1) 2 and E11, 2	52
33	Section of fill in D12/13, A	53
34	Plan of "Second Artemisium"	64
35	Elevation of walls of Artemisium pronaos and naos	64
36	Elevation of wall of Artemisium	65
37	Elevation of walls of Artemisium pronaos and naos	65

38	Elevation of cross-wall and inner door of Artemisium	68
39	Elevation of cross-wall and marble outer door of Artemisium	68
40	Phase plan of Artemisium	71
41	Elevation of S3 structure	73
42	Elevation of S21 Propylaeum Court	75
43	Section of fill accumulated against S21 and S3	76
44	Elevation of W21 and W24 walls across south end of C12/13, 1	77
45	Section of fill over S4 building	45
46	Section of fill at south end of C11, 1 and C11, 2	83
47	Combination elevation and section, illustrating S2's east wall	84
48	Section of fill at south end of C11, 1 and C11, 2	85
49	Section of south balk of C15/16, 1	85
50	Section of north balk of C15/16, 1	86
51	Plan of S1 Sacred House	89
52	Section of balk covering W1 wall and S1	91
53	Section of balk covering W1 wall and S1	91
54	Plan of S5 Sacred House	92
55	Elevation of west wall of S5	96
56	Elevation of south wall of S5	96
57	Elevation of east wall of S5	97
58	Section of E13/F13, 1 fill	100
59	Elevation of north face of southeast corner of Middle Sanctuary	110
60	Elevation of walls of S23 Late Structure	110
61	Section of fill between T8 peribolos and S15 Colonnaded Vestibule	111
62	Section of fill in D14, 1 and C14, 1	111
63	Section of east balk of D11/12, 1	112
64	Section of west balk of D11/12, 1	112
65	Section of D12 balk	113
66	Section of D12 balk	116
67	Elevation of interior face of T9 peribolos	122
68	Section of fill east of S20 Propylaeum	123
69	Section of fill east of T14 peribolos wall	125
70	Elevation of T14	126
71	Perspective drawing of fill deposited against T14	127
72	Section of fill across S20	132
73	Drawing of fragmentary limestone door jamb	133
74	Section of fill across S20	134
75	Plan and elevation of G1 threshold	135
76	Elevation of wall of F2 water tank	136
77	Drawing of marble lion's head water spout	137
78	Section of fill between S17 Southwest Building and wall W29	138
79	Section of fill covering F2	140
80	Plan of F1 fountain	142

81	Elevation of F1's walls	142
82	Section of east balk F11/12	144
83	Elevation of T8 wall	150
84	Section of G5 and G6 doorways	151
85	Plan of S7 Sacred House	152
86	Elevation of S7's west wall	153
87	Elevation of S7's east wall	153
88	Elevation of east wall and cross-section of south wall of S7	154
89	Elevation of S7's south wall	154
90	Elevation of south wall and cross-sections of east and west walls of S7	154
91	Plan of S7 with blocking	155
92	Section of F11, 1 fill	156
93	North facade of S7	164
94	Restored elevation of south wall of S7	164
95	Restored exterior of S7	165
96	Restored west wall of S7	165
97	Pilaster capital, doorway of S7	166
98	Horizontal cornice from S7	167
99A	Type **C:2** cover tile	167
99B	Type **D:2** pan tile	167
100	Elevation of facade of naiskos of Thea Basileia	168
101	Plan of naiskos of Thea Basileia	169
102	Cross-section of naiskos of Thea Basileia	169
103	Elevation of W10 wall of S12 Chamber and its W9 capping	174
Plan A	Plan of early Archaic sanctuary	follows page 198
Plan B	Plan of later Archaic, early Classical sanctuary	follows page 198
Plan C	Plan of later Classical sanctuary	follows page 198
Plan D	Plan of Hellenistic, pre-Imperial Roman sanctuary	follows page 198
Plan E	Plan of sanctuary at its fullest development	follows page 198
Plan F	Evidential plan of sanctuary	follows page 198
Plan G	Phase plan and elevation of Middle Sanctuary's north wall system	follows page 198

Plates

1	Sanctuary of Demeter and Persephone	2
2	Middle Sanctuary grounds	3
3	Early Archaic and later Archaic sanctuary walls	6
4	Central section of P3 south wall	9
5	East end of P3 southern peribolos wall	9
6	South face of P3 peribolos wall	10
7	Wall P2	10
8	North face of peribolos wall P11	13
9	South face of P11	14
10	Southwest end of P11	15
11	Traces of compacted yellow earth floor (St. 3a)	16
12	Section of D15/16, 1 fill	17
13	D15/16, 1, 6 argillaceous floor	18
14	Southwest corner of S8 Sacred House	18
15	Center of Middle Sanctuary	19
16	P7 southeast corner of peribolos	20
17	F14/G14 trench	22
18	F14/G14 test sounding	23
19	P8 wall interfacing with P9 wall	24
20	Fill across east end of F14/G14 sounding	26
21	P9 wall	27
22	P10 peribolos west wall	28
23	Rubble wall P1	29
24	Spur walls to north of T1	31
25	Detail of P6 wall	32
26	Detail of P5 wall	32
27	South face of T1	33
28	Walled Structure P14	34
29	P15 rubble wall	35
30	Southeast corner of Middle Sanctuary	45
31	Southeast corner of pseudoisodomic bislab peribolos	46
32	South face of T1 in D12/13, B	47
33	Detail of south face of T1	47
34	Iron drove-chisel	49
35	Section of T1 bislabs in area D12/13	50
36	West end of south wall of T6 peribolos	51
37	Southwest corner of peribolos	54

38	T5 west wall of peribolos	54
39	East end of Middle Sanctuary retaining wall system	55
40	Detail view of wall T3	56
41	Later Classical and Roman period Artemisium	61
42	Frontal view of Roman period porch of Artemisium	61
43	Detail of Artemisium door	62
44	Detail of Artemisium's lintel inscription	62
45	Marble door of Artemisium	63
46	Northern exterior of Artemisium	66
47	North and west walls of naos of Artemisium	66
48	Artemisium interior bislab	67
49	Detail view of Pl. 48	67
50	Cross-wall separating original pronaos from naos of Artemisium	69
51	Cross-wall separating original naos of Artemisium from its pronaos	69
52	Detail of junction between cross-wall and north wall of Artemisium's pronaos	70
53	Cut-down Doric capital used in north wall of Artemisium	70
54	Northeast corner of S3 structure	72
55	East wall of S3	74
56	Detail view of eastern face of east wall of S3	76
57	S4 building	77
58	Interior cross-wall and west wall of S4	78
59	Northwest corner of S4	80
60	Juncture of S4 with S2 pseudoisodomic bislab masonry building	81
61	East wall of S2	82
62	Zone west of Hellenistic F2 fountain complex	87
63	S1 Sacred House	90
64	S1 Sacred House	90
65	S5 Sacred House	93
66	Stone bench at rear of S5	94
67	West wall of S5	95
68	Southeast corner of S5	97
69	Triglyph block found in S5	99
70	S6 Sacred House	100
71	S6 Sacred House	101
72	Section of W2 peribolos wall	108
73	W2 peribolos wall	109
74	T8 peribolos wall and S23/S24 Late Structure	114
75	F3 water channel	115
76	T13 northwest corner of Middle Sanctuary	124
77	T14 west wall of Middle Sanctuary	128
78	Inner face of T14 wall	128
79	Earthquake-toppled upper courses of T14	129
80	Detail of wall masonry of Cyrene Agora Portico B5	131

81	Propylaeum wall W3	134
82	Limestone door jamb fragment	135
83	G1 and G3 doorways	136
84	F2 fountain tank	139
85	F1 fountain house and S7 Sacred House	143
86	F1 fountain house and R3 steps	143
87	R4 steps	148
88	R2 steps and blocked-up G5 and G6 doorways	149
89	S7 Sacred House	156
90	S7 Sacred House	157
91	Interior of S7	157
92	Detail of southwest corner of S7	158
93	Shrine of St. Nikalaos Marmarenios or Marmaritis	168
94	South wall (W10) of S12 Chamber	173
95	S12 Chamber	173
96	Temple-tomb at Messa	181
97	Side/rear view of temple-tomb, Cyrene West Necropolis	182

Minor Abbreviations

The abbreviation *Arch. Cat. No.*, followed by a letter A-P, that occasionally appears below in the figure and plate captions as well as in the main body of the text refers to the *Architectural Catalogue* developed to inventory architectural *frusta* separately from the project's general catalogue system. Letters indicate the following sub-categories:

A. Marble column shafts or drums
B. Limestone column shafts or drums
C. Engaged columns
D. Spiral columns
E. Capitals
F. Bases
G. Pilasters
H. Rabetted and L-shaped blocks
I. Door jambs and lintels
J. Blocks with mouldings
K. Triglyphs and metopes
L. Denticulated blocks
M. Arch and vault components
N. Altars
O. Statue bases
P. Miscellaneous blocks

Bibliographical Abbreviations

This series of reports adopts the standard abbreviations used by the *American Journal of Archaeology*. The works listed below are supplementary.

Acrocorinth V	N. Bookidis and J. Fisher, "Sanctuary of Demeter and Kore on Acrocorinth. Preliminary Report V: 1971-1973," *Hesperia* 42 (1974) 267-91.
Agora I	S. Stucchi, *L'Agorà di Cirene* I: *I lati nord ed est della platea inferiore* (*Monografie di archeologia libica* 7, Rome 1965).
Agora II,1	L. Bacchielli, *L'Agorà di Cirene* II,1: *L'Area settentrionale del lato ovest della platea inferiore* (*Monografie di archeologia libica* 15, Rome 1981).
Agrigento	P. Marconi, *Agrigento. Topografia ed arte* (Florence 1929).
Apollonia	R. Goodchild, J. Pedley, and D. White, *Apollonia, the Port of Cyrene. Excavations by the University of Michigan 1965-1967* (*Supplements to Libya Antiqua* 4, Tripoli 1977).
Applebaum, *Jews and Greeks*	S. Applebaum, *Jews and Greeks in Ancient Cyrene* (*Studies in Judaism in Late Antiquity* 28, Leiden 1979).
Béquignon, *Déese acropolitaine*	Y. Béquignon, "Déméter, déese acropolitaine," *RA* 2 (1958) 149-77.
Bergquist, *Temenos*	B. Bergquist, *The Archaic Greek Temenos* (Lund 1967).
Bohtz, *Pergamon*	C. Bohtz, *Altertümer von Pergamon* XIII: *Das Demeter-Heiligtum* (Berlin 1981).
Bruneau, *Cultes*	Ph. Bruneau, *Recherches sur les cultes de Délos a l'epoche hellenistique et a l'epoche impériale* (Paris 1970).
Chamoux	F. Chamoux, *Cyrène sous la monarchie des Battiades* (*Bibliothèque des Écoles Françaises d'Athènes et de Rome* 177, Paris 1953).
Coldstream, *Knossos*	N. Coldstream, *Knossos, the Sanctuary of Demeter* (*BSA* supp. vol. 8, Oxford 1973).
Dinsmoor	W. Dinsmoor, *The Architecture of Ancient Greece* (1950 3rd ed. rev. New York 1975).
Farnell, *Demeter Cult*	L. Farnell, *The Cults of the Greek States* (Oxford 1907).
Farnell, *Mystery*	L. Farnell, "Mystery," *Encyclopaedia Britannica* 1 (11th ed. Cambridge 1911) 117-23.
Final Reports I	D. White, *The Extramural Sanctuary of Demeter and Persephone at Cyrene, Libya, Final Reports*, vol. I: *Background and Introduction to the Excavations* (Philadelphia 1984).

Final Reports II	G. Schaus, *The Extramural Sanctuary of Demeter and Persephone at Cyrene, Libya, Final Reports*, vol. II: *The East Greek, Island and Laconian Pottery* (Philadelphia 1984).
Final Reports III	S. Lowenstam, M. Moore, P. Kenrick, and T. Fuller, *The Extramural Sanctuary of Demeter and Persephone at Cyrene, Libya, Final Reports*, vol. III: *Scarabs, Incised Gems, and Engraved Finger-Rings; Attic Black Figure and Attic Black Pattern Pottery; Hellenistic and Roman Fine Wares; Conservation of Objects* (Philadelphia 1987).
Final Reports IV	P. Warden, A. Oliver, P. Crabtree, and J. Monge, *The Extramural Sanctuary of Demeter and Persephone at Cyrene, Libya, Final Reports*, vol. IV: *Miscellaneous Small Finds; Faunal Remains; Glass* (Philadelphia 1990).
Freese, *Demeter*	J. Freese, "Demeter," *Encyclopaedia Britannica* 7 (11th ed. Cambridge 1910) 980-82.
Gabrici, *Malophoros*	E. Gabrici, "Il santuario della Malophoros a Selinunte," *MonAnt* 32 (1927).
Goodchild, *Cyrene*2	R. Goodchild, *Cyrene and Apollonia, an Historical Guide* (2nd ed. Libya 1963).
Goodchild, *Kyrene*	R. Goodchild, *Kyrene und Apollonia* (Zürich 1971).
Gruben, *Greek Temples*	H. Berve, G. Gruben, and M. Hirmer, *Greek Temples, Theaters and Shrines* (London 1963).
Kerenyi, *Eleusis*	C. Kerenyi, *Eleusis. Archetypal Image of Mother and Daughter* (New York 1967).
Kraeling, *Ptolemais*	C. Kraeling, *Ptolemais, City of the Libyan Pentapolis* (Chicago 1962).
Le Dinahet, *Sanctuaires*	M. Le Dinahet, "Sanctuaires chthoniens de Sicile de l'époque archaïque a l'époque classique," *Temples et sanctuaires*, ed. G. Roux (*Travaux de la Maison de l'Orient* 7, Paris 1984) 137-52.
Martin, *Manuel*	R. Martin, *Manuel d'architecture grecque 1, Matériaux et techniques* (Paris 1965).
Mylonas, *Eleusis*	G. Mylonas, *Eleusis and the Eleusinian Mysteries* (Princeton 1961).
Nilsson, *GGR* 1, 2	M. Nilsson, *Geschichte der Griechischen Religion* 1 (2nd ed. Munich 1955) and 2 (2nd. ed. Munich 1961).
Pacho	J.-R. Pacho, *Relation d'un voyage dans la Marmarique, la Cyrénaïque et les oasis d'Audjelah et de Maradeh* (reissue of the 1827 ed. Marseilles 1979).
Pernier	L. Pernier, "L'Artemision di Cirene," *AfrIt* 4 (1931) 173-214.
Priene	T. Wiegand and H. Schrader, *Priene* (Berlin 1904).
Princeton	*The Princeton Encyclopedia of Classical Sites*, ed. R. Stillwell (Princeton 1976).
Stucchi, *Architettura*	S. Stucchi, *Architettura cirenaica* (*Monografie di archeologia libica* 9, Rome 1975).
Thompson, *Thesmophorion*	H. Thompson, "Pnyx and Thesmophorion," *Hesperia* 6 (1936) 151-200.
Thompson and Wacherly	H. Thompson and R. Wycherley, *The Athenian Agora* 14: *The History, Shape and Uses of an Ancient City Center* (Princeton 1978).

Tocra I	J. Boardman and J. Hayes, *Excavations at Tocra 1963-1965. The Archaic Deposits* I (Oxford 1966).
Tomlinson, *Sanctuaries*	R. Tomlinson, *Greek Sanctuaries* (London 1976).
Travlos, *Pictorial Dictionary*	J. Travlos, *Pictorial Dictionary of Ancient Athens* (New York 1971).
White, *Summary*	D. White, "Cyrene's Sanctuary of Demeter and Persephone: a Summary of a Decade of Excavation," *AJA* 85 (1981) 13-30.
White, *Suburban Expansion*	D. White, "Cyrene's Suburban Expansion South of its Ramparts," *Cyrenaica in Antiquity*, eds. G. Barker, J. Lloyd, and J. Reynolds, *Society for Libyan Studies Occasional Papers* I: BAR International Series 236 (1985) 105-20.
Zuntz, *Persephone*	G. Zuntz, *Persephone* (Oxford 1971).

Preface

"Who are you?" Statue: "Opportunity, the all-conquerer." ... "Why is the back of your head bald?" Statue: "Because nobody, once I have run past him on my winged feet, can ever catch me from behind, even though he yearns to!"

An awareness of opportunity, often gained but occasionally dissipated or misspent, underlies the writing of this preface. Richard Goodchild offered to share the excavation of the Wadi Bel Gadir site in 1967 while still Controller of Antiquities for eastern Libya. His death in the following year deprived me of the chance to collaborate with the finest interpreter of walled remains of his generation to work in Libya, but it is to be hoped that some of the lessons gained through repeated discussion of his favorite Pentapolis sites as well as Utica and Carthage visited together shortly before Goodchild's untimely passing, have survived to benefit the present study.

Help in unraveling the complexities of the site's architecture has come from many sources whom I am happy to be able to thank at last. The first architectural survey of the sanctuary grounds was jointly carried out by Matthew Stolper and Henry Moss, with Moss responsible for drawing the detailed plans and elevations of the opening 1969 season. In 1971 Herbert Stoughton set the stage for all subsequent research by laying out the site's grid plan, which covered an extensive tract of broken, sloping terrain on both sides of the wadi. In the same year Edward Keall produced a preliminary study of the basic periodization of the walls uncovered at the level of the Middle Sanctuary that continued to help in interpreting the site's major phases until the conclusion of fieldwork in 1978. As project architect, Woodard Openo carried forward the graphic survey between 1973 and 1976 when the site's clearance went through its most extensive and in many respects most baffling expansion; his labors, which were carried out with no trained assistance, deserve special praise. Miriam Liddell and Fred Guthrie devoted considerable effort in 1977 to improving the site's plan as well as producing, in the case of Mrs. Liddell, individual drawings that were to set a high standard for graphic excellence.

While every person connected with the project between 1969 and its final 1981 study season contributed in his or her own way to the making of this book, the field notebooks and final reports of five individuals have proven to be of particular help not only because of the clarity and fullness of their narratives but also because of their specific interpretations of the site's development. Delays systemic to long-range publication projects have prevented my expressing the depth of my gratitude before now, and I am happy to have this occasion to acknowledge the special contributions of Matthew Stolper, Edward Keall, Steven Lowenstam, Philip McAleer, and Murray McClellan. The excavation's conservator, Joan White, occupies a category by herself. After initially helping to survey its grounds in 1968 before the fieldwork began, she returned as field excavator during the opening 1969 season while simultaneously establishing the system for cleaning and preserving the finds used for the remainder of our time in Libya. She devoted the next decade to conserving with inexhaustible skill and care every category and type of object from the sanctuary's grounds. As its most senior staff member, Joan deserves the project's special thanks and her husband's everlasting gratitude.

Help has come from other quarters, most particularly the Italian mission led by the late Sandro Stucchi, the leading authority on the sites and architecture of the Libyan Pentapolis. The opportunity to discuss with him the daily progress of our own work was of great benefit, and Professor Stucchi's generosity in sharing the resources of his time and knowledge will long be remembered. Dr. Claudio Frigerio, head of the Italian mission's ongoing restoration of the Cyrene Zeus Temple, understands more about the characteristics and uses of stone than any person I know. On numerous occasions the American mission came to him for help in dealing with a broad range of problems. He was unsparing in his willingness to share equipment, experience, and ideas, to say nothing of the warmth of his friendship. He often came to Wadi Bel Gadir in the company of the Italian mission's master-mason, Gastone Buttarini, to help us straighten out a problem in stratigraphy or wall sequence. One suspects that neither could have guessed that ideas shared from the side of a trench or from the heights of the Zeus Temple's scaffolding would end up in print. But such is often the case, and I am permanently indebted to all our Italian colleagues for all they have done.

In 1978 the project was joined by Alan Cook. With his assistant, Jeffrey Cohen, Cook undertook the concluding and most rigorous phase of the site's graphic recording. The site's eleven trans-site sections (Figs. 1-11) and the photo-rectified documentation of the complicated retaining wall system separating the sanctuary's middle and lower levels (Plan G) were carried out by a team of surveyors under his direction in 1978 and 1979. During the same period Cook and his assistants surveyed the Artemisium in the nearby Sanctuary of Apollo, some of the results of which appear below in Chapter Three on the Later Archaic and Early Classical Sanctuary. While in the field Cook also began the final study of the Wadi Bel Gadir sanctuary's architectural phase development. He continued to refine his analysis until his departure from The University Museum in 1983. The resulting phase plans (Plans A-E) are largely his creation. The format for the site's detailed plans, cross-sections, and elevations was worked out by Alan and Jane Cook. Many of the drawings used for the first as well as the present volume of this series were drawn by Jane Cook. I cannot overstate the importance of their contributions, and I am especially pleased to have this chance to record once again the project's thanks.

The last field architect to work at Cyrene was James Thorn, who joined the 1981 study season to record the site's wide selection of architectural *frusta* lying in the field and in storage. Working under especially trying circumstances Thorn drew the entire corpus during a single season. Some of his drawings accompany the present volume on the site's Imperial architecture. In addition Thorn has executed the restoration of the S7 Sacred House that accompanies Chapter Five. The project owes him a major debt of gratitude.

Work on the project's plans and drawings were continued after the departure of the Cooks from The University Museum by Dr. Carl Beetz, who either redrew or produced for the first time seventeen of the 1:200 scale plans and sections included with this study (Plans A-F; Figs. 1-11), as well as creating a series of new detailed plans, sections, and elevations. Beetz's advice in dealing with a wide range of interpretive problems was a constant help, and I am pleased to be able to acknowledge his important contributions here.

I am also very pleased to be able to record how the Department of Antiquities at Cyrene under the leadership of Ess. Breyik Attiyeh provided direction and support during all the years our mission worked in Libya. Our special gratitude and respect are due Ess. Breyik for all of his invaluable contributions, but most particularly for his unfailing friendship during times that were not always so easy. His various technical assistants were named in the preface to the opening volume of this series, but deserve to be mentioned once again, since without their active and positive collaboration the work on the site's architecture could never have gone forward. Salah Wanis, departmental librarian, Abdulkarim Mayyar, Keeper of Collections, Muhamad Bu Sherit, departmental secretary, Fadlallah Abdussalam, assistant to the Controller and liaison officer to the expedition, and Abdul Hamid Abdussaid, departmental director of technical affairs, all deserve great praise for their many acts of friendship and assistance. Additionally, we were truly fortunate to be able to draw upon the enthusiastic talents of three young departmental inspectors who agreed to join our team for two seasons in order to supervise and record the excavation of a number of key archaeological sectors. The field notebooks kept by Ramadan Kwader, Abdulgadr al Muzeine, and Fadel Ali Muhamad (now Controller of Antiquities for eastern Cyrenaica) document key information for the understanding of the site's architecture, and we are most grateful to their authors for their responsible participation.

A word of thanks must also be directed to the Publication Section of The University Museum. The volume's final editing was undertaken by Helen Schenck. Otherwise, responsibility for every facet of its production was carried by Karen Vellucci, manager of the Publication Section. Between them this study has been provided from beginning to end with the kind of supportive and intelligent guidance that authors dream about but can seldom expect to find in parlous times like these.

In a related vein Dr. Jamal el-Harami, graduate of the University of Pennsylvania, veteran of many seasons at Cyrene, and now Professor of Classical Archaeology at the University of Riyadh, has once again most generously contributed his time in translating the Arabic summary.

Finally, I would simply like to acknowledge the roles of my various teachers, both living and dead, Peter Von Blanckenhagen, Sterling Dow, Eric Sjöqvist, and Richard Stillwell, and my deceased and sorely missed Princeton friends, Kyle Phillips and Kenan Erim.

I

Introduction

The focus of the following work is on the architectural development of the extramural Sanctuary of Demeter and Persephone at Cyrene (Pl. 1) from its foundation late in the seventh century B.C. to the end of its pre-Imperial Roman phase (31 B.C.). The site's excavation has already been the subject of an extended introductory analysis by the present writer[1] as well as sections of three additional volumes that treat in detail various categories of the sanctuary's objects.[2] It may therefore be anticipated that the reader will have already acquired a basic familiarity with the Demeter and Persephone Sanctuary before undertaking to read the present study, and no attempt is being made now to describe its location, general appearance, and exploration, together with the basis for its identification and other introductory matters.

Any archaeological site reflects the overlay of time and space. One that lasts in continuous use for nearly a thousand years can be expected to present an especially intricate web of decay and renewal, laid bare in many ways, but perhaps in none more expressive of the growth patterns of the social organism that gave it birth than in its architecture. The principal periods of sanctuary architecture selected for treatment here took shape in the shadow of the major events in the history of Cyrene, the parent city, starting with its later seventh century colonial foundation and continuing through its brilliant and rapid expansion under the early Battiad monarchs, its early collisions with the native indigenous Libyan population, and its eventual struggle with Persian-occupied Egypt. This is then followed by Cyrene's apparently tumultuous but still poorly understood fifth century development that ended with the assassination of its last king, its protracted and unstable experiment with Republicanism that eventually led to its loss of independence under the Ptolemies and, in time, its ultimate absorption by the Romans.[3]

Chapter Two deals with the sanctuary's earliest walled remains which belong to Cyrene's early Battiad period (ca. 620 to 500 B.C.). Chapter Three takes up the later Battiad period sanctuary (ca. 500 to 440 B.C.). Chapter Four covers the Republican period sanctuary (ca. 440-330 B.C.). Chapter Five is concerned with its Hellenistic, early Roman period (330-31 B.C.), frequently referred to throughout simply as the Hellenistic phase. During these four periods the sanctuary undergoes significant internal change without sacrificing its original character as an extramural hillside precinct enclosing a variety of independent cultic installations. The principal concessions to its steeply rising setting involve organizing the sloping hillside into a series of terraced zones that are themselves in time organized into three separately defined zones: the Upper, Middle, and Lower Sanctuaries.

Enough architecture survives from the later Battiad period to enable one to speak with some confidence of the existence of an Upper Sanctuary and a Middle Sanctuary (Pl. 2). While the identity of the Upper Sanctuary's Classical buildings remains on the whole unclear until as late as the Hellenistic period, the artifactual evidence for cultic activity on this level is extremely good. The sanctuary's expansion north or down the wadi slope to the level of the Lower Sanctuary does not occur until the early Imperial period when both the Upper and Lower Sanctuary levels take on the architectural features of what will remain their characteristic layouts until the earthquake of A.D. 262. For example, the Upper Sanctuary's colonnaded Southwest Building (S17) and Propylaeum entrance (S20) belong to this period, together with the bridge entranceway (W14 and S28) that connects the Lower Sanctuary with the city's Agora quarter (Plan E). Most of the site's architectural limestone and marble *frusta* found scattered throughout earthquake levels across the Middle Sanctuary appear to have first originated with Imperial period Upper Sanctuary additions, and it is these which supply most of the sanctuary's restorable monuments. In addition, while the bulk of the surviving evidence for building activity down to the end of the Hellenistic period has to do with the Middle Sanctuary, in the years leading up to the sanctuary's earthquake destructions in the third and fourth centuries of this era,[4] little new architecture is

---

1. *Final Reports* I.
2. See *Final Reports* I, 119-120; *Final Reports* II, III, and IV.
3. Cyrene's independence ceases when its final Greek ruler, Ptolemy Apion, dies in 96 B.C. after willing Cyrenaica to the Senate of Rome. Its period of Roman Republican administration therefore overlaps by some 65 years what is conventionally taken elsewhere throughout most of the eastern Mediterranean to be the final years of the Hellenistic period. The latest of the artifacts associated with this phase of the architecture belong to the late Hellenistic period in that larger sense.

4. See *Final Reports* I, 1, 61-63.

Plate 1: The Sanctuary of Demeter and Persephone seen from the northeast across Wadi Bel Gadir following the conclusion of the 1978 season of excavation.

added across most of its ca. 1900 sq. m. interior.[5] Instead, what new construction takes place occurs mainly at the Upper Sanctuary level.

It is, moreover, the earlier periods that persons familiar with the first four volumes of this series will remember as having produced the overwhelming majority of the sanctuary's votives and other types of small finds. The site's total number of Roman period lamps, pottery, coins, and most of the other miscellaneous objects is far lower than the pre-Roman examples of the same classes of artifacts. The terracotta figurines and incised gems go essentially unrepresented in the later period. The major exceptions to this are the glass, inscriptions, and stone sculptures, which are more evenly balanced between the two periods.

The publication of the sanctuary's Archaic East Greek, Island, Laconian,[6] Attic B.F., and black glaze pottery,[7] Hellenistic and Roman Fine Wares,[8] Archaic/Classical scarabs, incised gems, and engraved finger rings,[9] glass,[10] miscellaneous small finds,[11] and faunal remains[12] has preceded this study. The publication of the Attic R.F. pottery and coins forms Volume VI. What remains to be accounted for are the site's Corinthian pottery, coarse and plain ware pottery, lamps, terracotta figurines, stone sculptures, and inscriptions.

In summary then, what the present volume represents is the publication of the architectural setting of the Demeter and Persephone Sanctuary's first major physical expansion, covering approximately six hundred years of the occupation of its Upper and Middle Sanctuary grounds. It is offered at mid-point in the publication series in order to provide a better understanding of the archaeological context in which the bulk of the site's objects were found, including those already in print as well as the remaining awaiting publication. While its presentation now rather than at the end of the publication series as was first announced somewhat arbitrarily divides the sanctuary architecture into two overarching periods, our belief is that the practical benefits to persons wishing to follow the complete results of the published series will outweigh any theoretical disadvantages.

---

5. An approximate rectangle, the Middle Sanctuary grounds measure ca. 67 m. east to west by 28 m. north to south. The natural rise in bedrock measured from the northeast to the southeast corners of the Middle Sanctuary amounts to ca. 6.75 m. For more on the overall topographical setting of the sanctuary and its individual parts, see *Final Reports* I, 31-53, esp. 48.
6. G. Schaus, *Final Reports* II.
7. M. Moore, *Final Reports* III.
8. P. Kenrick, *Final Reports* III.

---

9. S. Lowenstam, *Final Reports* III.
10. A. Oliver, *Final Reports* IV.
11. P. G. Warden, *Final Reports* IV.
12. P. Crabtree and J. Monge, *Final Reports* IV.

Plate 2: Middle Sanctuary grounds from across the wadi at the conclusion of the 1978 season, seen from north.

Given the site's longevity, it is understandable that its earliest architectural phases are preserved in what can be charitably described as threadbare condition. Later construction overlies most of the walls built before 480 B.C. Their remains are consequently apt to represent mutilated truncations of the original structures to which they once belonged. In addition, the pre-31 B.C. components that managed to retain their integrity to the end of the sanctuary's use, such as the Middle Sanctuary's main west wall (T14) and several of the various independent shrine houses, were severely destroyed by the mid-third and mid-fourth century A.D. earthquakes and are therefore often little better preserved than their contemporary structures that were partially dismantled in Hellenistic and Classical times. The passage of time has not always dealt kindly with this site.

The first of the two keys needed for sorting out the architecture's complicated periodization is the site's stratigraphy, which has received an introductory description in the series' opening volume.[13] The following chapters are accompanied by graphic sections to help clarify the discussion in the text of the archaeological contexts associated with each individual walled component.

The second key has to do with the structural interrelationship of the individual walled features to one another, which frequently turns on questions of relative level. These relationships are illustrated by a series of graphic elevations sometimes supplemented by photographs. Further information is provided by the series of eleven trans-site sections reproduced at 1:200 scale (Figs. 1-11). Because of their relatively small scale the trans-site sections do not attempt to indicate stratigraphical levels. The reader referring to the trans-site sections should be aware that the features drawn in bold or heavy black line indicate walled remains that are cut by the line of the actual section. Features drawn in fainter line refer to whatever elements were visible to the draftsman behind the plane of each given section and are included in order to provide a closer approximation of the appearance of the site along each of its eleven planes. Two of the trans-site sections (Figs. 10 and 11) are drawn east to west, while the remaining nine (Figs. 1-9) run north and south. The lie of each of the trans-site sections is plotted on the site's 1:200 scale evidential or stone-by-stone plan (Plan F).[14] Reference to this plan will indicate that the nine north-south sections are alternatively drawn from the east (Figs. 2, 4, 6, 8, 9) and the west (Figs. 1, 3, 5, 7). The two east-west sections (Figs. 10, 11) are both drawn from the north.

The sections and elevations are supplemented by additional drawings that include the site's five 1:200 scale phase plans (Plans A-E) and a series of detailed plans of individual features drawn at 1:100, 1:50, or 1:10 scale. The photo-rectified elevation and plan of the Middle Sanctuary's important forward wall is reproduced at 1:200 scale (Plan G). Finally, the by now familiar site Area and Trench plan that has accompanied each of the series volumes since Volume III here reappears in modified form (Fig. 12) in order to display the site's network of trenches superimposed over a composite drawing of the site's Archaic through Classical walls (omitting, in other words, the post-31 B.C. walls). In regard to Fig. 12 it should be under-

---

13. *Final Reports* I, 56-116.

14. Plan F is based on Plan A incorporated into the *Final Reports* I, back cover pocket.

stood that not all of its walls remained in use until the end of the Hellenistic period; instead, the plan's inclusion of all the known pre-31 B.C. walls is intended simply to help the reader locate where individual stratigraphical contexts appear in relation to given structures or features.[15] For the periodization of structures the reader should refer to Plans A-E. Figures 1-12 and Plans A-G are placed together at the end of the volume.

The chronological evidence accumulated from the site's various finds is tabulated below in Appendix I. The Appendix is organized to display the chronological range of each individual class of artifact that provides evidence relevant to the dating of a given individual archaeological context, here designated by Area, Trench, and Stratum.[16] The chronological data summarized by the Appendix derives from l) the final studies of artifacts that have been either published before or accompany this study or 2) lists of dates that have been transmitted to me in anticipation of their future publication.

Each final study is indicated by the following abbreviations:

EG   G. Schaus, *Final Reports* II: *The East Greek, Island, and Laconian Pottery*
BF   M. Moore, *Final Reports* III: *The Attic Black Figure and Attic Black Pattern Pottery*
FW   P. Kenrick, *Final Reports* III: *Hellenistic and Roman Fine Wares*
IG   S. Lowenstam, *Final Reports* III: *Scarabs, Incised Gems, and Engraved Finger Rings*
G   A. Oliver, *Final Reports* IV: *Glass*
MF   P. Warden, *Final Reports* IV: *Miscellaneous Small Finds*
C   T. Buttrey, *Final Reports* VI: *Coins*
RF   I. McPhee, *Final Reports* VI: *Attic Red Figure Pottery*
TC   J. Uhlenbrock, *Final Reports*, forthcoming: *Terracotta Figurines and Plastic Vases*
S   S. Kane, *Final Reports*, forthcoming: *Stone Sculpture*
CP   A. Kocybala, *Final Reports*, forthcoming: *Corinthian Pottery*
L   E. Fabbricotti, *Final Reports*, forthcoming: *Lamps*
I   J. Reynolds, *Libya Antiqua*, forthcoming: *Inscriptions*

Where a given class has received final publication, its appropriate abbreviation and its final catalogue number are incorporated into the fourth column of the Appendix ("artifact type/catalogue number") to indicate where it has been published within the current series of final studies. For example, "EG/125" refers to a Laconian stamnos attributed by Schaus to the years 525-500 B.C. in *Final Reports* II, p. 29.

In the case of still unpublished objects awaiting their final catalogue number, an asterisk in place of a catalogue number indicates that the dates included in the Appendix have been communicated to me in anticipation of their future publication. For example, "TC/*" refers to a terracotta awaiting its final catalogue number in J. Uhlenbrock's forthcoming study of the site's figurines, while "L/*" refers to a lamp awaiting publication by E. Fabbricotti.

Finally, in a few rare instances an object providing significant information for a given context has failed to be included in a final study. If its date seems noncontroversial, it has been included under its own short descriptive title (e.g. "lamp") without reference to either author or catalogue number. Longer descriptions of such objects usually appear in the main body of the text.

Objects are included in Appendix I only when they contribute relevant chronological information. In other words, reference to objects occupying the chronological middle range of any given class of objects is omitted. When more than two objects from any given study are included, it indicates a major change of category within the actual study. For example, two silver coins might be included to indicate the full range of that particular class of currency, while the inclusion of a third coin would indicate the presence of a bronze coin of later date.

Finally, Appendix II lists the block height-to-length proportions of masonry blocks described in the text where these dimensions are available. The table utilizes the two principal block dimensions visible to the observer in any given wall elevation (i.e., height and length) and does not take into consideration the normally hidden third dimension (width), since it is assumed that if these statistics have any relevance, it lies in what people were able to see and not in some abstract formula known only to the wall builders. The results are organized into the broad chronological periods of sanctuary development followed throughout this study, i.e., early Archaic, later Archaic/early Classical, later Classical, and Hellenistic/pre-Imperial Roman. While these data seem to provide some indication of period, the reader is cautioned against placing excessive reliance on them for dating purposes in the absence of other contributing factors.

---

15. Most of the trenches drawn on Fig. 12 conform to the slightly irregular, squared or rectangular units normally laid out in order to excavate walled sites, but D14/E14, 2 looks more like a cartoon gerrymander. In this case the trench incorporated the line of the site's main wheelbarrow path connecting the Upper Sanctuary with the Decauville railway across the forward edge of the Middle Sanctuary. Most of it was only excavated to the top of the St. 2 earthquake destruction level at the end of the project's 1978 final digging season and therefore does not constitute a normal trench. For the railway line see *Final Reports* I, Plan A, back cover pocket.

16. See *Final Reports* I, 56 for a full description of the site's survey and grid system. For purposes of the present volume the main point to remember is that the Cyrene grid is read by referring to the *upper left-hand corner* of each square. Each gridsquare is bound by four grid points, e.g. E-10, F-10, E-11, and F-11. The proper reference here is therefore *F11*. Trenches that extend into more than one square are referred to, for example, as E11/F11.

II

The Earliest Walled Remains Ca. 620-500 B.C.

The sanctuary's foundation, which can be placed around 600 B.C., coincides with one of the most eventful periods in Cyrene's history, the first generation or so following its well-attested colonial foundation. In addition to the various standard discussions of this event and its aftermath that are too familiar to require detailed citation here,[1] volumes I and II of the present publication series have devoted a fair amount of space to an analysis of the role played by the sanctuary in the affairs of the city in the years that follow the sanctuary's initial foundation.[2] Scattered observations dealing with the same subject appear in the publications of the Attic Black Figure, miscellaneous small finds, scarabs, incised gems and engraved finger rings, and coins (volumes III-VI). Further analysis has taken place elsewhere of the contributions made by the early sanctuary to an understanding of religious and economic relations between the first Greek colonists and their Libyan neighbors.[3]

While the evidence preserved for the earliest architectural layout is sparse, it is apparent that the sanctuary experienced a remarkably rich and diversified influx of votives during its first 125 years of use. It is, for example, during this time that the greatest amount of imported pottery is introduced, while there is simultaneously a considerable buildup of locally made plain and coarse wares. A wide range of local as well as imported personal jewelry makes its way into the sanctuary during the sixth century, along with much cored glass and lesser amounts of faience, bone, and shell objects. Some of the site's very earliest finds are imported lamps that predate by a considerable interval what is taken to be the sanctuary's foundation. Both imported and locally made terracotta figurines have accumulated in relatively large numbers by the end of the sixth century but are already well represented by the later seventh century. Even more noteworthy in light of the city's early history is the accumulation of a small collection of imported figurines, whose date of manufacture seems to go back to as early as the beginning of the seventh century. Metal products, mainly bronze but including silver and gold as well, are reflected in the sanctuary's important series of locally minted silver coins and its local and imported bronze animal figurines; and its various metal pendants and other types of personal jewelry provide additional significant concentrations of sixth and early fifth century finds. Large-scale stone sculpture is mainly conspicuous by its absence in the Archaic period and does not start to accumulate in any great quantity until later times. Even here, however, there are exceptions, of which the most important is the sanctuary's mid-sixth century marble kore.[4] It is against the backdrop of these finds that the sanctuary's initial architectural development is to be understood.

RECOVERY

As has been already pointed out, the earliest wall remains (Plan A) have come to light mainly in the area of the later Middle Sanctuary (Pls. 1-3). The Area and Trench plan (Fig. 12) illustrates their location in relation to the site's ten-meter-square grid and trench layout. The P7 southeast corner of the early Archaic peribolos was discovered in E11, 1. Traces of the peribolos's P3 south wall came to light in D12/13, A, E12, 1, D12/E12, D, and E12/13, C. More traces of the peribolos's south wall (P11, P12) and the junction of its north walls (P8, P9) were excavated in D15/16, 1, D15/E15, 1, and F14/G14, 1. A section of its west wall (P10) was found in F16, 1.

The attached but apparently semi-independent series of spur walls (P2, P4, P5, P6) south of the peribolos was discovered in D12/13, A, D13 (Area 2), 2, and E12/13, C, along with the short spur (P3a) north of the same wall. A short length (P1) of what may have been part of a separate structure indepen-

---

1. See however Stucchi, *Architettura* 3-5. Add Applebaum, *Jews and Greeks* 8-73. M. Vickers and D. Gill, "Archaic Greek Pottery from Euesperides, Cyrenaica," *SLS* 17 (1986) 106. For general bibliography including references to historical studies see L. Gasperini, "Bibliografia archeologica delle Libia. 1967-1973: Cirenaica," *QAL* 7 (1975) 189-96. J. Humphrey, "North African Newsletter 2," *AJA* 84 (1980) 76-78.
2. *Final Reports* I, 23-30. *Final Reports* II, 2-4, 96-107.
3. D. White, "Demeter Libyssa, her Cyrenean Cult in Light of the Recent Excavations," *QAL* 12 (1987) 67-84.

4. Awaiting final publication in a future volume of this series by S. Kane, cat. no. **81**. In the meantime see S. Kane, "An Archaic Kore from Cyrene," *AJA* 84 (1980) 182-83.

Plate 3: Early Archaic and later Archaic sanctuary walls seen from the west, embedded in the fabric of later building.

dent of the peribolos, along with a neighboring scrap of wall (P13), was found in E13/14, 1 and D14/E14, 1.

Two sets of walls of similar period and construction (P14, P15) were excavated in the area of the later Upper Sanctuary in C12/13, 1, C13, balk, C13/D13, 1, D12/13, F, and C15/16, 1. The southern extension of the four spur walls (P2, P4, P5, P6) was disrupted by the line of the T1 later Archaic pseudoisodomic peribolos. Originally the spur walls may have continued onto the level of the Upper Sanctuary where, along with walls P14 and P15, they would have been part of a major southern extension of the primitive sanctuary, whose existence has been otherwise thus far only attested by the presence of exceptionally rich Archaic occupation levels.

Most of the Middle Sanctuary was excavated to bedrock south of the line of the expedition's Middle Sanctuary Decauville railway line,[5] and it is fairly certain that later construction must have eradicated nearly every trace of early Archaic building from the center of this zone. On the other hand, most of the Upper Sanctuary remains to be dug to its lower strata,[6] and it is correspondingly less clear how widespread the damage caused by later renovation and replacement has been to the earliest walls at this level.

No sub-surface exploration was carried out by the present expedition to determine whether or not early walls occur north of the later retaining walls (T11, T12, T13, T20) that separate the Middle from the Lower Sanctuary (Plans D and E). Ghislanzoni's pre-1916 test of the sanctuary's Roman period northwest corner (Plan E, S27, W14) and the bridge abutment (Plan E, S28) across the wadi drain brought to light no

---

5. See *Final Reports* I, Plan A, for line of railway.

6. For a description of what the University of Pennsylvania Expedition was able to excavate by the conclusion of the project's final 1978 season of fieldwork, see *Final Reports* I, 54-56, 117.

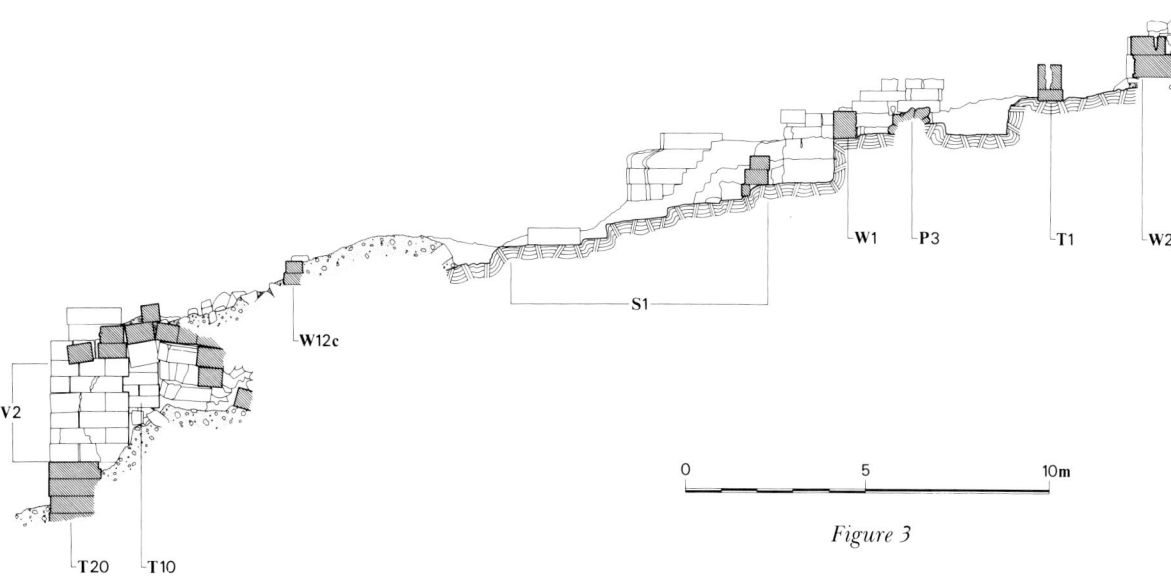

Figure 3

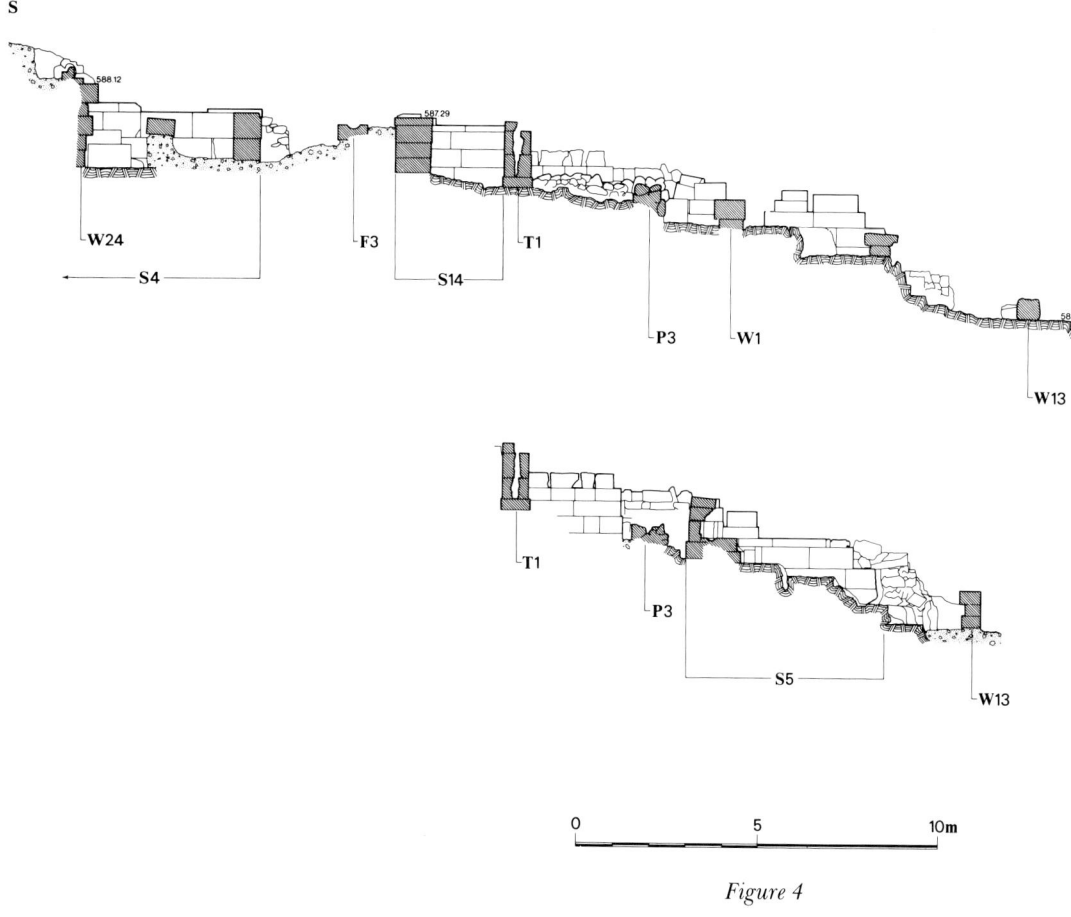

Figure 4

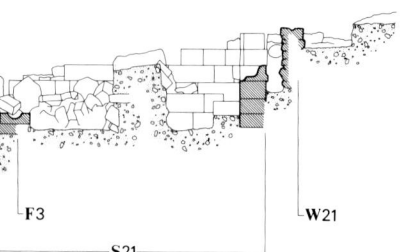
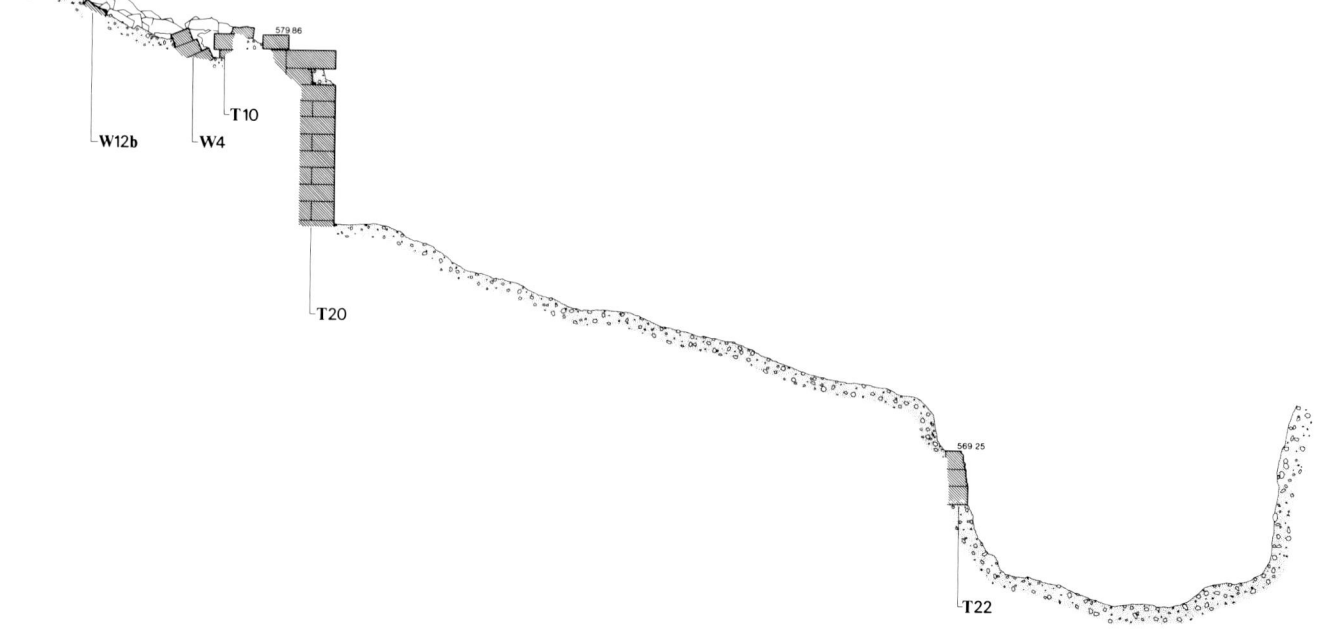

N

S

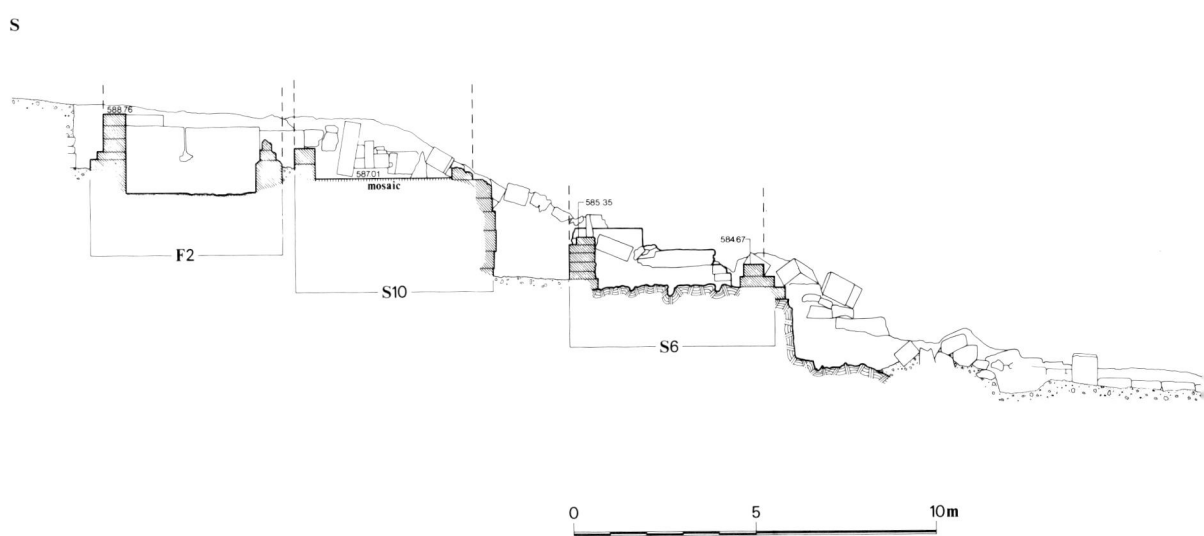

Figure 8

S
S22
588.37
587.37
586.95
586.49
T16
582.06
584.66
R5
P12
S10
582.85
S29
581.46
579.92
W12a
T11
0
5
10m

Figure 7

N
578.10
G2

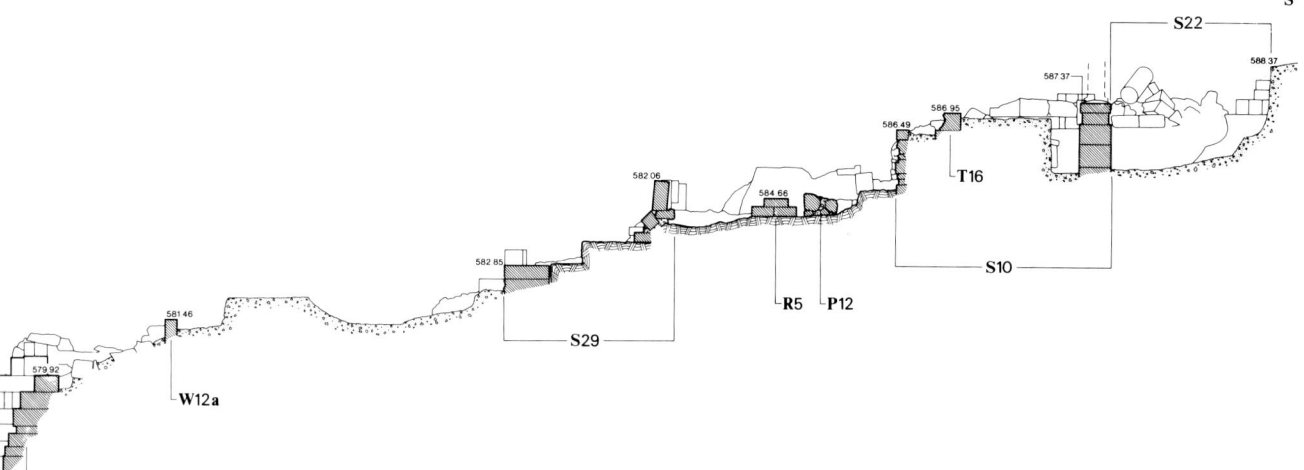

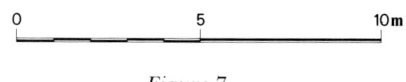

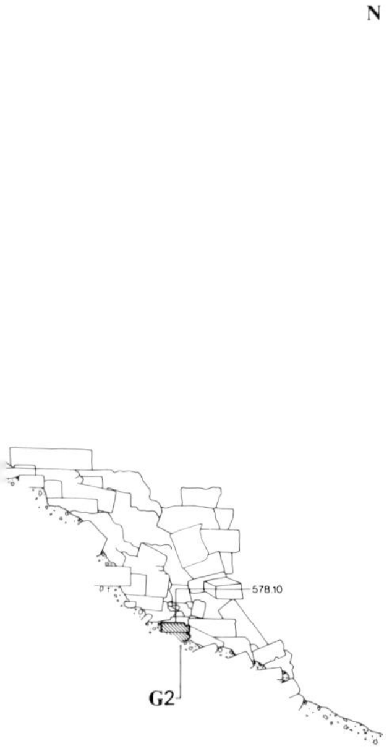

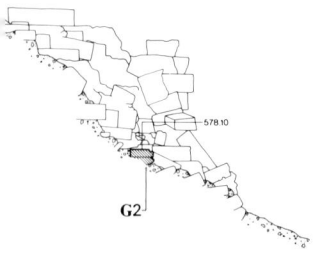

Figure 11

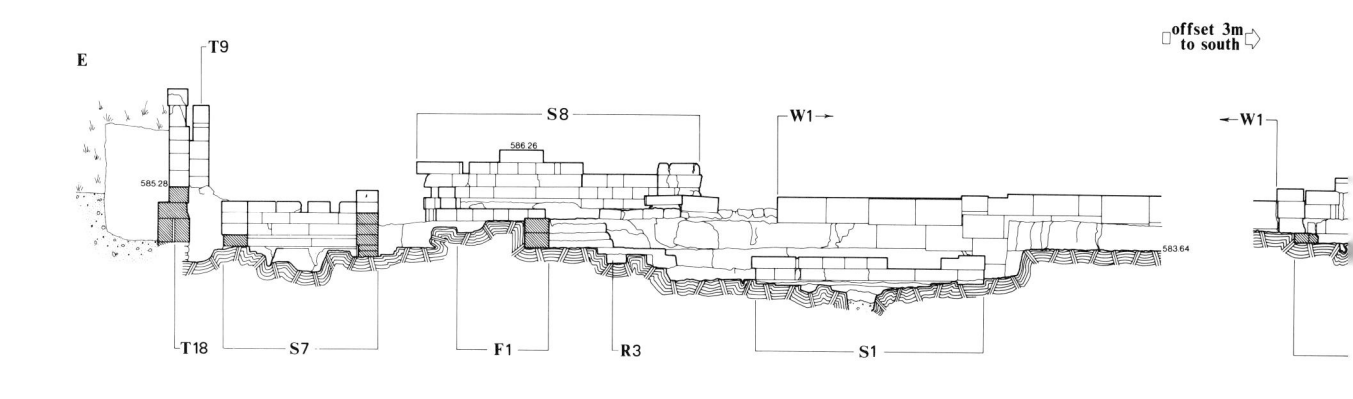

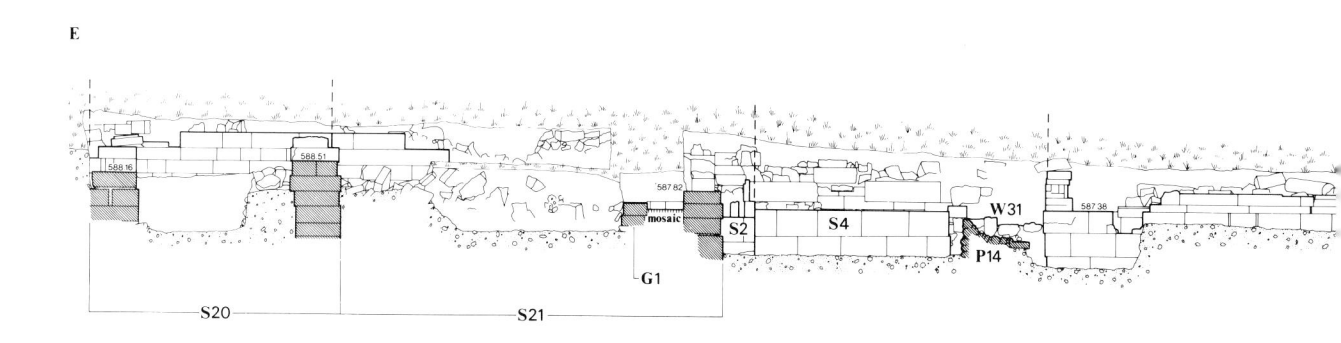

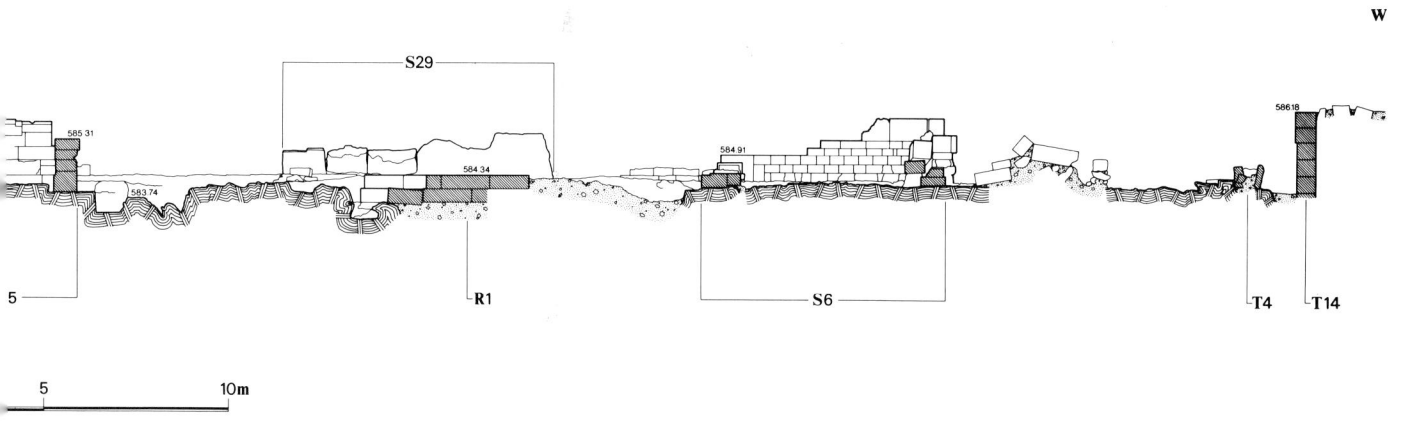

Figure 10

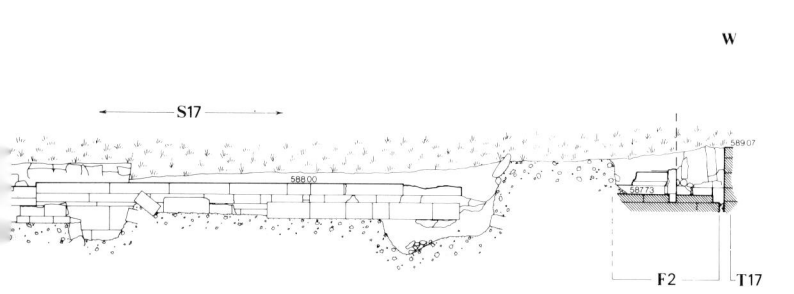

Figure 12

traces of Archaic walls that are still visible.[7] Hillside sanctuaries as a rule occupied their higher levels in the early phases of their development and then in time spread down. There is no reason to suspect that the present example contradicts this basic pattern.

In summary, the majority of the earliest walls appear to have been part of a stone peribolos, which surrounded a temenos occupying the level of the later Middle Sanctuary. Apart from the vestiges of what may have been an independent east-west wall (P1), there is no evidence for what construction occupied the interior of this temenos. In effect, from the point of view of what survives of its architecture, the early sanctuary is mainly the peribolos. On the other hand, there exist traces of possibly two early independent structures (P14, P15) on the higher ground south of the peribolos, along with four north-south walls (P2, P4, P5, P6) that might have belonged either to a single unified structure or to a group of semi-independent rooms attached to the exterior face of the peribolos wall.

The Earliest Peribolos

Eight sections of the peribolos have been unearthed. These make up parts of its south wall, southeast corner, north wall, and west wall. Because masonry as well as perhaps chronological differences exist between the various surviving peribolos sections, the procedure that has been adopted below is to describe and, where possible, to date each wall segment separately.

PERIBOLOS SOUTH WALL

Five sections (P11, P12, P13, P2, P3) survive, although the status of two (P13 and P11) as parts of the original peribolos is uncertain.

WALL P3

Throughout its entire length the south wall was set either directly on bedrock or on a thin layer of earth over bedrock. Wall P3 (Figs. 3, 4, 13; Pls. 4, 5, 6, 27) represents its longest preserved stretch. It consists of a rubble foundation that averages ca. 0.20 m. high. Over this rises the wall's superstructure, preserved to a maximum height of three courses. The courses are made up of small-to-medium-sized natural stones that have been roughly shaped into truncated cones or plugs (Pl. 6). Their outer faces are dressed flat in the vertical plane. Small rubble stones and chips are used to fill the interstices in its outer face and core. What results is a form of simple polygonal masonry. The north face of P3 has tended to collapse down the slope and therefore is apt to present a generally less finished polygonal appearance than the corresponding south face. The total width varies from less than 0.50 m. to over a meter, depending on the state of preservation. The wall nowhere survives to more than a meter in height and furthermore reveals no evidence for ever having continued vertically in mudbrick.

WALL P2

The segment represents the nearly unbroken continuation of wall P3 to the west. It consists of identical polygonal masonry founded on rubble (Pl. 7). As preserved, P2 describes a right-angled turn to the south. Its northwest corner is composed of a single squared block (0.54 by 0.30 by 0.28 m.). Intensive later rebuilding in this area makes it impossible to determine whether P2 stopped its passage west at this point or continued on to connect with P12. Since squared blocks are occasionally used in combination with rubble and polygonal masonry along other parts of the early peribolos, the appearance of the single squared block here does not necessarily argue that the wall changed direction. In other words, the polygonal construction could theoretically have continued straight west to connect with wall P12.

Wall P12, on the other hand, may also have extended south. Hence, if wall P2 turned south without continuing west, it could have linked up with wall P12's southern extension to form a southern annex that may have encroached on at least some of the terrain later incorporated into what is designated the Upper Sanctuary.

WALL P13

All that survives is a short stretch of foundation preserved to a height of ca. 0.30 m. As we have it, wall P13 is less than a meter long and only ca. 0.45 m. wide. In its surviving condition where it is merged into a considerably later early Imperial rectangular structure of unknown purpose (S9, Plan E) wall P13 consists of a single badly shattered squared block set over the rubble foundations. This could have been either part of P13's original superstructure or a later replacement. If P2 and P12 once formed an unbroken east-west line of peribolos, P13 would have been included in the same stretch of wall. Alternatively, it could have also been attached to the east-west line of

---
7. See *Final Reports* I, 11-12, figs. 14, 15.

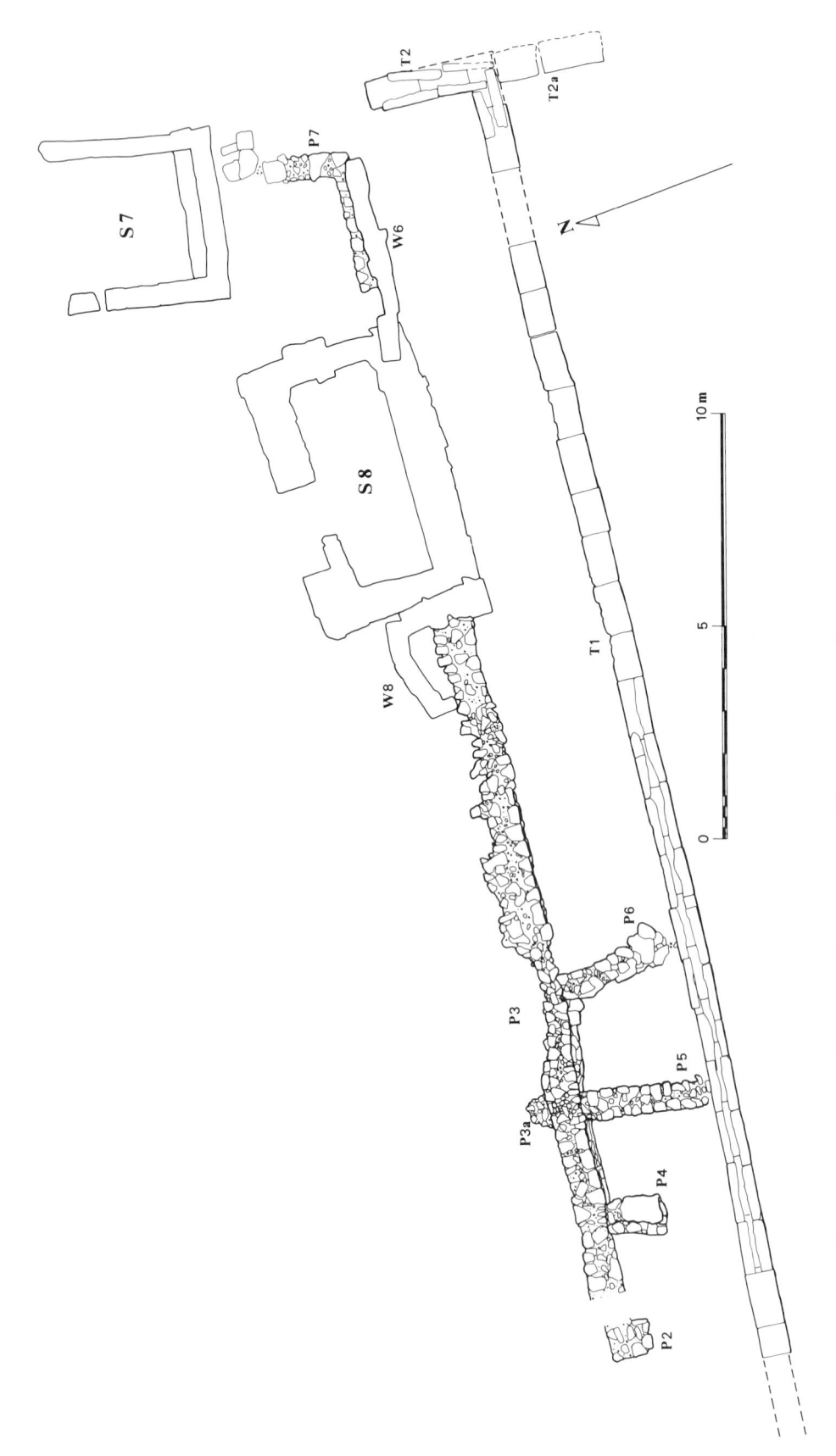

Figure 13: Plan of the southeast quarter of the early Archaic (P3, P7) and later Archaic, early Classical (T1, T2) sanctuary periboloi. The rubble walls (P2, P4, P5, and P6) may represent one or more semi-detached early Archaic structures. 1:150 scale.

Plate 4: Central section of the P3 south wall of the early Archaic peribolos, seen from south.

Plate 5: East end of the P3 early Archaic southern peribolos wall as it disappears under the early Imperial S8 Sacred House. Seen from southwest.

wall P1 to its north to form part of a structure that was either partially or even fully separate from the peribolos. In its present meager state of preservation it is, however, impossible even to determine whether P13 originally ran north-south or east-west.

WALL P12

Located some 17 m. to the west of wall P3, this short section of rubble (Fig. 7) can only be assumed to have once belonged to a continuation of the peribolos's south wall on the strength of its alignment with the nearby stretch of wall designated P11. In other words, since a fairly strong case can be built for regarding wall P11 as part of the peribolos, wall P12 should be part of the same architectural component. Its construction closely resembles that of wall P3 but in this instance survives to only the height of a single course of plug-shaped polygonal stones, ca. 0.75 m. wide. The east end has collapsed, making it impossible to

Plate 6:   South face of partially excavated early Archaic P3 peribolos wall in background, early Archaic spur walls, P4 to left, P5 to right, seen from south.

Plate 7:   Wall P2 seen from west in midst of the later Imperial S24 Late Structure. The eastern half of the early peribolos and its spur walls continue east of S24 in the upper half of the picture.

determine whether wall P12 originally merely continued in a straight line to the east to link up with walls P2 and P3 or split off at this point to form a right-angled turn to the south, eventually connected up with wall P2. Its total east-west length is 1.60 m., while its maximum north-south spread is 1.30 m.

WALL P11

Constructionally unlike the rest of the southern peribolos, the superstructure of P11 (Figs. 8, 14, 15; Pl. 8) is composed of regular courses of ashlars instead of plug-shaped polygonal blocks. The ashlars from the four courses above its rubble foundation course level measure only ca. 0.20/0.30 m. high, 0.60/0.80 m. long and 0.40 m. wide. They are, in other words, as far as later sanctuary ashlar masonry goes, unusually small. The lower three courses above the foundations are laid as headers, the fourth as modified perpends[8] or extra-wide stretchers, ca. 0.55 m. deep and spanning much of the wall's width. Although eroded, the inner (i.e., north) faces of the ashlars preserve beveled joints and are marked by traces of broad, parallel chisel strokes. The outer wall faces survive in a much rougher condition. For the most part the vertical plane is left untrimmed (Pls. 9, 10), while in some places the headers run less than the full width of the wall. A single block from the perpend course appears to be a reused L-shaped quoin. Stratified debris accumulated against the south face suggests that P11 was backfilled to the top of its fifth course, counting the foundations (Fig. 15, St. 3), either at the time of its construction or possibly shortly afterward and therefore was never intended to be seen.

The east end of wall P11 is made up of a single large ashlar block (1.00 by 0.58 by 0.44 m.), carefully leveled with the top of the remaining headers of the second course. At the opposite, west end, the fifth course above foundation level is composed of a single vertical slab (1.70 by 0.65 by 0.38 m.). The stretcher upon which the upright block rests is cut with a raised flange, designed to hold in place a now missing parallel slab (Fig. 15).

The foundations consist of a single course of rubble set into the red earth fill that covers the natural limestone pavement. The north face is more carefully trimmed than on the south.

Of all the elements making up wall P11 only its foundations are indisputably early Archaic, being buried in early fill. The foundations, moreover, closely resemble the rubble foundation of the remainder of the peribolos to the east. The upright course and possibly the perpend course that carries it must be later and indeed appear to be part of the later Archaic peribolos (T7) that eventually replaced the primitive early Archaic peribolos (Plan B). Wall T7 took the form of a pseudoisodomic sequence of parallel orthostates tied across by low binding courses. Consequently, in this sector of the Archaic sanctuary the later peribolos was constructed directly on top of the line of its early Archaic predecessor.

It is less clear whether the four courses of low headers and stretchers that presently make up most of what is left of wall P11 represent 1) the original superstructure of P11, built to go with its early foundations, 2) a localized reinforcement of this wall, added to support the later Archaic peribolos (T7), or 3) an intermediate phase of P11, set up at some time between the original erection of P11 and its later replacement, wall T7. As shall be shown, however, the stratified fill against the south face of the wall to some extent seems to favor the first interpretation.

CONTEXT AND DATE OF THE PERIBOLOS SOUTH WALL

Walls P3, P2, and P13 all share what basically appears to be a common stratigraphy.

WALL P3

The south face of wall P3 between the two spur walls, P5 and P6, rests on a dense argillaceous D12/13, A, 4 fill (Fig. 16), burying its foundations in places to a depth of ca. 0.15/0.29 m. This is overridden with patches of a densely compacted yellow fill (St. 3a, not present in the Fig. 16 section) that represents the remnants of an earth floor (Pl. 11). This was later covered with a dark brown earth fill (St. 3) that masks what is preserved of wall P3. The D12/13, A, 3 finds range from a late seventh century lamp to a standard selection of sixth/fifth century sherds, coins and other artifacts, mixed with a fifth-fourth century B.C. terracotta figurine and a marble head tentatively assigned to the late Hellenistic period. The figurine and marble head could be intrusive, in which case St. 3 represents a gradual accumulation of occupation debris against the outer face of the peribolos from the time that the wall was initially built. If on the other hand the marble head dates the stratum, St. 3 represents a relatively late backfill that utilizes mostly early fill to cover wall P3 from view.

D12/13, A, 4 underlies wall P3's foundations and spreads to its south. Since not all of its surface was sealed by the St. 3a floor at the time of its excavation, it represents both a pre-construction period fill as well as an early post-construction occupation fill. St. 4 contains a silver pin that has been dated to the late seventh century B.C., along with some MC and possibly LC sherds and a pre-560 B.C. East Greek dish. Since the pottery may have been dropped onto St. 4 after the wall's erection, the pin perhaps provides the best indication of the wall's early construction date.

In E12/13, C north of walls P5 and P6 the north face of P3 lies on bedrock and St. 4 fill, which partially buries its footings. The upper 0.30 m. of St. 4 contains ashes and bones, Corinthian sherds that range from perhaps MC to LC, and three terracotta figurines, whose dates run from ca. 600 to the third quarter of the sixth century B.C. The otherwise early contents are offset by lamps that date to the

---

8. For a fuller explanation of perpend, see infra chap. 3, n. 11.

12 CYRENE FINAL REPORTS: VOLUME V

☐ early fifth century B.C. ☐ post-A.D. 262 debris
☐ early Imperial

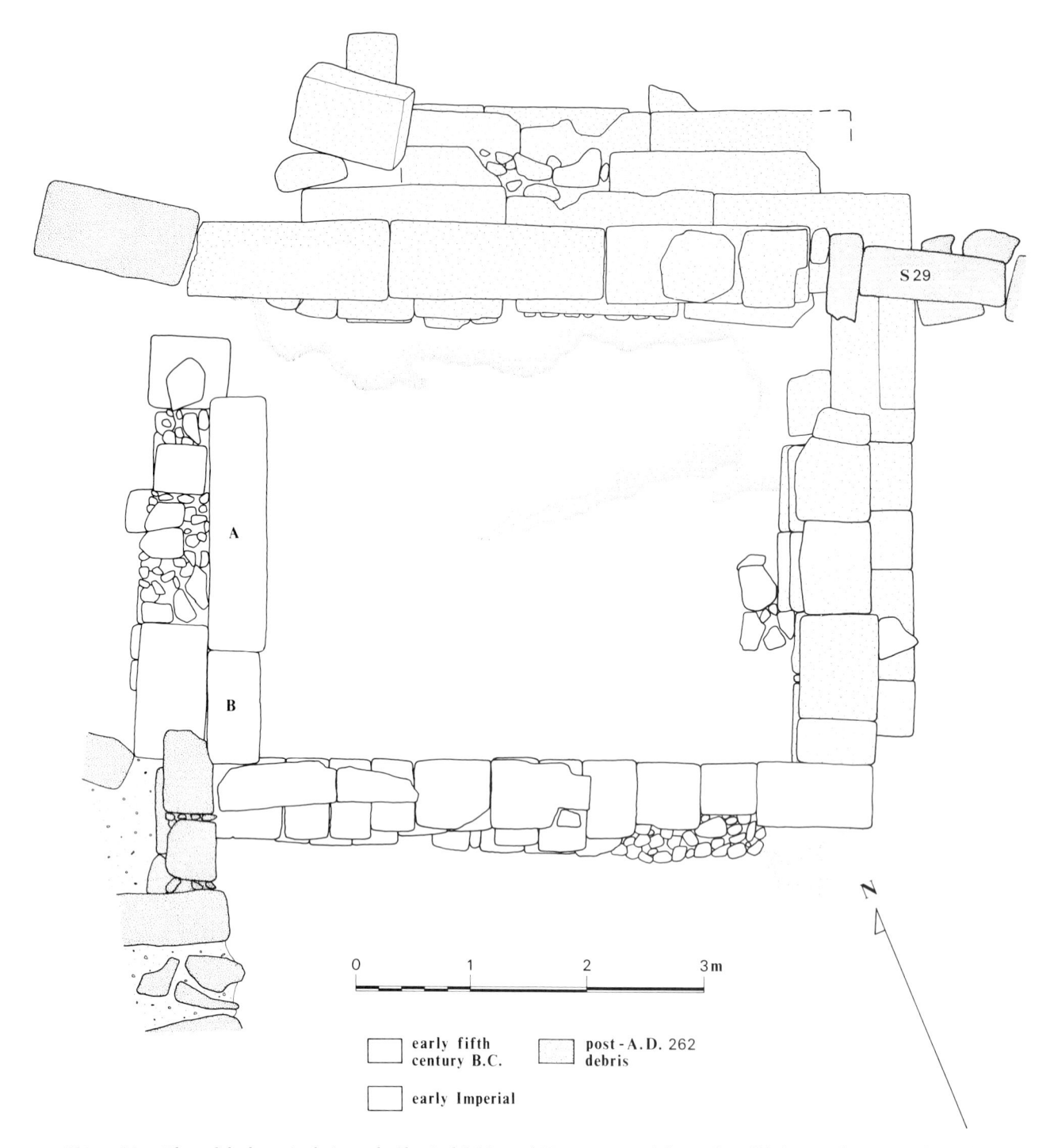

Figure 14: Plan of the later Archaic, early Classical S6 Sacred House. Parts of the south wall belong to the P11 early Archaic peribolos. 1:50 scale.

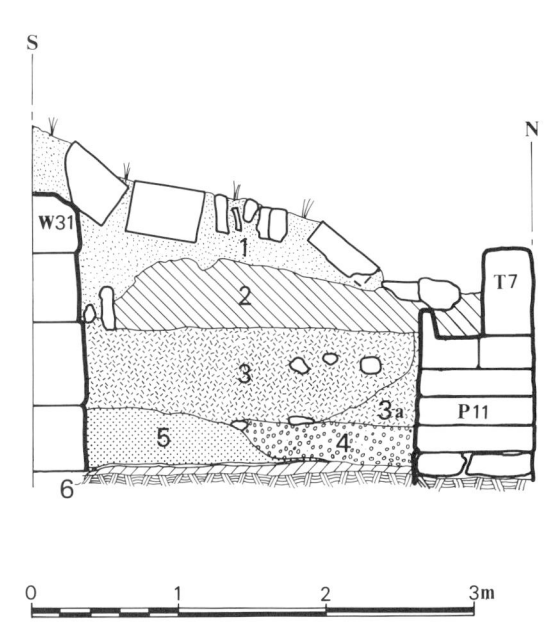

Figure 15: North-south section of D15/16, 1 fill south of the P11 early Archaic peribolos and the south wall of the later Archaic S6 Sacred House. Drawn from east. 1:50 scale.

Plate 8: North face of the early Archaic peribolos wall P11, seen from north. This wall also constitutes the south wall of the later Archaic, early Classical S6 Sacred House.

Plate 9: The south, outer face of the early Archaic peribolos wall P11, partially cleared and seen from south. The large block in the foreground has fallen from the early Imperial S10 structure to the rear.

fifth and fourth centuries B.C., and the fill is once again best interpreted as an early occupation fill that was gradually added to after the wall was erected.

East of the spur wall P6 wall P3 continues to rest on a combination of bedrock and a thin layer of St. 4 fill (not indicated in the Fig. 16 section because of a later 2a intrusion directly east of wall P6). About six m. east of wall P6 the natural bedrock pavement south of wall P3 forms a natural sink hole in D12/E12, D, filled with mostly sterile St. 6 terra rossa[9] (Fig. 17). This was covered with a hard-packed brownish red St. 5 layer which in late Hellenistic or early Roman Imperial times was dug into to make a disposal pit (St. 4). The St. 4 contents of the pit now cover wall P3 which has collapsed back up the slope to the south. St. 5 must represent an Archaic occupation, which, to judge from its level relative to wall P3, post-dates the wall. Its contents, moreover, are contaminated with finds spanning the late fifth to second-first centuries B.C. that appear to have worked their way into its upper surface from the St. 4 pit fill. Although not directly associated with wall P3, St. 6 appears to have been coeval with its period of initial use. Several pieces of LC I pottery were excavated from its surface, along with an undateable piece of alabaster, which provide at least an approximate indication of the wall's Archaic date.

WALL P2

The wall is built over a red argillaceous D13 (Area 2), 2, 4 soil layer overlying bedrock which contains traces of ashes and animal bones but otherwise no man-made artifacts.

WALL P13

A similar red argillaceous soil designated D14/E14, 1, 3 overlies bedrock and underlies wall P13. The layer contains Archaic sherds, including Corinthian dating from MC to the end of the sixth century, mixed with some later material, of which the latest dateable artifacts appear to be locally made Hellenistic and Eastern Sigillata A wares of the second and first centuries B.C. The context clearly fails to shed any light on the wall's construction date.

WALL P12

The foundations are once again set into a thin layer of dense, argillaceous red earth covering the bedrock, designated variously D15/E15, 1, 3 and E15, 1, 3. The E15, 1, 3 context appears to have been contaminated with later intrusions. In the case of D15/E15, 1, 3 the evidence, which

---

9. For the character of terra rossa fill, see *Final Reports* I, 58.

Plate 10: Detailed view of the southwest exterior end of the P11 early Archaic peribolos wall, seen from south.

basically turns on a single fourth century B.C. figurine, is ambivalent but could reflect a sixth century date. The bulk of the St. 3 potsherds and other artifacts from both trenches belongs to the sixth century. Otherwise St. 3 is contaminated with a later second century coin and second/first century B.C. pottery. While the late coin reflects the generally disturbed condition of P12 and may in fact be an intrusion from the earthquake stratum above, the same could be argued for the pottery. On balance, however, both contexts appear to point to a sixth century date for wall P12.

WALL P11

At some time after ca. 480 B.C. wall P11 (i.e., what is here argued to be the ashlar masonry, western extension of the peribolos) and its later replacement T7 were incorporated into the small sacred building designated S6.[10] Construction taking place at the time of the conversion obliterated all traces of the fill that must have been originally associated with the north face of wall P11 (i.e., from what in time became the interior of the Sacred House S6). On the other hand, its stratigraphy is preserved between the exterior of the building and the wall W31 that constitutes the north wall of the early Imperial period Porticoed Chamber (S10) lying to its south (Plan E). Here the uneven natural bedrock pavement is covered with a typical overlay of terra rossa stereo (Fig. 15, St. 7; Pl. 12). The stereo in turn is coated with a thin, patchy layer of glutinous brown mud (St. 6) that seems to represent what remains of an early floor (Pl. 13). The "floor" is buried beneath a ca. 0.35 m. thick layer of reddish brown soil that was found to contain a scattering of bone fragments and badly preserved pottery fragments (St. 5).

It has proven impossible to extract a precise date for St. 5 from its D15/16, 1, 5 sherd material. It should, however, represent an early Archaic occupation layer that pre-dates wall P11, since the wall's builders cut into St. 5 to lay their foundations. As wall P11 rose, the masons filled their foundation trench with stone chips left over from trimming the wall's outer face (St. 4). Since the chip fill rises to the top of the lowest course of wall headers, the P11 foundations and superstructure should in fact belong to a common building phase at least to the level of the fourth course. Unfortunately, D15/16, 1, 4 contained no man-made detritus and cannot be dated.

When the wall reached the level of its stretchers, the builders covered it from view by a backfill of light brown earth (St. 3a). The only block at the level of the stretchers to project above the top of St. 3a is the flanged stretcher cut to receive the orthostate slabs. The likelihood is that the former was a later insertion. Most of St. 3a appears to have been removed when wall W31 was erected in the early Imperial period. The zone was then back-filled with a slightly darker earth fill (D15/16, 1, 3), which contained miscellaneous Archaic period artifacts along with Archaic and Classical

---

10. The S6 Sacred House is associated with the Middle Sanctuary's later Archaic and early Classical phase. See infra foldout, Plan B.

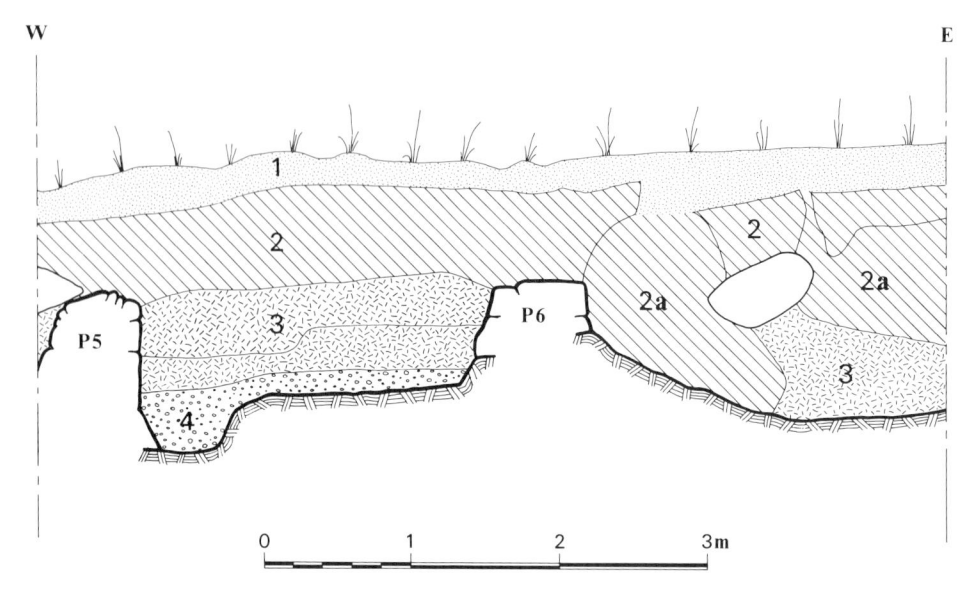

Figure 16: East-west section of D12/13, A over south face of wall P3 between the two spur walls, P5 and P6. Drawn from south, before final clearance of wall P3. 1:50 scale.

terracotta figurines and silver coins. These were further mixed with late Hellenistic bronze coins and a late Roman period lamp. Because St. 3 is close in color and texture to St. 3a and contains in particular a large number of Corinthian sherds from before 550 B.C., it seems at least possible that the Roman period builders of wall W31 used St. 3a fill to make up most of their St. 3 backfill and that this explains the presence of the late finds within what is otherwise a predominantly early level. Once again nothing was recovered from St. 3a to provide a close date, leaving only the early sherds recovered from the Roman period St. 3 backfill for wall W31 as the only indication for P11's sixth century date.

SUMMARY OF THE DATING EVIDENCE FOR THE PERIBOLOS SOUTH WALL

Walls P12, P13, P2, and P3 were all built into basically the same dense argillaceous fill, composed of disturbed terra rossa that occurs as a natural deposit across the site mixed with some man-made detritus. The most convincing chronological evidence for the construction of the southern peribolos stems from the fill associated with wall P3 as well as perhaps to a lesser extent the portions of wall P12 falling in D15/E15, 1. It is important to understand that this fill, where excavated both north and south of the foundations of walls P3 and P12, must have lain open for objects to drop onto its surface long after the wall had been built. In other words, it nowhere represents a closed deposit. This presumably explains why, leaving aside what may have been the odd late intrusion into the levels directly associated with wall P12, the red earth fill contains some Archaic artifacts that date as late as the last quarter of the sixth century as well as objects

Plate 11: Traces of compacted yellow earth floor (St. 3a) in interior corner formed by walls P3 and P6, seen from west.

THE EARLIEST WALLED REMAINS

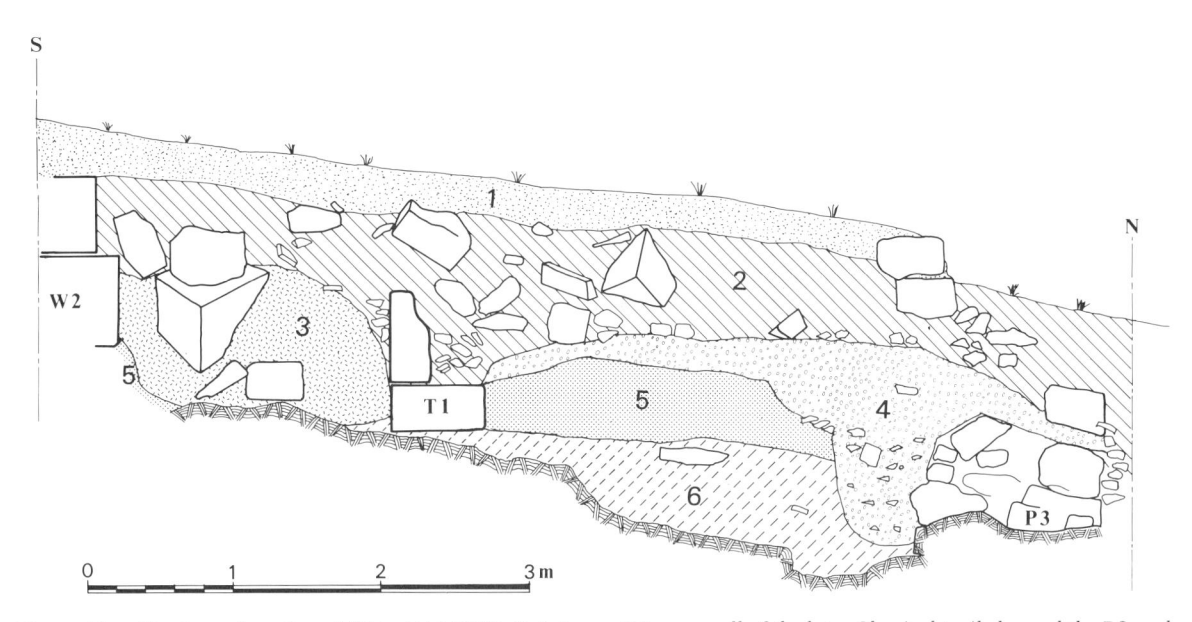

Figure 17: North-south section of fill in D12/E12, D, between W2 rear wall of the later Classical peribolos and the P3 early Archaic peribolos wall, drawn from east. The fill engulfs the later Archaic pseudoisodomic peribolos wall T1. 1:50 scale.

Plate 12:   North-south section of D15/16, 1 fill south of the P11 early Archaic peribolos wall, seen from east.

Plate 13: D15/16, 1, 6 Archaic period argillaceous floor south of the P11 early Archaic peribolos wall.

Plate 14: Southwest corner of the S8 Sacred House, with line of the P3 south wall of the early Archaic peribolos continuing to its west. Viewed from east.

that go back to the seventh. It seems apparent that as far as the date for the actual commencement of religious activity within the sanctuary grounds goes, the important objects are probably the first generation of early objects, which include the lamp from D12/13, A, 3, the jewelry from D12/13, A, 4, and the terracotta figurines from E12, 1, 6. All date around 600/590 B.C. or slightly earlier. Given the general paucity of objects of all kinds from the strata directly associated with the walls, these admittedly few artifacts represent a significant concentration and, as such, provide a fairly reliable indication for a date of the wall's erection around 600 B.C.

As said, the construction of wall P11 differs sharply from that of the remaining sections of the southern peribolos. Since it was built over ground that, unlike the fill surrounding the rest of the peribolos, shows evidence of previous occupation, it seems fairly likely that wall P11 represents a later replacement. How much later is a moot point, but the lack of any dated material before ca. 580 B.C. from the D15/16, 1, 3 fill to its south suggests that it was probably built not long after that time.

PERIBOLOS SOUTHEAST CORNER

Interrupted by the early Imperial Sacred House S8 (Fig. 13; Pls. 5, 14, 15), the line of the southern peribolos continues to run east for another 3.60 m. where it turns north to form the southeast corner (Fig. 1; Pl. 16) of the primitive temenos (P7). The north leg runs 2.0 m. before its line disappears immediately south of the Hellenistic Sacred House S7. The bedrock sheers away north of wall P7 to form a natural sinkhole.[11] This forced the builders of the wall's east-west line to thicken their foundations to a width of ca. 1.20 m. Above this there rises today a single course of plug-shaped polygonal blocks that carry a second course of larger, more irregularly shaped rubble stones, which may represent a later replacement. There is no evidence for the superstructure having continued in mudbrick.

The north-south leg of P7 survives in a more ragged condition. Most of its elevation was removed in antiq-

---
11. For sinkholes across the site see *Final Reports* I, 58, fig. 50.

Plate 15: Center of Middle Sanctuary from west, with line of the P3 south wall of the early Archaic peribolos together with spur walls P3a, P4, P5, and P6 occupying the middle ground.

uity above foundation level. The width varies from ca. 0.50 to 0.60 m.

CONTEXT AND DATE OF THE PERIBOLOS SOUTHEAST CORNER

The same moist, argillaceous red soil that underlies the south peribolos reappears under and around the foundations of wall P7 wherever they do not rest directly on bedrock. As recorded south of wall P7, this layer, designated E10/11 (Area 1) 1, 5 (Fig. 18), contains a sparse number of diagnostically useless black glaze sherds on its surface, contaminated with what are probably objects from St. 3 and 4 above. A short distance to the west, however, in the area of the D11/E11 balk (Fig. 19) the St. 3 reddish clay earth above bedrock held ceramic material dating to the first half of the sixth century as well as a late fourth century B.C. bronze coin that is probably intrusive. The fill (St. 4) surrounding the lower levels of wall P7's north-south leg is largely empty of dateable finds in the area of E11, 1, 4 (Fig. 20), apart from terracotta figurines dated from the early fifth century to the Hellenistic period, which once again seem intrusive. Less than a meter further north in fill directly south of the Hellenistic period Sacred House S7 the same fill (E10 balk S, 2/3 and 3; Fig. 21) has Archaic pottery and glass dated between 600 and 500 B.C., and Attic Red Figure dated between 500 and 480. It also contained terracotta figurines dating from the mid-sixth to the late fifth centuries B.C.

On balance, what all this seems to indicate for wall P7 is that its construction probably does not date much before 600 B.C. and that the fill to either side of the southeast corner lay open, as did the fill around wall P3 to the west, gradually accumulating finds until ca. 500-475 B.C., when the bulk of the finds cease. The upper layers in the general vicinity are

Plate 16: P7 southeast corner of the early Archaic peribolos viewed from northwest.

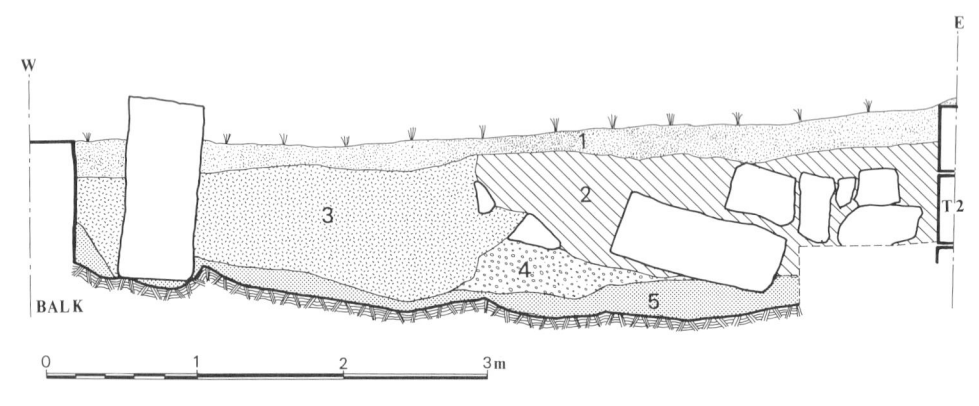

Figure 18: East-west section of fill in E10/11 (Area 1) 1, drawn from south. 1:50 scale.

badly disturbed by earthquake activity, and it seems likely that any later material here is intrusive.

PERIBOLOS NORTH WALL

No trace of the east wall of the peribolos survives beyond the point of its disappearance a short distance south of the Hellenistic Sacred House S7. For purposes of the restoration of its outline as indicated on Plan A the remainder of the peribolos, including the northeast corner and its return west, are assumed to follow the direction of its subsequent replacements, which all adhere to essentially the same format.

What survives of the north wall is located in area F14/G14 where there occurs a dog-leg junction in the line (Plan A, walls P8 and P9). Both wall sections (Pls.

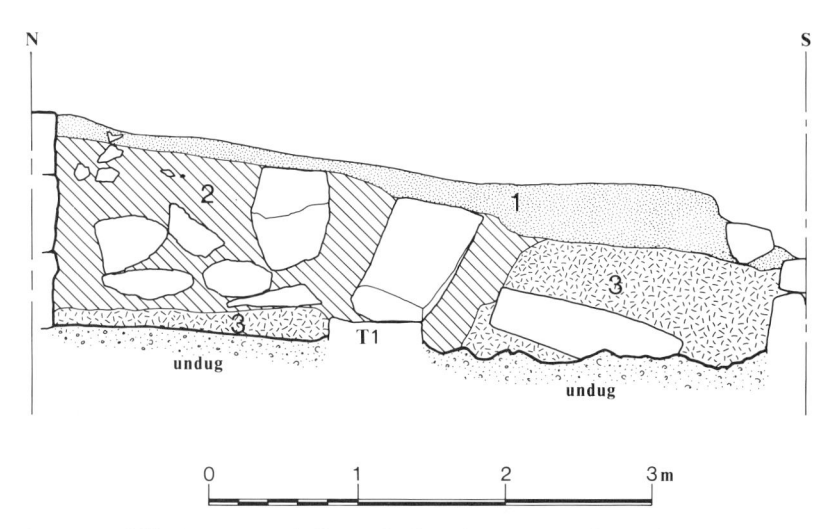

Figure 19: North-south section of fill of D11/E11 balk, south of southeast corner of Sacred House S8, drawn from east. 1:50 scale.

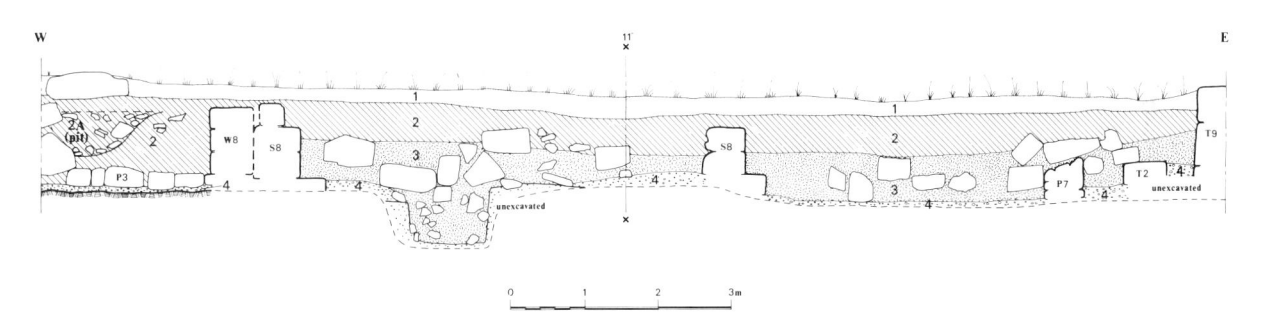

Figure 20: East-west section from the P3 early Archaic peribolos wall west of the early Imperial S8 Sacred House to the T9 main east wall of the Hellenistic Middle Sanctuary, drawn from south. Line of section undergoes twenty-degree shift to south at S8's east wall. 1:100 scale.

17-21; Figs. 22-24) have been cleared on their exterior faces as part of a restricted deep-level probe of the fill directly south of the later Archaic peribolos wall T4, which in turn backs against the heavy Imperial period retaining wall T20. Wall P8 (Pl. 19; Fig. 23) is constructed of mainly polygonal masonry of irregular shape and size. Its foundation course, resting on bedrock, is made up four large undressed stones. There then rise to the immediate east three irregular courses of roughly shaped polygonal stones, while to the west there is a large boulder (1.12 by 0.45 m.) which projects ca. 0.40 m. north of the face of P8. Above this there survives on the west four additional courses of dressed stones. Its exposed east-west length is ca. 1.80 m.; its maximum preserved height is 2.40 m.

Wall P8 rests on a lip of the sloping bedrock, which has been backfilled to the north with three strata of early fill (St. 4, 5, and 6; Figs. 23, 24). The lower half of the wall, up to the top of its large boulder, rests in St. 3 fill, while its upper half on the west lies in St. 2 fill. Its foundations and therefore presumably its construction are clearly associated with St. 4, 5, and 6.

Wall P9 (Pl. 21; Fig. 24) lying to the immediate west extends ca. 0.75 m. north of wall P8 with which it forms a dog-leg junction. Only 2.05 m. of its east-west length has been excavated because of the restricted nature of the F14/G14 sounding. Wall P9 is composed of three courses, each ca. 0.50 m. high, of squared blocks set on bedrock. These abut on the south but fail to bond with the foundations and projecting boulder of wall P8. There then rise perhaps five additional courses of superstructure, composed of a combination of rubble, rough polygonal, and squared blocks. The upper two have toppled over to the north and nearly rest against the inner face of the later Archaic peribolos wall T4 (Fig. 24). The maximum surviving height is 2.45 m.

As in the case with its companion wall P8, wall P9 rests on bedrock and a packing of deep fills to its north (St. 4, 5, and 6). Its foundations are partially covered with St. 3 fill. St. 2 fill buries the superstructure.

Wall P8 is similar to the main sections of southern and southeastern peribolos (walls P12, P13, P3, P7), while wall P9 more closely resembles walls P2 and P11 in its combination of rubble stones with occasional

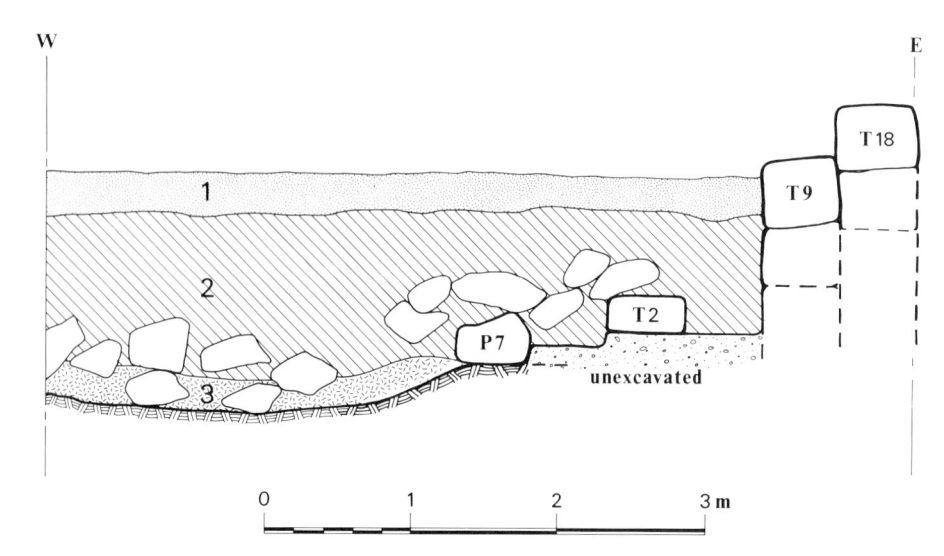

Figure 21: East-west section of fill in E10 balk south of the Hellenistic S7 Sacred House, overlying the P7 early Archaic peribolos wall. Drawn from south. 1:50 scale.

Plate 17: The F14/G14 trench against the inner face of the T20 Imperial period Middle Sanctuary retaining wall, from west. The upper courses of the T4 later Archaic peribolos wall rise against wall T20.

Plate 18: The F14/G14 test sounding seen from the south, with the P9 wall to left and the T4 wall at top of photo.

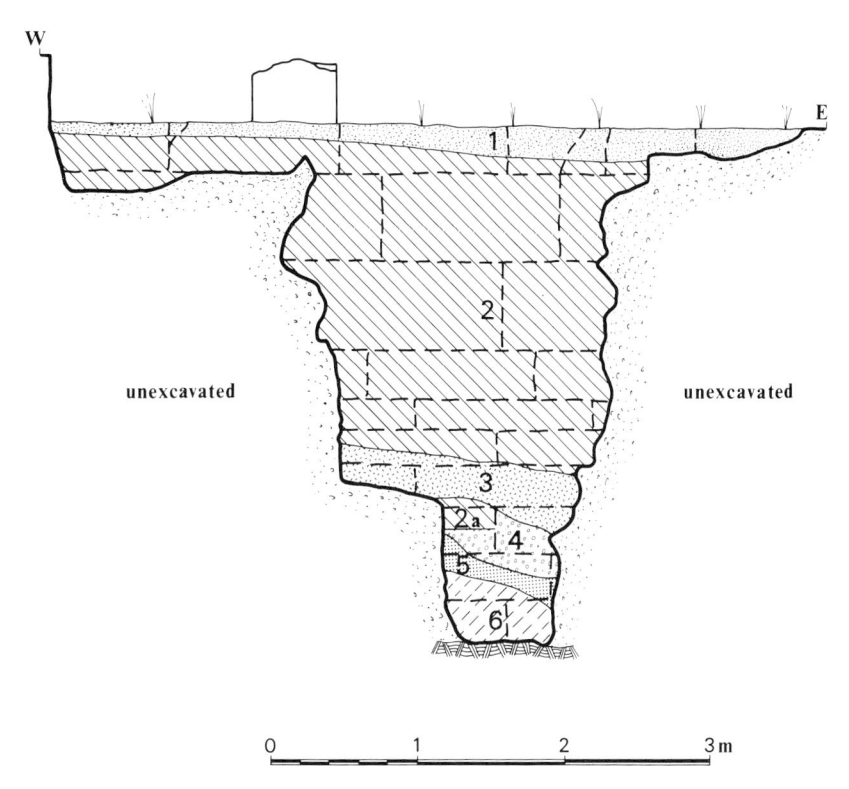

Figure 22: East-west section of F14/G14 fill between the outer face of the P8 early Archaic north peribolos wall and the inner, south face of its T4 later Archaic replacement, drawn here in broken line from south. 1:50 scale.

Plate 19: The P8 wall (center) interfacing with the P9 wall (right) seen from north, corresponding to Fig. 23.

polygonal and roughly squared blocks. To judge from the short exposed distance in which the two walls interface, they do not bond and therefore must represent separate, but conceivably contemporary builds. Since wall P9 preserves a right-angle turn to the south before it abuts wall P8, the possibility arises that its line continued south to divide the early Archaic temenos into two unequal parts. While such a cross-wall can be imagined to have linked up to wall P13 19 m. to its south, which in constructional terms it resembles, no trace of a north-south line has been recovered from the center of the Middle Sanctuary grounds. This leaves one's acceptance of its existence largely dependent on masonry differences between the two halves.

CONTEXT AND DATE OF THE PERIBOLOS NORTH WALL

The F14/G14, 1 test sounding brought to light six separate strata. Of these, the lower three levels (St. 4-6) represent backfills that occupy the space between the lowest courses of the late Archaic pseudoisodomic peribolos (T4) and the bedrock shoulder to its south which carries the foundations of walls P8 and P9. All three contain material that was introduced into the sanctuary at the time of the construction of walls P8 and P9, but the levels themselves appear to be part of later backfills made after the construction of wall T4.

Starting with the deepest level, St. 6 is a ca. 0.50 m. thick deposit of argillaceous brown soil mixed with numerous small stones and fragmentary bits of pottery. It covers the bedrock at the foot of the south face of T4. The dateable material includes a small number of what are apparently Attic Black Figure fragments not published by Moore, and a LC III sherd, dating to the late sixth, first half of the fifth century B.C. St. 5 is a narrow (ca. 0.10/0.15 m. thick) band of ashy black soil mixed with burnt bones, charcoal, and LC/LC II miniature hydriai. St. 4 is a ca. 0.50 m. thick layer of yellow, clay-like soil, mixed with patches of reddish clay, tiny white pebbles, broken roof-tiles, miscellaneous Corinthian sherds including a LC II kotyle, and a late sixth, early fifth century silver coin.

Judged from their contents, all three strata are chronologically undifferentiable and appear to represent separate tips or loads of fill thrown behind wall T4 at roughly the same time. Their latest object is the late sixth, early fifth century silver hemidrachm, which provides a good indication of the construction date for wall T4, but does little to date the earlier walls, P8 and P9.

PERIBOLOS WEST WALL

As was the case with its opposite number in the northeast corner, the northwest corner of the early Archaic peribolos lies beneath unexcavated fill, but its

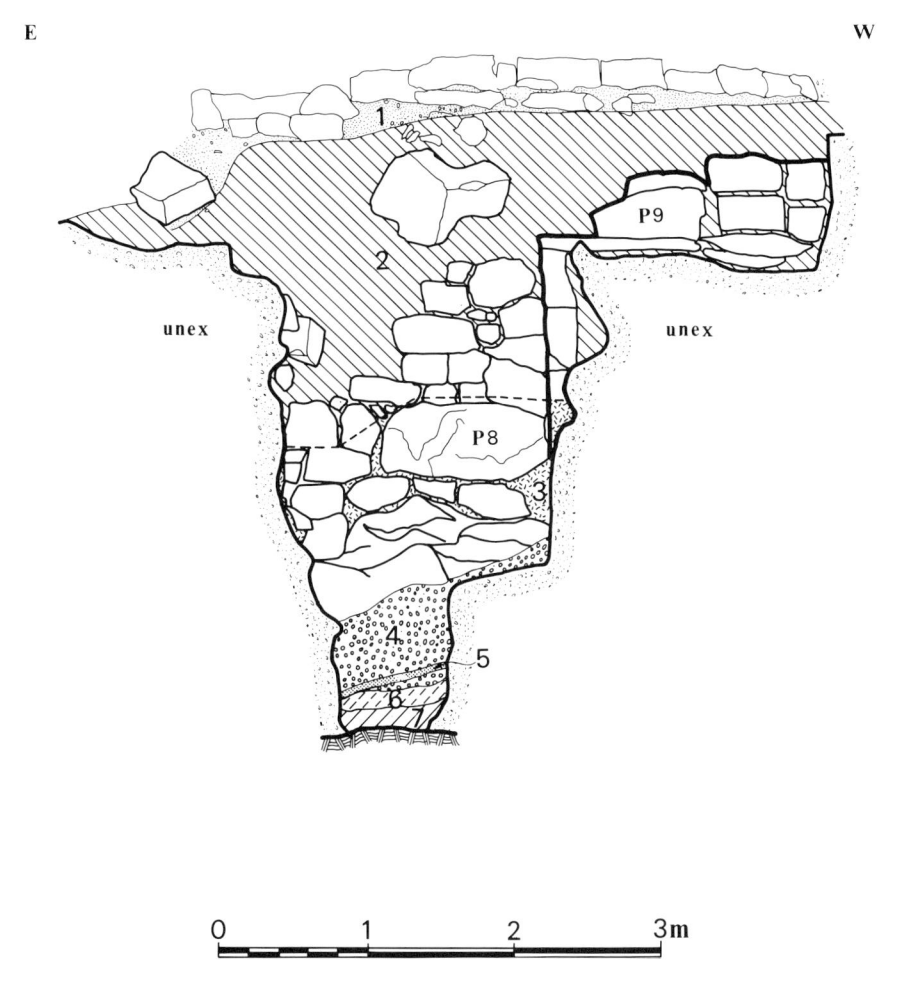

Figure 23: East-west section of fill associated with the early Archaic north peribolos walls P8 and P9, drawn from north. 1:50 scale.

approximate location can be fixed with reasonable certainty by the survival of a ca. 2.90 m. long stretch of the west wall P10 (Fig. 25; Pl. 22) in gridsquare F16, 1. The eastern face of wall P10 was carried away in antiquity, leaving only its western face intact to the height of a single course. This rises over low rubble foundations set on bedrock and earth fill. While the foundations are ca. 0.60 m. wide, its one preserved course of irregularly squared blocks is only 0.45 m. wide because of damage to its outer face. The employment here of rubble in combination with roughly dressed squared blocks resembles more closely the construction of walls P9, P2, P13, and, to some extent, wall P1 than that of the preserved sections which makeup the eastern half of the Archaic peribolos, walls P3, P7, and P8.

CONTEXT AND DATE OF THE PERIBOLOS WEST WALL

Wall P10 is bedded on a thin layer of terra rossa fill over bedrock (St. 4) Its foundations are covered with a light-red-colored soil (F16, 1, St. 3a) mixed with small stones, a small number of badly smashed and unidentifiable sherds, and an island gem dated to the final quarter of the seventh century B.C. By itself, the gem does little to date the wall, apart from providing a rough confirmation of its generally early date.

The Earliest Peribolos, Some Final Observations

The southern line of the peribolos, the southeastern corner, and the west peribolos wall all provide evidence of varying degrees of reliability for a general construction date around 600 B.C. The wall P11 addition erected in the western half of the southern peribolos must date either shortly before or after 580 B.C.

Plate 20: Fill across east end of F14/G14, sounding. Viewed from west.

If we disregard the solitary corner squared block built into the northwest corner of wall P2, what survives of the eastern half of the peribolos is built with a mixture of rubble and polygonal masonry, while the western half appears to combine squared blocks with rubble or, on occasion, roughly shaped polygonal stones, with the exception of the short stretch of P12, which apparently makes use of exclusively polygonal masonry over rubble. Our feeling is that, while it is extremely risky to generalize on the basis of such limited evidence, the constructional difference may perhaps supply some support to the hypothesis that the Archaic temenos was originally separated into two parts by a north-south cross-wall, preserved in the southern return of wall P9. If such a division in fact ever existed, the two parts cannot be dated separately.

Temenos Interior

WALL P3A

Turning now to construction occurring inside the early Archaic walled temenos, a glance at Plan A makes it readily apparent that little in the way of interpretable remains actually survives, however many structures may have originally occupied the grounds. There is, however, a short spur of rubble masonry (wall P3a), held together by a whitish limey clay, that extends for ca. 0.55 m. north of the peribolos's south wall P3. Its state of preservation is such that it is impossible to state definitely whether the spur represents collapsed stones from the superstructure of wall P3 or part of an independent wall. If it was in fact a separate wall, the clay might be the remainder of a mudbrick superstructure that has filtered down over

Plate 21: The P9 wall set between the P8 wall to left and the T4 wall to right, corresponding to Fig. 24. Seen from east.

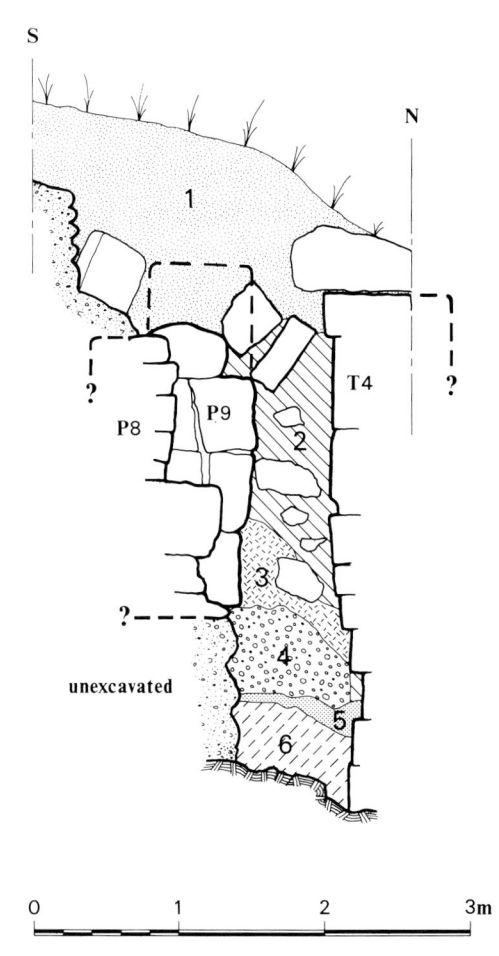

Figure 24: North-south section of fill between the P9 early Archaic north peribolos wall and its T4 later replacement, drawn from east. 1:50 scale.

its rubble core after most of the elevation had been demolished by later building. No evidence survives by which to date it.

WALL P1

In addition, a solitary 4.90 m. long line of east-west masonry, designated wall P1 (Plan A; Fig. 5; Pl. 23), has been preserved ca. 1.00/1.80 m. north of walls P13 and P2. It consists of a ca. 0.30 cm. high foundation of small rubble stones whose maximum width is ca. 0.70 m. Wall P1 otherwise rests on bedrock and a thin layer of red argillaceous soil (E13/14, 1, 3 and D13, Area 2, 2, Ext. N., 3) which has buried most of its preserved elevation. The only dateable object excavated from this context is a fragment of an East Greek round aryballos, dated ca. 575-525 B.C.

Given the poorly preserved state of the adjacent walls P12, P13, and P2, it is not possible to determine with any certainty whether wall P1 was once part of an independent structure, occupying the southern interior of the early Archaic temenos, or was instead integrated with the line of the southern peribolos. It has already been observed that wall P2 either could have continued west to link up directly with walls P13 and P12 to create a straight east-west peribolos or alternatively might have veered south to form an elbow in the peribolos associated with wall P12. Even a third possibility exists, which is that walls P2 and P13 were originally attached to wall P1.

On the other hand, surface indications suggest that wall P1 probably continued west to a point where it intersected with wall P13. This would seem to vitiate the possibility that wall P1 was originally part of the outer peribolos of the temenos. Unfortunately, as the reader is now doubtless acutely aware, none of these suggestions can be proven one way or the other. For purposes of the present discussion it seems best to treat wall P1 as if it were built independently of the line of the peribolos and otherwise leave unresolved the question of what it might once have been a part.

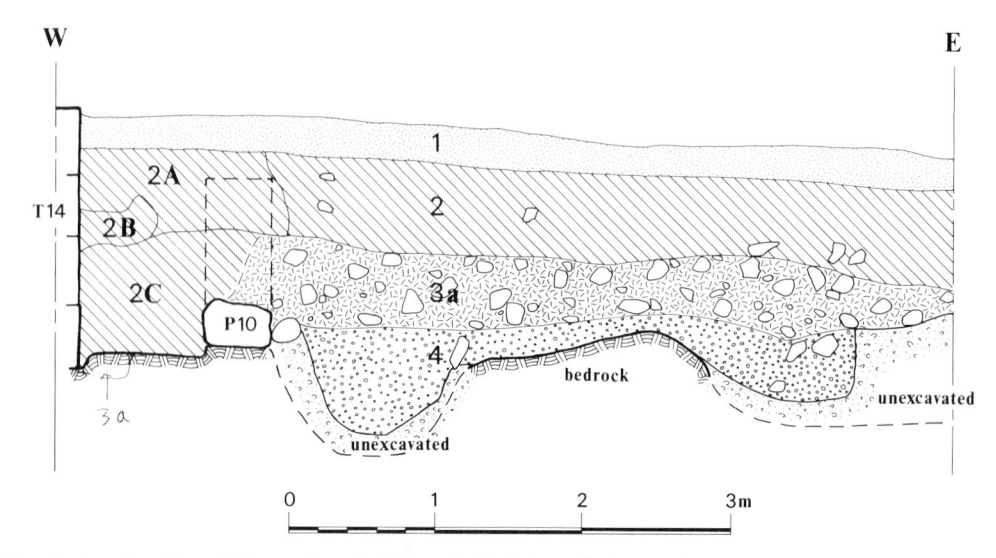

Figure 25: East-west section of fill covering the P10 early Archaic wall, drawn from south from the Middle Sanctuary's T14 Hellenistic west wall across north edge of F16, 1. 1:50 scale.

Plate 22: The P10 early Archaic peribolos west wall running parallel to the Middle Sanctuary's Hellenistic main west wall T14, to right, and at right angles to the later Archaic peribolos spur, wall W38. Seen from north.

Plate 23: Early Archaic rubble wall P1, seen from west, with the S5 Sacred House occupying the background.

Wall Features South of the Peribolos

The situation with the architectural remains south of what is here assumed to constitute the core of the early Archaic walled temenos is hardly less enigmatic, despite the fact that the evidence of actual walls is somewhat more abundant. Three separate clusters of walls have been unearthed in various locations south of the early Archaic peribolos. We may begin with an examination of the three or possibly four spur walls excavated in the immediate vicinity of the peribolos.

WALLS P2, P4, P5, AND P6

At least three of the four walls associated with the peribolos's south face run south at approximately right-angles to the principal surviving east-west segment of the southern peribolos, wall P3 (Plan A; Fig. 13). These are the three eastern walls, P4, P5, and P6 (Pls. 24-27), which abut wall P3 but otherwise fail to bond with its fabric. The western spur, P2, is separated by a gap of only 0.75 m. from the end of wall P3 and may be safely assumed to have once joined with it,

if it is indeed a spur at all. All four are made up of rough rubble stones, as opposed to the plug-shaped polygonal blocks that constitute such a distinctive feature of wall P3 (Pl. 27). The individual stones vary in length from ca. 0.25 to 0.80 m. and survive to a maximum height of ca. 0.60 m.

The southern course of walls P5 and P6 is interrupted by the line of the later Archaic pseudoisodomic peribolos, T1 (Pls. 24, 27). As excavated, walls P2 and P4 appear simply to peter out, but obviously at one time they continued further south. While the line of wall P6 diverges to the east from the lines of the remaining three spurs, it appears to have been pushed out of its original alignment by earth pressure in post-Archaic times.

CONTEXT AND DATE OF WALLS P2, P4, P5, AND P6

Bedrock under and around walls P2, P4, P5, and P6 is covered with a thin layer of red argillaceous soil, D12/13, A, 4 (Figs. 16, 26). St. 4 is then succeeded by a narrow (ca. 0.05

m. thick) "floor" (St. 3a) of coarse yellow earth, clay-like in texture and filled with ash and bones (Pl. 11). Traces of the floor are especially noticeable in the angle formed by P3 with the west face of wall P6 and therefore the stratum does not appear in Figs. 16 and 26. While passing beneath P5 and P6, the 3a floor halts at the south footings of P3 and does not reappear on its north. Consequently, wall P3 must be earlier than either wall P5 or P6.

The same layer, accumulating in places to a depth of ca. 0.30 m., continues east of wall P6 (Fig. 17) to where D12/13, A, 4 becomes D12/E12, D, 5. It also appears to spread south of the later pseudoisodomic peribolos T1 into D12/13, B where it once again appears as a St. 4 fill over bedrock inside the basement of the Roman period compartment S14. There exists no trace of the 3a clay floor recorded north of wall T1, but instead we have a layer of stone chips embedded in the surface of St. 4, which may relate to the construction of the post-A.D. 115 compartment S14. Possibly the St. 3a clay floor was destroyed in this sector at the time of the construction of the T1 later Archaic peribolos wall, which permitted a small number of relatively late objects to settle on the upper surface of D12/13, B, 4.

As for the chronological implications of this fill, D12/13, A, 4 in the immediate vicinity of walls P2, P4, P5, and P6 contained East Greek and Corinthian pottery dating from ca. 600 to 550 B.C., along with a terracotta duck figurine assigned to the late sixth century B.C. On the other hand, the miscellaneous items of personal adornment from the same context are somewhat earlier, dating from the late seventh to the early sixth century. Where the fill spreads east of wall P6 to become D12/E12, D, 5 it contained terracotta figurines dating from the mid to late sixth century B.C., East Greek wares spanning the years ca. 600 to 520 B.C., and a number of LC and LC I sherds.

The D12/13, B, 4 fill south of wall T1, representing almost certainly a continuation of the same occupation level as St. 4 to its north, contained one of the richest accumulations of early material encountered anywhere within the sanctuary. It covers a period from the end of the seventh century to ca. 475 B.C.

Among the more notable early finds are ca. 250 fragments of Corinthian pottery, dating from MC to LC II, various East Greek sherds including an early sixth century plastic aryballos in the shape of a bivalvular shell, Attic Black Figure and R.F that range from ca. 550 B.C. to the early fifth century B.C., mid-sixth to early fifth century B.C. terracotta figures, eight silver coins struck between ca. 570 and 475 B.C., jewelry, and miscellaneous bronze and terracotta items. The deposit of miniature Corinthian vessels included at least twenty kotylai, three bowls, two black glaze hydriai, three pixides, two kothons, and two lids.

This important assemblage is, however, contaminated with a relatively small number of later finds that presumably made their way into the upper surface of D12/13, B, 4 at the time of the construction of the Imperial period compartment (S14) that eventually occupied this sector of the Upper Sanctuary. These include a late second, early first century B.C. bronze coin, lamp fragments of the fifth/fourth centuries B.C., two third century B.C. fragments of vertically fluted black glaze wares, and an iron pickaxe that may be as late as the Roman period. Because the stratum shows signs of having been disturbed, its continuation north of the later Archaic peribolos T1 in the immediate proximity of the surviving spur walls provides a more reliable index for the date of the wall series. Here the bulk of the evidence from D12/13, A, 4 points to a construction period of ca. 560/550 B.C., that is to say, perhaps forty years after the initial construction of the southern peribolos against which the spur walls were built.

ORIGINAL APPEARANCE OF WALLS P2, P4, P5, AND P6

With only four short stumps of walls surviving, little can be reliably adduced of either their original plan or their use. They may have formed the side walls of a series of small but uniformly sized rooms, ranging between 2.00 and 2.25 m. in width, that attached to the exterior of the southern peribolos for any number of reasons. As we have seen, however, the ground south of walls P4, P5, and P6 contained an extraordinarily rich accumulation of early finds, including what seems to have been a deliberate deposit of miniature Corinthian vessels. This perhaps suggests that the wall series together formed part of some kind of single sacred—as opposed to utilitarian—edifice.

In closing this initial description it is perhaps not out of place to note that, despite their conspicuously small size, the internal widths of the three rooms thus formed by the wall series are marginally larger than the central and eastern chambers of the contemporary Shrine of Ophellas (E2) along the eastern flank of Cyrene's agora.[12] The E2 shrine has been restored with three small cellae erected across its rear and a single broad vestibule set across the front. The construction of the lower parts of its walls consists of rubble mixed with randomly spaced squared blocks in a technique that resembles much of the construction of the western half of the early Archaic peribolos of the Demeter Sanctuary. Its superstructure is said to have been completed in mudbrick, which, if ever used in conjunction with the present wall series, has left no trace of its presence. The western cella of the E2 shrine has been restored as only 1.15 m. wide. If correct, this would give a total width to the Agora monument of ca. 6.15 m. If walls P2, P4, P5, and P6 were once part of a similarly designed single structure, their total combined width would have been 9.60 m., with an orientation toward the south. While somewhat unusual for a sacred edifice, a southern orientation does not lack parallels in Archaic architecture.[13]

---

12. *Agora* I, 34-55, figs. 12, 15, 25. Stucchi, *Architettura* 7-8, fig. 1.
13. The later eighth, early seventh century mystery cult sanctuary building at Xoborgo on Tinos faces to the south-southwest. See H. Drerup, *Archaeologia Homerica* II (Göttingen 1969) 0 55, fig. 46. The familiar later seventh century temple of Apollo at Thermum is oriented south. Dinsmoor, 42, 49, fig. 14. The various stages of the Telesterion at Eleusis look southeast (the Roman period Temple L10 at that site incidentally faces south-southwest). Mylonas, *Eleusis* 103-04, 179, fig. 4. Locally, two of the later small temples within Cyrene's Sanctuary of Apollo open to the south, these being the so-called Temple of Hecate and the Temple of the Parallel Orthostates. Goodchild, *Kyrene* 128, fig. 13, no. 28 and Stucchi, *Architettura* pl. I, nos. 8 and 19.

Plate 24: Early Archaic spur walls to north of the later Archaic peribolos wall T1, viewed from east. Wall T1 lies to left. Wall P6 occupies foreground, wall P5 middleground. Partly excavated P4 wall visible against western end of D12/13, A.

Early Wall Remains at the Level of the Upper Sanctuary

Two additional sets of early walls have been brought to light in the center of the high ground later developed into what is eventually termed the Upper Sanctuary (Plans A, E). The first of these, here designated Walled Structure P14, was discovered along the southern edge of the D12 gridsquare in C13/D13, 1 and D12/13, F, about 6.50 m. south of wall P5. The second, wall P15, came to light in C15/16, 1 and is therefore separated from the first by some 28 m. The distance renders the likelihood that the two sets of walls were once part of a single monument somewhat implausible at first sight. On the other hand, it must be borne in mind that only the most minimal sort of deep-level investigation could be undertaken in the intervening space before excavation was terminated in 1978. If the plan of the early Archaic sanctuary at the level of the later Middle Sanctuary resembles a moth-eaten rug with most of its center eaten out, here at the level of the Upper Sanctuary what is left of the early sanctuary is more like the remains of a thoroughly cremated body, which has left us with only a few scattered teeth and a handful of ashes.

WALLED STRUCTURE P14

The principal wall remains of P14 (Pl. 28) run approximately east-west for a distance of 5.15 m. before the west end disappears beneath the unexcavated sub-mosaic fill of the early Imperial corridor (S22) (Fig. 27). The east end forms a corner and turns south for a distance of 1.80 m. before its line is lost west of the later Archaic period structure S4. Both of the P14 walls are constructed of a mixture of rubble and squared blocks, of which some of the latter attain lengths up to 1.30 m. In constructional terms their closest parallels are with walls P9 and P10 from the western half of the early Archaic peribolos.

Plate 25: Detail of the P6 wall from east.

Plate 26: Detail of the P5 wall from east. Trace of the P4 wall visible in background.

Plate 27: South face of later Archaic T1 peribolos wall with early Archaic rubble spur walls P4, P5, and P6 behind it. Seen from south.

CONTEXT AND DATE OF WALLED STRUCTURE P14

The stratigraphy (Fig. 27) consists of a thin layer of terra rossa over bedrock (D12/13, F, 4 and C13/D13, 1, 8) succeeded by a dark orange colored clayey fill (D12/13, F, 3 and C13/D13, 1, 7) that buries the foundations and part of the P14 superstructure. Both strata contain unusually rich concentrations of Archaic finds that are characterized by their unusual purity. What is meant by this is that neither level includes any find that is necessarily later than the first quarter of the fifth century, with the solitary exception of a single fourth century B.C. lamp fragment from D12/13, F, 4. This context would otherwise represent one of the very few examples of a sealed Archaic deposit produced by this site. Under the circumstances it does not seem unreasonable to attribute the presence of the fourth century lamp to error in the excavation's recording process.

In addition to the usual ceramic finds the two layers combined to produce a remarkable concentration of miscellaneous silver as well as bronze artifacts, eleven incised gems, and seven silver coins minted before 475 B.C. Since the coins appear to be later than all other classes of dated finds, which in the aggregate date before ca. 520 B.C., a construction date of 490 B.C. (the earliest date permissible for the coins) is appropriate for the Walled Structure P14.

WALL P15

The other Upper Sanctuary level early Archaic wall is constructed entirely from rubble stones that rest on bedrock (Pl. 29). Its preserved north-south length is 5.30 m. (Fig. 28). What is left of its original thickness

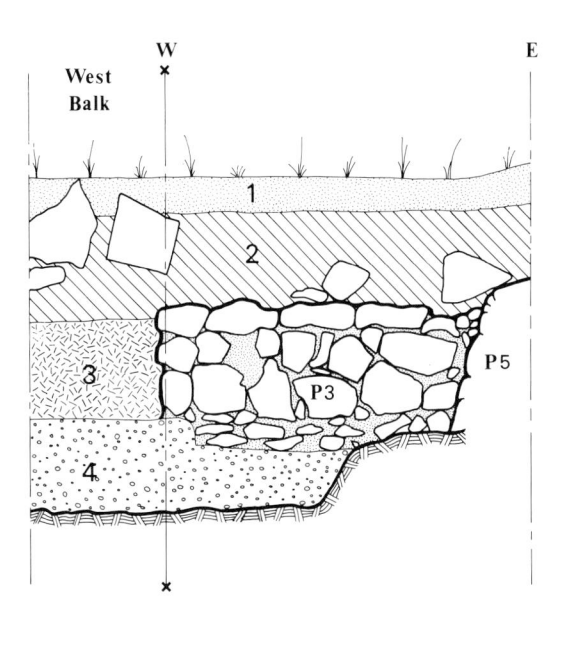

Figure 26: East-west section of fill over the P3 early Archaic wall and north-south fill ("west balk") at west end of D12/13, A, drawn before excavation of the P4 wall. 1:50 scale.

Plate 28: View from northeast of early Archaic Walled Structure P14 (foreground) as it disappears under S22 Mosaic Corridor fill.

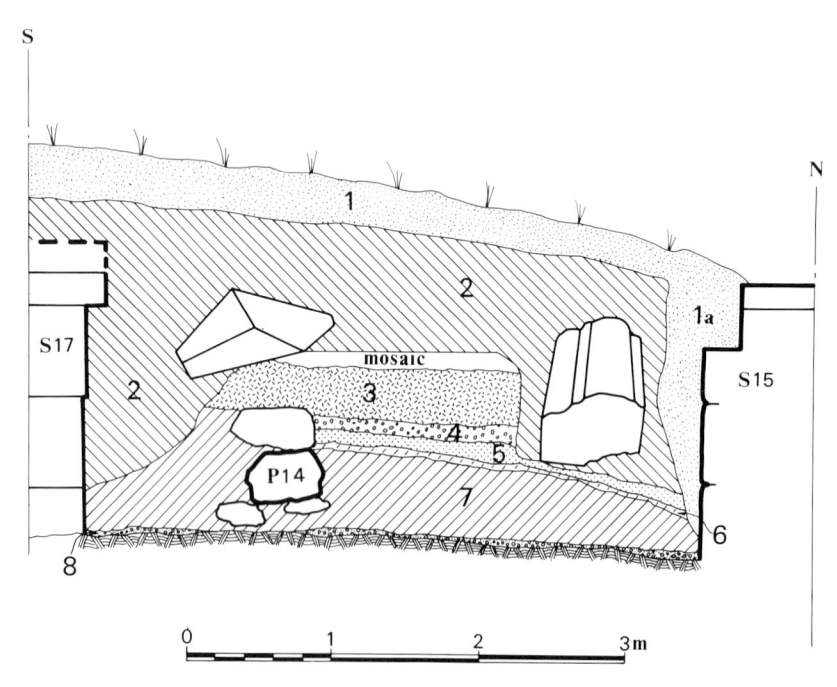

Figure 27: North-south section of fill between S15 Colonnade Vestibule and the Southwest Building (S17), drawn from east. The P14 early Archaic rubble Walled Structure is buried in C13/D13, 1 fill beneath the early Imperial S22 Mosaic Corridor. 1:50 scale.

amounts to no more than 0.40 to 0.50 m. Its east face is masked by the later pseudoisodomic wall W30 that in part rests on a foundation of P15 rubble. The construction of the later wall may explain the partial demolition of the western face of wall P15. It is possible that if its original east face could be exposed, it would display a polygonal technique similar to that of the southeastern peribolos, wall P3. In any event, P15 survives to a maximum height of only two courses ca. 0.60 m. high. Its purpose is unknown.

CONTEXT AND DATE OF WALL P15

The stratigraphy of C15/16, 1: W4 consists of pockets of a mostly sterile St. 5 terra rossa covered by a dense reddish brown St. 4 that seals the wall's western footings and much of its surviving elevation. The little dateable material that St. 5 contains belongs to the late seventh, early sixth century, while St. 4's early material is offset by several late Hellenistic bronze coins, lamps, and ceramics that may date as late as the first century B.C. The stratum was apparently contaminated by the nearby early Imperial pottery and lamp dump S18 (Plan E), and the wall is therefore associated with a disturbed early context that cannot be used to supply a construction date. On the basis, however, of the similarity of its construction to that of the early peribolos, along with its association with the two early strata directly over bedrock, its assignment to the early Archaic period seems secure.

Plate 29: Early Archaic P15 rubble wall seen from southwest covered by the later Archaic W30 bislab wall.

Commentary

What the earliest walled remains thus far described in association with both the principal walled nucleus of the early sanctuary occupying the level of the later Middle Sanctuary and the various more widely scattered remains across the site's upper levels add up to can be summarized as follows. The best-preserved architectural element to survive from the earliest phase of the Wadi Bel Gadir sanctuary is its peribolos enclosure, which is roughly rectangular in plan and measures ca. sixty m. east to west by twenty-two m. north to south. The ground inside the resulting temenos rises approximately six m. from north to south. When examined from the point of view of its masonry technique, the eastern half of the enclosure seems to be slightly different from the west insofar as the eastern half makes a more consistent use of a mixture of polygonal with rubble masonry, while parts of the western combine squared blocks with plain rubble. There appears, moreover, to be a shift in the alignment of the north wall of the peribolos at the point where wall P8 meets P9, which suggests that the sanctuary interior might have been divided by a now missing north-south cross-wall into two essentially contemporary but spatially unequal parts. This hypothesis, however, seems incapable of further demonstration at this time and should be treated with considerable caution.

The initial construction date for the overall peribolos enclosure, including both halves, occurs around 600 B.C. In addition, some alteration must have been carried out on its southern line some time after 580 B.C.; this is today embodied in the area of wall P11.

The remaining traces of early wall construction occur on the higher ground to the south that was later developed into what has come to be termed the Upper Sanctuary. Here, either a series of uniformly sized rooms or perhaps a single triple-celled sacred building (walls P2, P4, P5, P6) were built against the outer face of the southern peribolos around 560/550 B.C. In addition, the corner (wall P14) of an apparently independent structure of unknown character came to light a short distance to the south, dating to perhaps 520 B.C. Its masonry employs the same technique as the western half of the early peribolos. Lastly, a wall (P15) attached to what was probably a second Archaic structure was recovered from a disturbed context in the grounds of the western half of the later Upper

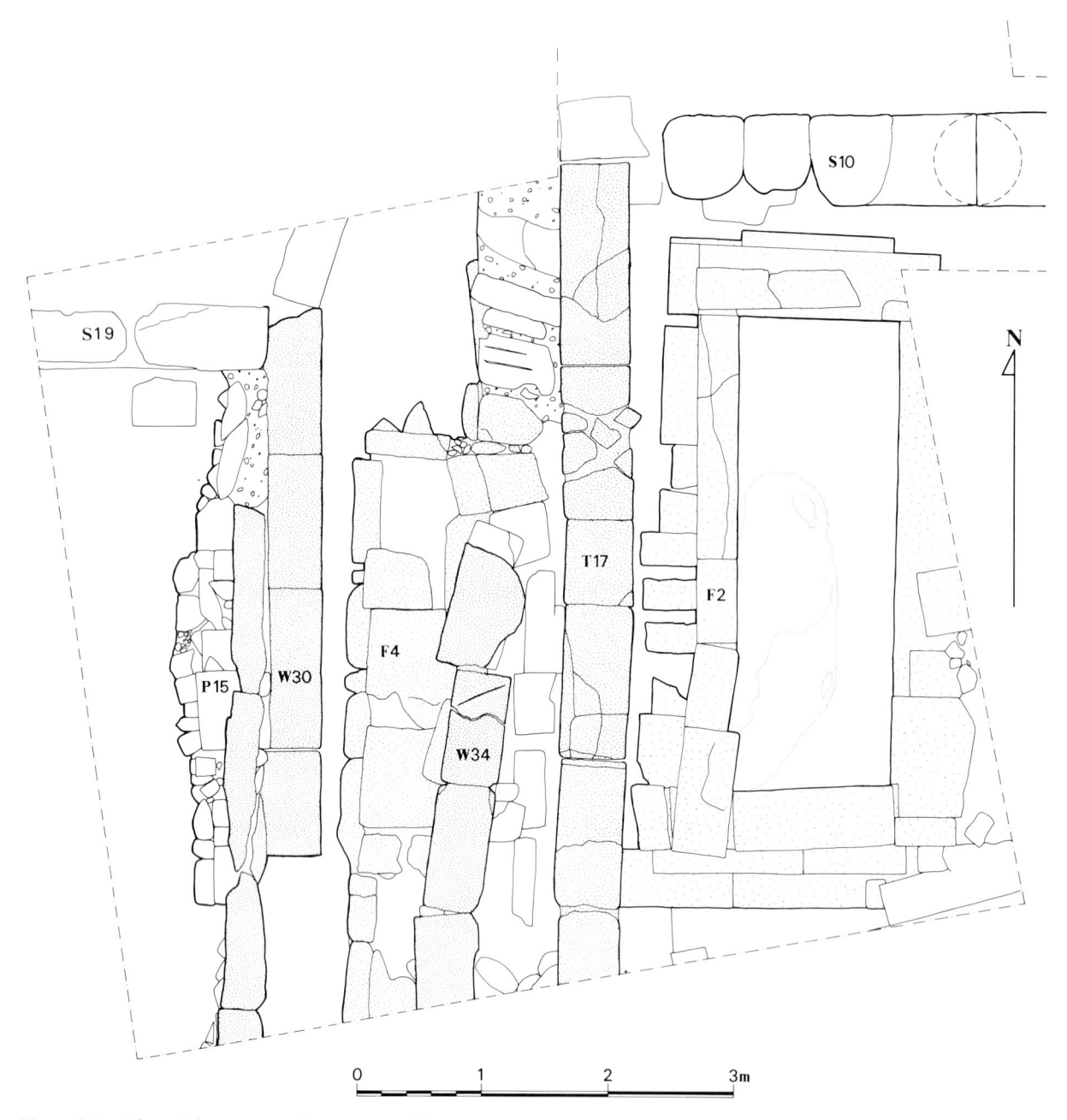

Figure 28: Plan of the upper southwest corner of the Sanctuary (C15/16, 1), illustrating the P15 early Archaic wall flanking the later Archaic wall W30. The Hellenistic F2 fountain complex lies to east. 1:50 scale.

Sanctuary. No trace of what can be plausibly identified as a continuation of the peribolos enclosure has been found at this level of the early temenos, unless of course the fragmentary P14 and P15 walls had something to do with such an arrangement.

The two construction periods of the peribolos proper therefore occur roughly a generation after Cyrene's initial 631 B.C. foundation and subsequently around the time of the city's so-called second colonization wave, carried out under Battus II around 580 B.C., whose historical significance has already been commented on elsewhere.[14] Further discussion of the sanctuary's development within the framework of the late seventh and sixth centuries is to be found below.[15] In the meantime the following more general points may be considered.

---

14. *Final Reports* I, 23-27. *Final Reports* II, 96-105.
15. See infra 177-179.

HILLSIDE SETTING

It has long been observed that Demeter sanctuaries were apt to be sited on slopes and hilltops.[16] Some of the better known of the later Demeter sanctuaries provide obvious parallels to the hillside setting of the Cyrene version, including Priene[17] and Pergamum,[18] to mention but two of the most obvious. The Sanctuary at Cnidus, which in many respects is one of the most important, albeit least well recorded, of all the known Hellenistic Demeter sanctuaries, was built on a terrace set on rising ground,[19] as was the apparently Hellenistic *Thesmophorion* at Eretria.[20]

More immediately relevant to the present discussion is the fact that the same pattern can be detected in the placement of a number of excavated examples of early Demeter sanctuaries that are in round terms roughly coeval with the Cyrene sanctuary. For example, the Sanctuary of Demeter occupying the slope of Acrocorinth was already in existence by the early seventh century B.C.[21] The seventh to fourth century B.C. Sanctuary of Demeter Thesmophoros at Troizen occupied a slope overlooking the village of Damala.[22] The largely destroyed *Eleusinion* at Kalyvia Sokhas near Sparta must date roughly to the same time. Its original location has never been precisely identified but appears to have been situated at the foot of a steep slope.[23] The later sixth century *Thesmophorion* at Evraiocastro, west of the ancient town of Thasos, occupied a terraced setting on rising ground.[24] The *Eleusinion* in Athens east of the Panathenaic Way on the northwest foot of the Acropolis occupied a gentle slope. It must have come into existence by at least as early as the end of the sixth century B.C.[25] Even the great sanctuary at Eleusis arguably made use of rising ground for its Archaic Telesterion.[26]

The evidence is also abundant from the west. While the controversial Archaic "cave sanctuary" at Acragas that was built on a rocky shelf on the precipitous eastern slope of the *rupe Atenea* may not be a Demeter sanctuary at all,[27] the late sixth century B.C. *Temple C*, constructed above the cave sanctuary on a hillside terrace beneath the Medieval Church of S. Biagio, is securely attached to the goddess's cult.[28] The extramural Sanctuary of Demeter Malophoros at Selinus, which began its existence in the late seventh century B.C., lay on the gentle slope of a low sandy hill a short distance from the west bank of the river Mudiuni.[29] The hillside Demeter-Kore sanctuary at Terravecchia di Cuti in western Sicily is evidently to be dated to the late sixth, early fifth century B.C.[30]

When combined with the numerous literary references to hillside Demeter sanctuaries collected by Béquignon,[31] this short overview of excavated examples makes it clear that the hillside setting of the sanctuary under discussion is fairly typical of many Demeter sanctuaries of nearly every period. Béquignon's view that the goddess's preference for slopes stems in every case from the early veneration of her mother Rhea as a Cretan mountain deity is unconvincing, especially when applied to the later sanctuary foundations, and it makes better sense to look for the reasons behind the selection of any given site in whatever conditions or circumstances prevail locally. As far as can be determined here, the crucial factors were the probability that an intramural Demeter Sanctuary had already been established more or less directly across Wadi Bel Gadir in the area that was to become Cyrene's agora,[32] the relationship of the site to the agricultural regions to its south,[33] the setting's relative privacy,[34] the availability of water for lustration and sacrifice throughout the year in a landscape that normally suffers drought during the summer,[35] and lastly the possible symbolic value of

---

16. Béquignon, *Déese acropolitaine* 149-77.

17. *Priene* 147-63.

18. Bohtz, *Pergamon* 10-14. Gruben, *Greek Temples* 490-91, figs. 151, 152, pls. 172, 173.

19. C. Newton, *A History of Discovery at Halicarnassus, Cnidus, and Branchidae* II (London 1865) 376-425. I. Love, *AJA* 76 (1972) 399-401, ill. 5.

20. *AR* 11 (1964-65) 18. K. Davaras, *ArchDelt* 208 (1965) 257. P. Auberson and K. Schefold, *Führer durch Eretria* (Bern 1972) 105.

21. *Acrocorinth V* 267, n. 1 for bibl.

22. Paus. 2.32.8. G. Welter, *Troizen und Kelaureiai* (Berlin 1941) 20 ff. The large cache of Archaic vases found in the corner of its temenos indicates that the sanctuary originated at least as early as the sixth century B.C.; the extant walls, however, appear to be later.

23. J. Cook, *BSA* 45 (1950) 261-63.

24. C. Picard, *CRAI* 1913, 365-68. G. Picard, *MonPiot* 32 (1932) 24. G. Picard, *RA*, ser. 6, 35-36 (1950) 125. J. Pouilloux, *BCH* 75 (1951) 90-96. C. Rolley, *BCH* 89 (1965) 468-83, esp. 478.

25. Thompson and Wycherley, 150-55. R. Wycherley, *The Stones of Athens* (Princeton 1978) 71.

26. Mylonas, *Eleusis* 67-70.

---

27. *Agrigento* 24-29. G. Cultera, *AttiPal* 1942, 609-27. G. Zuntz, *Klearchos* 20 (1963) 114-24. Le Dinahet, *Sanctuaires* 143-44. See *AR* 28 (1981-82) 97; *AR* 34 (1987-88) 127. Also see infra chap. 5, n. 58.

28. *Agrigento* 66-72. Gruben, *Greek Temples* 433. Le Dinahet, *Sanctuaires* 144.

29. E. Gabrici, *Malophoros* 4 ff. D. White, *AJA* 71 (1967) 335. Gruben, *Greek Temples* 421-22, figs. 82-85, pls. 124, 125. Le Dinahet, *Sanctuaires* 141-42.

30. *AR* 28 (1981-82) 100.

31. See the material collected by Béquignon (supra n. 16).

32. The sanctuary has already been identified according to its Italian excavators. See *Agora* II,1, 27-39. In my view the final identification must be regarded as still pending. *Final Reports* I, 23, n. 2. D. White, *AJA* 86 (1982) 606-07. For the topographical relationship of the Agora to the extramural Demeter and Persephone Sanctuary see *Final Reports* I, 3, figs. 3, 4.

33. *Final Reports* I, 53. White, *Suburban Expansion* 105-16.

34. *Final Reports* I, 48-53.

35. *Final Reports* I, 36, fig. 39.

certain terrain features, such as caves and springs that may have reminded the early worshippers of the occurrence of similar features in Demeter's myth.[36]

PERIBOLOS ENCLOSURE

The second distinctive feature of the early sanctuary is the peribolos enclosure itself, which is an element common to many Archaic *temene*,[37] despite the fact that too frequently it is the peribolos that is less likely either to survive or to be excavated than the structures it surrounds.[38] Because chthonian deities were customarily worshipped in secret, their precincts were frequently surrounded by outer walls which had the effect of restricting both visual as well as physical access to their interiors. A familiar example from the repertory of later Demeter sanctuaries is supplied by Priene where the intramural sanctuary lay inside a rectangular enclosure of strongly built ashlar walls that doubled as a framework for the interior buildings and a barrier to the outside.[39] In the Demeter and Kore Sanctuary at Iasos in Caria a small prostyle temple built ca. 510-480 B.C. was set inside a ca. 22 m. square structure toward the end of the fifth century. Its fragmentary walls are described as part of a "building," but they resemble more the outer walls of an enclosure designed along the same lines as the Priene sanctuary.[40] The polygonal peribolos wall of the *Thesmophorion* at Eretria, which ought to be earlier than the Hellenistic structures it surrounded, was architecturally detached from the inner cult buildings and served only as a barrier.[41] The late seventh, early sixth century rubble peribolos that surrounded the primitive megaron of Demeter Malophoros at Selinus provides an unusually close parallel with the Cyrene sanctuary.[42] Its later sixth century replacement was built of well-cut ashlar masonry.[43] A peribolos is epigraphically attested for the Delian *Thesmophorion*,[44]

---

36. A small rock cavity, which may have begun as a natural rock shelter and later was modified for cultic reasons, was discovered a short distance to the east of the Ain Bu Gadir. See *Final Reports* I, 44, fig. 39. Given that many natural caves are found in the wadis surrounding Cyrene, coupled with the geological instability of the local terrain, it is possible that a larger and poetically more evocative cave now sealed by earth slides at one time existed near the sanctuary and remains to be discovered. Caves are associated with Demeter and Persephone sanctuaries not only because in a fairly straightforward way they symbolize the underworld but also because in the various regionally localized versions of the stories of Persephone's rape Hades is made to enter and exit this world by means of a cleft or chasm. "But the wide-pathed earth yawned there in the plain of Nysa" (*Hymn. Hom Cer.* 15-17, Loeb trans.). "Near to it" (Enna, central Sicily) "also are sacred groves, surrounded by marshy flats, and a huge grotto which contains a chasm which leads down into the earth and opens to the north, and through it, the myth relates, Pluton coming out with his chariot, effected the Rape of the Core" (Diod. 5.3.3-4, Loeb trans.). See also ibid. 5.4.2. Claud., *Rapt. Pros.* 163-81. In addition, according to the Phigalian version of her legend, during Demeter's time of angry retirement when the earth bore no fruits, the goddess lived in a "black cave": Paus. 8.42.1. Freese, *Demeter* 981. Farnell, *Demeter Cult* 50-51, 320-21, n. 40. Thus Eleusis had its celebrated cave of Pluto, the "very gates of Hades." Mylonas, *Eleusis* 99-100. Kerenyi, *Eleusis* 80, fig. 27. The fissure through which Heracles dragged Cerberus near the Temple of Demeter and Persephone at Hermione was dedicated to Pluto: Paus. 2.35.7. At Hierapolis Nysa and Thymbria in Asia Minor caves that exhaled chemical vapors were called the *Plutonia* and *Charonia*: Strab. 13.629; 14.619. As we have already seen, according to Demeter's Sicilian myth, the cave into which Kore was drawn by Hades was located near Enna (*Mir. Ausc.* 82. Solin. 5.14-15) where traces of a Demeter sanctuary have been identified in a cave on the eastern tip of the acropolis. See O. Rossbach, *Castrogiovanni, Das Alte Henna in Sizilien* (Leipzig 1912) 9. P. Orsi, *NSc* 1931, 373 ff. A natural cave that contains early Demeter figurines has been found on the eastern edge of Megara Hyblaia. See P. Orsi, *MonAnt* 1 (1889) 723. F. Cavallari, *Bull. della commissione di antichita e belle arti in Sicilia* VI (1873) 5, 9-10. F. Winter, *Die Typen der Figurlichen Terrakotten* I (Berlin 1903) xcvi-xcvii. At Centuripe near the town cathedral a cave has been excavated which contained a significant cache of Demeter votive figurines. See G. Libertini, *Centuripe* (Catania 1926) 93-94. However, for a contrary view see Zuntz, *Persephone* 255, n. 2. In addition to the role played by water in preparing for the celebration of Demeter's rites, wells and springs constitute important topographical features in both the Athenian and Sicilian versions of the goddess's story. See infra chap. 4, 5, 144-147.

37. Bergquist, *Temenos* passim. Dinsmoor, 113.

38. Sicilian Gela supplies a case in point. Although the small Classical period Demeter shrine house at Vassalaggi located west of Caltanisetta was discovered with traces of a walled peribolos surrounding it, most of the remaining, similarly modest suburban and rural Demeter sanctuaries located in districts in and around Gela such as Bitalemi, Madonna dell'Alemanna, Carrubazza, Via Fiume, Predio Sola, Scalo Ferroviario, Feudo Nobile, Villa Iacona, and Molino a Vento, along with those further afield from Gela, such as Monte Saraceno, Monte S. Mauro, and Monte Bubbonia, have all been reported with no published reference to enclosures, despite the fact that most of them must have been set inside some kind of peribolos. For Vassalaggi see *Kokalos* 14-15 (1968-69) 334. The Predio Sola sanctuary was published by P. Orlandini, *MonAnt* 46 (1963) 1-78. See ibid. 1, n. 1 for bibl. for Bitalemi, Madonna dell'Alemanna, Carrubazza, Scalo Ferroviario, Villa Iacona, and Via Fiume. For Feudo Nobile see P. Griffo and L. von Matt, *Gela* (Greenwich, Conn. 1968) 24, 39, 66. For Monte Saraceno see P. Mingazzini, *MonAnt* 36 (1938) 671-79. D. Adamesteanu, *ArchCl* 7 (1952) 121-46. Monte S. Mauro: P. Orsi, *MonAnt* 20 (1910) 775-78. Monte Bubbonia: P. Orsi, *NSc* 1905, 447-49. D. Adamesteanu, *ArchCl* 7, fasc. 2 (1955) 179-86. See also Le Dinahet, *Sanctuaires* 138-40, 152.

39. *Priene* 148, fig. 119.

40. D. Levi, *ASAtene* 29-30 (1967-68) 569-72, fig. 37.

41. Auberson and Schefold (supra n. 20) 105.

42. Gabrici, *Malophoros* 16-21.

43. Gabrici, *Malophoros* 66-72.

44. Bruneau, *Cultes* 277, ns. 55-57.

Gambraion in Asia Minor,[45] and Koroneia.[46] Herodotus recorded a structure that appears to have functioned as the porch or gateway to Demeter's temenos wall on Aegina[47] and elsewhere related how Miltiades was injured by scaling the fence surrounding the sanctuary of Demeter Thesmophoros on Paros.[48] At Knossos only four blocks survive from what has been interpreted as the eastern peribolos that once surrounded the fifth century B.C. Temple of Demeter.[49] The *Eleusinion* on the northwest slope of the Acropolis at Athens preserves traces of a surrounding wall to the west of the late sixth century B.C. temple.[50]

The earliest Demeter sanctuary peribolos to survive may be the Lesbian polygonal walls Z11 and Z12 that formed part of the early Archaic enclosure and gate at Eleusis.[51] The approximately meter high stone superstructure of Z12 was continued in mudbrick. Toward the end of the seventh century, a new retaining wall Z20 replaced the older peribolos, again in Lesbian polygonal masonry. During the following century the Peisistratean sanctuary was set inside a strong peribolos constructed on a foundation of large, unworked flat stones. Its superstructure consisted of a socle of polygonal blocks topped with sun-dried brick.[52]

On Acrocorinth the north temenos wall of the Demeter Sanctuary, which doubled as a retaining wall, is preserved to a height of nearly a meter. A section was built as two rows of large boulders, set ca. two m. apart and packed with earth; other sections consisted of a facing of rubble.[53]

Finally, looking closer to hand, the layout of Tocra's Demeter Sanctuary largely remains to be laid bare. However, wall *alpha*, dated to ca. 560 B.C., may have belonged to its peribolos as well as having served as part of the town's early defensive circuit. The line of *alpha* was traced for over 40 m. Its considerable breadth of 2.60 m. was made up of rubble facings that sandwiched a sun-dried brick core.[54] At Cyrene itself, the small intramural "Temenos of Demeter and Kore," located toward the center of the west side of Cyrene's agora, has been restored with a modest, rectangular peribolos enclosure that surrounded two altars. Its walls, which have been dated to the third quarter of the sixth century B.C., were constructed from rubble mixed with occasional larger blocks that have been roughly squared.[55]

DUAL TEMENE

Potentially the most original feature of the layout of the early Archaic sanctuary is its hypothetical separation into two parallel but unequal *temene*. It has been suggested that some form of now totally vanished north-south division wall may have at one time separated the larger sector to the east from its smaller western counterpart.[56]

If the sanctuary was spatially divided into separate *temene* for its two resident goddesses, such a separation has left few clear parallels in antiquity. Pausanias refers to the *Holes* on the road from Troizen to Hermione where there were sanctuaries (pl.) consecrated to Demeter and the Kore,[57] but nothing further is said about how they were spatially organized. Strabo[58] and Pomponius Mela[59] both refer to a single temple dedicated to Demeter at Enna, but Cicero seems to know of a second, apparently quite separate temple consecrated to Persephone at the same site.[60] Again the difficulty is that nothing is known about the topographical relationship of the one to the other. The two may have shared a common temenos or, alternatively, Persephone's temple may have been located in another sector of the ancient town. The mystery cult at Phlya contained two temples. One of these housed altars of Zeus Ktesios, Demeter Ane-

---

45. Thompson, *Thesmophorion* 186, n. 3. *SIG*³, 1219, 31 ff.
46. Thompson, *Thesmophorion* 186, n. 3. *IG* VII, 2876.
47. Thompson, *Thesmophorion* 186, n. 3. Hdt. 6.91.
48. Thompson, *Thesmophorion* 186, n. 3. G. Picard, *RA*, Ser. 6, 35-36 (1950) 124-25. Hdt. 6.134.
49. Coldstream, *Knossos* 15.
50. Thompson and Wycherley, 150, fig. 37.
51. Mylonas, *Eleusis* 64-66, figs. 6, 23.
52. Mylonas, *Eleusis* 90-91, fig. 4, where the Peisistratean peribolos is shown in solid black.
53. *Acrocorinth* V 270.
54. *Tocra* I, 8-12, fig. 3, pls. 1, 2.

55. *Agora* II,1, 27-31, pl. VI, 3, 4, figs. 10, 11. For my doubts as to whether this complex should be associated with Demeter see supra n. 32.

56. The reasons for advancing this theory are, first, a section of the north peribolos wall, wall P9, forms a dog-leg return to the south that is coaxial with a short stump of the south peribolos wall, wall P13. Secondly, the deflection in the line of the north peribolos created by the junction of walls P8 and P9, which appears uncalled-for on structural grounds, is reflected in all subsequent phases of this wall's development down to the time of the terminal A.D. 262 earthquake. This suggests that the separate character of the eastern and western sectors was to some extent honored throughout the sanctuary's subsequent history, although it cannot be overemphasized that no trace of a north-south division wall has been discovered for any period. Finally, there exist constructional differences between the walls of the two sectors: the eastern uses a mixture of rubble foundations and rough polygonal masonry for its superstructure; the western combines occasional pieces of carelessly cut squared masonry with either rubble or polygonal masonry for its superstructure.

57. Paus. 2.34.6.
58. Strab. 6.271.
59. Pompon. 2.117.
60. Cic., II *Verr.* 4.49.

sidora, and Kore Protogene,[61] but the second is clearly disassociated by Pausanias from Demeter and her daughter, which invalidates Rolley's contention that the goddesses must have possessed twin temples.[62] Pausanias describes two temples that were associated with Demeter above the Enneakrounos in Athens, one being dedicated to Triptolemus and the other Demeter and Kore.[63] The latter has been associated with the Southeast Temple, which was assembled in the first century A.D. from materials taken from the Temple of Demeter at Thoricus.[64] The Triptolemus temple has not yet been securely located, but Travlos has raised the likelihood that it may have been excluded from the same precinct as Demeter and Kore.[65] In addition, the Eleusinion below the Acropolis at Athens was housed in a small non-peripteral temple of early fifth century B.C. date. Said to be dedicated to both goddesses, it was set inside a quadrilateral walled precinct to the east of the Panathenaic Way.[66] A second, still unidentified shrine has been found in its own walled-in triangular peribolos directly north of the Eleusinion precinct.[67] Could the one have been dedicated to Demeter and the other to Kore? Travlos has speculated that the Thesmophorion at Athens was located in the zone directly south of the Eleusinion.[68] This presumably could mean that perhaps two or even three sacred buildings associated with the cult in question at Athens theoretically could have been housed in neighboring but independently walled precincts. Finally, inscriptions from Delos refer to a temple of Demeter and a naos of the Kore; at the same time they also mention "the temple that is in the Thesmophorion."[69] While both goddesses could have been worshipped in a common temple, the evidence allows for the possibility that there may have been two shrines. If so, nothing definite is known about the specific topographical relationship of one to the other, since the monuments in question remain unexcavated.

Despite the fact that Demeter sanctuaries often contain more than a single shrine house,[70] there exists no hard archaeological evidence for their separation into parallel temene. Where separate temene are encountered the lesser precincts are reserved for deities other than Demeter and Kore,[71] apart from the problematic Athenian examples just mentioned.

This leads to Syracuse. Various later sources tell us that after the battle of Himera in 480 B.C. Gelon ordered the construction of twin temples to Demeter and Kore.[72] Plutarch implies that they were constructed inside a single temenos.[73] It is now generally accepted that their site lies in the area of the Piazza Vittoria on the mainland where one temple has already been excavated in association with traces of a temenos wall, together with astonishingly rich discov-

---

61. Paus. 1.31.4; 4.1.7. Plut., *Them.* 1. J. Harrison, *Prolegomena to the Study of Greek Religion* (3rd. ed. reprint 1966) 640-44. Nilsson, *GGR* 1, 669. Rolley (supra n. 24) 469, n. 3.
62. Rolley (supra n. 24) 469.
63. Paus. 1.14.1-4. Travlos, *Pictorial Dictionary* 199.
64. H. Thompson, *Hesperia* 29 (1960) 334-43.
65. Travlos, *Pictorial Dictionary* 199.
66. Travlos, *Pictorial Dictionary* 198.
67. Travlos, *Pictorial Dictionary* 198.
68. Travlos, *Pictorial Dictionary* 198.
69. Bruneau, *Cultes* 275-76.
70. The most instructive example of this is the Sanctuary of the Chthonian Gods at Acragas, for which see P. Marconi, *Agrigento arcaica* (Rome 1933) 20-28, 143. Gruben, *Greek Temples* 434-35, pl. 137, fig. 97. Le Dinahet, *Sanctuaires* 144, 148-50, 152. For further discussion see infra 98-104. A less common feature of Demeter sanctuaries is a single dominant temple of conventional peripteral design. Many of her precincts, including the present example so far as we know, do not have large-scale standard temples. For their general scarcity explained on grounds of the exclusion of male worshippers from certain of the goddesses' rites, see Thompson, *Thesmophorion* 186-87. On the other hand, leaving aside the various literary references that habitually fall short of explaining what sort of structures their writers had in mind, exceptions do exist. Thompson, *Thesmophorion* 186, n. 3, notes Pagasai-Demetrias: *Praktika* 1915, 192 ff. Two doubtful examples occur at Acragas where, east of the Sanctuary of the Chthonian Gods, lie two temples, "I" or the "Temple of the Dioscuri" and "L"; both have been linked in the past with the cult of Demeter and Persephone on the strength of their proximity to the nearby sanctuary, but this identification rests on no real proof. See Gruben, *Greek Temples* 435. On the other hand, the fifth century peripteral temple from Thoricus already mentioned (supra n. 64), transferred in Roman times to the southeast corner of the Athenian Agora, seems reliably to have been associated originally with Demeter and Kore, whatever its later identification might have been. See H. Mussche et al., *Thorikos* II (Brussels 1964) 73-74. But was it a temple? Its Doric colonnade is said to have been heptastyle by fourteen, which is scarcely a conventional temple arrangement for the fifth century. Both Thompson and Mussche carefully avoid labelling it a temple. For its later existence as the Agora's Southeast Temple, see Thompson and Wycherley, 167. Travlos, *Pictorial Dictionary* 104, 199. *The Athenian Agora. A Guide to the Excavation and Museum* (3rd. ed. Athens 1976) 139-41. Demeter was provided with a standard hexastyle by eleven temple at Lepreon. See H. Knell, *AAA* 12-13 (1979-80) 53-60. The Sanctuary of Despoina, an ancient chthonian deity identified with Demeter and Persephone, received at Lycosura west of Megalopolis a Doric hexastyle prostyle temple during the second century B.C. See Bermond Montanari, *Princeton* 537. E. Levy, *BCH* 91 (1967) 518 ff.
71. The Sanctuary of Demeter Malophoros at Selinus, for example, was architecturally attached to smaller walled precincts dedicated to Hecate and Zeus Meilichius; the latter was in later times converted to the worship of Baal-Hammon and Tanit. See Gabrici, *Malophoros* 74-75, 91-107. White (supra n. 29) 346-51. Le Dinahet, *Sanctuaires* 141-42, 147-48. Pausanias speaks of a Sanctuary of Demeter Chthonia near Hermione which included shrines to Pluto-Klymenos and Ares, "all surrounded by stone parapets." Paus. 2.35.7.
72. Diod. Sic. 11.27; 14.63. Cic., IV *Verr.* 53.119. D. White, *GRBS* 5 (1964) 264-66.
73. Plut., *Dion.* 56.3.

eries of terracotta figurines.[74] The recovery of the second, presumably nearby temple is reported to be imminent.[75] When it is found, its placement within the walled peribolos will be critical to the present discussion.

BUILDING TECHNIQUES

The final aspect of the early sanctuary for present consideration has to do with its masonry. Undressed or rudimentarily dressed stones were widely used for a variety of constructional purposes throughout Iron Age Greece.[76] In the case of the present sanctuary the types of stones that are used include untreated rubble, which has either been gathered from nearby fields (λίθοι αργοί) or broken from the outcroppings of the limestone pavement that occur both inside and immediately outside the sanctuary limits. The stones also include plug-shaped polygonal blocks with roughly dressed outer faces, and miscellaneously sized, dressed rectangular blocks. The post-580 B.C. addition to the southern peribolos (wall P11) employed relatively carefully finished ashlars, laid in low header and stretcher courses. Their inner, north faces were dressed with broad chisel marks and given bevelled joints. Apart from a single doubtful instance of spilt clay found next to the P3a spur wall,[77] the fill associated with the sanctuary's earliest walls produced no evidence for sun-dried brick. Evidence for flooring is equally slender, but what there is points to the use of compacted earth. No early roof tiles could be distinguished from the fragments of later tiles. No traces of exterior revetments or other forms of applied decoration were recovered that could be associated with the earliest walls.

Locally, the best analogies for the wall construction used in the sanctuary come from the east and west sides of Cyrene's agora, along with the earliest phase of the Artemisium in the nearby Sanctuary of Apollo. The first phase in the development of the agora's *Oikos* of Ophellas (E1), dated by its excavators to the last quarter of the seventh century B.C., makes use of courses of plain broken rubble stones for its foundations and sun-dried brick for the superstructure.[78] The shrine's mid-sixth century replacement (E2) combines rubble with roughly squared blocks.[79] The small sunken Archaic structure in the center of the agora's west side utilizes various sizes of rubble that have been laid up in courses.[80] The later sixth century open-air temenos to its north combines rubble with occasional larger rectangular blocks.[81] The late seventh century B.C. First Artemisium uses the same combination but restricts the squared blocks mainly to reinforcing the corners.[82]

The low ashlar courses used to build the Demeter sanctuary's wall P11, in which the course heights vary from ca. 0.20 to 0.30 m., are paralleled locally by the three socle courses of the mid-sixth century First Apollonium, where the course height averages only 0.26 to 0.28 m.[83] The way in which wall P11 juxtaposes a finished inner face with a ragged outer face also occurs in the treatment of the socle walls of the First Apollonium.[84] It also resembles to a somewhat lesser extent the treatment of the inner and outer wall surfaces of the early fifth century B.C. *Hestiatorium* in Cyrene's agora.[85]

---

74. *AR* 23 (1976-77) 66, fig. 31. *Kokalos* 22-23 (1976-77) 554. Le Dinahet, *Sanctuaires* 145-46.
75. *AR* 28 (1981-82) 87.
76. Martin, *Manuel* 372-73, n. 2. *Agora* I, 48-50, ns. 1-8. *Agora* II,1, 23, n. 6.
77. Supra 26-27.

---

78. *Agora* I, 34, pls. IX, 1; XXXII, 1. Stucchi, *Architettura* 7-8, figs. 1, 2. For sun-dried brick see ibid. 13.
79. *Agora* I, 34-35, 50-54, pls. VIII, 1-3; IX, 2, 3; XXX, 5, 6.
80. *Agora* II,1, 22-23, pl. VI, 1, 2, fig. 8.
81. *Agora* II,1, 27, 31, figs. 10, 11.
82. Pernier, 178-204, fig. 6. Stucchi, *Architettura* 8-9, fig. 4.
83. L. Pernier, *AfrIt* 5 (1935) 27. S. Stucchi, *QAL* 4 (1961) 61. See Martin, *Manuel* 395-97 for ashlar masonry in general use during the Archaic period.
84. Pernier, 27-29, fig. 28.
85. *Agora* II,1, 47.

III

The Later Archaic, Early Classical Sanctuary Ca. 500-440 B.C.

The earliest remains discussed below belong to the end of the city's 125 years that climax a period of aggressive economic and political expansion. Their addition to the sanctuary presumably coincides with the reign of Battus IV, the Handsome (ca. 515-470 B.C.), a regent about whom strangely little is known.[1] By way of partial compensation for the impoverished state of the historical record, what we find hinted at in the archaeological data is a high standard of living apparently achieved despite the turbulent conditions that must have prevailed in the city's domestic as well as external affairs toward the century's end. This is at least what *seems* to be reflected in the buildings,[2] sculpture,[3] and other material remains retrieved from late Archaic contexts across the city by traditional archaeological methods, including those used by the present expedition, to the extent that any of these can serve as reliable indexes for economic condition. Material remains other than large-scale sculpture and architecture are better represented by what has been recovered from the Demeter and Persephone Sanctuary than by artifact collections from anywhere else in the city. On the other hand, the building projects that unquestionably reflect the most ambitious and important architectural statements of the period are definitely associated with other cults. I have in mind in particular the colonnaded stage of the First Apollonion[4] and the city's massive Temple of Zeus.[5] Although in their own humble way the various structural elements added to the late sixth, early fifth century B.C. Demeter and Persephone Sanctuary mirror the larger projects, the circumstances surrounding their construction differ to the extent that the sanctuary buildings are matched by a surge of sanctuary votive offerings largely unparalleled by the artifacts recovered from the Zeus Temple, Apollo Sanctuary, agora zone, and suburban cemeteries.[6]

To some extent this is the result of factors that transcend the ancient past. Cyrene's necropolises had by and large been ransacked of most of their disposable contents before the beginning of the present century,[7] and much of the miscellaneous small-find material excavated in the Apollo Sanctuary and Agora before World War Two was dispersed during the chaotic early years of that conflict when Cyrene repeatedly changed hands between the Germans and the Allies.[8]

The point has also been made that a memory of the land hunger that initially drove Greeks from a broad range of mainland and island centers to emigrate to

---

1. Battus's reign was preceded by the deplorable careers of Arcesilaus III and the queen-mother, Pheretima, whose medizing policies must have ruined the anti-Battiad parties in Cyrene and Barca, established as a rival offshoot earlier in the century. A full regional history of the later Archaic Pentapolis still remains to be written, but see Chamoux, 144-68. Goodchild, *Cyrene* 2, 9-11. R. Goodchild, "Recent Discoveries of Archaic Sculpture at Cyrene," *LA* 3-4 (1966-67) 197-98. Goodchild, *Kyrene* 22-25. Applebaum, *Jews and Greeks* 25-29.

2. Stucchi, *Architettura* 15-43. *Agora* I, 67-105. *Agora* II,1, 35-50. Also Chamoux, 160-61.

3. For a sampling of some of the sixth, early fifth century sculpture recovered from Cyrene see E. Paribeni, *Catalogo delle sculture di Cirene* (Monografie di archeologia libica 5, Rome 1959) 5-17. A full set of references to Cyrene's sculptures will accompany Kane's forthcoming study of the present sanctuary's sculptures, including its sole mid-sixth century marble kore.

4. L. Pernier, "Il Tempio e l'altare d'Apollo a Cirene," *AfrIt* 5 (1935) 44-46. S. Stucchi, "Le fasi construttive dell'Apollonion di Cirene," *QAL* 4 (1961) 57-62. Chamoux, 303-10. Goodchild, *Kyrene* 116-18. Stucchi, *Architettura* 16-20, figs. 8-10. See esp. 17, n. 8 for bibl.

5. G. Pesche, "Il 'Gran Tempio' in Cirene," *BCH* 71-72 (1947-48) 307-58. Chamoux, 320-29. Goodchild, *Kyrene* 154-55. Stucchi, *Architecttura* 23-29, figs. 13-16. See esp. 23, n. 2 for bibl.

6. The grounds surrounding the Zeus Temple remain to be systematically excavated. Otherwise, the only other excavated sanctuary at Cyrene to rival the Wadi Bel Gadir sanctuary in terms of diversity, if not sheer numbers of votives, is the Artemisium located in the midst of the urban Apollo Sanctuary. See Pernier, 173-214.

7. Tombs excavated by the Manchester expedition during the nineteen-fifties provide the single most important exception to this statement. See A. Rowe, *Cyrenaican Expedition of the University of Manchester, 1952* (Manchester 1956). R. Rowe, *Cyrenaican Expeditions of the University of Manchester, 1955-57* (Manchester 1959).

8. R. Goodchild, "A Hole in the Heavens," *Libyan Studies. Select Papers of the Late Richard Goodchild* (ed. J. Reynolds, London 1976) 318-34.

Plate 31: Southeast corner of the later Archaic pseudoisodomic bislab peribolos from northwest. Walls T1 and T2 parallel the later Middle Sanctuary walls T18, T9a, and W2. The P7 early Archaic rubble peribolos wall occupies the lower left-hand foreground.

second course of paired bislabs. While the southeast corner survives to the height of only a single bislab course, the western end today preserves both complete as well as fragmentary flat bonding plinths or perpends over the second upright bislab course to verify the fact that the peribolos originally rose in an A-B-B-A pseudoisodomic sequence to a height of at least 2.20 m. (Fig. 30; Pls. 27, 32). Several of the individual upper level perpends that survive in D13 (Area 2) 1 and 2 were split either by the late earthquakes or by squatter-period builders and are missing their northern halves (Pl. 32).

The foundation slabs and their counterpart perpend courses average 0.28/0.30 m. high. Their lengths vary from 1.10 to 1.80 m., but most average ca. 1.40 m. The total wall thickness is 0.58/0.60 m. The upright bislabs are a uniform 0.60 m. high and vary in thickness between 0.25 and 0.30 m. Their lengths are similar to those of the foundation perpends. This gives the bislabs an average block height-to-length ratio of 1:2.33. Their inner faces have been left rough (Pl. 24), while their outer faces are dressed smooth. The south face of the lowest bislab course in D12/13, B preserves faint traces of five or six rows of broad, parallel chisel strokes where each stroke measures a uniform ca. 2 cm. in width. What results is a kind of herringbone pattern (Pl. 33). The second bislab course is more carefully smoothed, and the herringbone pattern is not detectable. The north faces of both bislab courses display the herringbone pattern on certain blocks. Where they are undamaged, the ends of the bislabs show traces of a rudimentary *anathyrosis*.

The sanctuary grounds have yielded five iron drove-chisels,[13] of which one (Pl. 34) was recovered from an Archaic stratum immediately south of wall T1 in

---

13. See P. Warden, "Miscellaneous Small Finds," *Final Reports* IV, cat. nos. **327-31**.

Plate 32: South face of wall T1 in D12/13, B, seen from southeast. The wall is preserved to the height of one complete pseudoisodomic A-B-B-A sequence. The upper perpend course has been damaged here on its north face where several of its individual blocks have been split down their long axes, leaving only the south faces intact.

Plate 33: Detail of south face of wall T1, showing herringbone pattern left on surface from use of a drove-chisel.

D12/13, B, 4.[14] Its blade is 3.5 cm. wide. The remaining chisel blades vary in width from 3.1 to 4.5 cm., i.e., as a group they all seem slightly too wide to have been used for dressing this particular set of blocks. On the other hand, three out of the remaining four chisels were recovered from Archaic levels and may have been used on other parts of the pseudoisodomic peribolos. The state of preservation of the wall's surface is not sufficiently good to generalize about the width of the chisel strokes used elsewhere along its line.

Both the foundation plinths and bislab courses occasionally retain traces of setting-out lines and notches on their upper surfaces. The former are scratched lines that bisect the blocks normally about 0.10 to 0.15 m. from their ends. Their purpose was presumably to guide the wall builders in positioning

---

14. Warden (supra n. 13) cat. no. **327**.

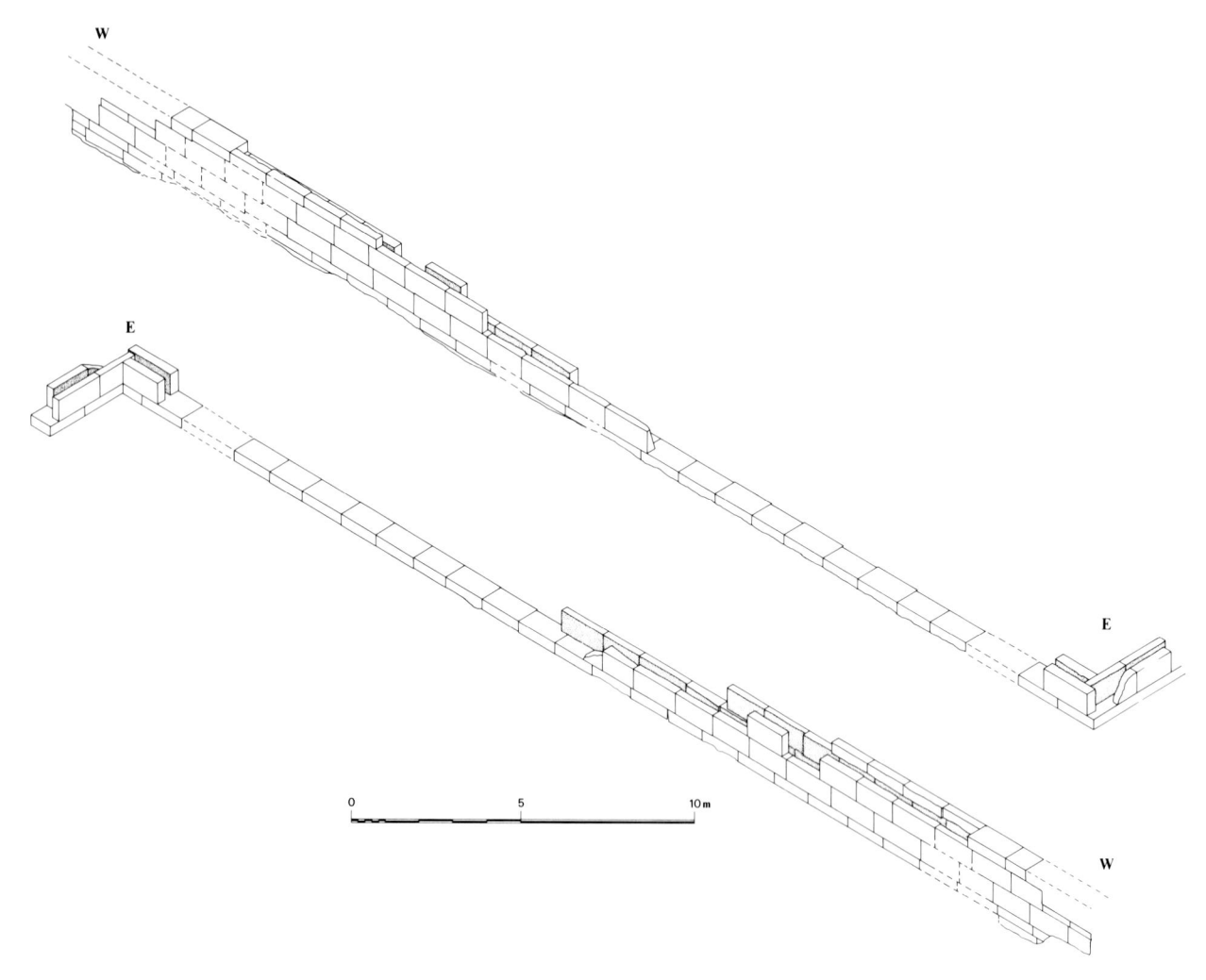

Figure 29: Perspective drawing of the southeast corner of the later Archaic peribolos, drawn from southeast (above) and northwest (below). 1:200 scale.

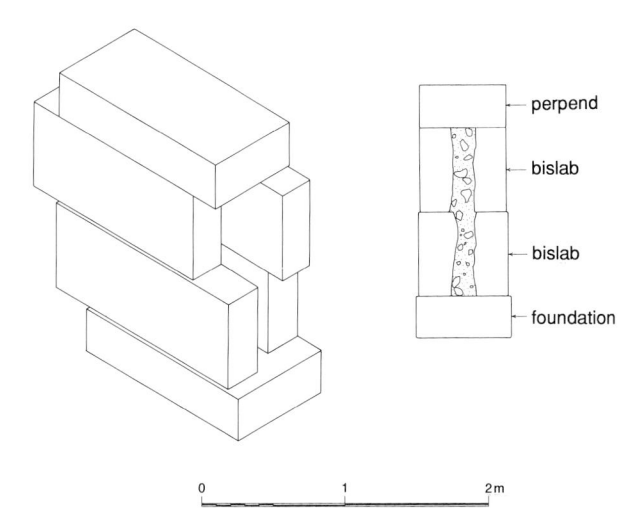

Figure 30: Reconstruction of the first four courses of wall T1, illustrating its A-B-B-A course sequence. 1:50 scale.

stones in the course immediately above.[15] The notches, small irregular oval slots set close to the block ends, usually occur in pairs on the foundation perpends and individually on the bislab blocks (Pl. 35). They must have functioned as pry holes[16] rather than gudgeons or mortises,[17] since the latter would require some kind of answering notch on either the perpendicular or lower surface of the adjacent block to be attached, and nothing approximating these are preserved.

WALL T7

Forming a continuation of the line of the southern peribolos to the west, in its current condition the wall is made up of a single bislab block, which, as has been already pointed out,[18] rides on top of four courses of ashlar masonry that belong to the early Archaic peribolos wall P11. The block in question (Pl. 10) measures 1.73 by 0.60 by 0.38 m. (block height-to-length ratio 1:2.88). The flanged stretcher block directly beneath it was cut to hold a pair of upright slabs and may be taken to belong to the later Archaic phase as well. The companion slab to the south is missing.

WALL T6

Constituting the final westward extension of the southern peribolos, wall T6 is here preserved for a

---

15. Martin, *Manuel* 231-34, fig. 108.
16. Martin, *Manuel* 236, fig. 110.
17. Martin, *Manuel* 279-82.
18. Supra 11.

*Plate 34: Iron drove-chisel, Inv. 71-516, Warden, "Miscellaneous Small Finds" Final Reports IV, cat. no. **327**, found in an Archaic stratum (D12/13, B, 4) south of wall T1.*

distance of 5.70 m. to a maximum height of one bislab course (Fig. 9; Pl. 36). The foundations throughout its length consist of badly weathered and cracked perpends that vary in height from 0.15 to 0.30 m. Their width is 0.77 m. The foundations support two pairs of bislabs at the east end of wall T6. The easternmost pair has not, however, been fully excavated. Fallen slabs

Plate 35: Section of T1 bislabs in area D12/13, illustrating pry-holes let into block ends.

that are visible in the scarp of the adjacent trench (D16/E16, 1) may once have belonged to a now missing second bislab course. When compared with the bislabs of wall T1, the western pair seem constructionally mismatched: while the south slab is a normal upright measuring 1.35 by 0.66 by 0.23 m. (block height-to-length ratio 1:2.04), dressed and finished like the T1 bislabs, the stone paired to it is badly dressed; its length, moreover, is only 0.65 m., while its thickness is nearly 0.40 m. (matching the unusually thick slab that makes up wall T7). This leaves little space between the two for the usual rubble packing. In addition, contrary to normal practice the wall here rests mainly on a red clay fill rather than directly on bedrock.

These small but telling constructional differences, taken along with the conspicuous lack of alignment between wall T1 and walls T6/T7, once again raise the possibility that the eastern half of the south peribolos (wall T1) represents a separate building operation from the walls to its west (T6 and T7). Yet it should be noted that walls T7 and T6, along with wall T5 that makes up the actual southwest corner of the peribolos, are all built on what appears to be the direct continuation of the lines of the earlier Archaic peribolos, as delineated by walls P11 and P10. This provides some circumstantial evidence that all three pseudoisodomic walls occupying the western half were originally part of the later Archaic temenos enclosure, despite the fact that they were not directly aligned with wall T1 to their east.

CONTEXT AND DATE OF THE PERIBOLOS SOUTH WALL

WALL T1

Both the north and south edges of wall T1's foundations are associated at a number of points along the preserved length with a compacted Archaic occupation fill whose contents provide some assistance in dating the construction of wall T1. The stratum designation for this fill varies from context to context. In E10/11 (Area 1), 1 the wall builders trenched into the dense, moist red earth over bedrock (Fig. 31, St. 6) in order to base their foundations on bedrock. When excavated, this layer proved to be entirely sterile. Ca. three m. north of the actual southeast corner of the peribolos an irregular depression was encountered in the red earth fill which the excavators designated the "NE Pit." Its latest object was a silver tetradrachm dated ca. 510-490 B.C. A substantially larger pit fill (St. 3) sunk into the surface of the red soil occupied the northwest quarter of the trench. The Fig. 31 section indicates how the southern edge of the pit (St. 3) encroaches on the line of wall T1. Its contents include large quantities of early pottery that run as late as the first quarter of the fifth century. The actual constructional relationship, if any, between the two pits and the pseudoisodomic wall system is anything but clear. The St. 3 "NW Pit," however, does appear to stop just short of the wall's north face (implying perhaps that the wall was already in place at the time that the pit was cut out).

At the time of their excavation it proved difficult to determine the sequential relationship between E10/11 (Area 1), 1, St. 3 and St. 4. The fill overriding wall T1's perpend course (which can only mean that the wall had been largely dismantled when the fill was introduced) was labelled "4" because, as the Fig. 31 section indicates, the southern edge of the NW Pit seemed to cut into St. 4 and thus had to be designated "3" in order to imply that it was sequentially later. Now, however, after the contents of the two strata have been fully analyzed, it becomes clear that St. 4 is an Imperial Roman period backfill, dating to the second century A.D., while St. 3 is an apparently uncontaminated late Archaic fill. It therefore seems probable that the southern edge of the NW Pit (St. 3) was simply undercut for a short distance at the time of the Roman period backfill over wall T1 and that its contents do provide at least some kind of a rough index of wall T1's relative date.

Two m. to the west at the east end of D11/12, A (Fig. 32), the south face of T1's foundations are associated with a greasy brown-colored fill (St. 3) that contains miscellaneous artifacts that yield no precise date, together with an Archaic silver and a fourth century B.C. bronze coin. The later coin may have been ground into the upper surface of the layer by the earthquake whose thick debris stratum, St. 2, overlies it, but the trench is itself largely useless for dating purposes.

THE LATER ARCHAIC, EARLY CLASSICAL SANCTUARY

Plate 36: The west end of the south wall of the later Archaic T6 peribolos appears to left of the collapsing T15 rear wall of the later Middle Sanctuary. Viewed from west.

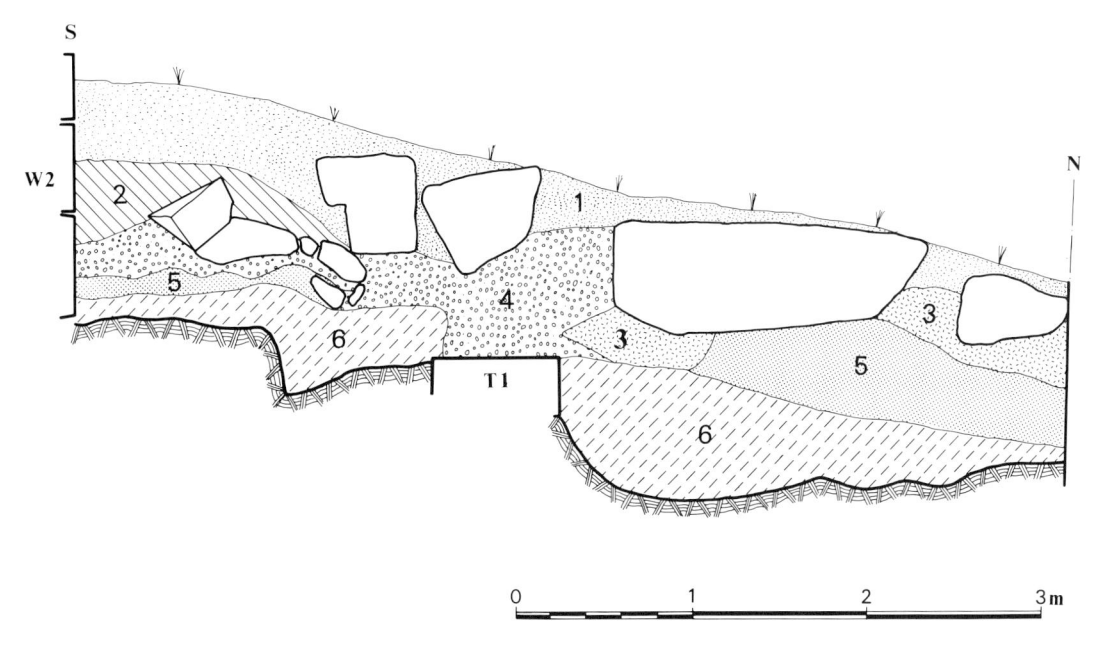

Figure 31: North-south section of fill covering the later Archaic T1 peribolos wall at the west end of E10/11 (Area 1), drawn from east. 1:50 scale.

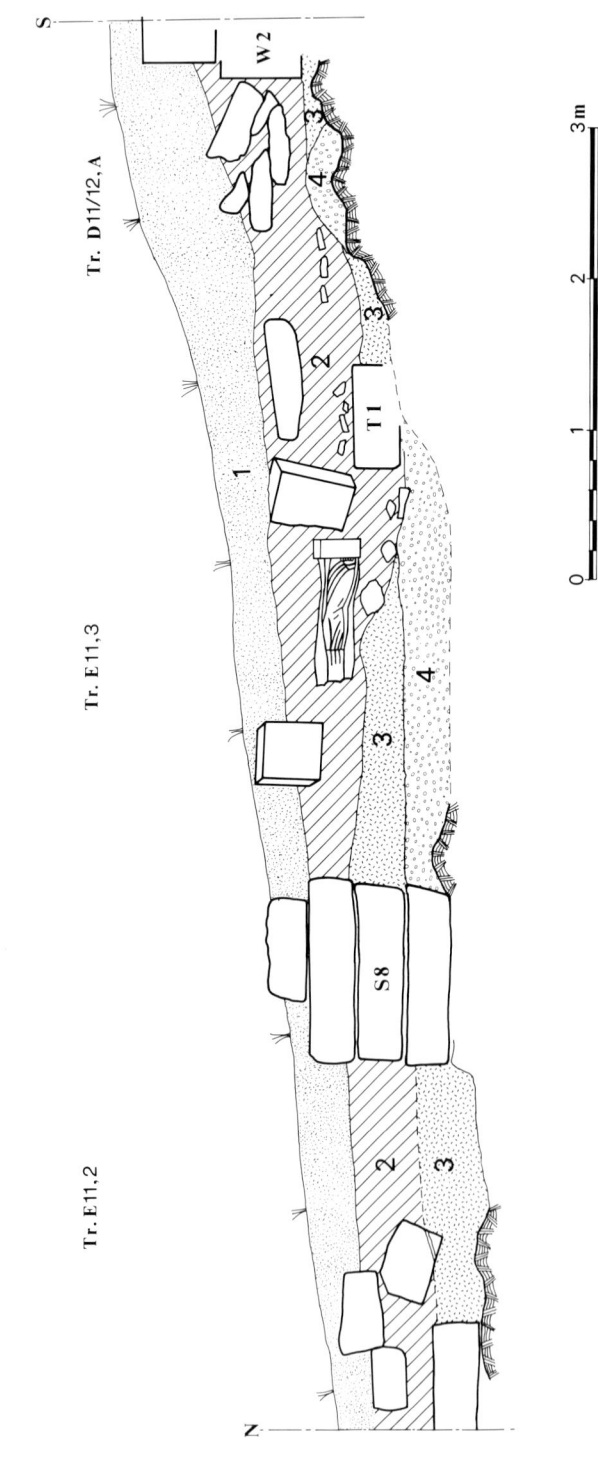

Figure 32: North-south section of fills in D11/12, A, E11, 3, (Area 1) 2 and E11, 2 covering the largely dismantled later Archaic T1 peribolos wall and the early Imperial S8 Shrine Building, drawn from west. 1:50 scale.

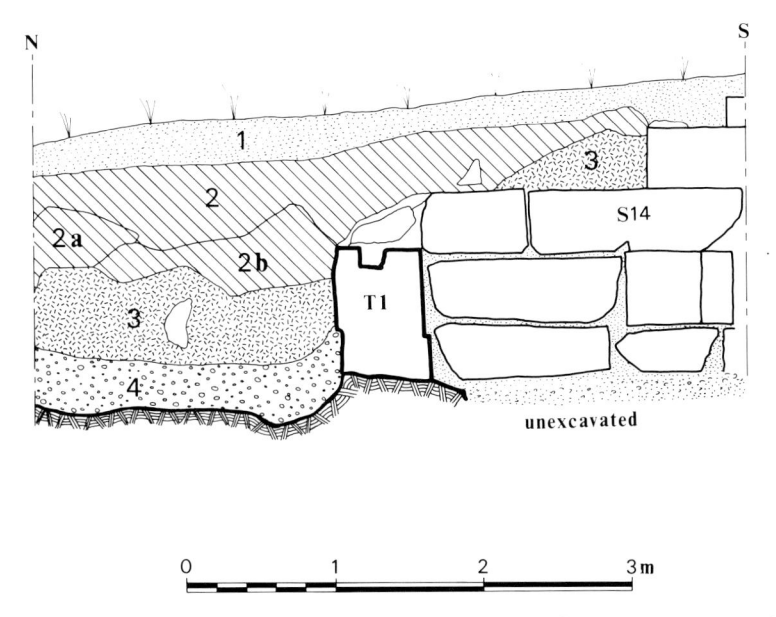

Figure 33: North-south section of fill in D12/13, A, north of the Roman period S14 compartment and the later Archaic T1 peribolos wall, drawn from west. 1:50 scale.

The St. 3 fill continues north of wall T1 but is not contiguous with the foundation perpend, as illustrated by Fig. 32. Its contents in E11, 3 are largely sixth century in date, but include some fourth century Attic Red Figure sherds and a third century bronze coin, which once more |may represent contaminations from the earthquake immediately above.

To the west of the southeast corner of the peribolos much of the eastern half of T1 is preserved only in the foundation courses. The bislab elevation, however, picks up again about fifteen m. to the west in D12/E12, D where the cross-section (Fig. 17) intersects with the first upright bislab. The fill over bedrock (St. 6) is largely sterile terra rossa into which is intermixed a scattering of LC I sherds. This layer here partially supports the foundation perpend.[19] St. 5 is a dense reddish brown earth layer that lies up against the north face of wall T1's foundations. In addition to a large quantity of Archaic material, St. 5 contains what may have been an intrusive Attic Red Figure sherd and a fine-ware sherd of second or first century B.C. date. The level has been disturbed by the Hellenistic votive pit to its north (St. 4), but, apart from the two exceptions just mentioned, appears to date down to ca. 520 B.C.

Finally, a meter east of the Early Archaic spur wall P6 the north face of the T1 foundations is built against a hard-packed dark brown earth fill (St. 4) over the bedrock (Fig. 33). The D12/13, A, 4 contents include exclusively Archaic material, the latest of which appears to be LC II pottery.

To summarize the chronological evidence for wall T1, allowing for intrusions, the eastern half of the south wall of the peribolos dates some time after ca. 510 B.C. but no later than 480 B.C.

WALL T7

No stratified evidence was recovered for the construction date of wall T7 because of the building activities associated with wall W31 to its south and its own eventual integration into the independent S6 sacred house.[20] Its association with the peribolos rests on its use of a single bislab and its apparent coaxiality with wall T6 to its immediate west.

WALL T6

The D16/17, 1, 4 red clay fill underlying wall T6 and separating it from bedrock contained at least one terracotta late Archaic figurine that may have intruded into the stratum from St. 3 and a few badly preserved Corinthian sherds that seem to range from MC to LC. The hard reddish brown soil filled in around the bislabs at the wall's east end (D16/17, 1, 3) represents an Imperial period dump and tells us nothing about the wall's date.

PERIBOLOS WEST WALL

In its preserved condition, the later Archaic temenos's western edge was defined by a short stretch of new peribolos wall (T5) added to its southwest corner which aligns axially with the older, early Archaic rubble peribolos P10, described in the previous chapter. Whatever arrangement originally linked the two has been thoroughly obliterated by later building. The northwest corner has not been excavated, and it

---

19. See supra 14 for a discussion of this stratigraphy in association to wall P3.

20. Supra 11 and infra 94.

Plate 37: Southwest corner of the later Archaic peribolos formed by the junction of walls T5 and T6 in front of the T14 Hellenistic main west wall of the Middle Sanctuary. Taken from east before the final excavation of T5 wall.

Plate 38: The T5 west wall of the later Archaic peribolos, shown in front of the T14 Hellenistic west wall of the Middle Sanctuary. Viewed from east.

Plate 39: East end of Middle Sanctuary retaining wall system. The upper surface of the later Archaic T3 peribolos wall appears to the immediate left of ranging rod. Taken from west.

is therefore impossible to say whether it consisted of a continuation of the older rubble peribolos or of new pseudoisodomic bislab construction.

WALL T5

Wall T5 has a total preserved length of 2.05 m. Its south end firmly abuts wall T6 (Pl. 37) to form a proper corner. The two walls, however, are not bonded. The builders were forced to drop the bislabs making up T5 to the level of T6 to compensate for the falling-off in the bedrock to the north. The south end is made up of a pair of upright blocks (Pl. 38). Its outer or western bislab, 0.57 m. high, rests directly on a red clay packing over bedrock. The inner or eastern slab, which is only 0.33 m. high, is built over a rubble footing that may have been left over from the line of the earlier peribolos. The remainder of wall T5 to the north consists of a second pair of uprights. The outer slab is of normal dimensions, set on red clay. However, its inner facing consists of rubble which may be all that remains of a single bislab block shattered during the third century A.D. earthquake.

CONTEXT AND DATE OF THE PERIBOLOS WEST WALL

The same dense red argillaceous soil that surrounds the foundation course of wall T6 is associated with the footings of wall T5. Its early contents (D16/17, 2, 4), which should date both walls, appear to have been contaminated by fourth and third century B.C. lamp and terracotta figurine material as well as late Hellenistic coins from the overlying stratum 3 that represents a continuation of the same late dump reported in connection with the St. 3 fill surrounding wall T6. The generally disturbed and therefore unreliable character of the D16/17, 2 stratigraphy is further indicated by the fact that an eighth century A.D. Islamic coin was retrieved from St. 3, while St. 4 produced a modern (1926) coin of Italian origin!

Plate 40: Detail view of wall T3 from east.

PERIBOLOS NORTH WALL

Two sections of the north or forward wall of the later Archaic temenos overlooking the wadi drain survive. These are walls T3 and T4. The latter came to light in the same F14/G14 test trench that revealed the early Archaic peribolos walls, P8 and P9, at the approximate center of the temenos grounds, while the former occupies the northeast corner. Plan B demonstrates how the two align.

WALL T4

Wall T4 (Figs. 5, 22, 24; Pls. 17, 18), 5.20 m. long, preserves ten courses of masonry that rise 3.40 m. above the sloping bedrock pavement. Since its north face tightly abuts the massive T20 Imperial period retaining wall, it was possible to clear only the south face. Its builders carefully founded wall T4 directly on bedrock. The lowest seven courses are all foundation perpend-blocks that vary in height from 0.20 to 0.32 m. The apparent purpose behind such a deep foundation was to bridge over or, perhaps more accurately, to fill in a localized fault or crevice in the wadi's limestone shoulder. The eighth and ninth courses are composed of paired vertical bislabs, utilizing the same variety of fossil-free limestone as wall T1 and marked with a similar surface finish of parallel rows of herringbone chisel strokes. The slabs appear to average 1.20 m. long and are a standard 0.60 m. high (block height-to-length ratio 1:2). The uppermost, tenth course is composed of perpend-blocks, 0.32 m. high and 0.58 m. thick, which in turn allow us to estimate the wall's total thickness. With the stone type, surface finish, and overall dimensions all resembling those of wall T1, there can be little doubt but that wall T4 represents a continuation of the same peribolos enclosure.

WALL T3

The upper surface of some 14 meters of the later Archaic northeast temenos wall was exposed in gridsquares G11 and G12 during the course of cleaning the back of the Imperial period retaining wall T20 (Figs. 1, 2; Pls. 39, 40). Of the eleven pairs of bislabs that were cleared, most measured a normal 1.03 to 1.18 m. in length, but three were made up of "half-slab" lengths of only 0.45 to 0.57 m. long, which indicates some breakdown in the extreme regularity of coursing that typifies wall T1. The block heights could not be measured.

CONTEXT AND DATE OF THE PERIBOLOS NORTH WALL

WALL T4

As has been already indicated,[21] the lowest three levels between the foundations of the early Archaic peribolos (P8/P9) and the south face of wall T4 represent backfills to the latter and therefore ought to assist in establishing its construction date (Figs. 22-24). F14/G14, 1, 4, the highest and presumably the latest of these fills, partially masks the second and third T4 foundation courses above bedrock. Its latest finds are a silver coin struck by Cyrene between 510 and 490 B.C. and several examples of LC II pottery, including a nearly intact miniature kotyle that could depress the date of the level into the early fifth century B.C. St. 5 contains only LC II sherds. St. 6, however, produced a fragmentary LC III kotyle, which could theoretically date wall T4 to as

---

21. Supra 24

late as the first half of the fifth century. All three strata could easily represent separate tips of a single backfill. Given the character of the rest of the material associated with them a date around 490-480 B.C. seems appropriate for the wall.

WALL T3

Since only the upper surfaces of the bislabs making up wall T3 were cleared, no evidence was recovered to date this stretch of the north peribolos.

PERIBOLOS EAST WALL

Beginning at its southeast corner ca. seven m. of the east wall (T2) is preserved before the north end disappears into the later S7 Sacred House (Figs. 13, 20, 21, 29, 31; Pls. 3, 16, 31). Otherwise, the entire northern two-thirds of the later Archaic peribolos's east wall is either lost or not yet excavated. Of what survives of wall T2 the northern half consists of only a disturbed line of foundation slabs that ride on red clay fill over bedrock. The southern half preserves two pairs of uprights, one course high, with foundations set on rubble and red clay.[22] The foundation perpend slab are 0.13 to 0.15 m. high; the orthostate bislabs are 1.12 to 1.40 m. long and 0.56 m. high (average block height-to-length ratio 1:2.25). The corner pair of bislabs bonds with the corner of wall T1. The two walls share the same stone, surface finish, and block dimensions and appear to be coeval.

CONTEXT AND DATE OF THE PERIBOLOS EAST WALL

The same E10/11 (Area 1), 1 fill associated with wall T1 is found west of the foundations of wall T2. Its contents are diagnostically useless. A short distance further north the E11, 1, 4 fill (Fig. 20), which seems to be equally associated with wall P3 as well as wall T2, contains a sparse number of Corinthian sherds as well as an early fifth century B.C. figurine. It, however, also yielded a Hellenistic terracotta head, which dilutes the chronological value of its contents.

SOUTHERN EXTENSION OF THE PERIBOLOS

Low foundations perpends, designated wall T2a, continue the line of T2 south of its junction with wall T1 for ca. 2.50 m. before becoming lost under the corner of Hellenistic peribolos T9 and T9a (Plan B; Fig. 13). The fact that they are thinner and more roughly dressed than the foundations of wall T2 opens the possibility that they represent a separate build. They appear to be associated with the same stratum of red clay fill over bedrock as wall T2 but the fill failed to produce independent evidence for their date.

Summary: Date and Layout of the Later Archaic Peribolos

The best-preserved section of the south wall of the peribolos, wall T1, is relatively securely dated to the last quarter of the sixth century B.C. or slightly later. This agrees in general terms with the date that emerges for the west wall, wall T5. The small section of north wall to emerge, wall T4, could, however, depress the date of the entire enclosure to the second decade of the fifth century B.C.

As to its original appearance, with the exception of the now lost connecting link between the eastern and western halves of the southern peribolos, the main outlines of the later Archaic enclosure emerge with a fair degree of clarity. It took the form of an approximately rectangular temenos with a maximum width of 64 m. east to west and a total depth of 28 m. north to south. In terms of such details as the care with which the bedrock and foundations were prepared, the selection of the stone, and the precision in the shaping of the individual blocks, the north, east, southeast, and perhaps the west walls all appear basically alike. The southwest section (walls T6 and T7) is less carefully made and, in the one case of wall T7, makes use of a previously existent wall (P11) for its foundations. The southwest peribolos also fails to align directly with the southeastern half. Yet, as has already been observed, the southwest peribolos uses the same line as the early Archaic peribolos, and, whatever its period, its function as part of the overall later Archaic peribolos seems reasonably certain.

---

22. One of these was discovered fallen east of the line of the actual wall.

Commentary

PERIBOLOS PLAN

As far as can be presently determined, the plan of the later Archaic peribolos conforms in rough terms with the layout of its early Archaic predecessor (Plan A). It in fact directly overlies the line of the latter's walls in the southwest quadrant of the temenos and along its west side, while running closely parallel to its north, east, and southeast sides. The later Archaic temenos represents a modest increase in the total amount of interior space enclosed by its outer walls, gained mainly in the southeast corner. While the north wall shows no evidence for the abrupt angled change of direction that permitted speculation that the earlier precinct might have been divided into two parts,[23] its alignment must undergo a ca. six-degree deflection at some point along its eastern half where walls T3 and T4 meet, and this should echo a similar division. There is, consequently, little to add to the general comments already made in the previous chapter about the planning of early peribolos enclosures.[24]

Probably the layout of the later Archaic Sanctuary of Athena Pronaia at Delphi comes closest to that of the present example, since it too is approximately rectangular in plan and shares the latter's hillside setting. The outer peribolos walls of the Delphi sanctuary enclose at least seven independently sited structures which, like those in the Cyrene version, face down a hillslope, spread across the long axis of the interior space.[25] The fact that the Delphi sacred buildings open to the south, while those at Cyrene are, with the apparent exception of the S6 Sacred House, oriented to the north, probably has less to do with ritual considerations than it does with local topography.[26]

PSEUDOISODOMIC MASONRY

The distinctive masonry associated with the later Archaic peribolos requires some discussion. The type of masonry employed throughout its walls (and associated, as we shall see, on the level of the later Upper Sanctuary with the more or less contemporary W30 wall unit and S2 structure) consists of foundations constructed from one or more carefully executed plinth or perpend courses.[27] Over these rise two courses of paired orthostate-like upright slabs referred to here as "bislabs." The space between the bislabs appears to have been filled with earth and small rubble stones, in a technique that recalls what has been termed *emplecton* (Fig. 30).[28] The two faces of the wall are bonded by a course of flat perpends or *diatones*,[29] which in their overall dimensions are similar enough to the foundation courses to describe the wall's rise as an A-B-B-A pseudoisodomic sequence. Since the peribolos nowhere survives above the height of its second perpend course, we do not know how the sequence continued above this level.

An A-B-B-A alteration of perpends with bislabs is a variation of a type of masonry that is fairly broadly distributed throughout the pre-Roman eastern Mediterranean from the sixth century onwards.[30] Probably its most common appearance takes the form of a plain isodomic sequence (A-A1-A or in some instances A-A1-A1-A1-A) that is documented on both the mainland and the islands, as well as at least once in Magna Graecia,[31] but not, so far as I know, in Cyrenaica. A second common variation consists of the regular alteration of a low perpend course with a single course of higher bislabs to create a pseudoisodomic A-B-A-B rhythm. The walls of the Cnidian Treasury at Delphi employ this sequence,[32] while the Massiliote Treasury

---

23. For consideration of the possibility that the early Archaic peribolos was divided into two parts see supra 39-41.

24. Comparable Archaic peribolos layouts are discussed supra 38-39.

25. Bergquist, *Temenos* 32-33, pl. 14. Tomlinson, *Sanctuaries* 68-69, pl. 17.

26. Bergquist, *Temenos* 70. For further discussion of the possible cultic implications of differences in orientation between the northern-facing independent houses that occupy the eastern half of the Middle Sanctuary and the apparent eastern orientation of the S6 Sacred House set over on the west, see 95.

---

27. The use of multiple foundation plinth courses appears mainly along the T4 north wall, although two foundation courses may have been used at the western extremity of wall T1 in D13 (Area 2), 1, where examination was hampered by the overburden of later building. Otherwise the peribolos seems to rise on a single course of perpend foundations.

28. R. Tomlinson, "*Emplekton* Masonry and 'Greek Structura'," *JHS* 81 (1961) 139-40.

29. "They insert special stones facing on either front of unbroken thickness. These they call *diatones* (through-stones), and they, by bonding, especially strengthen the solidity of the wall." Vitr., 2.8.7 (Loeb. trans.).

30. Discussed by Martin under the general heading of "les murs à carreaux" (bislabs) "et à parpaings" (perpends) "isodomes et pseudo-isodomes." Martin, *Manuel* 400-09.

31. Martin, *Manuel* 400-03, ns. 1-4, fig. 174 a and b. Add F. Winter, *Greek Fortifications* (Toronto 1971) 137, fig. 109 for the Hellenistic tower in the northern walls at Assos, which intersperses two paired stretcher (i.e., bislab) courses between single perpend courses: A-A1-A1-A.

32. W. Dinsmoor, *BCH* 37 (1913) 24-25, fig. 5. Martin, *Manuel* 400, fig. 175.

in a burst of Gallic originality varies the number of perpend courses intercalated between bislabs.[33] Other examples of structures using this block sequence for at least the treatment of their wall bases are relatively well known and range in date from the Archaic to Hellenistic times.[34] Apart from three Attic monuments, every example of this construction comes from either the islands or Asia Minor.

Direct parallels with the Demeter Sanctuary's use of multiple bislab courses between perpends are less frequently encountered. Martin lists the mid-fourth century B.C. Ionic Temple of Athena at Priene,[35] the agora stoa and a heroon at Assos,[36] the Portico of Philip on Delos,[37] and the post-fifth century B.C. Ionic temple at Messa on Lesbos.[38] The walls of the Lesbian temple rise in the same A-B-B-A sequence as the Cyrene peribolos but replace the rubble and earth fill between the bislabs with a third upright block, which creates in effect a solid stone wall that was presumably better able to withstand earthquake shock.[39] The Portico of Philip also departs from the Cyrene arrangement to the extent that its wall inserts three courses of bislabs between perpends. The walls of the fourth century B.C. Athena Temple at Priene are poorly preserved but nevertheless appear to employ a modified A-B-B-A sequence that may approximate the Cyrene peribolos.[40] A second close analogy with Cyrene is provided by the Hellenistic southwestern defensive walls of the acropolis at Sillyon, set on the edge of a high cliff where they were immune from attack by siege-engines.[41] The inherent instability of this form of construction would under normal circumstances prohibit its use along a defensive enceinte. For this reason its employment for the outer walls of the Wadi Bel Gadir sanctuary can only have been for non-defensive reasons.

Finally, there are the walls of other structures at Cyrene itself. The socle of the outer walls of the Agora's Portico A1, dated to the third quarter of the sixth century B.C., consists of a course of bislab orthostates capped with a course of perpends; the core between bislabs is packed with earth.[42] The mid-fifth century walls of the Temple of the Dioscuri in the northwest corner of Cyrene's Agora use the same technique, i.e., a single course of paired bislabs surmounted by perpends.[43] The earliest phase of the Hypaethral Temple east of the House of Jason Magnus, which perhaps belongs to the later sixth or first half of the fifth century B.C., uses paired bislabs in its lower walls.[44] The fifth, fourth century B.C. Tempietto of the Paired Orthostates is too poorly preserved above the level of its stylobate to be certain of its elevation but appears to use bislabs at least for a socle course.[45] The Temple of Apollo Archegetes, dated by

---

33. Dinsmoor (supra n. 32) 25-27. G. Doux, *FdD* II: *Topographie et architecture. Le sanctuaire d'Athena Pronaia*, fasc. 1 (1927): *Les deux trésors*, 53-58, figs. 71, 75, 76, pl. XXVI. As restored, the sequence runs: B-A-B-A-A-A-B-A-A-A-B-A-A-B and is, as far as I know, without parallel.

34. Martin lists the Archaic Altar of Monodendri at Miletus, the later fifth century B.C. Temple Poseidon at Cape Sounion, the late fourth century *paradoi* of the Theater of Dionysus at Athens, several small agora structures from Thasos, the *Ptolemeum* at Samothrace, the small Agora temple and the Temple of Athena at Pergamum, the Stoa of Attalus in Athens, the skene of the theater at Priene, and the Bouleuterion at Miletus. See *Manuel* 403-04, ns. 1-8 for bibliography. To these add the Stoa of the Naxians on Delos dating to the second half of the sixth century B.C. whose walls consist of a single course of bislabs above a course of perpends. See R. Vallois, *Les constructions antiques de Délos, Documents* (Paris 1953) pl. III, fig. 16. The West Building and South Portico at Argos employ the same system. See P. Amandry, *Hesperia* 21 (1952) 242, 254, 273, pls. 64b, 68a and b; the former structure dates 525-500 B.C., while the latter belongs to the years 450-40 B.C. Also the Archaic agora wall at Gortyna, which appears to preserve only a single course of bislabs. L. Pernier, *ASAtene* 8-9 (1925-26) 14, pl. V. The city wall at Lycian Isinda (Isionda) preserves at least seven courses of pseudoisodomic perpend and bislab masonry and constitutes what is probably the best early example of the type. See G. Perrot and C. Chipiez, *Histoire de l'art* VII: *La Grèce de l'épopée. La Grèce archaïque* (Paris 1898) 330, fig. 152. *RE* 9, 2 (1916) 2083, s.v. Isinda (Bürchner). The cella walls of the Archaic Temple of Athena at Assos may have been erected in an A-B-A sequence, but their ruinous state (only four blocks survive, and these appear to be all bislabs) makes it impossible to be certain. See J. Clarke, "Report on the Investigations at Assos, 1882, 1883," *Papers of the Archaeological Institute of America* II (1898) 74-75. The city walls at Isaura in Asia Minor provide another example from the post-Classical period. See Winter (supra n. 31) 136-37, figs. 106-08. Finally, examples of pseudoisodomic bislab walls too badly preserved to be certain of their precise block sequences are listed by Martin, *Manuel* 404-05, ns. 13-17; all come from Asia Minor and are, with the exception of the Hecatompedon on Naxos, Hellenistic.

35. Martin, *Manuel* 404, n. 9. *Priene* 86-88.

36. Martin, *Manuel* 404, n. 11 where he cites Clarke (supra n. 34) 41 and 116, which, however, provides no detailed description of the walls in question.

37. Martin, *Manuel* 404, n. 12, fig. 178. R. Vallois, *Délos* VII: *Le Portique de Phillipe* (Paris 1923) 38-40.

38. Martin, *Manuel* 404, n. 10. R. Koldewey, *Die Antike Baureste der Insel Lesbos* (Berlin 1890) 49-50, pl. 22.

39. The structural weakness inherent in this form of compartmentalized wall construction was aptly described by Clarke in his analysis of the walls of the Athena Temple at Assos. See Clarke (supra n. 34) 75.

40. *Priene* 85, 95, fig. 52. Gruben, *Greek Temples* 478, fig. 140. As restored, the walls rise off a low perpend course which supports two courses of high orthostate bislabs; above this follows a sequence of A-B-B-A perpends and normal bislabs.

41. Winter (supra n. 31) 137, fig. 110.

42. *Agora* I, 74, foldout plan d, fig. 33.

43. *Agora* II,1, 56-58, figs. 35, 36, pls. X, 2 and XI, 2, 3.

44. Goodchild, *Kyrene* 78. Stucchi, *Architettura* 22, pl. I, no. 112. *Agora* II,1, 58, n. 4. It is not clear what is the exact block sequence above the initial course of bislabs.

45. Stucchi, *Architettura* 53, pl. I, no. 8, fig. 41.

Plate 43: Detail of Artemisium door leading from its porch to pronaos, seen from east.

Plate 44: Detail of Artemisium's lintel inscription.

ty.[53] Along the outer face of the south wall and in the southwest corner of the naos individual upright slabs were replaced by stretchers. On the north side, over the first course of original bislabs, the outer face of the second course was built up with blocks of squarish orthostates. Proof of the general lateness of these repairs is provided by the fact that three reused members, possibly removed from the nearby Apollonion after its destruction in A.D. 115, made their way into the fabric. These are two triglyphs and a trimmed-down Doric capital (Pl. 53), the latter not mentioned by Pernier. Again, the only bonding that takes place between both cross-walls and the north and south side walls occurs at the level associated with these late repairs. It therefore follows that the marble doorway, with its inscribed lintel, separating porch from pro-

naos argues nothing about the date of the original structure in its pseudoisodomic phase.

On the strength of the presently available information, there seems to be no compelling reason to date the original A-B-B sections of the side and rear walls of the Artemisium's pronaos and naos later than the later Archaic/early Classical period.[54] In addition, following Pernier's original sequence, it seems probable that both the late repairs to the side walls and the insertion of the cross walls are related to the addition of the tetrastyle porch, but the precise chronology of the total structure cannot be argued in detail here, and our sequential plan (Fig. 40) should be taken as provisional.

To sum up, variations of the type of masonry used for the Demeter Sanctuary's later Archaic peribolos occur throughout the eastern Mediterranean from the sixth century B.C. until at least as late as the Hellenistic period.[55] Exact parallels with its sequence of perpend foundations, two bislab courses, and a perpend binding course (A-B-B-A) are much harder to isolate. The post-fifth century Ionic temple at Messa

---

53. Pernier, 206.

54. In support of this, it might be argued that the survival of a primitive rubble shrine in the very center of the city's principal sanctuary until as late as the opening of the fourth century is intrinsically unlikely. On the other hand, based on what is known of the history of similar rubble buildings in Cyrene's agora, it must be admitted that such survivals seem to occur routinely. The largely rubble Temple E2 was replaced by E3 in ashlar masonry by the third quarter of the fifth century B.C. See *Agora* I, 118. The Archaic rubble temenos of Demeter and Kore disappears under the *Building with Parascenia* by the final quarter of the fifth. *Agora* II,1, 87. The entire problem requires further work.

55. For some regional late survivals of pesudoisodomic walls see Stucchi, *Architettura* 543, 570-71, figs. 582, 583.

Plate 45:   Marble door of Artemisium leading from its pronaos to its Roman period porch. Seen from northwest.

on Lesbos[56] substitutes a third upright slab for the more normal earth and rubble fill. The fourth century B.C. Temple of Athena at Priene[57] and Hellenistic city walls at Sillyon[58] provide further examples. Locally, the fourth century Temple of Apollo Archegetes[59] and possibly earlier so-called Second Artemisium[60] also appear to approximate the same system. Thus, while contemporary sixth century variations of this masonry technique exist,[61] the monuments which most closely approximate the Demeter Sanctuary walls are, with the probable exception of the Artemisium, a century or more later. Lastly, most of the known parallels from all periods were part of buildings, attached to adjacent walls, i.e., forming corners. Only four examples are known to have been part of free-standing walls, the Hellenistic city walls at Sillyon[62] and Isaura,[63] the Archaic agora wall at Gortyna,[64] and the apparently Archaic city wall at Isinda.[65] Ancient builders must have been reluctant to trust what was, in aesthetic terms, an attractive building technique, but one which, in more practical terms, resulted in unstable masonry, poorly designed to withstand sudden shocks and shifts in horizontal pressure.[66] The corners of the Demeter Sanctuary peribolos would have lent some stability toward the interior, but the fact remains that its use in a largely free-standing temenos circuit wall is unusual.

BLOCK PROPORTIONS

A factor that has been introduced wherever recoverable into the above description is the ratio of bislab

---

56. Supra n. 38.
57. Supra n. 40.
58. Supra n. 41.
59. Supra n. 46.
60. Supra (60-62).
61. Most notably the two Delphic treasuries. Supra ns. 12, 32, 33.

62. Supra n. 41.
63. Supra n. 34.
64. Supra n. 34.
65. Supra n. 34.
66. Again see the remarks of Clarke, supra n. 34.

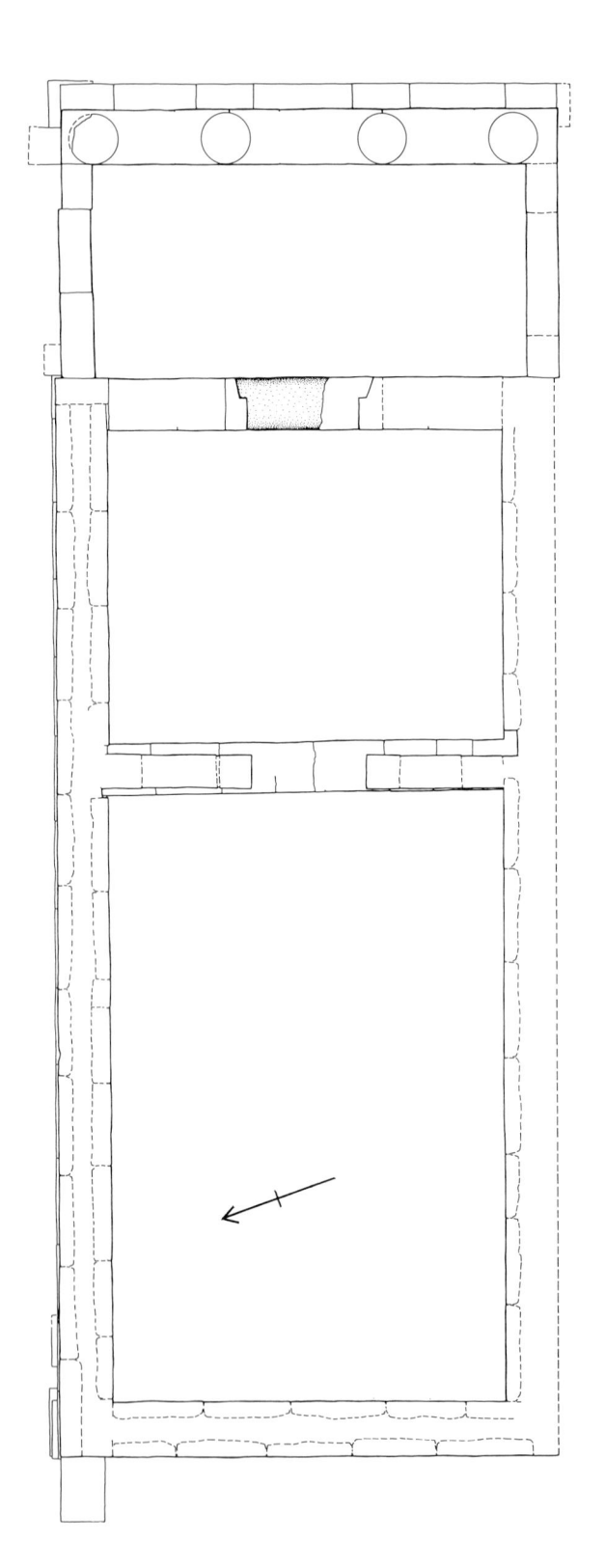

Figure 34: Plan of the "Second Artemisium" in the Sanctuary of Apollo at Cyrene. Drawn by C. Beetz from initial survey and drawing of A. Cook. 1:100 scale.

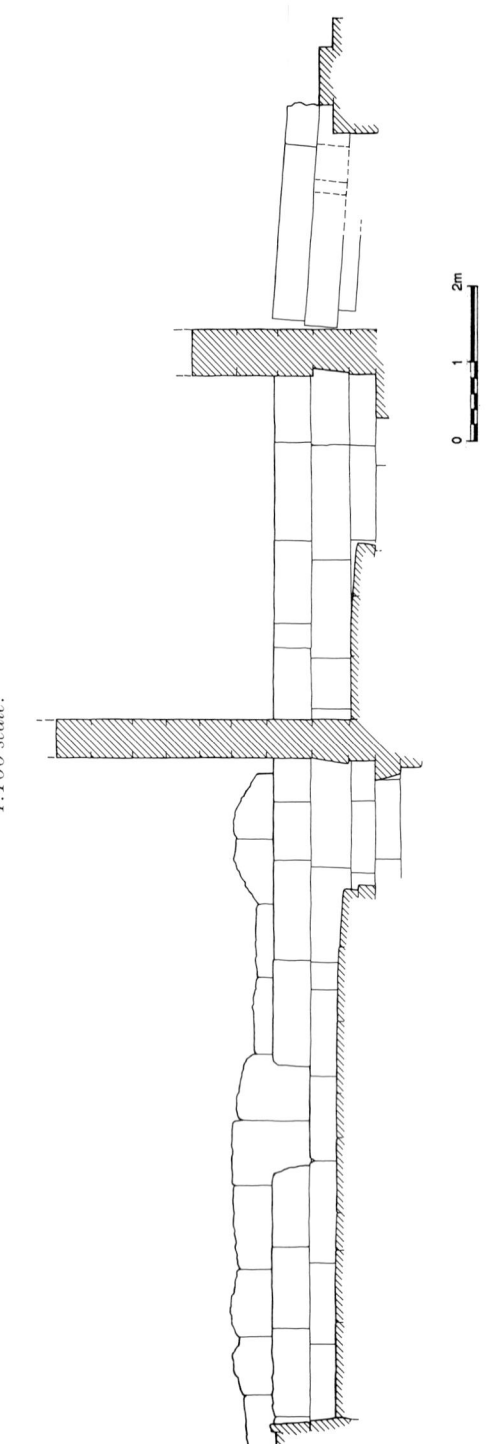

Figure 35: Elevation of the interior north walls of the Artemisium pronaos and naos, drawn from the south. 1:100 scale.

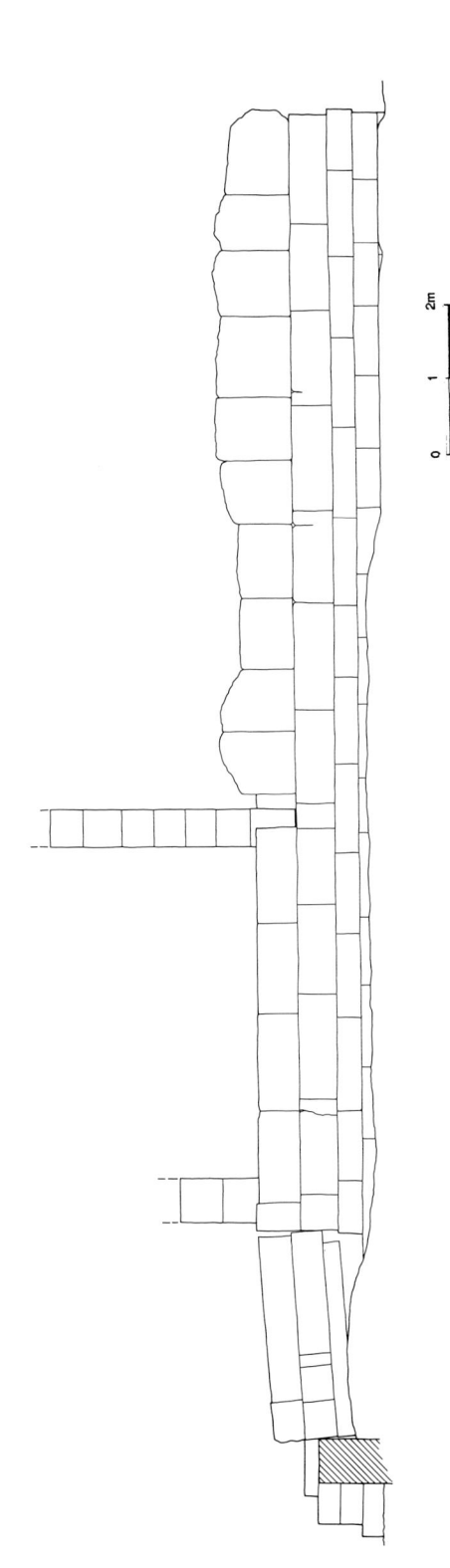

Figure 36: Elevation of exterior north wall of Artemisium, drawn from the north. 1:100 scale.

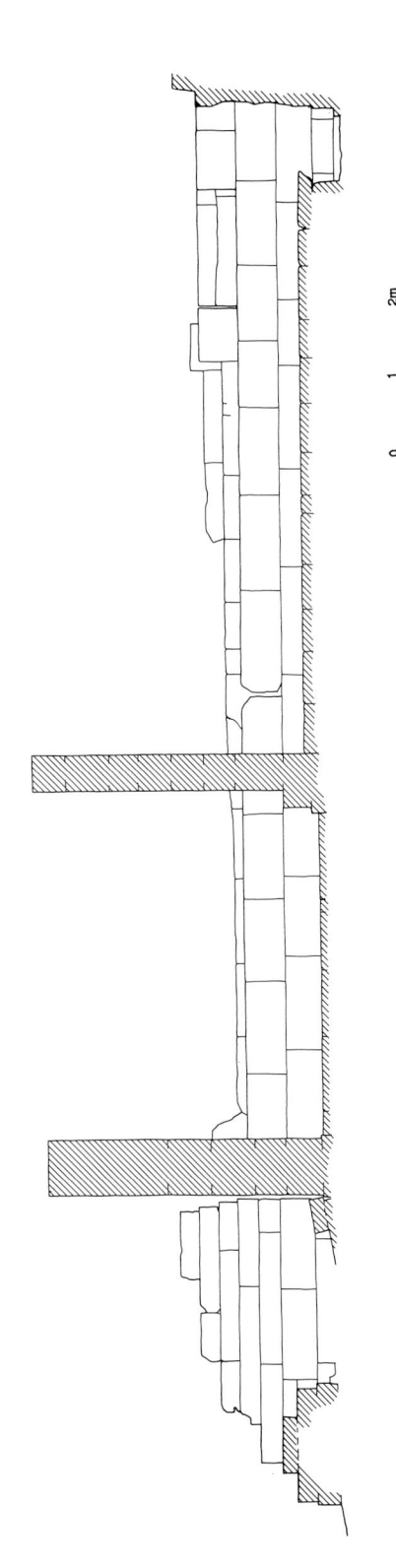

Figure 37: Elevation of the interior south walls of the Artemisium pronaos and naos, drawn from the north. 1:100 scale.

Plate 46: Northern exterior of the Artemisium, illustrating the pseudoisodomic construction of its original pronaos and naos. Seen from north.

Plate 47: The interior of the north and west (rear) walls of the naos of the Artemisium, illustrating their pseudoisodomic masonry. Seen from south.

Plate 48: Artemisium interior bislab displaying parallel strokes of drove.

Plate 49: Detail view of Pl. 48.

Figure 38: Elevation of the cross-wall and door leading from the naos into the pronaos of the Artemisium.

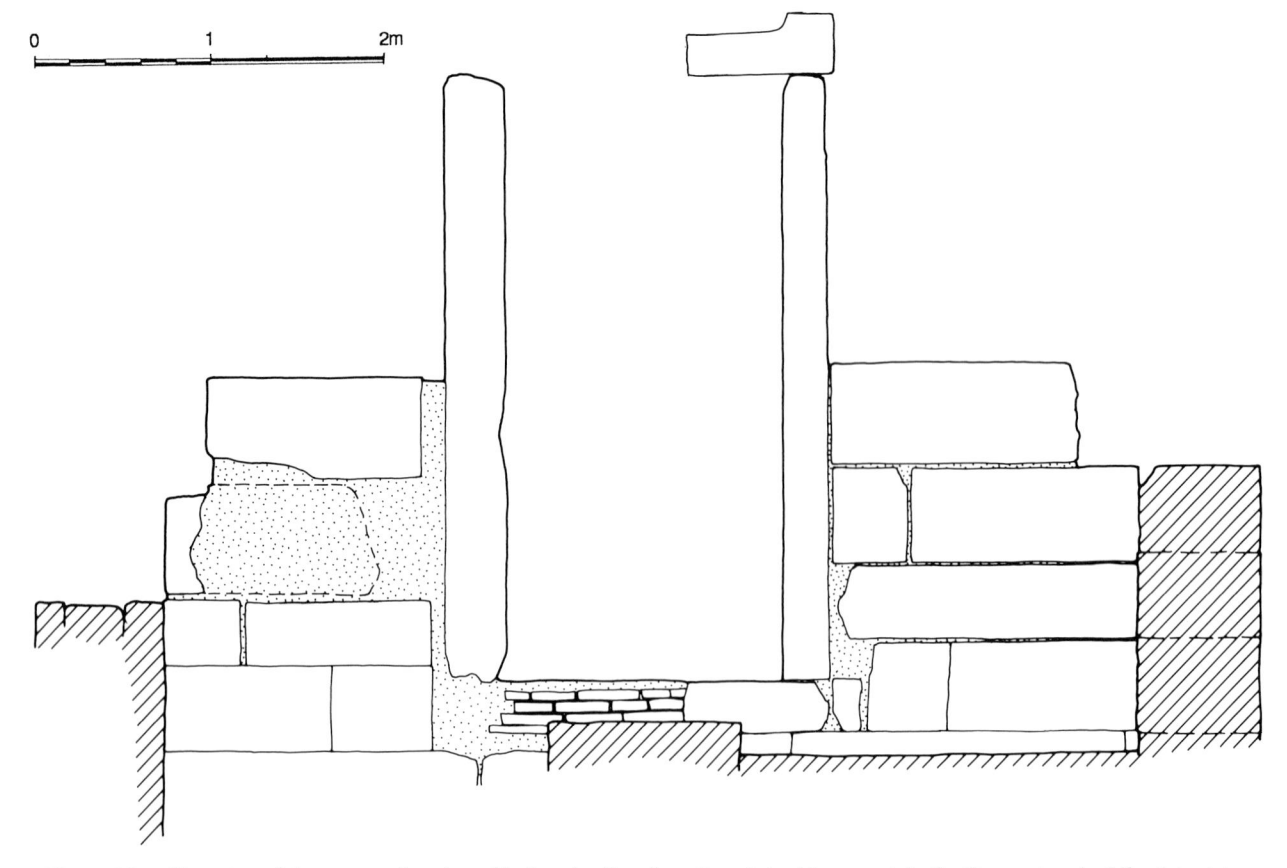

Figure 39: Elevation of the cross-wall and marble door leading from the original pronaos into the Roman porch of the Artemisium.

Plate 50:   Cross-wall separating the original pronaos from the naos of the Artemisium, seen from pronaos looking northwest.

Plate 51:   Cross-wall separating the original naos of the Artemisium from its pronaos, seen from the naos looking east.

Plate 52: Detail of the junction between cross-wall and main exterior north wall at northeast corner of the Artemisium's pronaos. The cross-wall overshoots the upper pair of bislabs to bond with north wall at the time of their latest repair.

Plate 53: Cut-down Doric capital used in north wall of Artemisium.

block height-to-length. The cumulative results from the later Archaic peribolos are tabulated in Appendix II, along with similar data gathered from other select sanctuary ashlar masonry structures. The picture thus far developed is that the later Archaic blocks from the sanctuary have rather squarish proportions, fluctuating between 1:2 (Wall T4) and 1:2.88 (Wall T7). Leaving out Wall T7, the ratios of the remaining wall sections average 1:2.15, which conforms closely to the 1:2.18 ratio of the second course of the Artemisium bislabs. Since our so-called "bislabs" appear to be made from conventional ashlars split in two, the ratios are not restricted to merely orthostates but apply to conventional masonry blocks. What this exactly proves is difficult to argue at this point, but on the basis of the aggregate of presently available information, much of the sanctuary's masonry follows proportional formu-

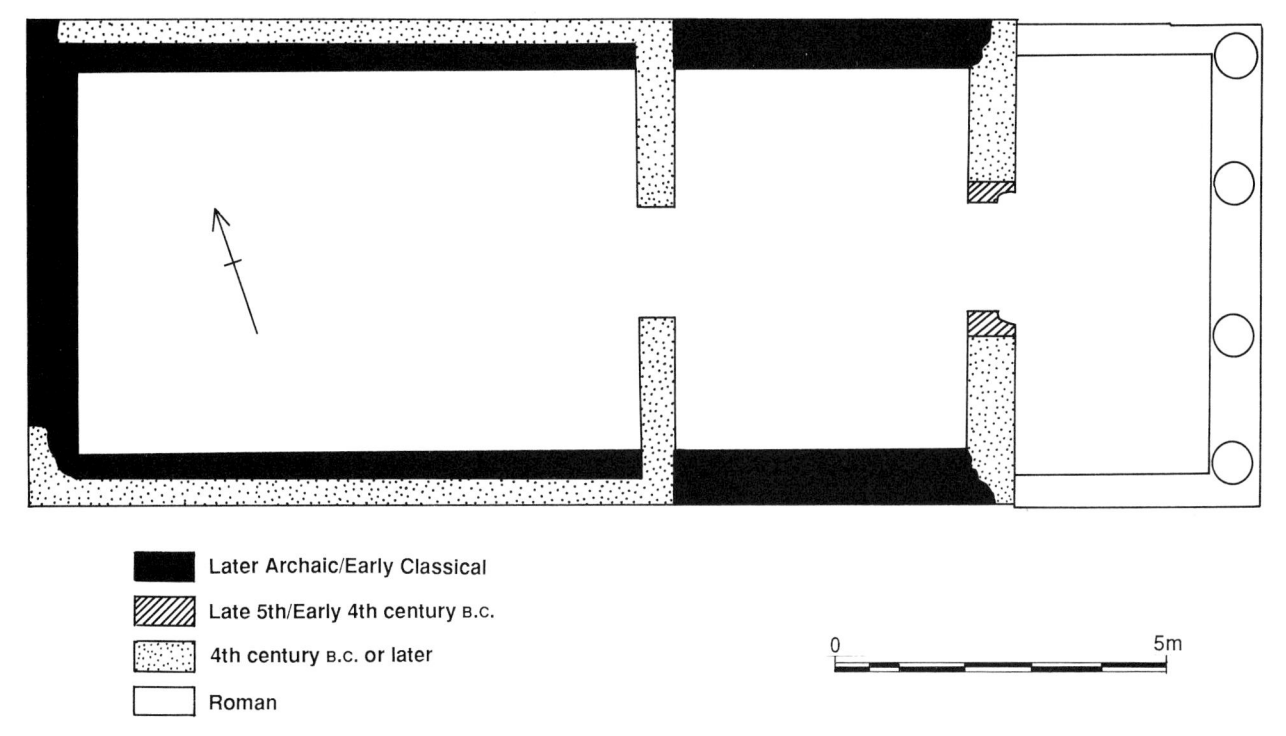

[Figure 40: Phase plan of the Artemisium.]

Legend:
- Later Archaic/Early Classical
- Late 5th/Early 4th century B.C.
- 4th century B.C. or later
- Roman

las that seem to have some broad chronological relevance for at least the sanctuary. Generally speaking, the later Archaic and Classical masonry tends to adopt the 1:2 ratio just observed. The Hellenistic period masonry frequently approximates a 1:4 ratio. And to anticipate the results of our future analysis, the early Imperial masonry fluctuates around 1:3, while the later Imperial reverts to something around 1:2.5.

Later Archaic, Early Classical Structures South of the Peribolos

S3 ASHLAR STRUCTURE

A number of walled elements belonging to this general period in the sanctuary's development came to light at the level of what eventually developed into the Upper Sanctuary. The earliest of these is the S3 Ashlar Structure. Its location is ca. nine m. south of the T1 peribolos wall in C11, 2 and the southern extremity of D11, 1 (Fig. 12; Plans B, E). Its walls were sharply modified by later building and therefore survive in only fragmentary condition. The north wall of S3 (Pl. 54) consists of a short spur (1.70 m. long and truncated at its west end by the later S2 pseudoisodomic masonry structure) that turns south at an obtuse angle to run under the south wall of the S21 Imperial period Propylaeum Court for a distance of 4.50 m. before disappearing beneath an unexcavated balk (Fig. 41; Pl. 55). What survives then appears to be the northeast corner of a chamber otherwise buried beneath a deep overburden of earth fill and later walls.

The north wall was fully exposed only on its south side. It consists of three courses of low (each ca. 0.30 m. high) finely dressed foundation stretchers. The lowest foundation course is offset as well as slightly skewed in relation to the foundation courses above it. The same is true of the course immediately above it. The wall-proper, ca. 0.85 m. wide, then rises above its foundations for two courses of variously sized ashlar blocks that are more roughly finished than their foundations and carry on their upper preserved surface traces of a crude plaster. Their coarser finish and lack of precise coaxiality with the foundations raise the possibility that the upper courses were a later addition that made use of reused blocks. Their stratigraphical context fails, however, to clarify the precise sequence.

Plate 54: Northeast corner of the later Archaic S3 structure undersailing south wall of the Imperial S21 Propylaeum Court in the lower left-hand corner, seen from east.

As said, the western continuation of the wall is interrupted by the east wall of the S2 pseudoisodomic bislab structure, which must definitely supersede the S3 structure by some indeterminate interval of time.

The east wall of S3 runs at a slightly obtuse angle to the northern spur but was probably pushed out of right-angle alignment by later construction. The width of the wall-proper (Figs. 41, 42) is 0.60/0.65 m. Its three ca. 0.30 m. high, offset foundation courses of finely dressed ashlars are well preserved north of the point where at a later time the south wall of the Imperial S21 Propylaeum Courtyard bisects their line. South of the courtyard wall the west face of the east wall of S3 is largely concealed by the later wall construction as well as by incomplete excavation, but its exposed east face (Fig. 43; Pl. 56) shows that the triple offset foundations continued south to the edge of the balk where the wall's progress is lost. Above the foundations a single ca. 0.50 m. high course of the wall-proper is preserved beneath the line of its later Imperial successor, wall W20, and the W19 squatter period wall. To the extent that its blocks can be observed, the block lengths appear to be ca. 1.00 m. and its height-to-length ratio therefore 1:2.

In effect then, the S3 structure survives fragmentarily as a narrow compartment or chamber, measuring in its preserved state internally only 1.50 m. east-to-west. Its original extension west was obliterated at the time of the construction of the S2 pseudoisodomic masonry structure. The context fails to settle definitively whether the cut-back walls of the S3 structure continued to survive above ground after its S2 replacement was built or were left buried, but to judge from its constricted and oddly shaped interior it seems likely that S3 disappeared from use at that time. It therefore may be somewhat misleading to see both features appearing contemporaneously on the phase plan (Plan B).

CONTEXT AND DATE OF THE S3 ASHLAR STRUCTURE

The interior fill at the north end of the S3 compartment (Fig. 42) consisted of a deposit of earth over bedrock (C11, 2, 3 NW) that buried the lowest two courses of its north and east wall. This fill was largely barren of finds but did contain a single good-quality Attic black glaze sherd that probably dates to the fifth century B.C. or earlier.

C11, 2, 3 NW is then overlain by a deep St. 2D fill of loose red argillaceous soil (cf. left edge of Fig. 42) that engulfs the surviving upper courses of the S3 east wall as well as portions of the S21 Propylaeum Court wall rising above it. C11, 2, 2D contains roof tiles, a fourth century lamp, and a sparse number of largely diagnostically useless sherds. Owing to the fact that the excavated area was so hemmed in by later building, the stratigraphy fails to clarify whether the builders of the S21 Propylaeum Court dug away all of the fill previously concealing the S3 structure in order to establish their wall or whether S3 remained visible until the post-A.D. 115 period when the court was introduced. But, as previously stated, the latter possibility seems intrinsically implausible.

The C11, 2 fill against the outer face of the east wall of S3 south of the S21 Propylaeum Court reflects a complex accumulation of eight levels over bedrock (Fig. 43), of which levels 5 through 8 appear to be associated with the S3 wall's construction. St. 8 is sterile terra rossa over bedrock. St. 7 is again sterile, consisting of disturbed terra rossa soil mixed with pockets of decaying yellow limestone and small stones. Levels 6 and 5 are basically the same reddish brown argillaceous fill, separated by a thin layer of crushed limestone; they may represent separate tips of the same period. St. 5a is a sterile backfill against the lowest two courses of the east wall of S3 and cuts into St. 6 and 7. The only dateable find comes from St. 5, which contains a LC II trefoil-lipped miniature olpe. The stratigraphical evidence developed for the S3 structure is therefore not especially helpful but nevertheless produces nothing to indicate that its walls are later than the sixth, possibly fifth century B.C.

On the other hand, for purely constructional reasons the S3 structure must be earlier than the S2 pseudoisodomic

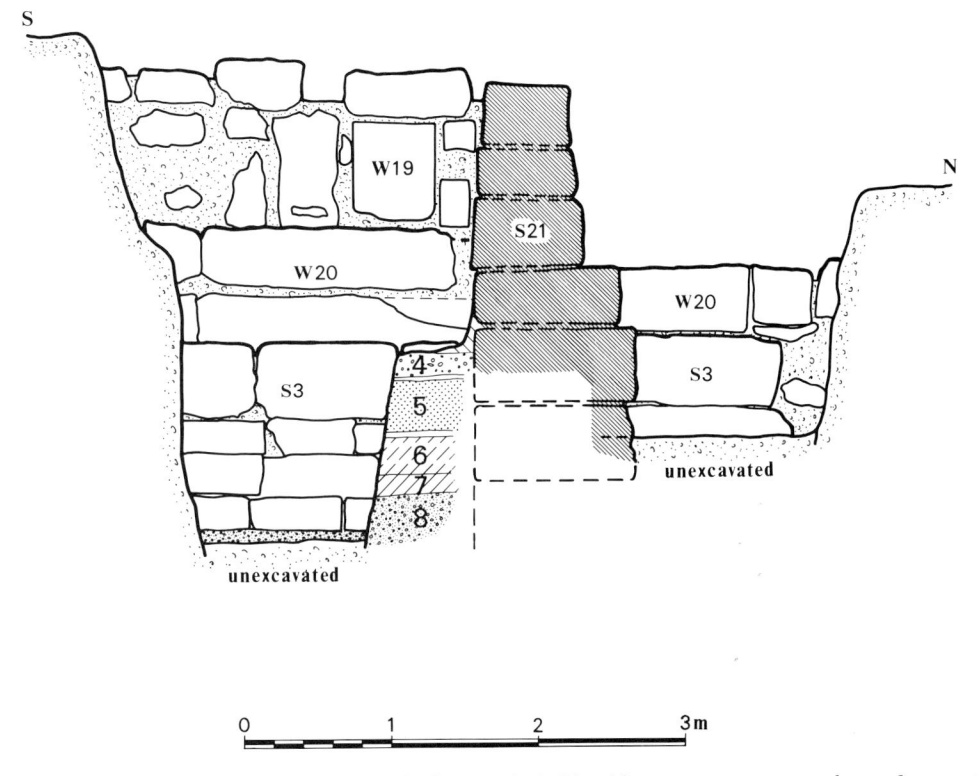

Figure 41: North-south elevation of the east wall of the later Archaic S3 ashlar masonry structure, drawn from east. 1:50 scale.

bislab masonry structure to its immediate west. For what it is worth chronologically, the one preserved course of the superstructure of S3's east wall has a block height-to-length ratio of 1:2 that conforms with the pattern already observed in the case of the later Archaic peribolos wall system.

S4 ASHLAR STRUCTURE

The second ashlar masonry component erected at this level during the later Archaic, early Classic phase of the sanctuary's development is designated as simply the S4 building. It is located to the west of the S3 ashlar masonry structure in C12/13, 1 and 2 and C12/D12, G (Plans B, E; Figs. 4, 11, 12; Pl. 57). The S4 building measures 5.40 m. east to west and 4.20 m. north to south before its extension south becomes lost beneath the Imperial period wall W24, the post A.D. 262 earthquake period wall W21, and the unexcavated trench balk (Fig. 44; Pl. 58). At some point subsequent to its initial construction S4 was subdivided by an inner east-west partition wall that had the effect of creating a narrow room to the north (interior measurements 4.70 by 1.60 m.) associated with a larger chamber to the south. No trace of an entrance is visible through its exterior north and west walls, and while it perhaps may be assumed that the structure was entered from the south, there is also no obvious indication of how entry was managed between the two interior rooms. It is therefore likely that whatever survives today belongs mainly to the structure's sub-pavement levels.

NORTH WALL

The surviving elevation (Fig. 45) consists of two courses of bulkily proportioned ashlars 0.60 m. wide, 0.60/0.63 m. high, and 1.11/1.32 m. long (i.e., a height-to-length ratio varying from 1:1.8 to 1:2.2). The S4 blocks echo the actual heights and lengths of much of the bislab masonry of the later Archaic peribolos. Since the bislabs were themselves evidently prepared from large ashlars split in two, the blocks for the two sets of structures may stem from a common quarry source.

Another indication of this stems from the physical characteristics of the actual stone. While the limestone surface is here weathered a dark reddish brown, its core is beige-white in color and essentially free of microshell inclusions, thus resembling the stone used for wall T1. Despite the difference in their surface colors, which are largely a product of exposure to

Plate 55: *The east wall of the later Archaic S3 structure passing to the south through the foundations of the S21 Propylaeum Court. Two later walls, W19 and W20, override the line of the S3 wall. Seen from southeast.*

weathering and surrounding soil conditions (i.e., they represent a post-quarrying patination), the stones again appear to derive from the same source. Both differ from the limestones used for later sanctuary additions in their smooth surface textures and absence of fossilized shells. Samples of limestone broken from the natural bedrock pavement north of the S4 structure as well as from the vicinity of the Sacred House S5 (Plan E) exhibit widely scattered but nevertheless clearly visible microshell inclusions, which suggests that the bedrock immediately in the vicinity of the S4 building and wall T1 was not used to supply the stone for their masonry.

A third characteristic is the treatment of the upper surface of the north wall's top surviving course (Pl. 59). This is distinguished by a smooth margin, ca. 0.04 to 0.08 m. wide, set around each block's outer edge. The remainder of the block surface is then dressed with a mallet-driven mason's point to produce a pecked or pockmarked surface. What is perhaps most noteworthy about this dressing is the fact that it appears to be associated with no other structure found within the sanctuary.

The west wall of the neighboring S2 pseudoisodomic bislab structure forming the east side of S4 overshoots the north wall of S4 by ca. 0.20 m. (Plans B, E). The top of S4's second course rises approximately the same amount above the top of S2's second course (Pls. 57, 60). No attempt was made by their respective builders to bond the two walls together, and it seems a fair assumption that they represent separate builds. The easternmost block of S4 abutting the northwest corner of S2 is roughly 0.60 m. square, but there exists no indication that it was cut down from a normal stretcher ca. 1.20 m. long. On the other hand, there exists some constructional evidence to support the idea that the west wall of S2 originally continued further north down the hill.[67] The likelihood is that, whatever plan the S2 structure initially possessed, it

---

67. The exposed end of the bislab surviving at S2's northwest corner has traces of anathyrosis, and cuttings are preserved in the bedrock for a now missing foundation slab that would have continued the line of the west wall down the slope.

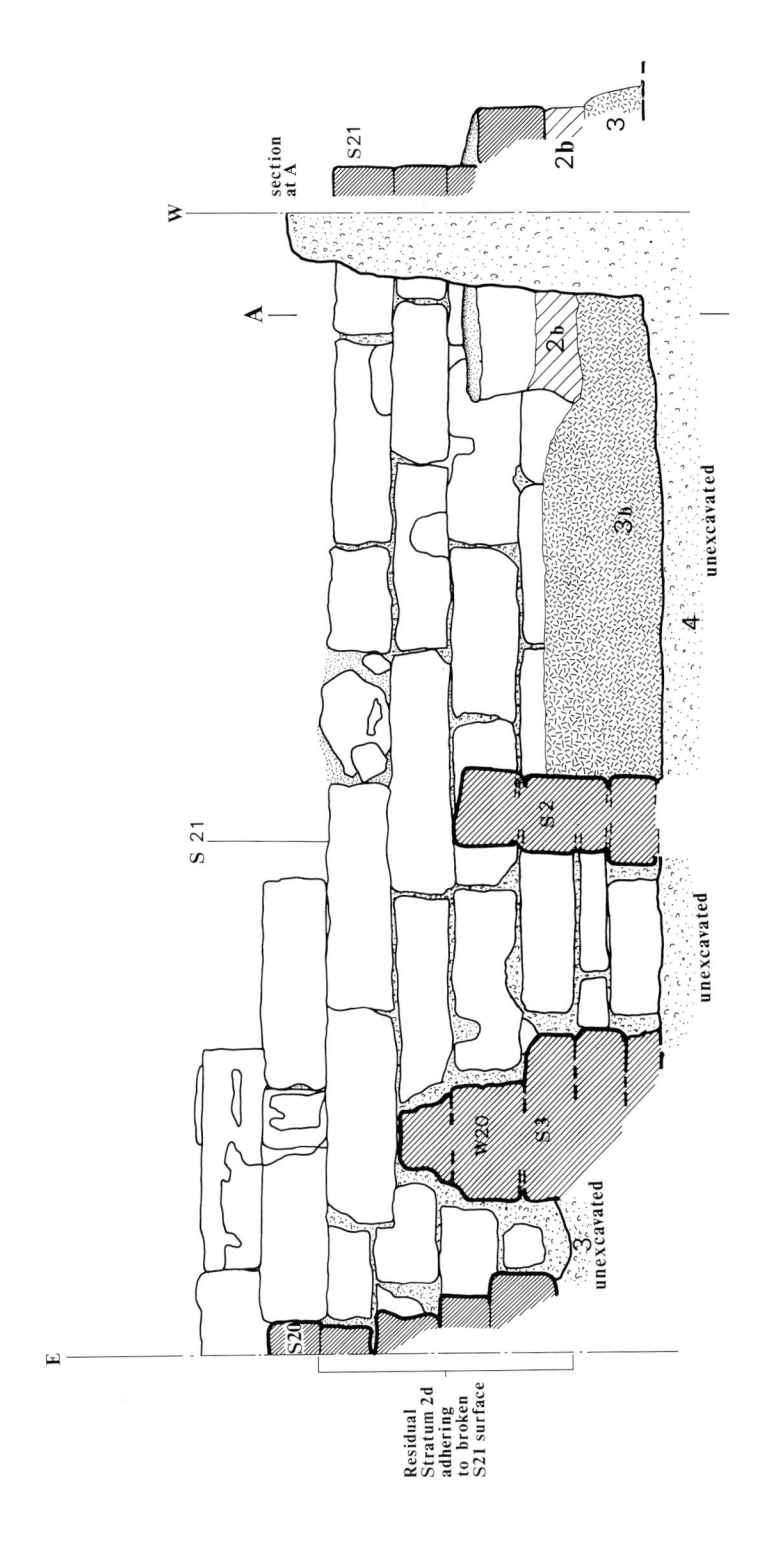

Figure 42: *Elevation of the north face of the south wall of the Imperial S21 Propylaeum Court to illustrate passage through its foundations of the east wall of the later Archaic S3 structure and the pseudoisodomic bislab S2 structure. Drawn from north. 1:50 scale.*

Plate 58: Interior cross-wall and main west wall of the later Archaic, early Classical S4 building, with the latter disappearing under the Imperial walls, W21 and W24. Seen from north.

be early. Some of the miscellaneous small finds designated by Warden as "probably Archaic" in date arguably could be as late as the first quarter of the fifth century.[68] Otherwise the structure appears to be connected stratigraphically with the Archaic period but should be later than both the S3 ashlar masonry structure and S2 pseudoisodomic bislab masonry building to its immediate east. As, however, shall be argued below, the S2 building could belong to the opening two decades of the fifth century, putting the S4 structure possibly as late as the beginning of the Classical period.

COMMENTARY

Given its incomplete state of preservation there is little to say about this building other than the fact that two of its masonry characteristics may have some external parallels whose possible relevance remains to be established. The approximately 1:2 height-to-length ratio of the blocks of its main north and west walls has already been commented on in respect to the later Archaic peribolos system. Without possessing sufficient information to make general comparisons between this and other Archaic, early Classical masonry found elsewhere in Cyrene, it is perhaps worth at least noting in passing that these proportions are shared by the orthostates of the city Agora's Portico A1 (block measurements: 55.12 by 117.60 cm., giving a ratio of 1:2.13), dated to the third quarter of the sixth century.[69] On the other hand, the more elongated proportions of its interior partition or cross-wall (1:2.9) may be another sign of the latter's secondary character.

The point-dressed surface represents another piece of incomplete research where the abrupt conclusion of our work at Cyrene prevented searching for additional examples of this distinctive type of stone finish on masonry found in other parts of Cyrene and elsewhere throughout the Pentapolis. My guess is that they exist. In the meantime, Martin has established the fact that point-dressed finishes were standard for

---

68. P. Warden, *Final Reports* IV, cat. nos. **96**, **131**, **132**, **133**.

69. *Agora* I, 72, fig. 31.

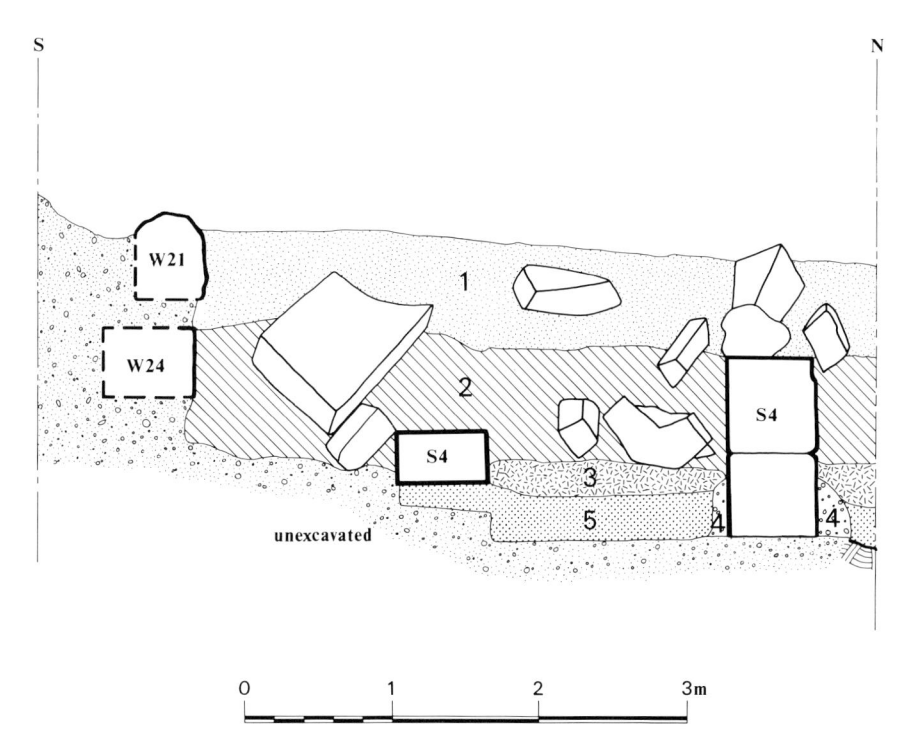

Figure 45: North-south section of fill over the north wall and interior cross-wall of the later Archaic, early Classical S4 building, drawn from east when the latter's west wall was still unexcavated. 1:50 scale.

Greek architecture from Archaic times into the fourth century B.C. and illustrates the technique with a wall from Thasos whose surface is remarkably similar to the S4 blocks.[70] What Dinsmoor described as the pock-mark effects of the point on the outer pink foundations of the ca. 570 B.C. Hekatompedon on the Athenian Acropolis again bears a close resemblance to the dressing of the S4 masonry.[71]

Pseudoisodomic Bislab Walls South of the Peribolos

S2 BUILDING

As has been mentioned, a set of pseudoisodomic bislab walls was discovered slightly more than seven m. south of the peribolos wall T1 between the two ashlar wall units (S3 and S4) just described (Plans B, E; Pls. 60, 61; Figs. 3, 11, 42, 46-48) in Trenches C11, 1 and C12/D12, G. Despite the constructional similarity of its walls to the T1 peribolos wall, the S2 structure apparently belongs to the north end of an independent building rather than reflecting either an extension of the sanctuary's main enclosure wall or a separate, secondary peribolos. The north wall measures 8.70 m. The maximum preserved length of its west wall is 3.85 m. The east wall is 5.20 m. Owing to the lack of excavation in this sector, it is not possible to say whether we are dealing with a relatively small structure whose principal axis ran east-to-west or instead a potentially long, narrow building that ran north-south.

In contrast to the limestone used for the pseudoisodomic peribolos T1, which is almost entirely free of fossilized shell inclusions, the surface of the S2 blocks displays occasional traces of shell matter. There is, however, insufficient evidence to say whether the blocks from both walls came from the same quarry source or not. The outer surface is weathered light to medium brown, while the core is chalky grey in color.

The north wall remains largely unexcavated. However, its two interior corners have been cleared. Their alignment, together with the close similarity in the masonry used for the east and west walls, leaves little doubt that all three formed a rectangular unit. Future

---

70. Martin, *Manuel* 180, pl. xiv, 3.

71. W. Dinsmoor, *AJA* 51 (1947) 116-17, pl. xxvii, 4.

Plate 59:   Northwest corner of the later Archaic, early Classical S4 building, showing the pockmarked top surface of its masonry. Seen from northwest.

excavation will be required to determine whether the north wall possessed a door.

EAST WALL

Resting on terra rossa, the flat foundation perpends of the east wall (width, 0.61/0.64 m.) support for their entire length a single course of paired bislabs 0.63/0.64 m. in height (Figs. 46-48) and, where measurable, 1.22 m. long (block height-to-length ratio 1:1.94). This in turn supports a single vertically placed block, 0.41 m. high, belonging to a second course of bislabs, otherwise completely embedded in the southern scarp of the trench. No traces of pryholes or setting-out lines, similar to those preserved on wall T1,[72] are visible. The north end bonds with the return of S2's north wall to the east at the level of the first bislab course.

---

72. For pryholes, etc., see supra 49.

WEST WALL

A gap of ca. 1.50 m. exists in the center of the west wall (width 0.62 m.), where its line is interrupted by the later south wall of the S21 Propylaeum Court and the post A.D. 262 earthquake squatter wall W21. Resting on largely sterile soil over the bedrock, S2's west wall consists of the normal flat foundation slabs, surmounted by two upright courses of bislabs. The lower bislabs measure ca. 0.60 m. high. Their lengths vary between 1.00 and 1.50 m. (block height-to-length ratio 1:1.65/1:1:2.5). The second course is ca. 0.45 m. high, reflecting roughly the same reduced height as recorded for the second bislab of S2's east wall. The block lengths are ca. 1.00 m. (block height-to-length ratio 1:2.22). Its block sequence therefore seems to be A-B-B', as opposed to the A-B-B-A rhythm of the nearby peribolos.

Some evidence exists to support the conclusion that the west wall at one time may have continued further

Plate 60: Juncture of the northeast corner of the S4 building with the northwest corner of the S2 pseudoisodomic bislab masonry building, seen from northwest.

north down the slope and that originally the S2 structure had a more complex plan than presently survives. The northwest corner bislab shows traces of anathyrosis along its exterior vertical edge, while cuttings in the bedrock immediately north of the present northwest corner suggest that the limestone shelf was prepared to receive a now missing foundation slab.

CONTEXT AND DATE OF S2 BUILDING

EAST WALL

The foundation course of the northern half (C11, 1) rests on nearly sterile C11, 1, 4 fill (Fig. 42), which contains a single glass fragment dated between the sixth and first centuries B.C. It is otherwise associated with a C11, 1, 3b level, ca. half a meter deep, covering the foundation to the tops of its slabs (Figs. 42, 47). The contents of St. 3b include pottery dating as late as 520 B.C. and a single Howland Type 21A Attic lamp, Inv. 76-249, not included by Fabbricotti in her study of the sanctuary lamps but clearly dating to the period of the late sixth century to 480 B.C.

The southern half (C11, 2) rests on a largely sterile St. 5 fill over bedrock (Figs. 46, 48). However, its upper surface east of the S2 wall produced an LC II miniature olpe, dating 550 to 500 B.C. The Archaic level associated with both the foundation and upper two-thirds of the bislab course is labelled St. 4a east of the S2 wall and St. 4 to its west. Nothing was recovered from its fill to provide a date.

WEST WALL

Built over a St. 4 layer of sterile terra rossa, the wall is undated by its associated stratigraphy. On constructional grounds it is, as has been argued, apparently earlier than the S4 ashlar masonry building to its immediate west.

In summary, the S2 pseudoisodomic bislab masonry building should date no earlier than the end of the sixth century B.C. but theoretically could have been built as late as 480 B.C. This in effect could depress the date of the adjacent S4 ashlar masonry building to slightly after 480 B.C. or into the early Classical period.

Plate 61: East wall of the S2 pseudoisodomic bislab masonry building passing beneath the south wall of the Imperial S21 Propylaeum Court and late squatter wall W21, seen from west.

COMMENTARY

Given the paucity of information that we have about both its interior and superstructure, little can be determined of the actual identity or usage of the S2 structure. There seems to be nothing to recommend the idea that it has to do with a second, independently walled enclosure, and it will be recalled that the bulk of the comparanda cited for the pseudoisodomic bislab masonry of the peribolos system to its north originated with independent buildings rather than temenos enclosures.

WALL W30

A second wall utilizing pseudoisodomic bislab masonry was brought to light in C15/16, 1 ca. 38 m. west of the first, at a distance of ca. nine m. south of the southwest corner of the peribolos (Plan B; Figs. 28, 49, 50; Pl. 62). As preserved, the W30 wall consists of a single course of four unusually thick foundation blocks (height ca. 0.50 m.). Two courses of bislabs were then set in conventional pairs over the foundations, averaging slightly less than 0.30 m. thick, 0.60 m. high, and 1.20 m. long (block height-to-length ratio 1:2). Four individual blocks of the first course of upright bislabs were recovered, together with two additional blocks from a second level of bislabs. Both courses appear to have belonged to the western face of the original wall; their counterpart blocks that originally formed its eastern face were removed in antiquity.

CONTEXT AND DATE OF WALL W30

The C15/16, 1, W4 fill directly west of wall W30 consists of pockets of St. 5 reddish clay fill over bedrock, associated with the wall's foundations. Its one dateable find belongs to the end of the seventh, beginning of the sixth century B.C. This in turn is covered with a 0.60-m.-deep reddish brown moist earth St. 4 fill packed against the lower orthostate course as part of the construction of a Hellenistic period drain (F4). It contains lamps from the fifth to the second century B.C., fine wares of either the second or first century B.C., an early fifth century silver coin, and Ptolemaic period bronze coins as late as the later second century B.C. Neither layer therefore assists in dating the wall, whose construction is characteristically early.

The fill east of W30 (C15/16, 1, 4-2) consists of a shallow layer of St. 6 reddish clay lying in scattered pockets over the bedrock and in places under W30's foundations. This is then covered by a moist brown St. 5 earth fill, substantially thicker toward the southern end of W30 (Fig. 49) where the foundations were eventually removed and shallower when packed against the preserved foundations to the north (Fig. 50).

St. 6 contains a terracotta relief dated to the early fifth century. St. 5 includes an assortment of sixth century pottery, a mid-fifth century terracotta figurine and local bowls of the second or first century B.C. that Kenrick regarded as intrusive. St. 5 is, however, better interpreted as a backfill introduced after the removal of wall W30's foundation blocks at its south end during the late Hellenistic period. The wall should take its date from the early fifth century relief from C15/16, 1, 4-2, 6.

S19 STRUCTURE

At some indeterminable time the north end of wall W30 was joined at right angles by a second wall built of a single series of large upright slabs running west (Plans B, E; Fig. 28; Pl. 62). The latter rests on the same fill as W30 and indeed appears to have been levelled with it. The heights of its two surviving courses match those of W30, but the course thicknesses are approximately half a meter and thus the east-west spur is not strictly speaking of "bislab" construction. Its excavated length is ca. two m. before disappearing into the unexcavated balk west of the C15/16 trench. The junction of the two walls is in too ruinous a condition to be certain whether they were

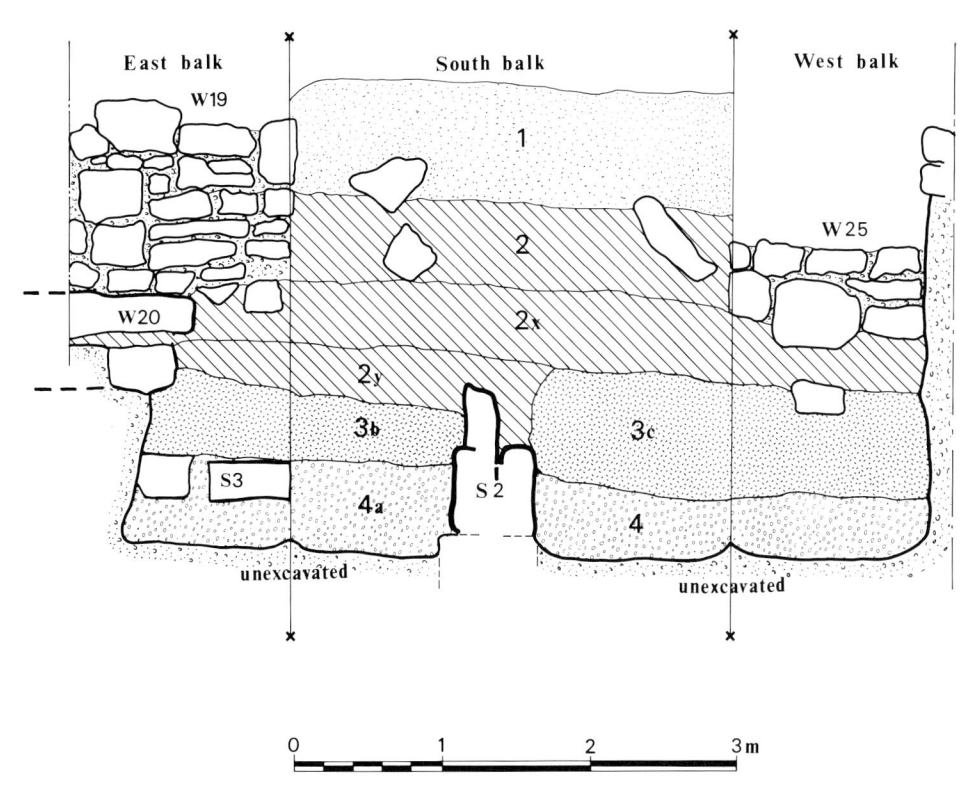

Figure 46: Wrap-around section of fill at south end of C11, 1 and C11, 2. The south balk covers the east wall of the later Archaic S2 pseudoisodomic masonry building. Drawn from north. 1:50 scale.

planned simultaneously or not. While the east-west wall appears to cut across the line of W30, this could have been part of the original arrangement to bond the two together to form the corner of a structure (tentatively designated S19), as opposed to a later interruption. The constructional difference (i.e., single slab orthostates versus paired bislabs) may indicate that the east-west wall was a subsequent addition. If so, no great interval of time may have separated the two events.

Interior of the Walled Temenos

The interior grounds of the walled temenos acquire in this period for the first time, as far as can be determined, separate buildings that are independent of the surrounding peribolos. In other words, whatever the architectural character of the early Archaic sanctuary might have been, it is only now that the series of small, independently sited shrine houses that together constitute the distinctive hallmark of its layout comes into focus. These shall be described and dated separately in the following pages and then discussed as a group at the chapter's end.

S1 SACRED HOUSE

Approximately centered in the eastern half of the later Archaic pseudoisodomic peribolos are the paltry remains of a largely dismantled independent shrine house (Plans B, E; Figs. 3, 10, 51-53; Pls. 63, 64). Its exterior measurements at foundation level are 6.24 m. east to west and ca. 7.00 m. north to south. With the exception of its south wall, a single block from its west wall, and a block perhaps displaced from its north wall, the entire superstructure of the S1 Sacred House was demolished in antiquity, leaving the outline of its exterior foundations in the bedrock pavement as the principal evidence for its shape. The cuttings are especially clearly preserved along the west side, where the bedrock was trimmed down ca. 0.10/0.20 m. to receive five foundation slabs, now missing, that ranged in length from ca. 0.40 to 1.30 m. To judge from the single block that survives *in situ* in its southwest corner, the width of the west wall was 0.60 m. In the

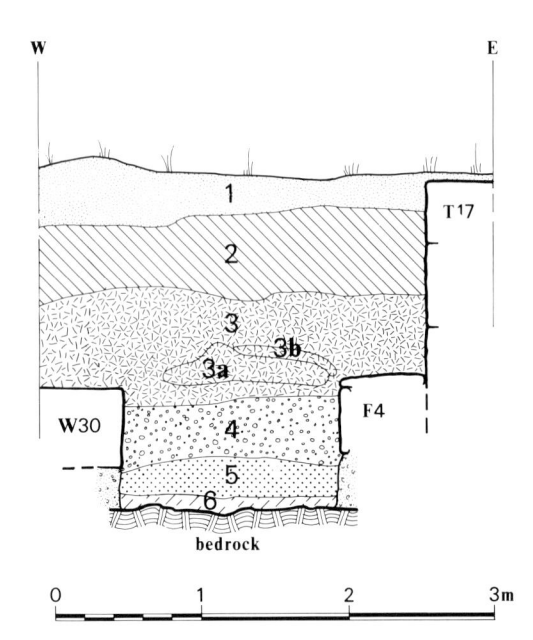

Figure 50: East-west section of north balk of C15/16, 1, showing fill between the T17 Hellenistic peribolos extension and the later Archaic W30 wall, drawn from south. 1:50 scale.

proper floor in place it is difficult to tell if these belong to the structure's period of early use or are associated with its initial construction. In either case the original phase of the S1 house would seem to belong to the sanctuary's later Archaic period. If its south wall is in fact a later replacement, no stratigraphical evidence was retrieved to verify that fact.

S5 SACRED HOUSE

This, the sanctuary's second independent shrine building (Plans B, E; Figs. 10, 54-57; Pls. 65-68,) was constructed ca. 4.75 m. west of the S1 Sacred House at a point slightly further back up the slope. Despite the fact that the structure underwent repairs to its superstructure prior to its total destruction in A.D. 262, its four original outer walls survive fairly well intact. In plan a small rectangular building, oriented to the north, the S5 house measures approximately 6.50 m. north to south by 4.60 m. east to west.[73] Its stone is an excellent quality limestone, relatively free of shell inclusions, and capable of maintaining precisely cut edges. Its surface is weathered grey-buff.

BUILDING INTERIOR

The principal feature to survive inside S5 is a limestone bench set flush to the rear or south wall (Pl. 66). Falling short of spanning the entire width of the building, the bench measures 2.20 m. in length. It is composed of two low blocks set in a cutting prepared in the bedrock; these carry a third, single large block, which, together with a small filler stone at its east end, brings the bench height to 0.68 m. above bedrock. Its width is 0.55 m.

The wall surface on most of the interior has suffered considerable erosion and crumbling, but small chunks of plaster attached to the top of the bench show that the back wall was originally stuccoed. On the analogy with the better preserved interior of the Hellenistic S7 Sacred House,[74] which also was provided with a bench across its rear, both bench and walls were probably originally painted with colored linear designs. If this was the case, no trace of the interior painted decoration has been preserved, since the bench plaster lacks traces of any color and the one fragment of detached wall plaster found in the earthquake debris from its interior is plain white. Moreover, no evidence was recovered to indicate whether the bench was part of the original building phase of S5 or an S5a later addition.

As was the case with the S1 Sacred House, the natural limestone pavement on the interior consists of a series of descending shelves and pits, which reflect a normal tectonic profile of the limestone slope once stripped of its earth cover. Again the oddity is that no trace could be found of an ancient floor level. It presumably was installed immediately above the bedrock shelf supporting the bench at the rear, which lies three courses higher than the bedrock across the building's front (north side). Two ashlar blocks, covered by a light brown loose earth fill (D13/E13, 1, 3) that may post-date the period of the structure's active occupancy, were excavated on a bedrock shelf close to the east wall in the building's center (Fig. 54), while a third ashlar lay closer to the west wall, supported on rubble and patches of a dark reddish soil (D13/E13, 1, 4). The upper surfaces of all three blocks lay either at the same level as the hypothetical floor or beneath it, but their use as part of a pavement fill belonging to the original building phase is ruled out by the interior's stratigraphy.

WEST WALL

In its present condition the wall (Pl. 67; Fig. 55) is preserved to a height of seven courses, or 2.60 m. The change in bedrock level from north to south is distributed over a series of rising foundation blocks set into the dressed surface of the natural stone pavement.

---

73. The precise wall measurements are as follows: East wall 6.38 m., west wall 6.53 m., north wall 4.29 m., south wall 4.58 m.

74. See infra 160-62 for the painted interior of the S7 Sacred House.

Plate 62: Zone west of the Hellenistic F2 fountain complex seen from south. The highest wall to right is the T17 Hellenistic peribolos extension. The wall carrying the meter scale is W34. The later Archaic W30 pseudoisodomic bislab wall crosses the trench north-to-south at left, joined at its far end by wall S19.

The two most northern foundation courses available for examination[75] project ca. 0.20 m. beyond the line of the courses set above them, while the one foundation block marking the southwest corner projects ca. 0.30 m. All remaining foundation blocks are set flush to the wall's surface.

The five lowest courses belong to the building's initial construction phase. The remaining upper two courses are part of a secondary Imperial phase (S5a). Starting from the north end, the masonry sequence consists of two projecting, 0.35-m.-high foundation courses, the lowest being only partially cleared and not included in the Fig. 55 elevation. Above this rise two stretcher courses, each ca. 0.50 m. high, 1.15 m. long, and 0.55 m. thick (block ratio 1:2.3). A 0.30-m.-high stretcher course is then inserted as the fifth course in order to level the northern two-thirds of the wall with its southern third, which is erected on the bedrock shelf ca. 1.20 m. above the level of the north

foundations. The change in level is compensated for by the use of two carefully prepared L-shaped blocks that form the corner with S5's south wall. A similar use of L-shaped bonding blocks appears in the south wall and is a mark of the elegant stonework that characterizes this structure's original building phase.

SOUTH WALL

The wall is here preserved to a height of four courses or ca. 1.80 m. above bedrock (Fig. 56). The northeast corner of the third century A.D. Late Building (S24) to some extent impedes a full understanding of the masonry sequence in the western third of S5's south wall. Nevertheless all four courses appear to belong to the building's original building phase.

The south wall rests on a ca. 0.40-m.-high foundation course that projects ca. 0.12 m. beyond the line of the regular courses above and is set directly on the dressed bedrock, which rises ca. 0.40 m. east to west. The change in level is initially absorbed by shallow L-shaped "step" joints that bond together the founda-

---

75. The actual exterior northwest corner was not excavated because of the presence of the late Imperial period E14 Mound (S29).

tion blocks. The southeast corner foundation supports a squarish ashlar, 1.25 m. long, 0.80 m. high, and 0.55 m. thick; the extra height is used to adjust the top of the second course to the changing bedrock level. The block's exterior face provides a well-preserved example of the wall's original smooth surface and closely fitted joints (Pl. 68). The second course block directly from the east has a shallow L-shaped step on its upper surface to bond with the third course of ca. 0.40-m.-high stretchers. Its length and height measure 1.22 by 0.60 (1:2.03). One of the two blocks preserved from the fourth course, is also cut with a shallow L-shaped step on its upper surface, which, together with its carefully finished exterior face, argues that it is part of the original superstructure. The shorter and more badly preserved stretcher to its west may be part of the later repair.

EAST WALL

Five courses, of which no more than four stand in any one place, are preserved to a maximum height of 1.80 m. (Fig. 57). The upper two courses at the south end belong to the structure's late S5a repairs, as do the second and third courses at the wall's center. The remaining original stretchers are more uniform in height than those on the south and west, averaging between 0.46 and 0.48 m. Their lengths vary between 1.10 and 1.40 (average ratio 1:2.65). Externally, the bedrock carrying the east wall drops off less sharply to the north than it does inside the building.[76]

NORTH WALL

Largely destroyed, the principal remains of the north wall are three crumbling first-course foundation blocks that support the wall's northeast corner and western half, together with a single corner stretcher (0.50 by 1.40 by 0.70 m.; block ratio 1:2.8) from what was probably the second course of foundations. There exist no traces of either a door threshold, which must have been supported by the missing third course, or of steps leading up to the building from the north.

SUPERSTRUCTURE

Little can be adduced about the original appearance of this structure, as opposed to what it looked like after its later S5a repairs. At the time of its clearance the interior was choked with a thick D13/E13, 1, 2 earthquake debris level, filled with numerous fallen building blocks. Some had clearly originated from the house's own back wall, which probably stood at least two courses higher immediately before the A.D. 262 earthquake than it did after its destruction. Others may belong to its side walls. On the other hand it is equally certain that many of the blocks plugging its interior belonged to buildings located on the wadi slope further south, especially the S23/S24 Late Building. That building elements were thrown down the slope into the broken interior of the the S5 House is made clear by the discovery in its St. 2 fill of numerous small moulding fragments detached from a large marble lintel and jamb fragment which had been carried by the earthquake against the outer north wall of the west chamber (S23) of the Late Building.[77] It is also likely that the single badly worn fragment of a limestone triglyph block (Pl. 69)[78] discovered inside the house also originated further up the slope. The ground to the east and in front of the S5 building contained virtually no architectural members that might help in restoring its original appearance. Numerous fragments were found to its west in fill associated with the E14 Mound (S29),[79] but these were collected from destroyed buildings across much of the site after the earthquake, especially from the grounds of the Upper Sanctuary, and do not have anything to do with S5.[80] Finally, the D13/E13, 1, 3 fill covering parts of S5's interior beneath the thick earthquake debris level produced numerous roof tile fragments, which suggests that the building in its late S5a phase had already been abandoned and to some extent dismantled before the earthquake took place. To this extent its late history resembles that of the S1 Sacred House.

---

76. The total internal dropoff amounts to three courses, while externally the total fall is the equivalent of only a single course.

77. Inventoried as Arch. Cat. No. **I:7**. A full discussion of this major building element will occur in the forthcoming study of the sanctuary's Imperial period development. See also *Final Reports* I, 96, fig. 102. For a further description of the spread of the various fragments of this marble doorway down the Middle Sanctuary slope, see ibid. 63.

78. Arch. Cat. No. **K:2**. Limestone triglyph fragment. MPH. 0.23 m. MPL. 0.56 m. MPTh. 0.35 m. Square mortise let into lower surface, 0.075 by 0.08 by -0.08 m.

79. For a preliminary discussion of this important feature of the late sanctuary, see *Final Reports* I, 99-103, figs. 103-06.

80. Two important examples are a limestone fluted column drum (Arch. Cat. No. **B:35**) that was built into the earthquake-ruined north corner of S5's west wall at the time of the construction of the E14 Mound (S29), and the handsome marble jamb fragment (Arch. Cat. No. **I:1**) left by the mound builders on top of the center of the same wall. See Fig. 55. Both will be discussed more fully in the forthcoming volume on the sanctuary's later architecture.

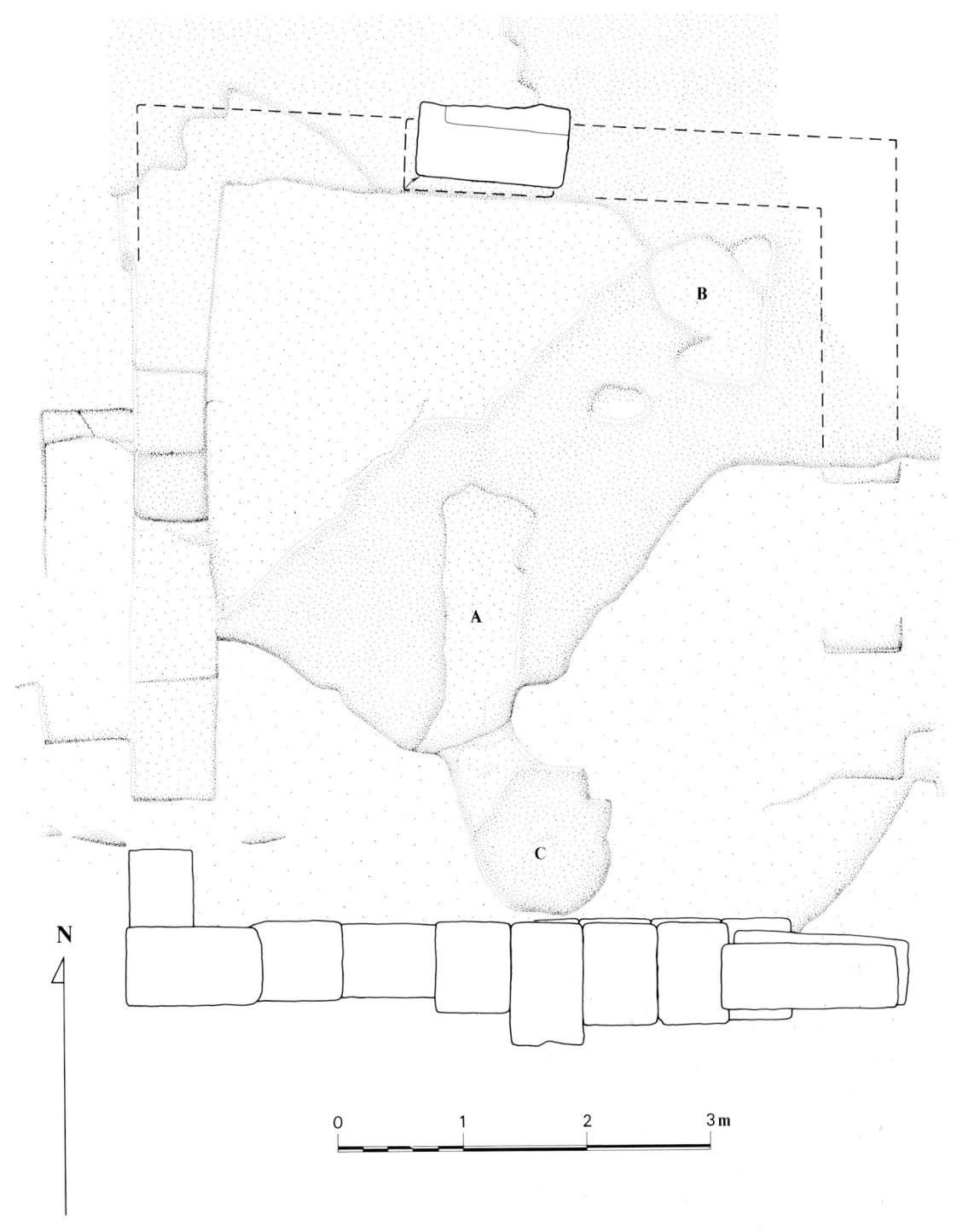

Figure 51: Plan of the S1 Sacred House. 1:50 scale.

Plate 63: S1 Sacred House, seen from northeast.

Plate 64: S1 Sacred House from west.

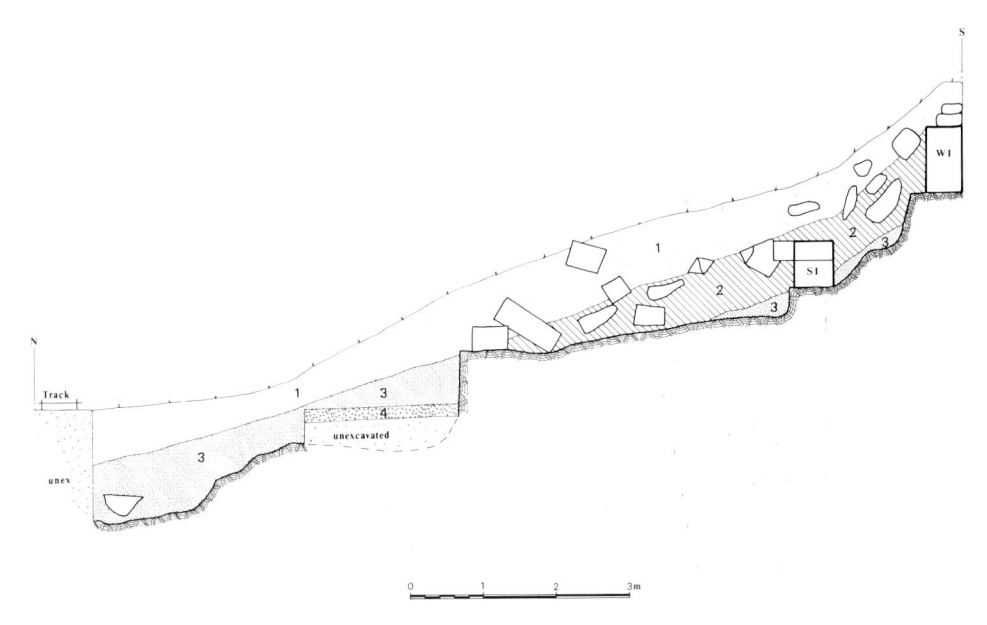

Figure 52: North-south section of balk covering the later Archaic, early Classical W1 wall and eastern edge of the S1 Sacred House. Drawn from west. 1:100 scale.

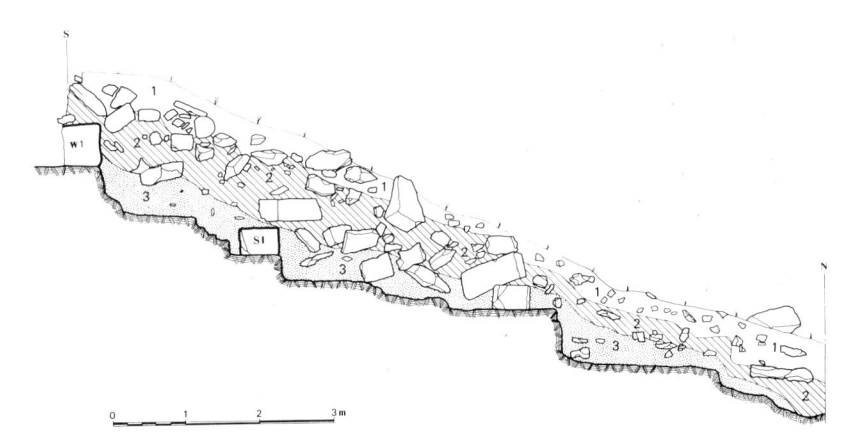

Figure 53: North-south section of balk covering the later Archaic, early Classical W1 wall and eastern edge of the S1 Sacred House. Drawn from east. 1:100 scale.

ASSOCIATED SCULPTURE

The earthquake stratum in and around the S5 house contained a substantial number of stone sculpture fragments,[81] but, owing to the relative steepness of the slope and the extent to which the earthquakes tended to move around objects, it is impossible to argue that any of these played a role in the function of the building, which as we have just seen appears to have been abandoned before the third century A.D. disaster. On the other hand, it seems reasonable to assume that the sub-earthquake level finds might have some greater relevance to the question of how the building functioned.

Essentially nothing can be learned of the original use to which S5 was put from the few artifacts retrieved from the early occupation fill (D13/E13, 1, 4) that overlay parts of its bedrock interior. Its later period is, however, perhaps better served. At some moment before the third century A.D. earthquake the mutilated lower two-thirds of a greater than lifesize

---

81. D. White and S. Kane, "Excavations in the Sanctuary of Demeter and Persephone at Cyrene. Fifth Preliminary Report," *LA* 13-14 (1976-77) 293, 314-17, pl. XCI, b, c. Also see the forthcoming study of the sanctuary's stone sculpture by S. Kane, cat. nos. **125** (Inv. 76-461) and **107** (Inv. 76-542).

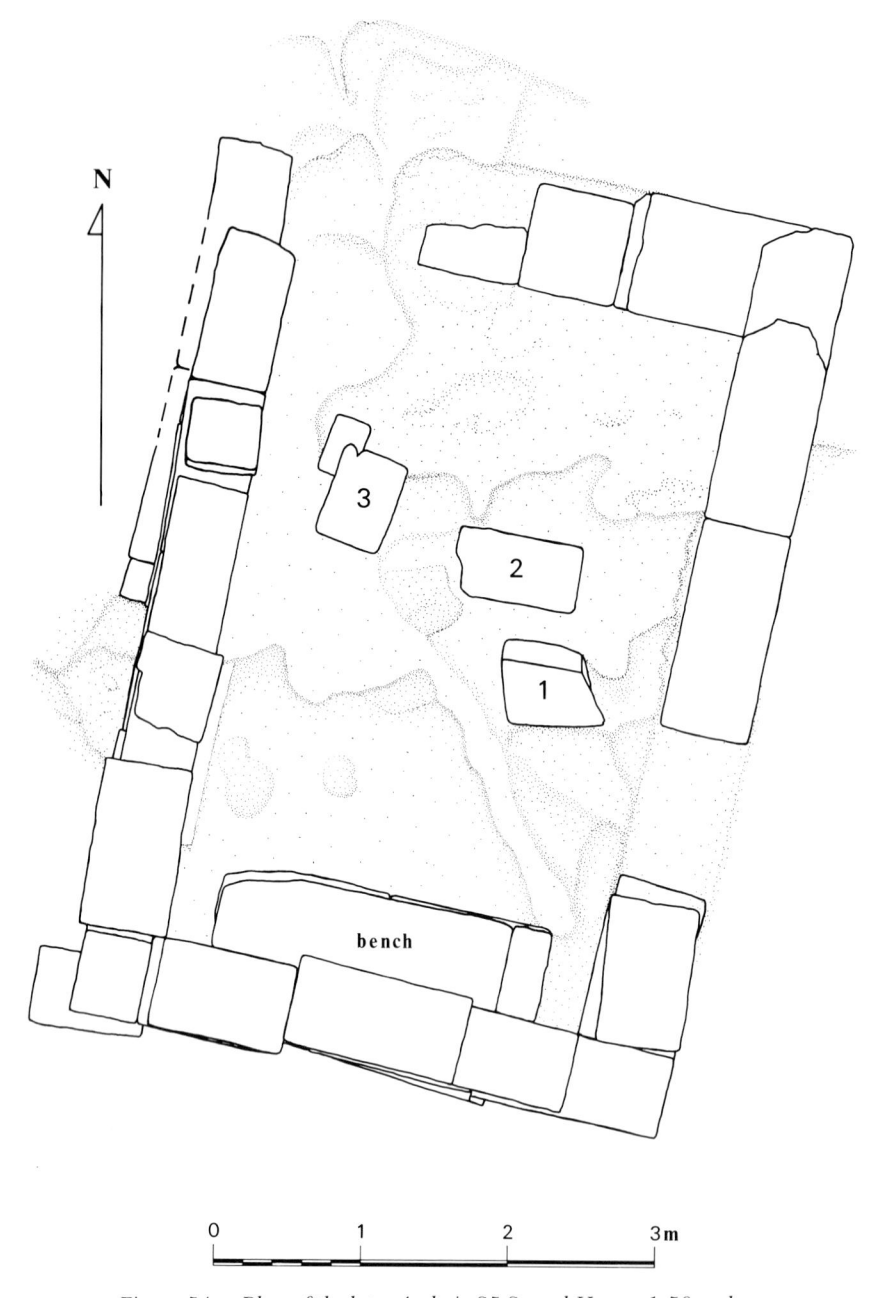

Figure 54: Plan of the later Archaic S5 Sacred House. 1:50 scale.

marble draped female statue[82] was discarded immediately in front of S5's northwest corner in fill associated with the destruction of the building's roof. The closeness of this unwieldy votive to the building suggests that it perhaps was originally housed inside and then dragged out to its final resting place after both it and the S5 house were damaged. A fragment of a marble pig statuette was found close by in the same fill.[83] It seems unlikely that storing sculpture was part of the house's original cultic function and instead seems more appropriate to the final half century before the sanctuary's destruction when the Wadi Bel Gadir

---

82. See Kane, sanctuary sculptures forthcoming, cat. no. **150** (Inv. 76-1308). See also White and Kane (supra n. 81) 293, 313-17, pl. XCI, a.

83. See Kane, sanctuary sculptures forthcoming, cat. no. **40** (Inv. 76-1037).

Plate 65: S5 Sacred House from north.

grounds were undergoing a significant cutback in religious activity.

CONTEXT AND DATE OF THE S5 SACRED HOUSE

The foundations of S5 are bedded on its exterior in a hard-packed red argillaceous soil, designated either St. 3 or St. 4, depending on its location. The early E13/F13, 1, 3 fill is as much as 0.60 m. deep on the slope north of S5 (Fig. 58). E13/14, 1, 3 is equally deep in the zone of the northwest corner of the building. The excavator found traces of a shallow construction trench cut into the same fill (D13/E13, 1, 4 south) along the exterior of the south wall of S5, which the builders refilled with a looser grey earth (D13/E13, 1, 3b), which regrettably contained no dateable material. Inside S5 the same pre-house fill, designated D13/E13, 1, 4 north, was much thinner and patchier than outside the building, reflecting the fact that its builders evidently wished to leave visible at least some of the bedrock features, unless they either covered the interior with a wood floor or covered it with an earth fill that was subsequently removed.

North of S5, the E13/F13, 1, 3 fill contains Archaic pottery, fifth-fourth century lamps, local pottery of the second half of the first century A.D., and marble sculpture as late as the Hadrianic period. Clearly the layer has been heavily contaminated by earthquake-borne debris from the destruction stratum immediately above it.

E13/14, 1, 3 in the vicinity of the house's northwest corner contained no reported artifacts.

South of its rear wall D13/E13, 1, 4 contained a sixth century B.C. faience ram's head seal and Archaic pottery dating to ca. 550 B.C. Inside the house the same stratum yielded nothing dateable. D13/E13, 1, 3, overlaying the Archaic occupation stratum, consisted of a light brown soil, loose in texture and filled with rubble stones and roof tile fragments, apparently reflecting some kind of pre-A.D. 262 earthquake destruction level. It contained a few early sherds, terracotta figurines dating from the late sixth to the fourth centuries, and marble sculpture of the late second or early third centuries A.D.

From what information is available it appears that the occupation layer preceding the actual erection of the S5 Sacred House contains nothing definitely later than the middle of the sixth century, but otherwise the building cannot be dated on the basis of stratified evidence. The use of L-shaped blocks in its masonry, discussed in greater detail below,[84] and the otherwise generally excellent quality of its

---

84. See infra 106 for parallels to the use of L-shaped blocks.

Plate 66: Stone bench at rear of the S5 Sacred House, seen from north.

masonry, combined with its block ratios, all point to the later Archaic or Classical period for the structure's erection.

SACRED HOUSE S6

The third in the sanctuary's series of shrine buildings, the S6 Sacred House is located ca. 17 m. west of the S5 house and some eight m. east of the southwest corner of the later Archaic pseudoisodomic peribolos enclosure (Plans B, E; Figs. 8, 10, 14, 15; Pls. 9-11, 70, 71). Attention has already been drawn to the fact that the S6 house's south wall (wall T7) is part of the line of the south wall of the peribolos. Three additional walls are subjoined to T7 at this time to form a small rectangular building. By the Hellenistic period the house stands free of the line of the old peribolos, which had been replaced by that time with an expanded system of enclosure walls (Plan C). Eventually, by early Imperial times, new walls are required for the east and north when the house, now designated S6a, takes on its present dimensions (5.20 m. north to south by 6.80 m. east to west). No traces of the original east and north walls survive beneath their later replacement, and the original size of the S6 house is therefore not securely known.

BUILDING INTERIOR

The bedrock over which the structure eventually rose is more level and less pitted than is the case inside the S1 and S5 Sacred Houses. A thin layer of red argillaceous E15, 2, 4 soil, reaching a maximum depth of ca. 0.30 m., fills the north half of the building's interior. As D15/16, 1, 3 the same fill can be traced across its southern half. Similar fill is traceable east of the house proper where it is designated D15/E15, 1, 3. Turning somewhat lighter in color toward its top, this fill (especially D15/E15, 1, 3) has the appearance of a rough, naturally deposited floor for the house during much of its active use. Otherwise, no interior features, such as a bench, survive.

SOUTH WALL

Since its earlier manifestations as walls P11 and T7 have already been described in connection with the sanctuary peribolos system,[85] the south wall's physical appearance needs only a summary description here (Pls. 9-11). Standing to a height of six courses or 1.50 m., its lower section consists of five courses of small ashlar blocks, whose north faces preserve beveled joints as well as the traces of broad, parallel chisel strokes. The initial four courses are laid up as headers, 0.20/0.30 m. high, 0.40 m. wide and 0.60/0.80 deep. The fifth course is treated as a series of modified perpends, averaging 0.25 high, 0.65 m. long (giving a block ratio of 1:2.6), and roughly 0.55 m. deep. The maximum wall width is 0.70 m., but the wall's outer, south face has been left untrimmed. In some places the headers fall considerably short of 0.70 m. The east end terminates in a single oversized ashlar, levelled with the top of the second course of headers. A sixth course survives at the west end in the form of an orthostate slab, socketed into the underlying perpend, whose shape has been modified to receive the slab (Fig. 15).

WEST WALL

The wall opposite the house's entrance is raggedly made. Starting with the southwest corner, it consists of a single trapezoidal ashlar, bonded and therefore coeval with the south wall at the level of the latter's fourth course. This overrides a foundation layer of small, irregularly shaped blocks, some of whose outer faces are dressed with the same broad, parallel chisel strokes that have already been noticed on the inner face of the stretchers and headers of the south wall. The foundations, which rest on bedrock, continue another ca. 1.95 m. north to where their line abuts a squarish ashlar, which does not connect with the S6a north wall, but instead leaves a narrow, 0.20-m.-wide gap between the two elements. Two stretchers that must originally been part of the west wall's otherwise largely destroyed superstructure came to light in the course of excavation immediately in front (i.e., east) of

---

85. Supra 11 for discussion of wall P11.

THE LATER ARCHAIC, EARLY CLASSICAL SANCTUARY

Plate 67: West wall of the S5 Sacred House, seen from west.

the west wall (Fig. 14, blocks A and B), riding on a thin layer of earth. The total wall thickness is ca. 0.50 m.

Despite its damaged condition and heterogeneous construction, the west wall appears to have been integrated with the south wall in order to form a proper corner. This can only have occurred after the south wall ceased to be used as a peribolos, since the small bonding block capping the trapezoidal block in the southwest corner interrupts the line of the south wall's orthostates. The chisel marks common to both walls indicates that the south wall cannot be a great deal older than the west. The two may therefore be assumed to be part of an independent building.

DOOR

Since neither the south nor the west walls preserve any traces of a doorway, it is probable that the building was entered either from the north, as in the case of the S1 and S5 houses, or from the east, which provided access to the house in its S6a Imperial phase. The fact that in its later phase the house faced east perhaps provides an additional reason for suspecting that it did so originally.

CONTEXT AND DATE OF THE S6 SACRED HOUSE

The stratigraphy and date of the south wall in its earliest P11 phase has already received discussion in connection with the peribolos system. As previously stated, no independent evidence is available for when the wall was developed into the later Archaic peribolos T7,[86] nor, unfortunately, is

---

86. For discussion of T7's date, see supra 53.

discussion here. On the other hand, both the S5 and S6 Sacred Houses appear to have been extensively rebuilt following the Jewish Rebellion of A.D. 115. Thus two of the epigraphically documented *naoi* could at least theoretically refer to them. The primary meanings of *naos* are of course "temple," "innermost part of temple," and "shrine containing the image of the god," but *naos* can also refer to a "portable shrine carried in processions" (*LSJ* 1160). *Naos* can therefore connote in a general sense a small sacred structure as well as a standard temple and inner chamber. There is nothing to support the notion that Claudia Venusta paid to renovate four separate full-size temples, and presumably her inscriptions refer to the sorts of secondary shrine structures that routinely occur in Demeter sanctuaries. If this is so, the individual Wadi Bel Gadir sanctuary houses under discussion may have been consecrated to the worship of separate deities, a point to which we will return in the final chapter.

Turning now to the archaeological evidence, the information is more abundant from the western Mediterranean than it is from the eastern sites. The coastal town of Carian Iasos, however, has produced traces of a Demeter and Kore sanctuary on the southern tip of the city's peninsula.[119] The remains include a small prostyle shrine, ca. 7.80 by 11.00 m.; its interior consists of a pronaos and adyton. The walls are made of poorly sawed ashlars, left rough on their inner faces but more carefully trimmed on the exterior. The obvious difference between this unpretentious structure, which is dated to ca. 510-480 B.C., and the contemporary Cyrene examples lies in its prostyle porch and bipartite plan. In other words, although comparable in scale, the plan of the Iasos shrine is more closely tied to that of a naiskos or scaled-down temple. A more imposing but considerably later example is provided by the first temple erected by Philetaerus and his brother Eumenes I for the Demeter Sanctuary at Pergamum. Designated a "plain megaron" by Gruben,[120] its plan, which measures 6.40 by 12.65 m., consists of a distyle in-antis Ionic pronaos and adyton, to which was later added a Roman-period columnar porch. Although the exterior lacks a surrounding colonnade, it was attractively decorated with a conventional Hellenistic marble frieze, sculpted with bucrania set between swags and in that sense is hardly "plain." The late sixth century B.C. Eleusinion on the north slope of the Acropolis at Athens had a similar bipartite plan, only without the distyle in-antis arrangement; the scale is also larger, measuring 11.00 by 17.70 m.[121] Its poor state of preservation makes it impossible to determine much of its appearance above ground level, but, as is the case with the Pergamene example, both the larger size and bipartite plan set it apart from the Cyrene house series. The even less well preserved Solonian Telesterion at Eleusis may have had a similar plan, only built once again on a larger scale.[122]

The Demeter Sanctuary at Knossos has preserved some sparse traces of a small (ca. 10.00 by 5.50 m.) rectangular shrine with perhaps either a Doric tetrastyle prostyle or distyle in-antis porch, dated to the later fifth century B.C.[123] While poorly understood, the plan of this structure must belong to the porched naiskos tradition. A small sixth century B.C. in-antis Doric temple dedicated to Demeter and Kore has been reported at Krania near Argostoli on the island of Kephallenia; its interior was apparently divided into the usual pronaos porch and cella.[124]

Remains of two small suburban Demeter sanctuaries have been brought to light on Cos, each preserving traces of small, independent sacred buildings. The site of Panagia Palatiane in the deme of Isthmos produced a small fifth century B.C. in-antis Doric naiskos that consists of a pronaos and adyton; overall, it measures approximately 7.00 by 13.00 m.[125] A local red trachite was quarried to provide ashlar blocks for its walls. The resident goddess was named on two inscriptions. The second sanctuary is located between the villages of Pyli and Asphendiu. Here was discovered a small square building, measuring ca. 6.00 on each side.[126] Its date is placed at the beginning of the fourth century B.C. Fragments of flat and curved roof-tiles make it clear that the structure was roofed. Its interior contained a series of important marble dedicatory statues, statuettes, and inscriptions. According to the excavators, the sculptures were found close to the actual positions they were occupying inside the building before it was destroyed by an earthquake, and from this it is clear that the pieces were not on display but rather were simply being stored. Consequently, the building is best interpreted as a magazine for preserving sacred votives, as opposed to a ritual place. In addition to resembling rather closely the Cyrene sanctuary's S1 Sacred House in size and plan, it matches as well what may have been the secondary use to which the S5, S7, and S8 Sacred Houses were put during the years preceding their third century A.D. destruction when they apparently stored discarded sculptures and other votives.

The Demeter Sanctuary on Acrocorinth was provided with a series of three small roughly square

---

119. D. Levi, *ASAtene* 29-30 (1967-68) 569-72. *AR* 25 (1978-79) 82.
120. Gruben, *Greek Temples* 490, figs. 151, 152. Bohtz, *Pergamon* 40-48, pls. 52-54, figs. 8-11.
121. Travlos, *Pictorial Dictionary* 198. R. Wycherley, *The Stones of Athens* (Princeton 1978) 71-72.

---

122. Mylonas, *Eleusis* 67-68, fig. 26, A.
123.. Coldstream, *Knossos* 12-15, figs. 10, 11.
124. P. Kalligas, *ArchEph* 1978, 136-46, esp. 142. *AR* 27 (1980-81) 28.
125. R. Herzog, *AA* 18 (1903) 2-3, fig. 1. G. Pugliese Carratelli, *ASAtene* 25-26 (1963-64) 148.
126. L. Laurenzi, *Clara Rhodos* V, 2 (1932) 157-85.

structures (Building G 1-2, the Mosaic Building, and the Building above the Theater Cavea) across the level of its Upper Terrace that resemble in broad terms the Cyrene examples in plan and size, but not date, since all three appear to belong to the early Imperial period.[127] The eastern Building above the Theater Cavea measures 5.60 by 4.80 m. The central Mosaic Building measures 5.60 by 5.65 m. The western Building G 1-2 in its latest, southern phase measures 4.65 by perhaps 5.10 m. Like their earlier Cyrene counterparts, they do not appear to have been subdivided and lack porch colonnades. Single entrances are restored in their north walls. The central Mosaic Building contained in its late fourth century A.D. destruction level a marble table top, a fluted table stand, moulded altar or statue base fragments, fragments of several marble statues, and seven pieces of unidentified horn-shaped objects, along with a wide variety of pottery, in other words an agglomeration of material that compares rather closely with the contents of the Cyrene buildings in their latest phases.

From this survey of eastern Mediterranean sanctuaries it is apparent that most of the examples cited of small independent buildings do not directly resemble the three late Archaic, early Classical period buildings in the Cyrene sanctuary, mainly because the majority adhere to a naiskos plan consisting of at least two chambers and a colonnaded porch. The interesting exceptions are the early fourth century B.C. Coan structure near Pyli and the three early Imperial houses on Acrocorinth. These seem to share a common function as storage areas for ex-votos with the S5 Sacred House, and the Hellenistic period S7 Sacred House and early Imperial period S8 Sacred House. It seems unlikely to me, however, that votive storage (as opposed to votive display) represents the original and primary purpose of any of these structures, including those from Cyrene.

The western Mediterranean has a somewhat broader range of chthonian sanctuaries associated with Demeter that typically contain various kinds of independent buildings. Some conform to the prevailing Greek mainland, island, and Asia Minor shrine type, i.e., small rectangular temple-like structures that internally have two or more rooms entered through a simple in-antis colonnaded porch or plain door.[128] But significant numbers of a second type occur that parallel more directly the Cyrenean series. These represent a plainer variety of building and consist simply of a single room entered through a door usually set on one of the shorter sides, if the structure itself is not square. Examples of such types are especially prevalent in the southeastern corner of Sicily and incorporate a fair percentage of the buildings associated with the small Geloan extramural sanctuaries at Carrubazza,[129] Via Fiume,[130] Bitalemi,[131] and

---

127. N. Bookidis and J. Fisher, *Hesperia* 41 (1972) 309-13, fig. 6, pl. 60, b. *Acrocorinth V* 278-85, fig. 5, pl. 56.

128. The mid-sixth century B.C. so-called megaron of Demeter Malophoros at Selinus has three interior rooms, a pronaos, naos, and adyton. Its overall measurements are 20.40 by 9.53 m. It lacks a colonnaded porch. It nevertheless clearly functioned as the central focus for ritual within the sanctuary, as opposed to providing merely storage, as did presumably its primitive single-chambered predecessor. Gabrici, *Malophoros* 21-52, pls. 1, 2, 11-13. Gruben, *Greek Temples* 421-23, pls. 124, 125, figs. 82-85. Le Dinahet, *Sanctuaires* 147-48, fig. 7. For a recently discovered second Demeter "megaron" ca. 50 m. southeast of the Malophoros temenos walls, see *AR* 34 (1987-88) 146. The ca. 500 B.C. Temple C or the Temple of Demeter beneath S. Biagio at Acragas could qualify in terms of size (measuring 30.20 by 13.30 m.), as a full-fledged temple. Its internal arrangement, however, of a columnless pronaos fronting a simple naos associates it with the eastern type. See *Agrigento* 66-72, fig. 38. Gruben, *Greek Temples* 433-34. Le Dinahet, *Sanctuaires* 144. The large Sanctuary of the Chthonian Gods at the same site has three small naiskoi. One has a pronaos and naos, a second a pronaos, naos, and adyton. Both represent variations of the megaron type of shrine building. The third has a broad prostyle porch, equipped with four piers, and naos. See P. Marconi, *Agrigento arcaica* (Rome 1933) 28-33, figs. 5, 8, 9. Gruben, *Greek Temples* 434, fig. 97. Le Dinahet, *Sanctuaires* 144, 148-50, fig. 6. Preliminary notice has been given of a fifth century B.C. extramural "temple" of Demeter at Monte Adranone near Sambuca in central Sicily. It is described as having a "remarkable bipartite cella." See *AR* 23 (1976-77) 72; *AR* 34 (1987-88) 130. The intramural Sanctuary of Demeter at Vassallaggi is of potentially great significance, since it has been described as a "small temple with temenos and altar, and it is *surrounded by rectangular structures, some of which contained votive offerings*" (my emphasis). See P. Orlandini, *Princeton* 957-58. Also P. Orlandini, *Kokalos* 14-15 (1968-69) 334. Unfortunately what appears to be the principal report issued thus far on the architecture is presently not available to me, but see P. Orlandini, *CronCatania* 3 (1964) 20 ff. The site of Monte Saraceno near Ravanusa has produced traces of a mid-sixth century B.C. naiskos, arranged internally into a plain pronaos and cella measuring ca. 8.00 by 14.00 m. See P. Mingazzini, *MonAnt* 36 (1938) 671-79. D. Adamesteanu, *ArchCl* 8, fasc. 2 (1956) 121-46. The site of Madonna dell'Alemanna north of Gela may have originally included both a full-size temple and perhaps two smaller naiskoi or possibly treasuries, known mainly through their terracotta decorations. See D. Adamesteanu, *NSc* 1956, 382-92. P. Orlandini, *Kokalos* 12 (1966) 33. Le Dinahet, *Sanctuaires* 139. On the mainland, the pre-colonial site of Saturo near Taras has an Archaic naiskos evidently dedicated to Persephone, but details of its plan are still unavailable. See *AR* 23 (1976-77) 51-52. At Lucanian Heracleia (Policoro) the extramural Demeter and Kore Sanctuary has brought to light traces of three megaron-like structures. Megaron A and Megaron C, which are constructed of rubble, appear to date to the fourth and third centuries B.C., while Megaron B, which is partly constructed of ashlar masonry, may have originated toward the end of the fifth century. See B. Neutsch, *Quaderni urbinati di cultura classica* 5 (1968) 211-23.

129. D. Adamesteanu, *NSc* 1956, 242-52.

130. P. Orlandini, *NSc* 1956, 252-63, fig. 1. Le Dinahet, *Sanctuaires* 139-40, 147.

131. The site has brought to light traces of several rectangular structures (G1, G2, and G3) that date to the sixth and fifth

Predio Sola,[132] the hinterland site of Sabucina,[133] and the *Koreion* at Camarina.[134]

It is seldom clear when the single-chamber variety was serving exclusively as a storehouse for votives or was doubling as a small temple on which were centered ritual activities. Some of the sanctuaries just listed were extremely modest in scope and were undoubtedly designed to accommodate merely the limited suburban-rural population that lived in their immediate neighborhoods. At Bitalemi the small rectangular Archaic Stratum 5 Mudbrick Building is interpreted as a meeting-place for the cult's predominantly female worshippers, and the bulk of the votives appear to have been buried in the nearby sandy soil where they were sealed over with scraps of clay and potsherds.[135] The later fourth century B.C. temple in the intramural Demeter Sanctuary at Helorus near Syracuse was surrounded by small rectangular structures described as storage chambers for votives.[136]

Finally, there is Cyrene itself. The northwest quadrant of the city's Agora was occupied during the first half of the sixth century by a tiny one-room structure (2.25 by 1.65 m.), roofed with wood and built with walls of unshaped rubble. The building appears to have been partially sunk below the surrounding bedrock level and was entered through a door on one of its long sides.[137] Some time after 550 B.C. it was supplemented by a modest rectangular, open-air temenos that contained a raised altar for burnt offerings and a low rock-altar connected to a bothros.[138] Both the pre-550 B.C. rubble edifice and the open-air temenos associated with it later in the century have been linked with Demeter by its excavators. While evidently chthonian in nature, the sanctuary cannot be said as yet to be definitely associated with Demeter.[139] That fact notwithstanding, the plan of the little rubble structure does mimic the plan of the early Imperial S8 Sacred House in the Wadi Bel Gadir sanctuary as well as echoing in a more general way the square plan of the later Archaic S1 Sacred House previously described.

To sum up, the impression that all this leaves is as follows. 1) Small independent structures of an apparently sacral nature but not conforming to what is normally identified as a temple are a standard feature of Demeter sanctuaries throughout the Greek world. 2) A fluctuating percentage of these, depending on which one is dealing with, take the shape of simple one-room structures, either square or rectangular in plan, lacking porches, and entered through a single door. Sicily and South Italy contribute more examples than the eastern Mediterranean, but this may be more the result of the Italian archaeologists placing a greater emphasis on the investigation of suburban, rural sanctuaries than of any regional differences in cultic practice. 3) The one-room type of building, to which the Cyrene series (including the Agora structure) clearly belongs, can function in a number of different ways, including as a place for ritual practice, votive display, storage of discarded votives, and the housing of sanctuary magistrates or functionaries. 4) While a variety of terms were used in antiquity to refer to such buildings, the only name that can be linked with any assurance to the series under review is a relatively late use of *naos*. While its usage here may indicate the consecration of individual buildings to specific deities, there is otherwise little known about the specific function of the Archaic series, and this in turn has led to their being labelled throughout this study as simply "sacred houses."

CULT BENCH

The badly preserved condition of all three sanctuary shrine houses limits what can be said about their interiors. The intact bench across the rear of the S5 Sacred House does, however, carry some relevance for the entire series, including the later S7 and S8 Sacred Houses and the S11 and S12 chambers. We cannot be sure if the bench belongs to the original construction of the house or its later S5a phase. If early, it has numerous parallels from other sites. The existence of "cult-benches" in the Minoan-Mycenaean tradition is well attested,[140] and Drerup supplies a number of Cretan and mainland examples of Geometric period shrines with similar arrangements.[141] More

---

centuries B.C. The precise arrangement of their interiors is not fully known. The series is described as sacella, naiskoi, and in the case of one structure as a *lesche* or meeting hall. See P. Orlandini, *Kokalos* 12 (1966) 18, 19, 31, pls. 1, 6, 8. P. Orlandini, *Kokalos* 13 (1967) 177-79. Le Dinahet, *Sanctuaires* 139-40, 146-47.

132. P. Orlandini, *MonAnt* 46 (1962) 1-78. *Kokalos* 12 (1966) 33-34. Le Dinahet, *Sanctuaires* 139-40, 147.

133. Sabucina has brought to light two Archaic structures, of which one is circular and equipped with a rectangular porch; its date is said to be seventh-sixth century B.C. The other structure has an orthodox rectangular exterior plan (9.25 by 6.50 m.), but no details are available about its interior arrangement. See *AR* 28 (1981-82) 97. The presence of pig bones suggests that the resident cult was Demeter's.

134. P. Orsi, *MonAnt* 9 (1899) 226-27, fig. 17. F. Guidice, "La stipe di Persefone a Camarina," *MonAnt, Ser. Misc.* 2, pt. 4 (1979) [=Vol. 49 in gen. series] 287-90; 343-46, fig. 1. *AR* 28 (1981-82) 90.

135. P. Orlandini, *Kokalos* 13 (1967) 177-79, pl. 21; ibid. 24-25 (1968-69) 334-38, esp. 335 and 337, pl. 53.

136. G. Voza, *Kokalos* 24-25 (1968-69) 360-62, pl. 66. G. Voza, *Princeton* 382-83. P. Orlandini, *Kokalos* 24-25 (1968-69) 334-35. *AR* 23 (1976-77) 67; *AR* 28 (1981-82) 87.

137. *Agora* II,1, 21-23, figs. 6-8.

138. *Agora* II,1, 27-34, figs. 9-17.

---

139. D. White, *AJA* 86 (1982) 607. *Final Reports* I, 23, n. 2.

140. L. Banti, *ASAtene* 3-5 (1941-43) 40 ff. H. Gallet de Santerre, *Délos primitive et archaïque* (Paris 1958) 217, n. 4. H. Hermann, *Omphalos* (1959) 72.

141. H. Drerup, *Archaeologia Homerica* 0 55 (Gottingen 1969) 121-22, 132. W. Taylour, *Antiquity* 44 (1970) 277. The Geometric

to the point, the tradition continues into the Archaic period and beyond,[142] despite the fact that more normal procedure, at least in the case of temples, called for the substitution of bases for large-scale cult statues in place of narrow benches intended to carry portable offerings.

Shrine buildings with benches from other Demeter sanctuaries give some insight into the use of the present example. At Helorus in southeastern Sicily Room "B" associated with the Demeter sanctuary discovered outside the town walls[143] contained a low rubble stone bench attached to one of its walls. The room has been subsequently reassembled in the local antiquarium at Noto.[144] A series of stock Demeter terracotta figurines were displayed on the bench in antiquity with their backs stuck to the wall behind by a kind of plaster, indicating that they were intended to remain on display in this position for at least some period of time. Three *bothroi* were placed in front of the wall; two were lined along their rims with more figurines in an effort to bring the offerings of the dedicants into as direct contact with the powers of the underworld as was physically possible. At Morgantina the third century B.C. Area IV Demeter Sanctuary contains a similar room with a long stuccoed bench against one of its walls. Its excavators believe that the three terracotta busts found broken on the floor directly in front of the bench were originally set on the bench and that the bench served as a place for cultic offerings.[145] A similar use may perhaps be attributed to the three benches set along the inner walls of the entrance room to the shrine building in the Demeter sanctuary at Priene, as well as possibly the bench by the door of the cella-proper, although a better case can be made for the cella's two marble "Opfertische."[146]

Votives were evidently no longer displayed in the Cyrene sanctuary during the confused years between the early Severan period and the A.D. 262 earthquake destruction, when at least large-scale marble statues were still being dedicated to the resident goddesses. If functioning at all during this period, the S5 and S6 houses were used while in a semi-ruinous condition simply to warehouse the sorts of large sculptural votives that were in many cases later buried in the nearby E14 Mound (S29) (Plan F).[147] It is impossible to speculate about the S1 Sacred House, whose destruction appears to have taken place earlier than the other two houses. On the other hand, the great abundance of small marble statuettes and terracotta figurines found throughout most of the sanctuary's layers strongly suggests that the interior of the S5 Sacred House with its prominent bench was used to display these classes of votives on a rotational basis as part of the ceremony of ritual presentation. The Hellenistic period S7 Sacred House, which also has a bench across its rear, may be presumed to have served something of the same purpose. Its interior contained a marble togate statue when it was destroyed by earthquake.[148] Our preliminary analysis indicates that the greatest concentrations of all sculptural fragments found throughout the sanctuary occur in the vicinity of the independent sacred houses, particularly the S5 and S6 houses, but the largest percentage of stone statuettes is found north of the S1 and S8 Sacred Houses.[149] The Hellenistic period S11 and S12 Chambers, located in the southwest corner and midway along the western wall of the Middle Sanctuary (Plan E) are both associated with large concentrations of largely mid-fifth century or later terracotta figurines.[150] Neither of the chambers, which are semi-detached structures

---

period examples at Dreros, Sparta, Delos, Kavousi, and Vroulia are discussed by Drerup, ibid. 121-22.

142. As on Delos where both the Second Heraion and Temple G are provided with what appear to be offering benches. In the case of the former, a marble bench is wrapped around the interior of its distyle in-antis pronaos; the latter is a single cella shrine with a bench stretched across two-thirds of its rear in similar fashion to the bench across the rear of the S5 Sacred House. See P. Bruneau and J. Ducat, *Guide de Délos* (Paris 1965) 97, fig. 13, and 146. For further general discussion of benches used for offerings, see B. Alrothe, "The Positioning of Greek Votive Figurines," in *Early Greek Cult Practice*, ed. R. Hägg, N. Marinatos, and G. Nordqvist, *Skrifter Utgivna Av Svenska Institutet I Athen* Series in 4, 38 (1988) 195-202. No pre-Hellenistic Cyrenaican examples are known to me, and the single regional Hellenistic example is the S7 Sacred House discussed infra 159. Drerup (supra n. 141) 122, n. 133, cites the example of the second century B.C. double-temple at Olous on Crete. See also J. Bousquet, *BCH* 62 (1938) 386 ff., pl. 43. For an even later survival cf. the post-A.D. 115 Temple of the Palm Capitals at Cyrenaican Ptolemais. Stucchi, *Architettura* 240, 225. C. Kraeling, *Ptolemais* 90, N on plan X.

143. For general bibliography on this site see supra n. 136. Add Le Dinahet, *Sanctuaires* 145-46.

144. A. Van Buren, "Newsletter from Rome," *AJA* 70 (1966) 358, pls. 86, 87, figs. 13-16. *Noto Museo Comunale* (Noto 1967) 1-3, fig. 1. D. White, *Expedition* 17, 4 (1975) 12, fig. 1.

145. R. Stillwell, *AJA* 63 (1959) 169, n. 4. For the cult of Demeter and Persephone at Morgantina see M. Bell, *Morgantina Studies* I: *The Terracottas* (Princeton 1981) 81-88, 98-103, 249-56, figs. d and e.

146. For the porch benches D, E, and F see *Priene* 148, 152, fig. 119. The cella bench is set against the entrance wall next to the door: ibid. 154. The cella offering tables K and J occupy the northwest rear corner and the near center of the rear wall: ibid. 153-54, figs. 121, 122.

147. *Final Reports* I, 96-99, figs. 103-08. The southwest corner of the S5 Sacred House was partially dismantled and then covered over with E14 Mound debris after the A.D. 262 earthquake struck.

148. *Final Reports* I, 107, fig. 112.

149. *Final Reports* I, 105. Kane's final study of the stone sculpture will deal further with the question of distribution.

150. *Final Reports* I, 80, 89-92, figs. 78, 90, 91. See infra 170-72. J. Uhlenbrock has communicated the preliminary information that the ground north of the S11 chamber produced 311 catalogued complete or semi-complete figurines and 888 uncatalogued heads (duplicating types already catalogued). Of the catalogued examples, 82% date to the mid-fifth century and later; 95% of the heads post-date the middle of the fifth century.

built against the inner faces of the Hellenistic peribolos, has benches or interior *bothroi*, and therefore they appear to have been used more for storage than for display or ritual use as in the manner of the Helorus and Morgantina examples.

MASONRY

The final point to be considered in connection with the early house series has to do with the masonry employed throughout its various walls. Block proportions, surface finish, and a use of L-shaped blocks distinguish the stonework of at least two out of the three houses from the sanctuary's later structures as well as providing certain limited parallels with contemporary regional architecture.

Simply in terms of block size, there is little to bind the series together. The one partially surviving wall of the S1 house is the rear or south wall. Its blocks are too randomly sized for comparison. However, the one complete stretcher that survives from its second course measures 1.15 by 0.35 m. By way of contrast, the S6 Sacred House uses considerably smaller blocks along its south wall and more standard-sized blocks across the west return. The block heights of the south wall fluctuate between 0.20 and 0.30 m. Its series of modified perpends are only ca. 0.65 m. long. The west wall, like the south wall of the S1 house, is made up of an assorted mixture of ashlars, whose heights vary between 0.40 and 0.45 m. The longest is ca. 1.10 m. In the case of the S5 Sacred House the blocks belonging to the original construction of the west wall average 1.15 by 0.55 m., the south wall 1.22 by 0.60 m., and the east wall 1.25 by 0.47 m.

The block height-to-length proportions indicate a somewhat greater congruency between the S5 and S6 Sacred Houses. The blocks of the S6 south wall present an average ratio of 1:2.6 ratio; its west wall ratio, while hard to estimate, is ca. 1:2.4. The average ratio for all three walls of the S5 house is approximately 1:2.3. Both houses fall near the median of the statistical range of all of the ashlar structures surveyed from this period, with the clear exception of the south wall of the S1 Sacred House, which may be later than its associated stratigraphy is capable of demonstrating, and parts of the S2 Building.[151] The S5 and S6 proportions in turn echo the roughly similar proportions of the later sixth century Portico A1 in Cyrene's nearby Agora,[152] as well as the pseudoisodomic bislab masonry of its Second Artemisium already discussed.[153] The general impression this leaves is that an approximately 1:2.25 block height-to-length ratio is characteristic of later Archaic, early Classical ashlar masonry at Cyrene and in particular at the Demeter and Persephone Sanctuary.

The S6 Sacred House preserves traces of broad, parallel chisel strokes on both its south and west walls. Also marked in the same way are the southern line of the later Archaic pseudoisodomic peribolos[154] as well as the controversial Second Artemisium.[155] No traces of this finish have been detected on the blocks of either Sacred House S1 or S5.

Finally, there is the use of L-shaped blocks, which is a feature shared by both the S5 and S6 houses. It is not clear what, if any, chronological relevance the use of this technique has. Nevertheless, a similar use of an L-shaped block to compensate for a change in level in the coursing occurs in the west facade of the temenos wall of Cyrene's Agora E2 Oikos, dated by its excavators to the second half of the sixth century.[156] It also has been restored to the coursing along the base of the rear walls of both the Agora's Portico B1, which dates to the final quarter of the sixth century B.C.,[157] and its Portico A3, which dates to the second quarter of the fifth.[158] Similarly early examples of L-shaped blocks used to span the right-angle interface of two walls occur in the unusually well preserved sixth century B.C. masonry of the megaron of Demeter Malophoros at Selinus.[159] The continuation of the technique into the fourth century B.C. and later is likewise documented for Sicily,[160] the mainland,[161] and Cyrenaica.[162]

---

151. See Appendix II.
152. *Agora* I, 72: "Gli ortostati sono alti cm. 55,12 (I piede e 7/8), lunghi 4 piedi (cm. 117,6)." Ratio 1:2.13.
153. Supra 60-62 for the Second Artemisium.
154. Supra 46-47 for chisel strokes on southern peribolos.
155. Supra 60 for Second Artemisium chisel strokes.
156. *Agora* I, 36, fig. 13.
157. *Agora* I, 95, fig. 54.
158. *Agora* I, 103, fig. 54.
159. D. White, *AJA* 71 (1967) 338, pl. 102, fig. 7.
160. The fourth century city wall at Gela incorporates L-shaped blocks in its juncture with a postern gate. See L. Bernabo Brea, *Musei e monumenti in Sicilia* (Novara 1958) 140. P. Griffo and L. von Matt, *Gela, the Ancient Greeks in Sicily* (New York 1968) 179, fig. 132.
161. A fourth century B.C. tower along the city wall at Messene and the third century B.C. fortification wall at Sounion both display a tenative application of the technique. See A. Lawrence, *Greek Architecture* (London 1957) pl. 120, A. W. Wrede, *Attische Mauern* (Athens 1933) fig. 106. Systematic investigation of the problem would certainly turn up many more mainland and East Greek examples.
162. Towers V and XVII of the Apollonia city wall. *Apollonia* pl. XIII, b. D. White, *AJA* 70 (1966) 264, pl. 67, fig. 16.

IV

The Later Classical Sanctuary Ca. 440-330 B.C.

Compared with the phases that precede as well as follow it, the later Classical period in the sanctuary's development (Plan C) is marked by a relatively modest series of architectural changes that seem to be accompanied by a definite slackening off in the quantities of most votives contributed to the resident deities after ca. 450 B.C. This is perhaps most readily apparent in the case of the pottery, the imports of which virtually cease with the exception of Attic Red Figure, which is itself numerically far less plentiful than the Black Figure of the preceding period. In addition, of the total number of Red Figure sherds, which range in date from ca. 520 to 320 B.C., those dating before 450 B.C. greatly outnumber those that follow.[1] Moreover, the Archaic examples of the miscellaneous artifacts published by Warden greatly outstrip those produced during the later fifth and fourth centuries.[2] A total of 87 pre-475 B.C. silver coins was found throughout the sanctuary as compared to the 17 silver and four gold coins that date between 475 and the later fourth century when bronze currency was introduced.[3] The terracotta figurines comprise the sole category of mass dedications that partially counters this tendency before the Hellenistic period; post-450 B.C. figurines vastly outnumber the earlier variety[4] in the case of one at least of the several large concentrations of figurines excavated in the sanctuary. These figures are offset by data collected elsewhere, however.[5]

The last in the line of Cyrene's hereditary Battiad monarchs was Arcesilaus IV, whose rule began around 462 B.C. By most accounts he was an effective ruler,[6] but fear of what had happened to his forebears led him to develop as a refuge against domestic oligarchic opposition the city of Euesperides, modern Benghazi, which he stocked with colonists from mainland Greece.[7] Nothing is specifically known about where the colonists were recruited, and their presence at the opposite end of the Pentapolis has left no discernible trace in the archaeological record of the imports introduced into the Wadi Bel Gadir sanctuary. In any case, despite his precautions Arcesilaus was assassinated by internal enemies around 440 B.C.

Applebaum has suggested that after the death of the king the royal lands were entrusted to the city's elected officials. These included the demiurgi, a body of magistrates responsible for defraying maintenance costs of various of the city's cults with allocations of revenues collected from the ex-royal agricultural properties that were by then extensively enlarged through the expropriation of properties previously owned by the native Libyan element as well as the recently proscribed enemies of the new republic.[8] While not specifically named, it seems likely that the Demeter sanctuary, which abuts a rich agricultural zone to its south, benefitted from the arrangement,[9] which in theory should have been accompanied by a resurgence in independent, small allotment farming. This could be what lies behind the increase in the dedication of small, inexpensive terracotta votives in the second half of the fifth century, since it was the rural agriculturalists who had traditionally formed the backbone of the support of Demeter's cult since its seventh century foundation.[10]

---

1. See McPhee's remarks, *Final Reports* VI. The reduction in trade between Athens and Cyrene during the second half of the fifth century may indirectly reflect the disastrous conclusion to the efforts of the Athenians to help the Libyan king, Inarus, in his revolt against the Persians in Egypt in 454. Chamoux, 202-205.
2. P. Warden, *Final Reports* IV, 3, 12, 40.
3. T. Buttrey, *Final Reports* VI.
4. See supra chap. 3, n. 150 for a preliminary statistical breakdown of figurines reported between the S11 and S12 chambers.
5. The single largest concentration of sanctuary figurines comes from the late backfill dumped behind the Middle Sanctuary's T10 early Imperial retaining wall, described in *Final Reports* I, 83-88. J. Uhlenbrock reports that 94% of these date to the seventh through early fifth centuries B.C.

6. Chamoux, 173-210. Goodchild, *Cyrene*2, 11-12. Applebaum, *Jews and Greeks* 31: "If we attempt to summarize the little information we possess on Arkesilaos IV, we may see him an energetic autocrat, strengthening his power with new colonization, drawing closer his ties with the desert oases, increasing the circulation of his coinage, maintaining relations with the Greek sacred centres (Delphi, Olympia, Athens), claiming rule over the other cities of Cyrenaica, a patron of culture, and a breeder of thoroughbred horses."
7. Led by his own brother-in-law Carrhotas. Chamoux, 174-75, 198. R. Goodchild, *Benghazi* (Cyrene, Shahat, 1962) 2.
8. Applebaum, *Jews and Greeks* 33, 87.
9. White, *Suburban Expansion* 115-16.
10. *Final Reports* I, 27-30.

Plate 72:   Section of the W2 later Classical peribolos wall from north.

Apart from this, little of the historical record appears to be reflected in the sanctuary. While the small modifications that have been traced by the Italians in the development of the city's Agora during the period covered by Arcesilaus's reign give way to more elaborate projects during the Republican years down to the end of the fourth century,[11] they are not answered, so far as we can thus far determine, by any correspondingly major alterations to either the Wadi Bel Gadir sanctuary's overall layout or its individual internal components.

The main changes center on the southern line of the later Archaic peribolos where header/stretcher ashlar wall replacements supplement both ends of the pseudoisodomic wall T1. These are designated wall T8 to the west and wall W2 at the east. In addition, a strongly built east-west retaining wall (W1) is run across the Middle Sanctuary from the east wall of the S5 Sacred House to a point directly south of the southeast corner of the S1 Sacred House. Otherwise the Middle Sanctuary's three independent S1, S5, and S6 Sacred Houses that had begun their existence during the Archaic period continue in use without apparent change, while on the level of the Upper Sanctuary no evidence was recovered for fresh construction apart from a well-built water channel (F3) immediately north of the Archaic period S2, S3, and S4 room series.

The later Classical additions came to light in the following archaeological contexts (Fig. 12): Wall W2 and wall W2a in D10/11, B, D11/12, A, D11/12, 1, D11/E11 balk, D12, 1, D12/E12, D, and E10/11 (Area 1), 1. Wall T8 was cleared in D13, 1 (Area 2), D13, 2 (Area 2), D14 balk, D14, 1 D15, 1, sondage, and C14/D14, 1 and 2. The Middle Sanctuary retaining wall W1 came to light in E12/13, C and E, D12/E12, D, the E12/F12 balk. The Upper Sanctuary level F3 water channel was excavated in D11/12, 1, D12 balk, and D12/13, F.

---

11. *Agora* I, 100-43. *Agora* II,1, 53-107. Stucchi, *Architettura* 48-86. The years from ca. 450 to the death of Alexander have been described by Stucchi as the province's architectural "periodo d'oro" for reasons that have nothing to do with building output. See D. White, *ArtB* 54 (1977) 624.

Plate 73: W2 later Classical peribolos wall from east-northeast.

SOUTHEAST CORNER OF THE PERIBOLOS: WALL W2

During this period the previously described[12] short T2a southern extension of the T2 later Archaic eastern peribolos wall (Plan B) was integrated into what then became the southeast corner of the later Classical peribolos (Plan C). Some 12.5 m. of the old T1 pseudoisodomic bislab peribolos were dismantled to bedrock. In their place the line was supplemented by a new wall (W2) erected two m. to the south and built out of heavy headers, set directly on bedrock, and a second course of stretchers that together reach a height of 1.20 m. (Pls. 31, 72, 73; Figs. 2, 3, 17, 19, 31, 59, 63-65).[13] The block dimensions average ca. 1.25 m. long, 0.60 m. high, and 0.50 m. thick; the heights and lengths therefore closely resemble those of wall T1 as well as the S2 and S4 structures. On the other hand, the core beneath the weathered grey surface of the limestone used for the W2 wall contains abundant traces of fossilized shell inclusions that range in size from microscopic to nearly two cm. across. They form enough of a contrast with the relatively shell-free limestones used for the Archaic units to suggest the use of a different quarry source. The north faces of the lower headers are left untrimmed and consequently project rather untidily beyond the face of the finished stretchers set above them (Pl. 31). The impression this leaves is that the headers were intended to be left buried, while the stretchers were to be visible. With blocks so close in size and proportion to those used for the various later Archaic structures just listed, the possibility exists that W2 was constructed from reused earlier material.

The resulting 1.50 m. wide gap between what had been wall T2a and the east end of wall W2 appears to have been used for a time as a narrow entrance to the Middle Sanctuary from the level of the Upper Sanctuary (Fig. 1). This so-called G7 entrance was blocked during the Hellenistic period by the insertion of wall T9a (Plan D) and otherwise has left no evidence for its appearance.

---

12. Supra 57 for wall T2a.
13. A detailed 1:20 scale plan of the bulk of wall W2 may be found in *Final Reports* I, 104, fig. 110.

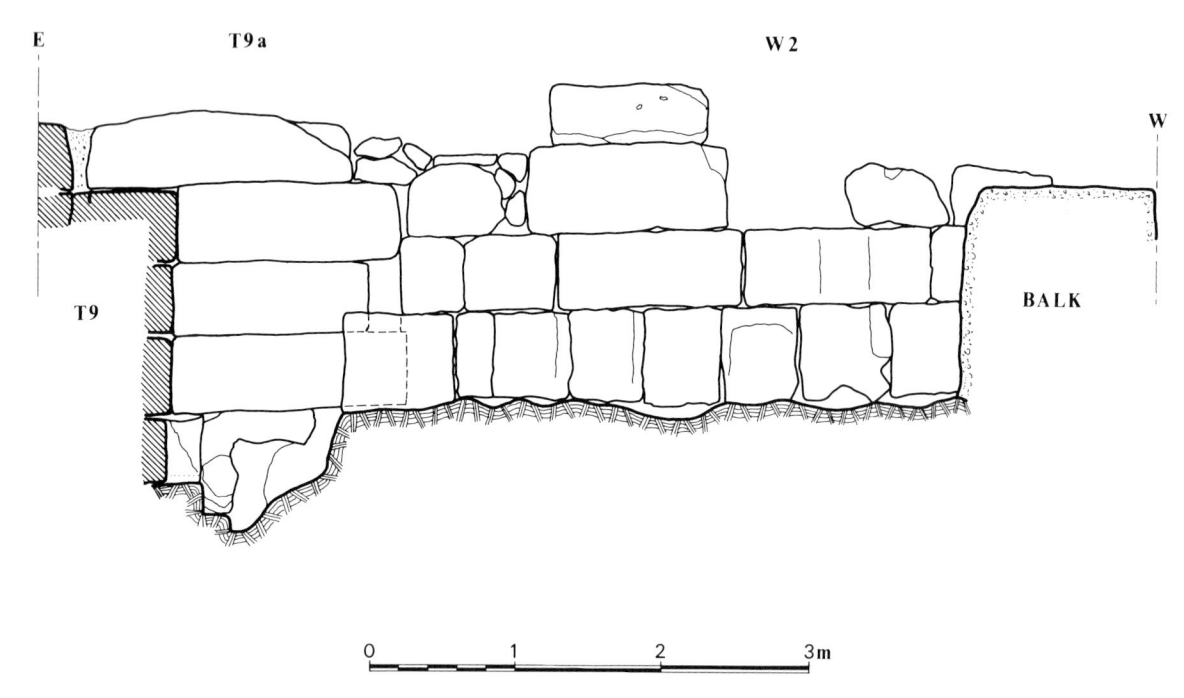

Figure 59: Elevation of the north face of the southeast corner of the Middle Sanctuary, showing the junction between the Hellenistic north-south T9 peribolos wall with wall T9a and the later Classical east-west wall W2. 1:50 scale.

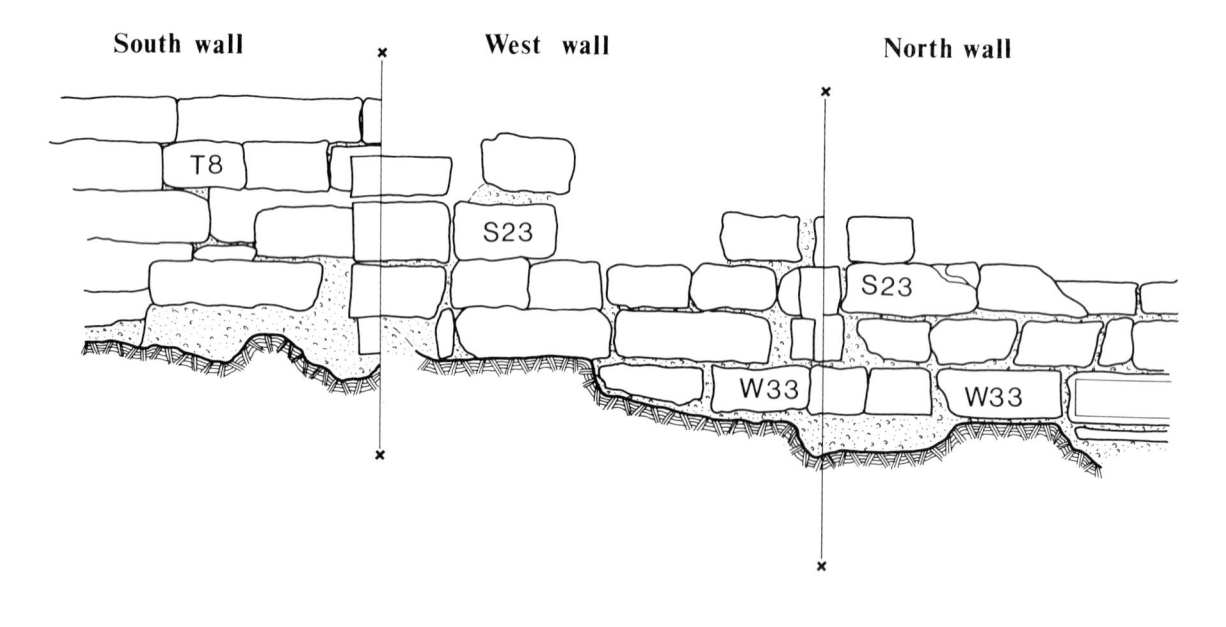

Figure 60: Elevation of the north, south, and west interior walls of the later Imperial S23 Late Structure. The south wall is the T8 later Classical peribolos wall; the W33 lower courses of the north and west walls belong to the Hellenistic S31 entrance enclosure. 1:50 scale.

THE LATER CLASSICAL SANCTUARY 111

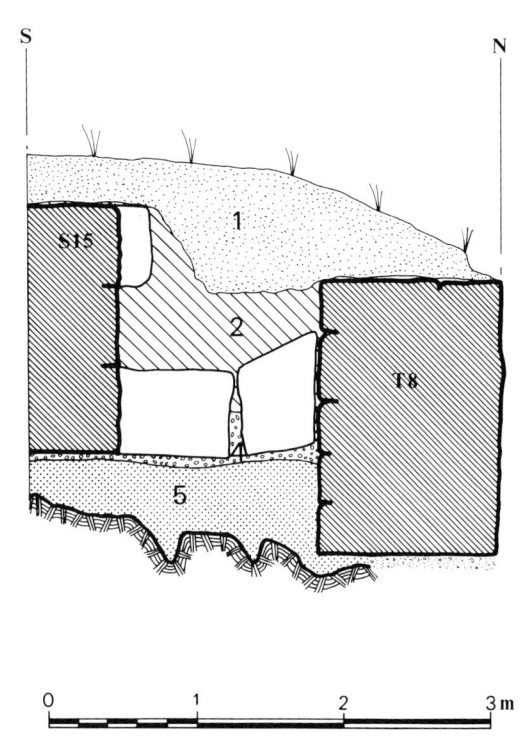

Figure 61: North-south section of fill between the T8 later Classical peribolos and the Imperial S15 Colonnaded Vestibule, drawn from east. 1:50 scale.

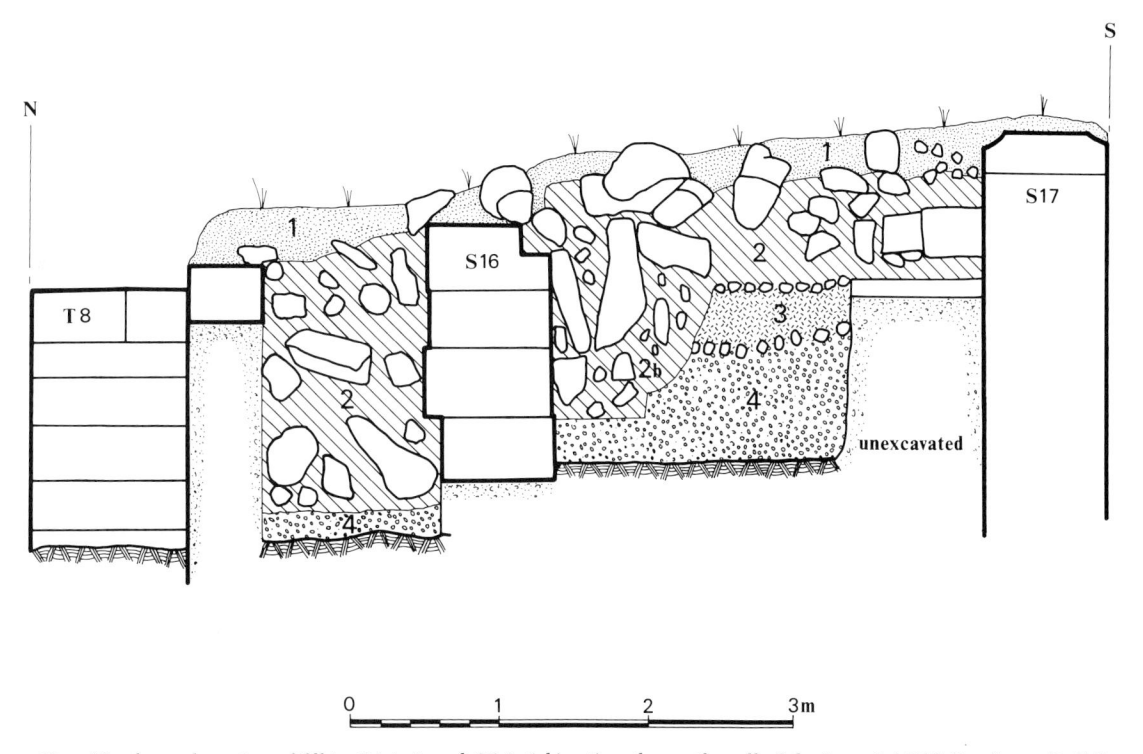

Figure 62: North-south section of fill in D14, 1 and C14, 1 bisecting the north wall of the Imperial S17 Southwest Building, the south wall of the S16 compartment, and the T8 later Classical peribolos wall, drawn from west. 1:50 scale.

112　　　　　　　　　　　　　　　　CYRENE FINAL REPORTS: VOLUME V

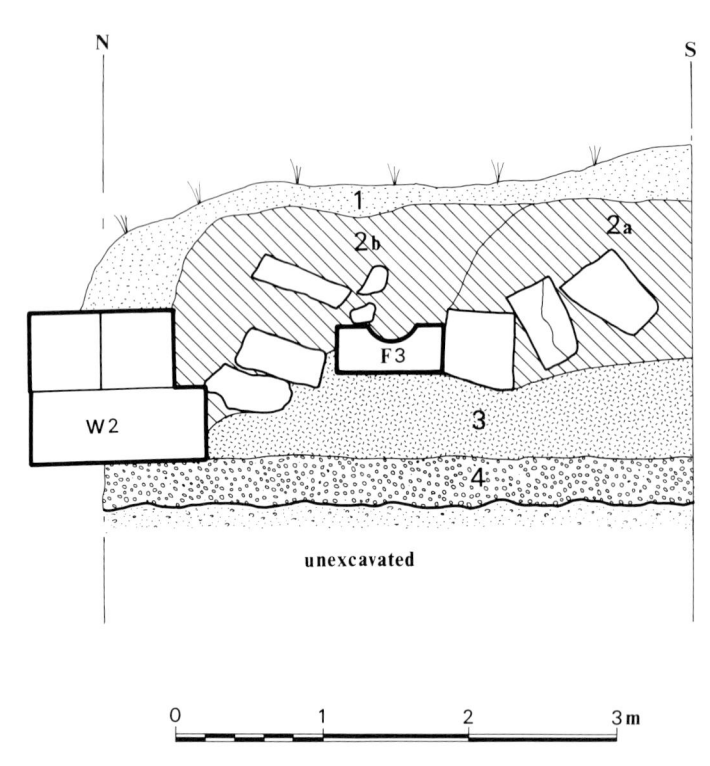

Figure 63: North-south section of east balk of D11/12, 1, covering the F3 later Classical water channel, drawn from west. 1:50 scale.

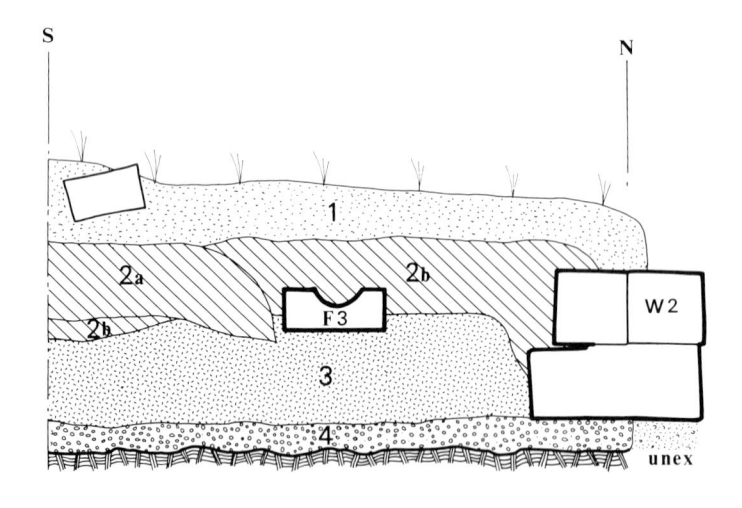

Figure 64: North-south section of west balk of D11/12, 1, covering the F3 later Classical water channel, drawn from east. 1:50 scale.

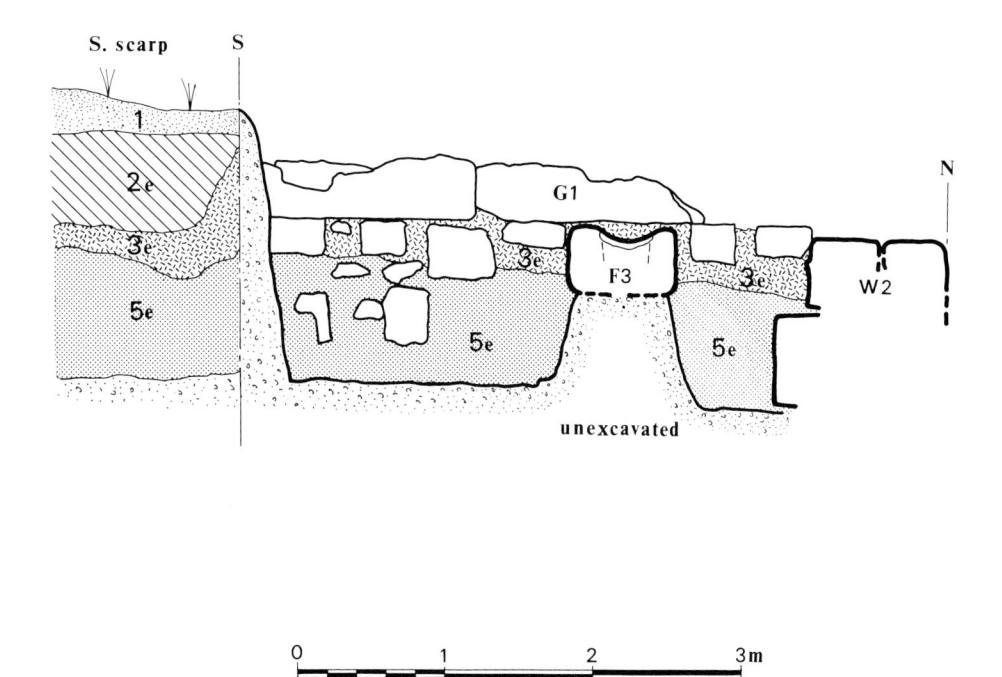

Figure 65: *North-south section of the D12 balk covering the G1 Hellenistic threshhold and the F3 later Classical water channel, drawn from east. East-west section of south end of D12 balk ("S. Scarp"), drawn from north. 1:50 scale.*

At the opposite end, a short north-south spur designated W2a connected wall W2 with wall T1 (Pl. 73). The spur consists of a single file of blocks, preserved to a height of two stretcher courses, the top of which was leveled with the top of wall W2's headers. Its width is ca. 0.55 m. A gap for drainage (?) ca. 0.35 m. wide was left between two of the spur wall's bottom course stretchers. Wall W2a abuts but does not bond with either wall T1 or W2.

In summary, the resulting rectangular cell formed by the W2 wall, the W2a spur at its west end, and the extension of the pseudoisodomic peribolos T2a on the east created what was in effect a 2.50 by 17.00 m. enlargement to the southeast corner of the later Archaic peribolos. Access to this extension was provided by door G7.

Plan C shows that a pair of uprights from the bislab wall T1a escaped demolition immediately in front of door G7. The same is true at the opposite, west end of wall W2, which raises the possibility that at the time of the construction of the W2 extension an earth fill covered the stumps of the earlier peribolos, walls T1 and T1a, as well as the unfinished bottom header course of wall W2. If this were the case, the fill was excavated away prior to the sanctuary's final destruction when the area was open enough to be inundated with earthquake debris (St. 2 in Fig. 32).

CONTEXT AND DATE OF WALL W2

The fill along much of the northern face of wall W2 was contaminated by later building activity and failed to yield any reliable dating information.

East of the W2a spur wall a large disposal pit (St. 3) was dug into the D12/E12, D, 5 Archaic occupation stratum (Fig. 17) and refilled by no earlier than the fourth century B.C. with bits of broken building blocks and lamp fragments. The southern edge of the pit is defined by wall W2, which clearly had to have been in place before the pit was created and therefore must be at least as old as the fourth century. D12, 1, 4, directly to its east, represents the Archaic occupation stratum originally associated with the T1 later Archaic peribolos, but here lying against the north face of the wall W2's headers. Its latest find is a mid-fifth century figurine, which in theory should predate wall W2.

WESTERN EXTENSION OF THE T1 SOUTH PERIBOLOS: WALL T8

At a point ca. 33.5 m. west of its southeast corner, the T1 later Archaic peribolos wall was absorbed into a strongly built wall of headers and stretchers (wall T8) that continues its passage west another 11.5 m. before forming a right-angled corner to the north (Plan C). The width of wall T8 is 1.30 m., or more than double the width of wall T1, while its preserved elevation reaches a maximum height of seven courses or 2.45 m.

Plate 74: T8 peribolos wall and S23/S24 Late Structure from southwest. S15 Colonnaded Vestibule and S16 Compartment occupy lower right-hand third of photo.

(Pl. 74; Figs. 5, 6, 60-62). Much of T8's length is made up of header courses that range from 0.30 to 0.55 m. in height. Where T8 serves as the back wall of the S23 Late Structure (Plan E, Fig. 60), the top course is composed of stretchers, ca. 1.20 m. long and only 0.30 m. high, thus yielding a height-to-length ratio of 1:4.[14] Immediately west of the S23 Late Structure the top course reverts to headers.

Wall T8's right-angled spur to the north is preserved for a distance of only three headers or ca. two m. before its line is lost. Because excavation around the spur in D15, 1 sondage was restricted to clearing away St. 2 earthquake debris, only its top surviving course has been exposed.

Both the variation in the course heights and the somewhat ragged appearance of the wall's north face (its one fully excavated face) contrast strongly with the careful pseudoisodomic masonry of T1 to its east. It is possible that T8 was partially fabricated out of reused blocks from earlier buildings.

CONTEXT AND DATE OF WALL T8

In the area of what was later to be developed as the S15 Colonnaded Vestibule (Plan E) the foundation course of the south face of wall T8 rests on a thin layer of a dark brownish red D13, 1 (Area 2), 5 soil over the bedrock (Fig. 61). This rises in places to nearly the top of T8's second course but regrettably failed to produce any identifiable finds to date the context. Ca. four m. further west the foundations are bedded on a sterile C14/D14, 1, 5 fill over which has accumulated ca. 0.20 m. of an orange-red soil (St. 4) packed against the lowest course of wall T8. While the lower levels of D14 were totally sterile, the same fill continues into C14, 1 (Fig. 62) where it contains exclusively early material, including an Attic Black Figure sherd dated to 550-540 B.C. and some fragmentary Corinthian sherds not examined by Kocybala. The north face of the foundations rests on rubble footings which in places ride over a D13, 2 (Area 2), 4 sterile terra rossa fill. The foundations are also associated with a ca. 0.30 m. thick greasy dark red argillaceous D13, 2 (Area 2), 3

---
14. Elsewhere in the sanctuary a 1:4 height-to-length block ratio is normally associated with Hellenistic masonry. See Appendix II. The upper course may possibly represent a later addition to T8's top.

Plate 75: F3 water channel, seen from west. Later Archaic S4 building to the center right.

layer, permeated with flecks of ashes (cooking debris?). St. 3 produced two late fifth, fourth century B.C. figurines that theoretically date the wall.

RETAINING WALL W1

Consisting of a single file of heavy ashlar blocks preserved to a maximum height of three courses, wall W1 runs for 11.10 m. across the rising ground of the Middle Sanctuary (Plan C; Figs. 3, 4, 52, 53). Its western limit is established by the east wall of the S5 Sacred House, while its eastern end stops just short of the southeast corner of Sacred House S1 (Pls. 3, 4). Its meandering course across the rocky slope, the ragged appearance of its south face, and the absence of side wall returns combine to argue that W1 served as a retaining wall rather than functioning as part of an independent structure.

The wall runs east to west across a natural lip of bedrock, which today drops down by ca. 1.25 m. beneath the eastern half of the north face of the wall, corresponding to the zone directly south of the S1 Sacred House (Figs. 52, 53). The presence of the trimmed shelf of bedrock west of the southwest corner of the S1 house argues that when its Archaic period builders flattened the sloping bedrock to receive the foundations of the house, they in effect artificially increased the dropoff of the lip that supports wall W1. While much of the wall rests directly on bedrock, its west end overrides a corner of a natural sinkhole at the southeast corner of the S5 Sacred House, so that here the wall rests on the sinkhole's terra rossa fill.

Most of the W1 blocks consist of randomly sized stretchers, ranging between 1.10 and 1.35 m. in length, 0.50 to 0.70 m. in width, and 0.60 m. in height. While their northern faces are fairly well aligned, the south faces present instead a ragged, jumbled outline that presumably was covered with the earth embankment which the wall was designed to contain behind the S1 Sacred House. Bedrock drops off beneath its

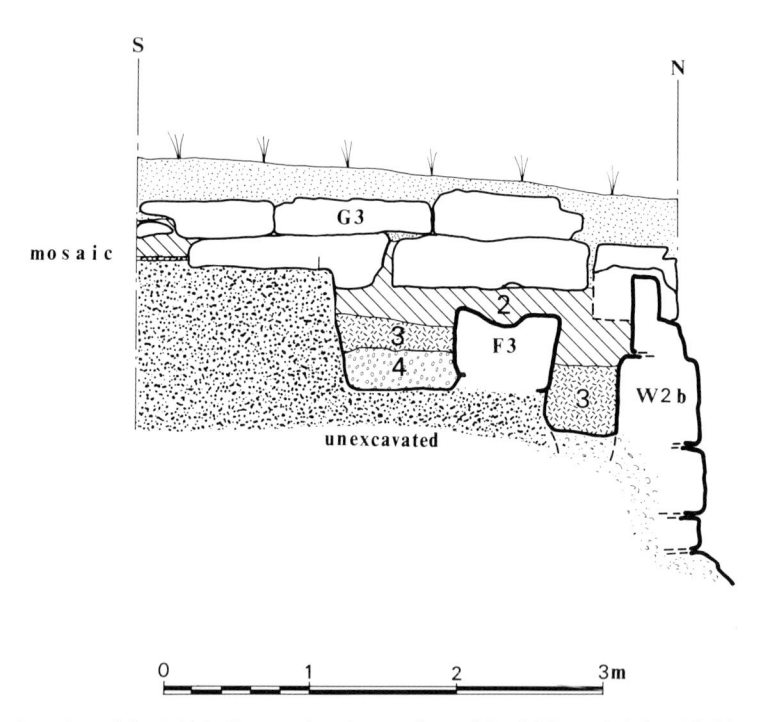

Figure 66: North-south section of the D12 balk, covering the east face of the G3 Imperial threshhold and the F3 later Classical water channel. Drawn from east. Inset: north face of balk left beneath mosaic floor west of G1 Hellenistic threshhold, drawn from north. 1:50 scale.

western half, and a low third course of stretchers was added to level W1 with the two courses of large stretchers that extend to the east. One of the leveling blocks has a low L-shaped cutback on its upper surface, which indicates its reuse here. Indeed, the general impression that the wall creates is that it was made up of stones salvaged from earlier building. The overall dimensions of the majority of its blocks and therefore their resulting block proportions echo those of the earlier structures already tabulated (Appendix II).

CONTEXT AND DATE OF WALL W1

The fill (Figs. 52, 53) north of wall W1 is mainly either earthquake debris or related specifically to the S1 house. The bedrock between the south face of W1 and the P3 early Archaic wall to its south formed a kind of natural shelf, against which the builders of W1 laid their wall after digging into the largely Archaic E12/13, C, 4 fill to form a foundation trench. This was then backfilled with St. 4a orange-colored soil and rubble, which preserves no dateable material. St. 4, however, contains fragmentary fifth and fourth century lamps near its surface, which may have become trapped at the time of W1's construction, thereby placing the wall's date within the later Classical period.

WATER CHANNEL F3

Fifteen m. of a cut-stone water channel (Pl. 75; Figs. 3, 4, 63-66) came to light between the Upper Sanctuary level Archaic S2, S3, and S4 structures and the line of the W2 later Classical peribolos extension (Plan C). Its construction consists of a single file of grey limestone blocks, of which nine have been excavated. Their lengths vary between 1.20 and 1.58 m.; heights range from 0.20 to 0.50 m. The widths, however, are a more or less standard 0.69/0.71 m. A semicircular trough, ca. 0.15 m. deep and 0.40 m. wide, was hewn into their upper surface and then coated with a waterproof yellow-white stucco to form the water conduit that flowed from west to east.

The west end of the channel abruptly terminates just short of the northeast corner of the early Imperial Southwest Building (S17), whose construction must have interrupted the channel's continuation west. Its progress east is lost under the unexcavated balk in D11, 1 occupying the eastern half of the later Propylaeum Court (S21). No sign of its line appeared beneath the floor of the Propylaeum (S20), whose erection shortly after A.D. 115 must have terminated its eastward extension. The channel was further interrupted by the west wall of the Propylaeum Court (S21) and the G1 Hellenistic portal. It may have continued to drain water after the G1 doorway was in place, since the door was associated with a mosaic floor to its west which theoretically could have covered the drain without halting its flow (Fig. 66). Both mosaic and G1 doorway were, however, put out of commission by the S21 Propylaeum Court, which perhaps ended the life of the F3 channel as well. On the other hand, the water channel was not originally designed as a covered drain,[15] and it is more probable that its usefulness was already curtailed by the Hellenistic period.

CONTEXT AND DATE OF WATER CHANNEL F3

For most of its length the F3 channel was sealed over with third century A.D. earthquake debris. Moreover, deep construction trenches filled with the same debris were discovered to either side of its line. While it is impossible to determine precisely when these trenches were opened, the hypothesis that has been adopted is that they are to be associated with an abortive attempt to reorganize the sanctuary immediately prior to its final destruction in A.D. 262.[16]

The fill on which the channel blocks rest does not contain a wide range of finds, but what there is points to the fourth century B.C. The D12 balk, 4 layer (Fig. 66) contains a third century lamp and an unidentifiable bronze coin, both of which may be intrusive. Otherwise its finds, as well as that of D12 balk, 3e which actually seals over the channel (Fig. 65) and D11/12, 1, 3 (Figs. 63, 64) are fourth century or earlier.

None of the Archaic construction known at the level of the Upper Sanctuary in the immediate vicinity of the F3 channel can be structurally directly related to it. It is certain from the way it inclines that the channel carried water from a source or building to the west, possibly from the area later occupied by the large colonnaded Southwest Building (S17), whose interior is still largely untested (Plan E). The shallow, wide profile of its trough, taken along with the fact that it was left uncovered, argues that the F3 channel functioned either as a gutter or a courtyard drain rather than a fountain conduit. Finally, its alignment with the Classical period W2 wall replacing the southeast corner of the later Archaic T1 peribolos perhaps adds some additional weight to the association of F3 with the Classical period.

---

15. Cf. the covered drain, dating from the third quarter of the sixth century B.C., on the north side of Cyrene's Agora. *Agora* I, 84, fig. 53.

16. *Final Reports* I, 93-94.

V

The Hellenistic, Early Roman Sanctuary Ca. 330-31 B.C.

The Hellenistic, early Roman period spans a number of major architectural changes that include, amongst other things, the creation of a genuine Upper Sanctuary that achieved parity of importance with the wall-enclosed Middle Sanctuary (Plan D), as opposed to its apparent earlier function as the location for a collection of miscellaneous extramural sanctuary outbuildings.[1] The peribolos walls that had previously enclosed the east and west ends of the later Archaic and Classical Middle Sanctuary were supplemented by new walls (T9, T9a, T13, T14, T15) that effected a modest increase in interior space, mainly in the southwest corner where the Hellenistic T15 peribolos wall was set ca. 3.50 m. south of the earlier line of the Archaic wall T6. A new independent Sacred House (S7) and two attached chambers (S11 and S12) were added at the same time, together with a rusticated fountain complex (F1) east of the old S1 Sacred House. Three sets of steps (R1, R3, R4) were constructed to provide access to the upper levels of the Middle Sanctuary, while a fourth set of steps (R2) allowed passage through the rear wall (T1) to the level of the Upper Sanctuary by means of a doorway (G5). The R2 steps appear to be associated with an irregularly shaped structure (S31) to the south-southwest of the S5 Shrine House, whose architectural function has been badly obscured by later building. The Upper Sanctuary saw the construction of what may have been the first version of a Propylaeum entranceway (W3) at its east end. The grounds directly north of the poorly understood S2, S3, and S4 later Archaic structures were bisected longitudinally by a large doorway (G1). A fountain house (F2) and what may have served as its enclosure wall (W29) were set at the western end of the Upper Sanctuary directly east of the extension south of the Middle Sanctuary's T17 peribolos. This separates the fountain house from the earlier and only partially excavated S19 structure to its west. A poorly engineered stone drain (F4) was constructed at the same time as T17, parallel to its outer, western face as well as to the rear wall of the F2 fountain's water tank.

While these architectural changes were taking place, the evolution in dedicatory practices already noticed in the later Classical period continues its movement away from the habits in votive giving established during the sanctuary's Archaic phase. In other words, terracotta figurines, metal statuettes, personal jewelry, and other types of miscellaneous small, inexpensive dedications now virtually cease to appear. This sets the stage for the apparent replacement of the older mass-produced, stereotyped dedications by more individualized as well as more expensive sculpted stone statues, statuettes, and reliefs,[2] along with a corresponding increase in dedicatory inscriptions. In the case of the pottery, locally manufactured fine wares as well as plain and coarse wares largely replace the imports.[3] On the other hand, a large dump[4] was recovered of discarded second and first century B.C. drinking and eating cups, bowls, and plates that may have been used in connection with ritual dining. These wares are matched by large quantities of coarse-ware food preparation vessels found in the same dump and behind the Middle Sanctuary's T10 retain-

---

1. Having made the point, it should be stressed that the distinction between the Hellenistic and pre-Hellenistic Upper Sanctuary is dependent on what has been excavated as well as what survives. If more were known of the full architectural extent of its early phases, the upper ground might conceivably emerge as *the* architectural focus of the Archaic sanctuary rather than a minor extension. But even at the height of the sanctuary's post-A.D. 115 development the upper level (Plan F) was apparently never fully enclosed by a protective peribolos.

2. The costliness of stone versus terracotta dedications turns on the simple and well-known fact that marble, the material from which ca. 90% of the sanctuary's 264 statuettes, 51 heads, and 692 statue fragments were made, had to be imported. The Cyrenaica of course possesses no marble. See S. Kane, "Sculpture from the Cyrene Demeter Sanctuary in its Mediterranean Context," *Cyrenaica in Antiquity*, eds. G. Barker, J. Lloyd, and J. Reynolds, *Society for Libyan Studies Occasional Papers* I: BAR International Series 236 (1985) 237-47.

3. See P. Kenrick, "Hellenistic and Roman Fine Wares," *Final Reports* III, 2-5, for the strikingly few examples of Attic black-glazed, Campana A, Apulian black-glazed, and Megarian bowls, found throughout all sanctuary levels. It is worth noting here that Ophellas's subscription of 10,000 Athenian volunteers to fight with him against Carthage in 321 B.C. has left no material trace of an increased Athenian presence in the late fourth century sanctuary. See A. Laronde, "Observations sur la politique d'Ophellas à Cyrène," *RHist* 498 (1971) 302, n. 5. Applebaum, *Jews and Greeks* 49.

4. The so-called Lamp and Pottery Dump (S18) was brought into existence during the early Imperial period and will be discussed in the final volume on the site's architecture. But see *Final Reports* I, 76, 99, n. 63, figs. 76, 77. *Final Reports* III, xi and Kenrick, ibid. 11, 14-16.

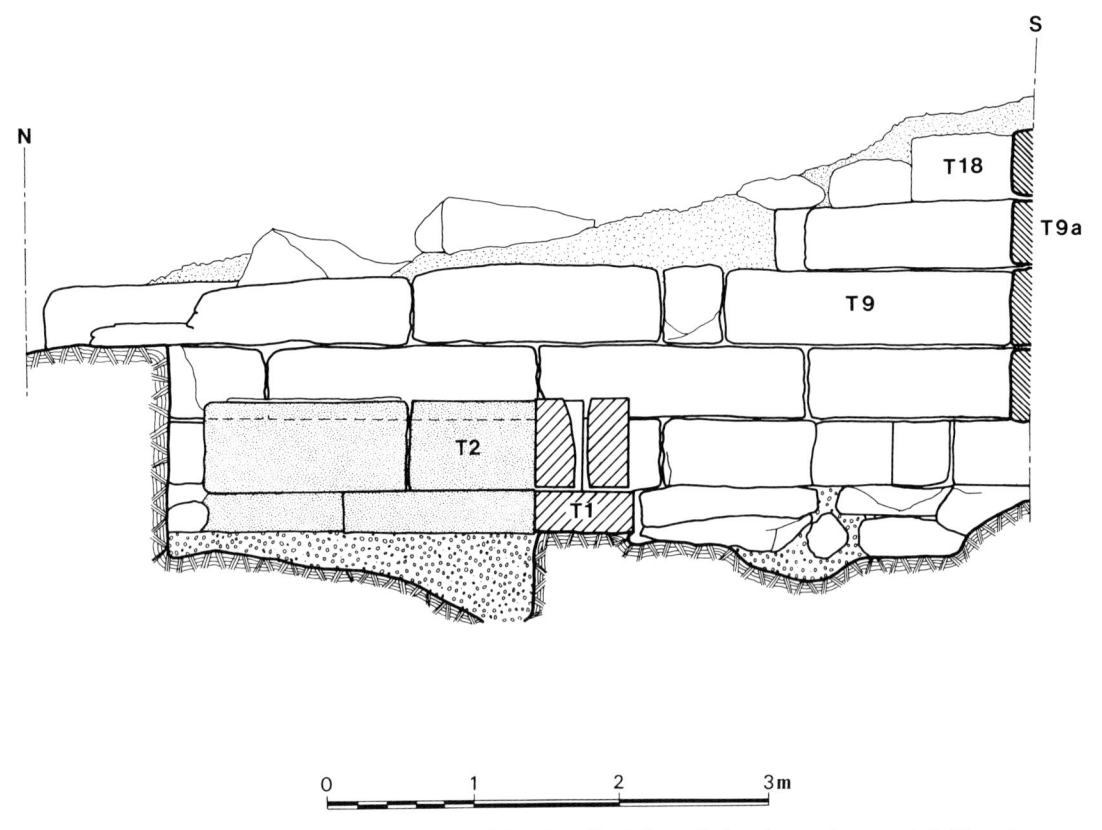

Figure 67: Elevation of the interior face of the T9 Hellenistic peribolos, drawn from west. 1:50 scale.

averaging 0.50 m. high, 1.70/80 m. long, and 0.60 m. wide, that survives to a maximum height of four courses. Its block height-to-length ratio averages 1:3.5. The surface of the limestone used throughout its length is weathered grey; its core, which is yellowish white in color, contains a greater number of microshell inclusions than its Archaic predecessor, the T2 wall, and must stem from a different quarry source.

In an interesting detail of how the wall was assembled, the bottom stretcher at the southeast corner of T9 was carefully chamfered back in order to slip the stone into position against the preexisting foundations of the southern extension of the later Archaic peribolos T2a (Pl. 16; Plan B).

CONTEXT AND DATE OF WALL T9

The fill accumulated against its inner (i.e., west) face in the vicinity of the southeast corner formed with wall T9a is largely E10/11 (Area 1) 1, 2 earthquake debris and thus is empty of much significance for the wall's date. At a point ca. eight m. north of the corner the E11, 1, 4 fill backing the inner face of the lowest course of T9 (Fig. 20) is the same dense reddish clay fill which here contains largely early material associated with the later Archaic pseudoisodomic peribolos T2. This would seem to indicate the T9 builders cut into the Archaic fill from the east in order to lay their wall, a view that receives some support from the presence of a single Hellenistic terracotta figurine in the St. 4 fill. E11, 1, 3 fill once again belongs to the time of the earthquake destruction. A short distance down the slope to a point just south of the S7 Sacred House the earthquake strata just mentioned coalesce into a single E11, 4, 2 earthquake layer, and St. 3 here is equivalent to St. 4 to its south (Fig. 21), but the St. 3 fill between wall T2 and wall T9 was never fully excavated and provides no date. In summary, the fill west of wall T9 associated with its lowest courses fails to provide conclusive evidence for its construction but tends to point to a post-fourth century B.C. date.

SOUTHEAST CORNER OF THE PERIBOLOS: WALL T9A

The narrow space marked G7 (Plan C), which has been tentatively identified as an entryway between walls T2a and W2, was filled by a short wall (T9a) bonded at an acute angle to wall T9 (Pl. 31). The fact that it bonds with T9 as well as sharing the same stone type and block dimensions suggests that wall T9a represents a contemporary build intended to convert the zone back to a blank, doorless corner of the peribolos. Taken together, walls W2 and T9a form the south wall attached to the southeast corner of the new

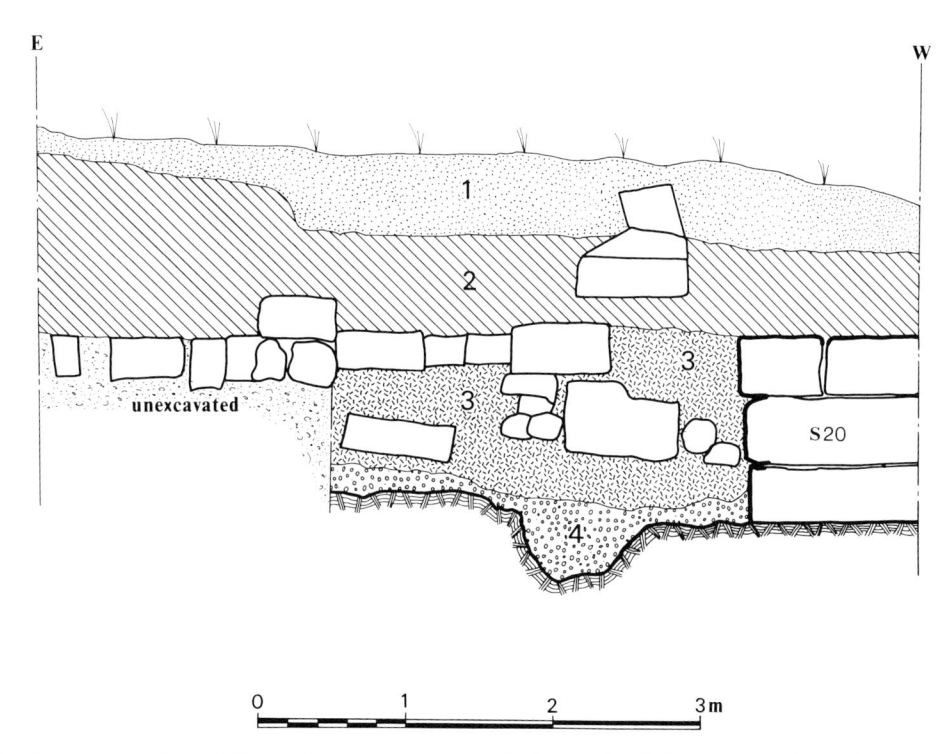

Figure 68:   East-west section of fill east of northeast corner of the Imperial S20 Propylaeum, drawn from north. 1:50 scale.

peribolos (Fig. 59). Resting on a low foundation of rubble that levels a depression in the bedrock pavement, Wall T9a has survived to the present as four courses of stretchers, ranging in length from ca. 1.80 to 2.00 m., and 0.50 m. in height.[17]

CONTEXT AND DATE OF WALL T9A

South of the wall and directly outside the northeast corner of the later Propylaeum (S20), the D10/11, A, 3 fill (Fig. 68) packed against the exterior of T9a rests on a St. 4 cover of Archaic soil filling the crevices that mark the natural limestone pavement. St. 3 contained a fourth century B.C. lamp, a fourth century figurine, fourth or possibly third century pottery B.C., and coins as late as the reign of Ptolemy Apion. This layer appears to be associated with the years directly following the construction of wall T9a, which, as we have seen, appears to be an integral part of wall T9. Therefore both walls are perhaps best regarded as the creation of the second half of the second century B.C.

NORTHWEST CORNER OF THE PERIBOLOS

Wall T13 (Plans D, G; Fig. 9; Pl. 76) consists of a ca. 5.50 m. long sequence of headers and stretchers cut from limestone weathered to a distinctive yellowy tan. A maximum of only five courses survives above the surface soil which rises as one moves west (Plan G). The course heights of the lower three courses are 0.25 m., while the stretcher elements average in length 1.20 m. (block ratio 1:4.8). The headers vary in width from 0.40 to 0.80 m. The fourth course consists of two oversized stretchers 1.90 and 2.10 m. long respectively and 0.44 m. high (block ratio: 1:4.5); their thickness is 0.55 m. The top course is made up of broken headers of approximately the same dimensions.

T13's fourth course seems to form a proper bond with the T14 west wall of the Hellenistic peribolos, and indeed the lower three courses have the appearance of foundations intended to level wall T13 with wall T14. The fourth course stretchers moreover share much the same dimensions as those of wall T14, creating the impression that the two features are coeval. Since the interior northwest corner of the peribolos system was not excavated and the inner face of wall T13 as a consequence never fully exposed, it is impossible to determine the exact total wall thickness, although the Fig. 9 transverse site cross-section provides an approximate idea of its considerable thickness, which was presumably required to enable the wall to retain the pressure of the soil backfilled against its inner face.

T13's eastern end does not form a proper bond with

---

17. Block height-to-length ratio 1:3.8. This falls within the normal range of the sanctuary's Hellenistic masonry. See Appendix II.

Plate 76: T13 northwest exterior corner of the Middle Sanctuary, from north.

its wall T12 continuation (Plan E); the respective courses of the two sets of walls do not consistently share the same levels and block dimensions. Wall T13 is furthermore considerably more worn and eroded than wall T12. In other words, for what it is worth, wall T13 looks older.

WEST WALL OF THE PERIBOLOS: WALL T14

Wall T14 is one of the most completely preserved stretches of wall found anywhere in the sanctuary (Plan D; Figs. 9, 10, 25, 69-71; Pls. 37, 77-78). It lies today as it was felled by the A.D. 262 earthquake, toppled over in thirteen or fourteen neat rows of courses (Pl. 79) in addition to the five to seven lower courses that are still standing. The type of limestone used throughout its length is relatively free of shell inclusions, although some large fossilized traces are scattered across the surfaces of its individual blocks. Where exposed to the weather, the stone surface has weathered to a whitish grey color. The parts of the wall sealed until recently by a cover of soil are a yellowish tan color that, perhaps only coincidentally, resembles the weathered face of wall T13.

Unlike wall T13, which had to bear the weight of a considerable earth mass to its rear, wall T14 served merely as a screen barrier similar to the companion T9 flanking wall on the east. For this reason its elevation rises as a single series of stretchers, ca. 0.55 m. thick. These average 0.45 m. high, which means that the wall must have risen at one time to at least 5.85 m. above bedrock. No traces of an original coping were retrieved. T14's stretcher lengths range from 1.60 to 1.80 m., creating a block height-to length ratio that varies from 1:3.5 to 1:4.

Where spared the worst effects of wind and water erosion, the inner faces of T14's stretchers preserve clear traces of diagonally slashed tooling (Pl. 78). Each block face was provided with a faint drafted margin ca. 0.03 m. wide. It is not presently known if the same dressing was employed on the outer wall face.

CONTEXT AND DATE OF WALL T14

The fill deposited against the inner face of T14 has been relatively well tested along approximately three-quarters of its length. The lower seven m. of fill in the precinct's northwest corner remains undug, as does the upper three and a half m. in the southwest where the earthquake-toppled T15 rear wall was left *in situ* (Pls. 36, 37; Fig. 69). Elsewhere, the fill shows a fairly consistent pattern. Starting at the southwest corner, the fill directly north of the collapsed T15 wall consists of a pocket of D16/17, 1, 5 soil against the inner face of T14's lowest stretcher course (Fig. 69) that probably represents a backfill at the time of the wall's actual construction. Unfortunately it produced no recognizable finds.

In the three m. of space to the north a roughly 0.45 m. thick layer of D16/17, 2, 4 dense reddish clay fill was cleared against the wall's inner face. This contains a mixture of early and late artifacts that suggests that St. 4 represents a standard Archaic occupation level contaminated with later material mixed into its upper surface. While the latter objects run as late as a third century B.C. lamp and three Ptolemaic coins that could be roughly coeval with the wall's erection, there is nothing in the relationship of St. 4 to the wall that argues conclusively for this association. The presence of a modern Italian coin in the same fill is a further indication of its chronological unreliability.

The area north of wall W9 in the vicinity of the Sacred

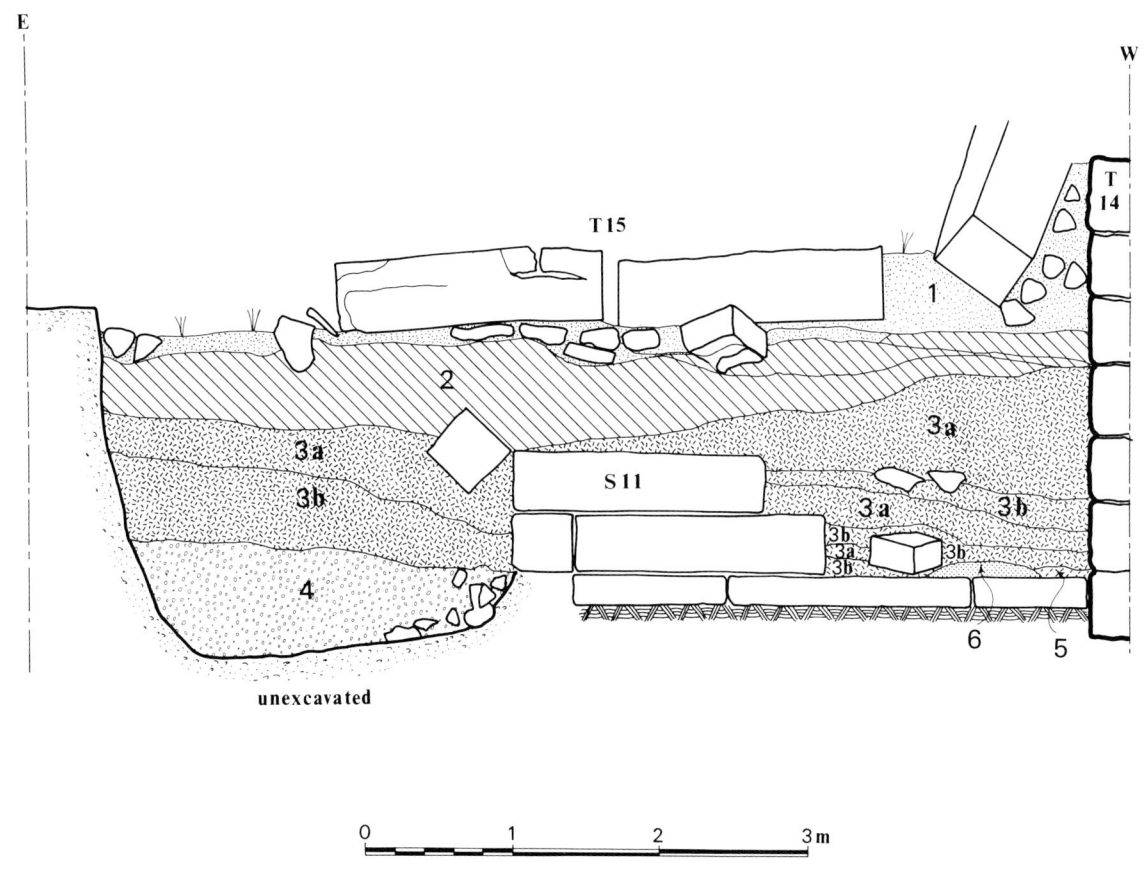

Figure 69: East-west section of fill east of the T14 peribolos wall over the north wall of the S11 Sacred Chamber, drawn from north. The stretchers marked "T15" have rolled forward of the line of the T15 rear wall of the Hellenistic peribolos but are themselves south of the plane of the actual section. 1:50 scale.

Chamber S12 produced more useful information. The bedrock pavement immediately east of wall T14 is irregular in level and broken in several places by sinkholes. When the wall builders erected wall T14 they utilized the natural bedrock shoulder created by one of these fissures for bedding their foundations (Figs. 70, 71). This created a narrow gap between the rim of the sinkhole and the inner face of the wall (Fig. 71: E16/17 [Area 3] 1, 2a), which they then backfilled at the time of the wall's construction with dirt mixed with sherds dating to the second or first centuries B.C.

In the final ca. three and a half m. of wall excavated north of S12 (Fig. 25) the same gap between the bedrock rim and the inner face of T14, now F16, 1, 3a, contained some dateable material of which the latest find was a fifth century B.C. lamp.

In summary, the latest objects associated with the construction of wall T14 are the second, possibly first century B.C. sherds from the gap between the sinkhole rim and the wall's inner face in the area of the S12 Sacred Chamber. Given the similarity between the block dimensions of wall T14 and of the T9 wall which frames the eastern side of the Middle Sanctuary, the second half of the second century B.C. date tentatively assigned to the T9 wall should probably be accepted for wall T14 as well. A post-ca. 150 B.C. date is otherwise consonant with T14's masonry finish.[18] Wall T14, moreover, in theory dates wall T13 to the same period.

SOUTHWEST CORNER OF THE PERIBOLOS: WALL T15

Wall T15 (Plan D; Figs. 9, 69; Pls. 36, 37) consists of a line of stretchers that returns ca. 10.75 m. east from the corner formed with wall T14 before apparently shifting south. Where still protected from weathering by soil the surface of the limestone is a soft yellow tan, while its core is off-white and relatively free of fossilized shell inclusions. Its weathered surface resembles the grey tone of wall T14, and stones for the two walls may have been supplied from the same quarry.

---

18. Infra 131 for comparative examples of diagonally dressed masonry.

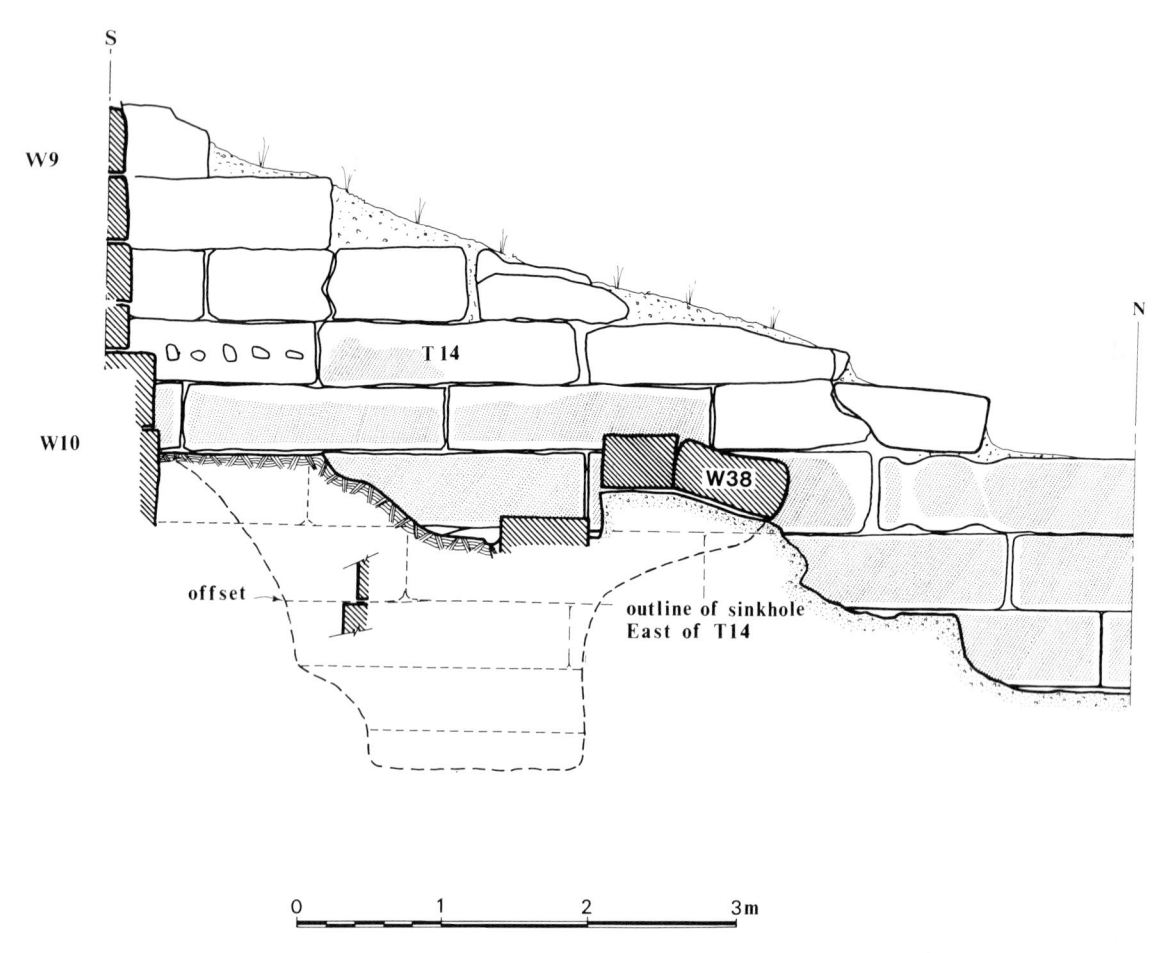

Figure 70: North-south elevation of the inner face of the T14 west wall of the Hellenistic peribolos, drawn from east in E16/17 (Area 3) 1. The wall also serves as the west wall of the S12 Sacred Chamber. Inset: drawn at right angles to plane of section, showing offset of T14. 1:50 scale.

The surviving portions of T15 in its southwest corner consist of three toppled courses of stretchers that correspond to the sixth through eighth courses of wall T14. These have been pushed forward, that is to say down the slope to the north, by the force of the earthquake and effectively seal from view the lower portions of the wall (Fig. 9), with the exception of the top of a fourth course, which was cleared in the course of excavation.

The stretchers average 1.80 m. in length, 0.40 m./0.42 m. in height, and 0.55 m. in thickness, i.e., approximately the same dimensions as walls T14 and T13. To judge from its fallen courses T15 rose as a single series of stretchers; however, its buried lower courses may have been thicker in order to hold back the weight of the earth fill to its south.

The exposed vertical faces of the fallen courses are carefully dressed but preserve no trace of diagonal tooling. Possibly the surfaces that originally faced north to form the wall's inner face are now turned into the earth, and if some day are restored to their original positions, will turn out to have the same distinctive obliquely slashed dressing as wall T14. The surfaces that presently make up the upper block surfaces have roughly tooled margins and slightly countersunk, pitted central panels that form a kind of crude *anathyrosis* that has no parallels elsewhere in the sanctuary.

DATE OF WALL T15

Because it was decided to leave T15's upper courses where they fell pending restoration, the foundation levels were left untested and no excavated evidence has been thus far recovered for a construction date. The similarity of T15's masonry to that of wall T14 is enough to indicate that the two are probably contemporary.

EXTENSION SOUTH OF THE PERIBOLOS?: WALL T17

Roughly eleven m. of wall T17 has been uncovered, running south at right angles from the east end of wall T15 (Plan D; Figs. 11, 49, 50). The actual junction

THE HELLENISTIC, EARLY ROMAN SANCTUARY

the unexcavated portion of the Upper Sanctuary grounds.

The most thoroughly exposed part of wall T17 lies directly west of the F2 Fountain House where its western face, running parallel to the Hellenistic period drain F4, was excavated nearly to bedrock (Pl. 62). Here four courses of stretchers are preserved, averaging between 0.70 and 1.10 m. in length, 0.45 m. in height, and 0.50 m. in width. The top preserved course is badly eroded, perhaps from modern plowing, while many of the lower stretchers were cracked probably during one or more of the site's earthquakes.

Ca. 4.50 m. of wall T17 came to light at the western edge of the S10 Mosaic Chamber (Plan E) where its maximum preserved height is 1.20 m. The top preserved course of T17 projects by ca. 0.10 m. above the level of the mosaic pavement, capped by a post-earthquake squatter wall (W35) that was built from reused blocks.

CONTEXT AND DATE OF WALL T17

West of the Fountain House (F2) the C15/16, 1:4-2 accumulation of fill against the wall's west face could not be exposed down to the T17 footings because of the presence of the F4 drain, which abuts its foundations (Fig. 50). C15/16, 1:4-2, 6 represents pockets of sterile terra rossa over the bedrock. C15/16, 1:4-2, 5 is a layer of heavy, moist brown soil, containing a mixture of both early and late objects that date as late as the second century B.C. It seems to belong to the partial dismantlement of the later Archaic wall W30. The significant layer for wall T17 is St. 4, a dense tan-brown earth stratum ca. 0.30 m. thick which largely buried the F4 drain at the same time that it was packed against the the lowest course of T17. In other words St. 4, having been used to cover the drain and backfill the extension of the peribolos, is contemporary with the construction of both. Eventually the drain ceased to work as a water conduit when its interior silted up with the same St. 4 fill in which it had been originally packed.[19] The late contents of C15/16, 1:4-2, 4 are late Hellenistic in date and include six bronze coins, of which the latest is assigned to ca. 145-116 B.C., and a Hellenistic terracotta plaque depicting Medusa. As a result Wall T17 ought not be later than the second century B.C. and thus appears to be contemporary with the rest of the peribolos.

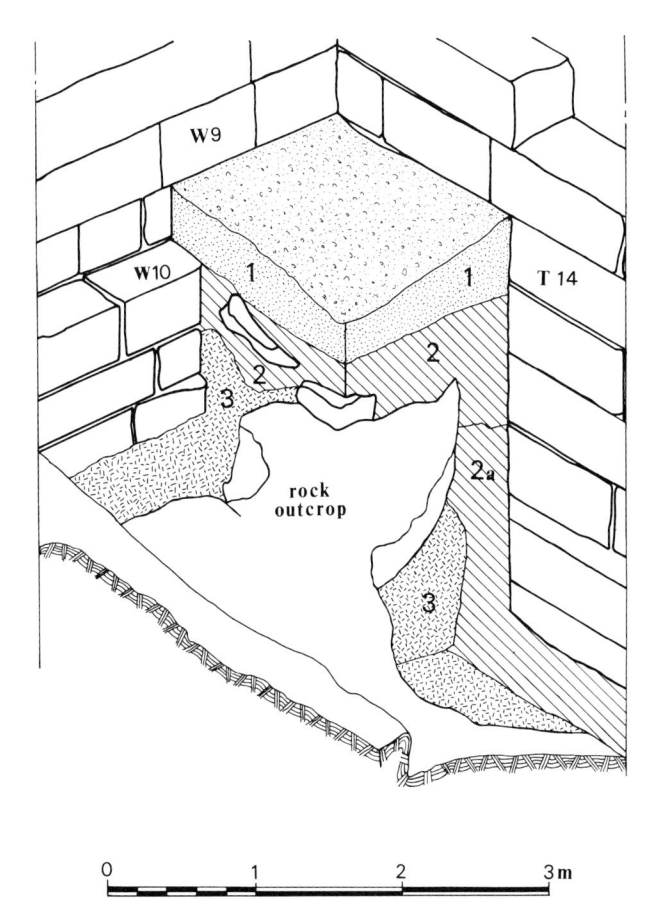

Figure 71: Perspective drawing of fill deposited against the inner face of the T14 peribolos wall in the southwest corner of the S12 Sacred Chamber. 1:50 scale.

between the two walls was insufficiently excavated to determine their structural relationship, but similarities in their respective masonry suggest that wall T17 may have formed an extension of the line of the peribolos to the south. How *far* south T17 extended is presently not known, since its continuation is lost in

Commentary

PERIBOLOS PLAN

Although adhering to much the same plan as its Archaic-Classical predecessor (Plans A-C), the late Hellenistic peribolos must have appeared more imposing when seen from the city because of the greater height of its side (east, west) walls. The alignment of the Hellenistic northwest corner (T13) with the center of the later Archaic north wall (T4) strongly suggests that the later wall either merged with the Archaic wall or, alternatively, masked its outer face in order to complete the front of the Middle Sanctuary. The precise way in which the two were joined is hidden by the massive later Imperial T20 revetment (Pls. 1, 2; Plan E) and will be properly clarified only when additional excavation has been carried out on its rear south face.

---

19. See infra 139-40 for the drain F4.

m. high as compared to the ca. six. m. high wall used by the smaller Cyrene sanctuary in its final Imperial phase (Plan G). The ends of the Pergamene sanctuary are enclosed by high screen walls restored as stepping down the hillslope at regular intervals,[25] which may well be the way in which the Cyrene walls were handled over similar falling terrain. Both systems shared the common purpose of protecting the flanks of their respective precincts from unauthorized entry and public snooping. The heavy retaining wall supporting the Pergamene sanctuary's South Stoa is capped with a meter-high parapet. In the case of Cyrene we do not yet know how its Middle Sanctuary's forward retaining wall was finished off because the nine or so meters of space behind its forward face have been only partially cleared of a massive buildup of earthquake debris (Pl. 1),[26] but some kind of similar arrangement, including perhaps a low portico across its front, cannot be ruled out until further excavation has been carried out.

In the west the later Classical-Hellenistic Sanctuary of Demeter Malophoros continues to make use of its Archaic peribolos walls into the Hellenistic period, and it may be safely assumed that some of the other early western Greek sanctuaries previously mentioned follow the same pattern.[27]

PERIBOLOS WALL MASONRY

The main criteria for discussing the masonry employed throughout the Hellenistic phase of the peribolos are its *stone type*, *block ratios*, and *surface finish*.

Of the three, *stone type* is the least reliable, since only a superficial ocular examination could be carried out to distinguish one limestone from another. Generally speaking, however, different quarry sources almost certainly were used for furnishing stone to the sanctuary at different periods in its history. The relatively clear-textured (i.e., free of fossil shell inclusions) limestone, with tan-to-yellowish brown surface coloration, used throughout much of the later Archaic pseudoisodomic peribolos, is sufficiently idiosyncratic that it can be argued that it came from a single quarry. But surface color is mainly a product of exposure to soil and air. Stones with widely differing surface patinations almost always present largely similar beige-to-white cores when broken open for inspection, although the cores of certain blocks veer toward a brownish yellow color. Texture is a more reliable distinguishing feature than color but not enough to yield definite information about sources, since it is not known, at least to me, how much variation in texture can be expected to occur within a single quarry bed.

Having said all this, the stones used for the T15 wall in the southwest corner are yellowish tan when covered with soil and weathered grey where exposed to the air. The same is true of the western peribolos, wall T14. By way of contrast, the weathered face of the northwest corner, wall T13, is yellowish tan; no sections of T13 were cleared below modern ground level to determine how their surface reacts to contact with earth. The eastern peribolos, wall T9, is uniformly weathered grey. Walls T9, T14, and T15 all contain some fossilized shell inclusions. In the case of T9 these range from small to medium-large shells visible on both the surface as well as scattered through its core. The stone in all the walls is coarser in texture than the stone used throughout most of the later Archaic peribolos, which in turn resembles the kind of fine limestone selected for the site's limestone sculpture. Based on these admittedly tentative observations the builders of the Hellenistic additions may have drawn their blocks from as many as two or three separate quarries.

A second consideration has to do with *block height-to-length ratios*. The results tabulated in Appendix II indicate that the ratio for the T17 southern extension falls outside the range of the remaining walls, which as a group are marked by their elongated block dimensions (maximum variation 1:3.5/1:4.8). This adds further support to the view that T17 represents a secondary expansion to the original Hellenistic unit, although to judge from the evidence of its associated stratigraphy, the wall ought to date to the same general period. Elsewhere in Cyrene elongated block proportions occur during the same period, as for example in the case of the Agora's two second century B.C. stoas, the North Portico B5[28] and Northwest Portico O2,[29] although it must be again stressed that the association of block proportions with period has

---

25. Bohtz, *Pergamon* pls. 5, 2; 9, 1, 2.
26. *Final Reports* I, fig. 54.
27. Supra 38. The Hellenistic Sanctuary of the Chthonian Gods at Acragas may have likewise continued to be enclosed with early walls. Although still awaiting a definitive study, the erection of its enclosure has been assigned to the second half of the sixth century B.C. See P. Marconi, *Agrigento arcaica* (Rome 1933) 17-18, 107-08, figs. 1, 5. P. Orlandini, *Princeton* 25, cautiously avoids giving it a precise date.

---

28. *Agora* I, 148, fig. 78 for the inner face of the east side of Portico B5 where the block ratios appear to be approximately 1:3.5.
29. Here the block proportions of the crepidoma are even more elongated, apparently ranging from 1:5.2 to 1:6.5. See *Agora* II,1, 113, fig. 82.

Plate 80: Detail of wall masonry of lower level shop, Cyrene Agora Portico B5.

not been tested on any kind of systematic city-wide basis.

Masonry finish constitutes the last and perhaps most informative masonry feature. Wall T14's diagonally dressed finish and drafted block margins have numerous regional parallels with other similarly dated monuments, of which several are supplied by the nearby Agora. The early second century B.C. basement level shops of Portico B5 that open to the north have their inner walls finished in the same manner (Pl. 80),[30] as apparently did the adjacent "Construction C."[31] The foundations of the early second century B.C. Portico O3 are similarly dressed, which is odd in the case of blocks not intended to be visible, but presumably they were reused in this context.[32] The south wall of Applebaum's so-called "Building A" south of the Sanctuary of Demeter and Persephone consists of "well cut drafted blocks whose bosses are obliquely tooled, dated from the mid Hellenistic period to the reign of Tiberius."[33] Elsewhere in the province the tower masonry of the early third century B.C. city defenses of Apollonia is built throughout with drafted edges and diagonally tooled faces.[34] The Hellenistic Tauchira Gate at Ptolemais is faced with carefully drafted ashlar blocks but without the diagonal dressing.[35] Similarly dressed masonry is preserved in the monumental structure of presumably Hellenistic date still partly visible beneath the walls of the East Church at Apollonia.[36] Outside of the Cyrenaica the combination of ashlar masonry with tooled (but not necessarily *diagonally* tooled) faces and drafted edges, to use Scranton's terminology, is said to be a largely fourth century technique.[37]

---

30. *Agora* I, 151, 177, fig. 82, pl. XXII.
31. *Agora* I, 179-80, pl. XXX, 2.
32. *Agora* II,1, 142, pl. XXIII, 1.

---

33. S. Applebaum, *IEJ* 7 (1957) 159-60. *Final Reports* I, 16, n. 79.
34. *Apollonia* 92, pl. X, d.
35. Kraeling, *Ptolemais* 58, 60, pls. VI-VIII.
36. *Apollonia* 37, 268.
37. R. Scranton, *Greek Walls* (Cambridge, Mass. 1941) 104-07, 179, figs. 20-22.

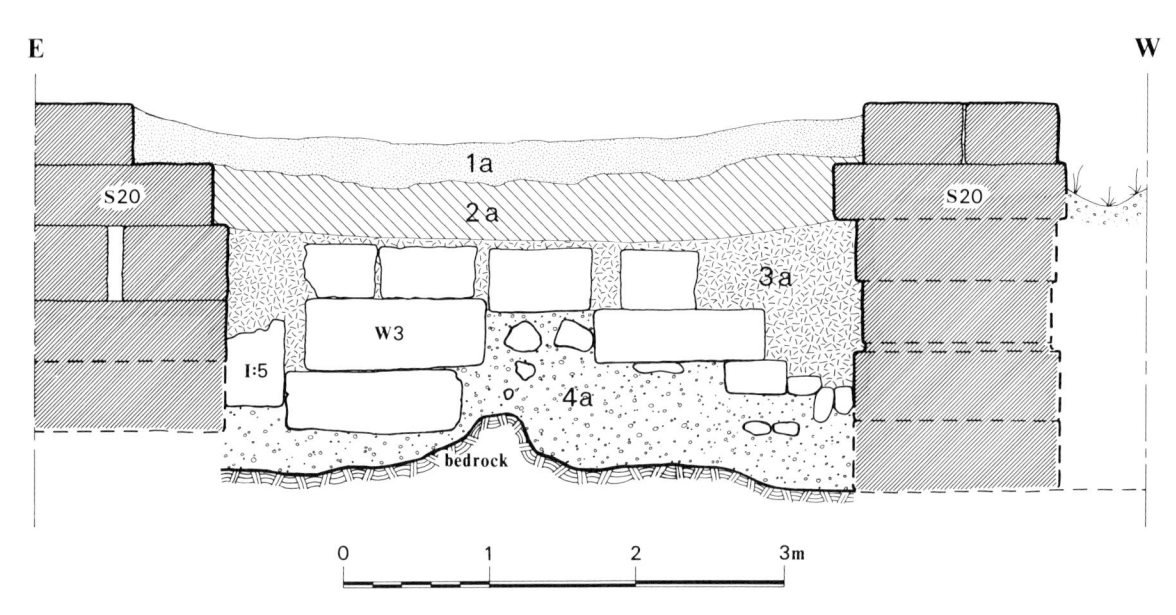

Figure 72: East-west section of fill across the interior of the Imperial S20 Propylaeum, covering the surviving wall W3 of its Hellenistic predecessor. Drawn from north. 1:50 scale.

Earliest Version of the Upper Sanctuary Propylaeum?

The wall remains (W3) that can be tentatively associated with a first version of a propylaeum entranceway to the Upper Sanctuary came to light in the course of excavating the foundations of the later, post-A.D. 115 Propylaeum (S20) in D10/11, C (Plan D; Figs. 12, 72, 74; Pl. 81). They consist of a three m. long east-west line of ashlar blocks that lie slightly out of alignment with the outer walls of the later structure in which they were eventually buried. The east end of W3 is made up of three courses of blocks that stand to a combined height of ca. 1.20 m. above the red clay fill over bedrock on which the lowest course is founded (Fig. 72). The lower two courses are standard limestone stretchers ca. 1.20 m. long and 0.45 to 0.50 m. high. Taken by themselves, they appear to represent part of the foundation of a well-built wall. On the other hand, the two ashlars making up the third course are broken headers that must be reused in the present context. Moving west, the center of W3 consists of an unbroken header supported on D10/11, C, 4 a red clay mixed with rubble. The western end is made up of a stretcher founded on the same fill and supporting once again a broken header. The lower coursing of W3 therefore mainly functions to level its top course and was never intended to be visible. Despite the tidy alignment of its south face it is unclear whether the third course was exposed to view or not. We are therefore dealing mainly with foundations that may be carrying a single surviving course of superstructure, interrupted and then subsequently buried by the foundations of the later S20 Propylaeum.

A fragmentary limestone door jamb (Arch. Cat. No. **I:5**)[38] was excavated at the east end of wall W3 immediately north of its north face and flush against the east wall of the S20 Propylaeum. Its top lay 0.15 m. below the top of the second course of W3. The stratigraphical context indicates that the fragment was dropped into a construction trench cut for the later Propylaeum, leaving open the possibility that the jamb was once part of an Upper Sanctuary monument that was dismantled to make way for its later Propylaeum.

Arch Cat. No. **I:5** (Pl. 82; Fig. 73).

Limestone fragment of door jamb. MPH. 0.90 m. MPW. (observable before stone disappears under east wall of later Propylaeum) 0.42 m. MPTh. 0.62 m. U-shaped lifting loop on outer face indicates fragment originally part of upper left-hand corner of a moulded door jamb, whose principal decoration consists of a cyma recta

---

38. The site's miscellaneous architectural *frusta* are catalogued separately from the remaining artifacts; a representative selection was drawn by J. Thorn in 1981. Most fragments belong to post-Hellenistic buildings and will, if selected for publication, appear in the forthcoming study of the site's Imperial period architecture.

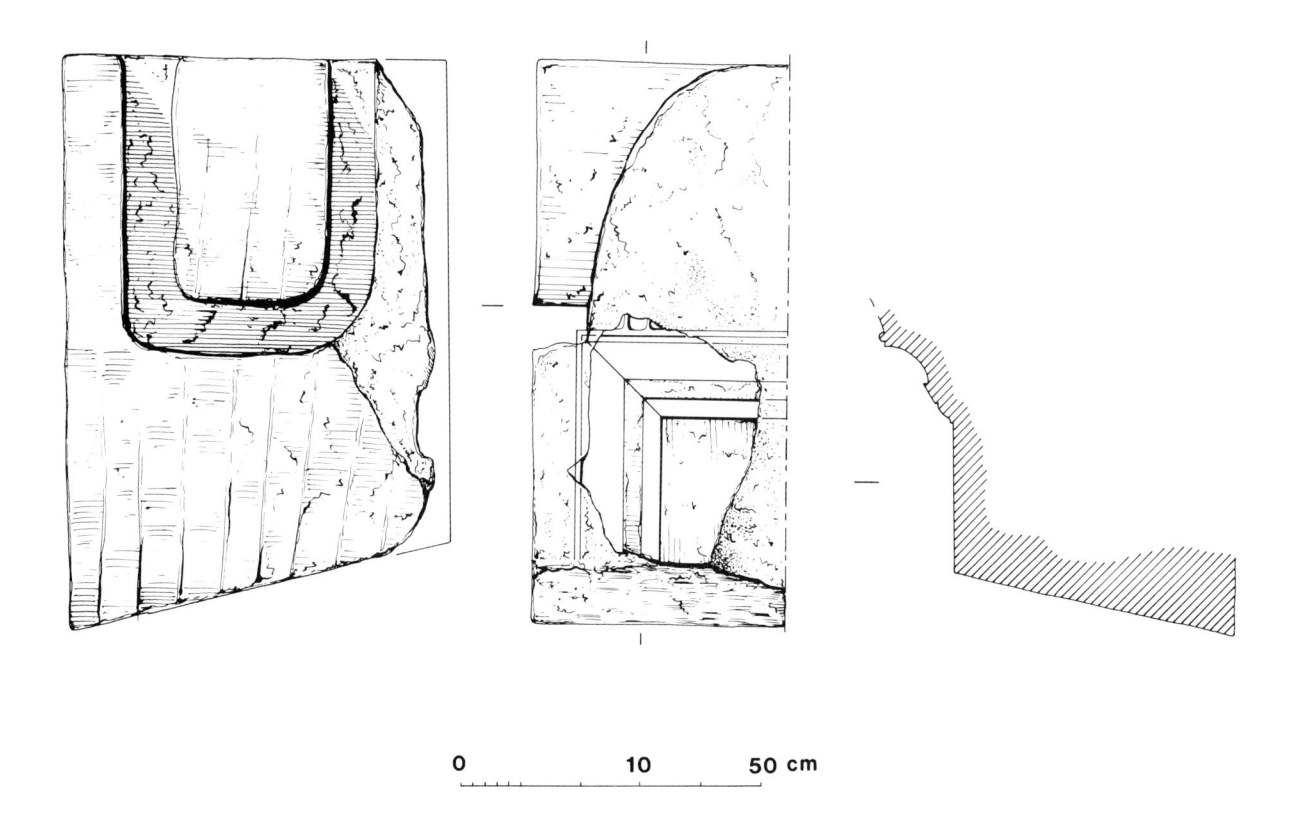

*Figure 73: Drawing of fragmentary limestone door jamb, Arch. Cat. No. **I:5**.*

moulding surmounted by an astragal. Similarly plain moulded doorways can be found in association with Cyrenaican tombs dating from the late fifth century through Hellenistic times. See Pacho, pls. XIX, XXXI, XXXVI and Stucchi, *Architettura* figs. 70, 71, 131, 133, 181.]

Exiguous as the evidence may be, the presence of foundations buried by, and roughly coaxial with, the north and south walls of the later Propylaeum raises the possibility that the W3 wall represents a survival of an original entrance-way to the Upper Sanctuary from the east. Later building has destroyed most of the material evidence for what is at best an extremely hypothetical phase, but the possibility exists that future excavation beneath the earthquake destruction level still blanketing the eastern half of the later Propylaeum Court (S21) to the west as well as the unexcavated fill east of the colonnaded front of the S20 Propylaeum would bring to light additional traces. The jamb fragment **I:5** may belong to this same early phase of entrance, but there is no binding proof of this fact.

CONTEXT AND DATE OF WALL W3

The stratigraphy north of W3 consists basically of four levels of D10/11, C fill (Fig. 72). The wall is supported by St. 4a fill over the bedrock. It is typical argillaceous red stereo, largely sterile of finds. St. 3a, chocolate brown in color, is backfill covering both the broken **I:5** jamb block and wall W3, whose contents belong to the construction of the later S20 Propylaeum. The latest object from 3a is a much battered early Trajanic marble male head.[39]

The western half of the fill south of wall W3 exposed a relatively complicated buildup of shallow layers that appear to be the leftovers of superimposed floor and construction levels. When first excavated strata 6 and 7 buried wall W3's two lowest foundation courses (Fig. 74, drawn after the relationship had been dug away) while leaving exposed the upper half of what may have been the first course of its exposed elevation. The latest find from St. 6 is a bronze Ptolemaic coin dated to the reign of Apion, which places wall W3 in the late Hellenistic period and thus makes it contemporary with the peribolos renovations.

---

39. Kane, sanctuary sculptures forthcoming, cat. no. **222** (Inv. 73-977). Also D. White, "Excavations in the Sanctuary of Demeter and Persephone at Cyrene 1973, Third Preliminary Report," *AJA* 79 (1975) 43, pl. 7, fig. 28.

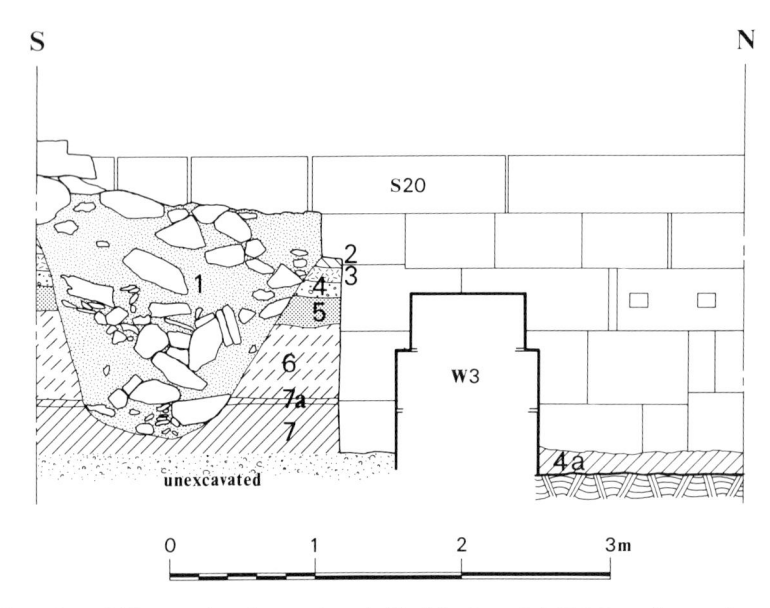

Figure 74: North-south section of fill across interior southern half of the Imperial S20 Propylaeum, drawn from east after removal of fill from northern half that buried wall W3. 1:50 scale.

Plate 81: Hellenistic Propylaeum wall W3 in midst of foundations of the Imperial S20 Propylaeum, from east.

Plate 82:   Limestone door jamb fragment, Arch. Cat. No. **I:5**, *buried by foundations of the Imperial S20 Propylaeum.*

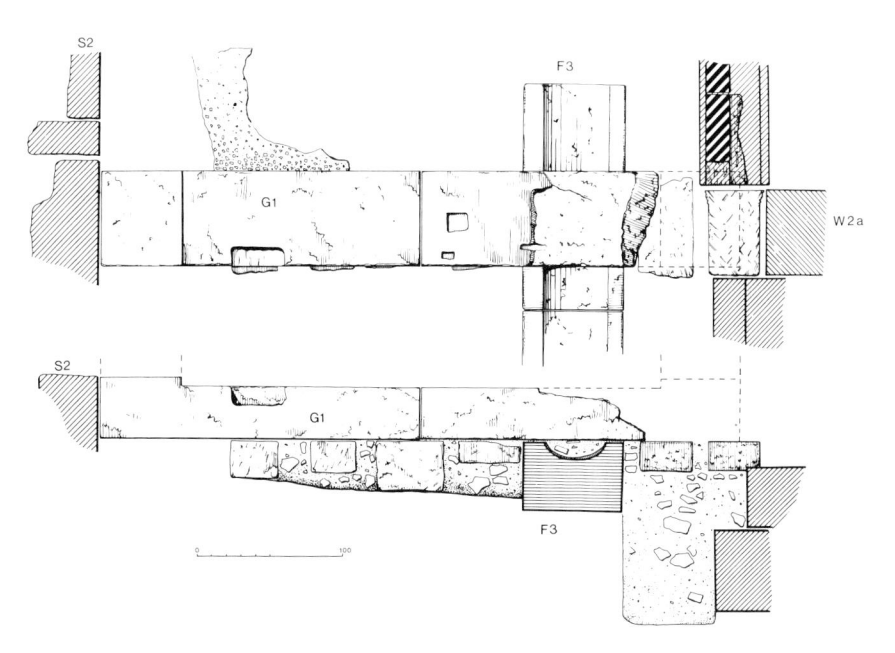

Figure 75:   Plan and north-south elevation drawn from east of the G1 Hellenistic threshold. 1:50 scale.

Plate 83: The G1 (center) and G3 (left) doorways from south.

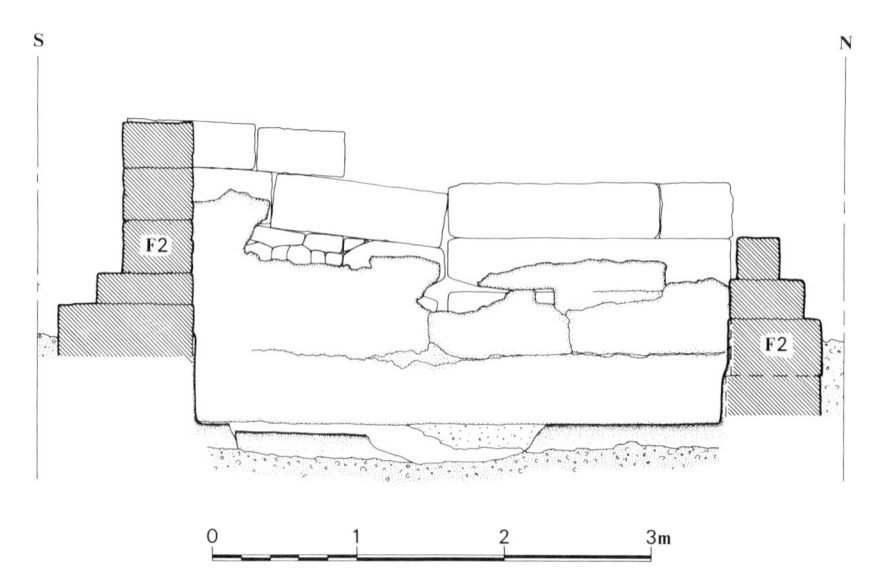

Figure 76: North-south elevation of west wall of the F2 fountain water tank, drawn from east. 1:50 scale.

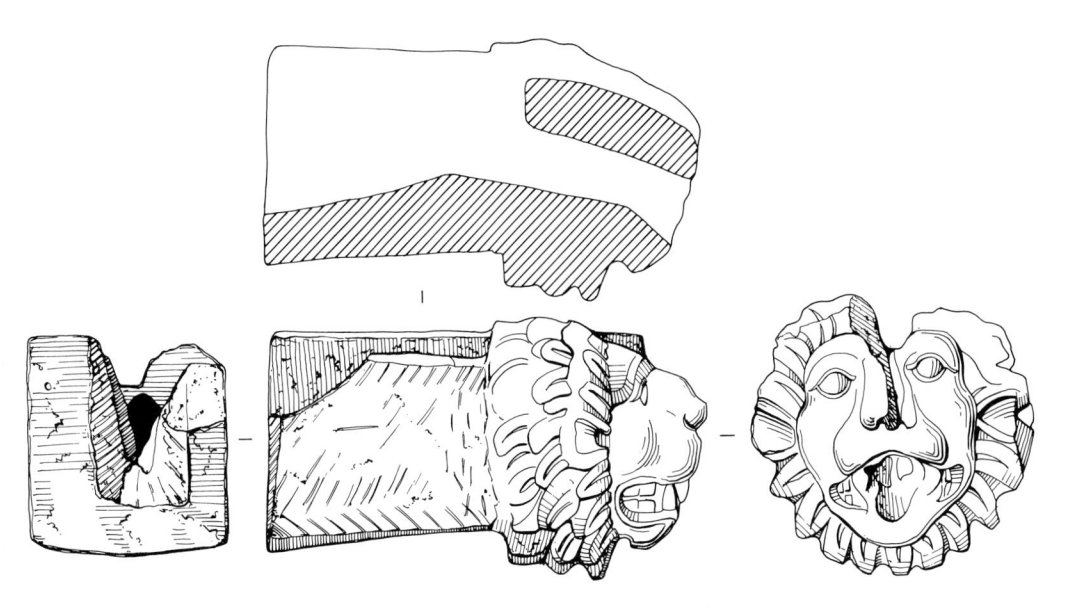

Figure 77: Drawing of the marble lion's head water spout, Inv. 73-979.

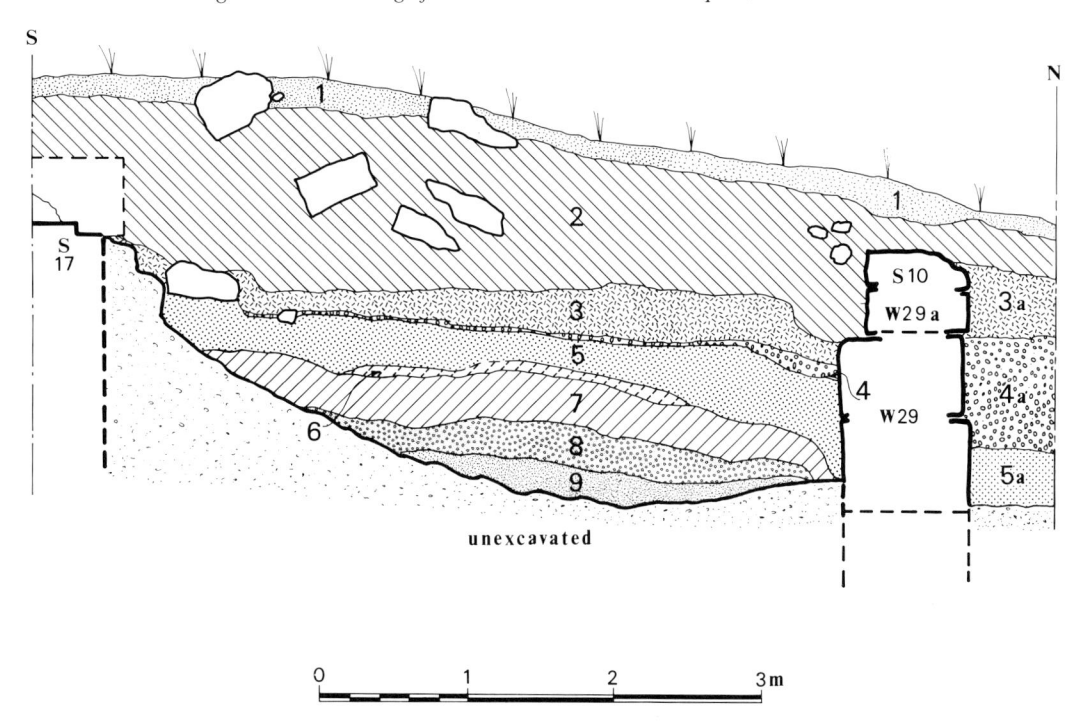

Figure 78: North-south section of fill between the Imperial S17 Southwest Building and the Hellenistic wall W29 carrying the south wall of the Imperial S10 Mosaic Chamber, drawn from east. 1:50 scale.

Courtyard Entrance?

Roughly nine m. west of the remains of what may have been the Upper Sanctuary's first propylaeum (W3) there came to light a short line of masonry that runs north to south for a distance of ca. 3.8 m. It seems clear that this stretch of masonry, designated G1 (Plan D; Figs. 11, 65, 75; Pl. 83), had at one time functioned as the threshold for a ca. 3.3 m. wide door. Its remains were excavated in D11/12, 1 and D12, balk (Fig. 12). Its broad width, together with its near proximity to the west entrance (G3) of the later Propylaeum Court (S21) with which it shares an approximately similar orientation (Plan E), suggests that the G1 doorway may at one time have given access to a similar type of court arrangement, now otherwise totally lost, that was set up north of the early Classical period S2 complex (Plan D) in association with the hypothetical W3 gateway. Arguing against such a reconstruction is the fact that wall W3 fails both to describe a true right angle with the G1 threshold as well as to align itself with the latter's north end. With so much missing between the two elements, it is difficult to restore how the two were linked, unless one is to imagine that wall W3 was shifted from its original position at the time of the construction of the later S20 Propylaeum (Plan E).

As preserved, the G1 threshold (Fig. 75) consists of two blocks. The block to the south is 2.20 m. long, 0.36 m. high, and 0.63 m. wide (block height-to-length ratio 1:6.1). As preserved the block to the north is 1.54 m. long, but its north end is broken and its original dimensions must have been similar to those of its companion. The upper surface of the south block is cut down 0.06 m. to provide a clear indication of the southern limit of the actual threshold. The shoulder left to support the missing vertical jamb-post is 0.55 m. wide. If the same total length is restored to the north block, the threshold width works out to approximately 3.30 m. and the combined width of both blocks to ca. 4.50 m. Three or possibly four differently sized cuttings that functioned to secure twin wooden doors are preserved in the threshold floor.

CONTEXT AND DATE OF THE G1 THRESHOLD

The line of the G1 threshold cuts across the later Classical F3 water channel. The D12 balk, 3e fill on which the G1 threshold rests (Fig. 65) plugged the water course and put the latter out of use. There can be no doubt that the doorway post-dates the water channel. St. 3e was a ca. 0.40/0.50 m. thick layer of dense light brown soil whose latest contents include lamp material dated to the fifth and fourth centuries B.C., plus an engraved bronze finger ring dated to the first half of the fourth century. Given the rather shaky grounds cited above for associating the F3 water channel (F3) with the Classical period,[40] the most that can be said for the construction of G1 is that it appears to date some time after the middle of the fourth century B.C.

Upper Sanctuary Fountain Complex and Drain

The waterproof tank and stepped base (F2) belonging to a fountain complex was brought to light 35 m. west of the G1 doorway directly east of the T17 Hellenistic peribolos wall (Plan D; Figs. 8, 11, 28, 49, 50, 76, 79; Pls. 62, 84). Their remains were excavated in C15/16, 1: 4-2; C15/16, 1, tank; D15, 2. A poorly constructed drain (F4) was unearthed directly west of wall T17 (Pl. 62) and the F2 stepped platform that may have been been associated with the F2 fountain complex. Lastly, a short line of wall (W29) that extends west from the T8 later Classical wall (Plan D) was excavated in C15/D15, 1 and C14/D14, 2 balk. It may have been part of a short-lived porch enclosure for the F2 complex.

Apart from the nearby drain, a further reason for associating the F2 steps and water tank with a fountain is the fact that a marble lion's head water spout (Fig. 77) of a type frequently used with fountains was discovered in earthquake debris a short distance to the west of the tank.[41]

The fountain steps measure 5.20 m. north-south by 2.65 m. east-west. The tank-proper measures externally ca. 4.60 by 2.20 m., while internally it is 3.60 by 1.25 m. Its greatest preserved depth occurs at the southwest corner where it is 2.10 m. deep. Both its walls and floor were originally waterproofed with at least two coats of unpainted stucco that has cracked and flaked away above the height of ca. 1.75 m. The southwest corner of the floor has broken and then settled around what may once have been a drain hole ca. 0.10 m. in diameter. There is no apparent connec-

---

40. Supra 117.
41. Inv. 73-979. White marble. L. 0.35 m. H. 0.14 m. W. 0.17 m. The piece was found between the S19 structure and the T17 wall amidst C15/16, 1, 2 earthquake debris. This means that its original location also could have been the nearby S17 Southwest Building or the colonnaded entrance to the S10 Mosaic Chamber as well as the F2 fountain (Plan E). If in fact it came from either S17 or S10 it presumably would have been a roof drain spout. But see infra 141 for fountain spouts.

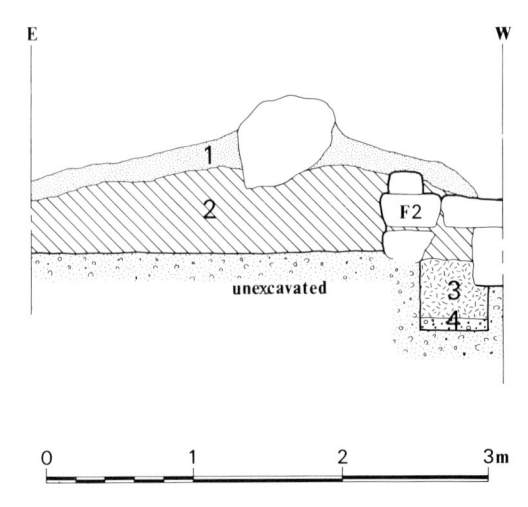

Figure 79: East-west section of fill covering the northeast corner of the F2 water tank, drawn from north. 1:50 scale.

Plate 84: The F2 fountain tank from south.

tion between this drain hole and the F4 conduit west of the T17 wall.

While traces of the F2 steps appear along the north and west exterior sides of the tank, they survive best across its south side, where they are preserved as a series of two precisely cut risers (Fig. 76). The upper step projects 0.20 m. beyond the outer face of the tank. The lower treader is 0.27 m. wide. The upper riser is 0.20 m. high, the lower 0.30 m. At the southeast corner both steps were trimmed back to allow passage of the stereobate course of the Southwest Building (S17), which accordingly has to postdate their construction.

Whatever stepped arrangement existed across the principal, east face of the tank is still buried under the unexcavated east balk of C15/16, 1. The steps, however, on the north and south sides are placed ca. 0.50 to 0.60 m. above the level of the tank bottom (Figs. 8, 76). It seems likely that the steps across the east face were set at a lower level, since bedrock appears to fall away to the east. Otherwise, too little is known of the front of this hypothetical fountain house to suggest any restoration of its appearance, including the placement of the marble lion's head spout found directly to its rear.

The W29 wall to the north and northeast of the F2 steps abuts the end of the continuation of the later Classical peribolos T8 wall but then deflects from its line by ca. fifteen degrees to the north (Plan D). Approximately three m. of W29's length has been exposed beneath the euthynteria (wall W29a) of the entrance colonnade to the S10 Mosaic Chamber (Plan E). Its width is ca. 0.85 m. (Fig. 78). Three of its courses are preserved to a combined height of 1.50 m. Its top preserved course is leveled with the bottom of the F2 tank; bedrock beneath its lowest course is ca. 1.15 m. lower than the tank bottom.

Since W29 parallels the north and south walls of the F2 steps, it may have originally risen to a higher level to form part of a porch in front of the fountain complex. If a similar wall ever existed to the south, it must have been removed at the time of the construction of the Southwest Building (S17).

The F4 conduit west of the F2 tank and steps is roughly constructed out of two parallel rows of blocks, ca. 0.40 m. high and set 0.30 to 0.40 m. apart. It is covered with slabs of varying widths and does not seem to have been furnished with a stone bottom but instead relied on a hard-pan floor to carry away its contents. This argues that the F4 conduit was built either as a storm drain or to empty the adjacent tank, i.e., its use was occasional and it did not serve as a fill-pipe carrying water on a continuous basis.

Its line runs tangentially to the west face of wall T17 for ca. two m. where it jogs to the west for a distance of ca. one m. and then resumes its parallel course to T17 for another 4.60 m. Both its beginning and end are lost under the unexcavated balks surrounding C15/16, 1. Where excavated, the drain nowhere passes through wall T17 nor does it appear to connect directly with the F2 tank. On the other hand, it is at least theoretically possible that its line turned east beneath the north balk of C15/16, 1, crossed under wall T17, and doubled back to establish some kind of linkup with the tank from its north.

While the level of the drain's earth floor is today slightly higher (ca. 0.14 m.) than the bottom of the tank, given the amount of disturbance experienced by the tank, the difference is not enough to rule out a link between the two.

CONTEXT AND DATE OF THE F2 PODIUM AND WALL W29

The fact that the terrain immediately surrounding the F2 steps could be only partly explored complicates the dating of its construction.

Starting with the C15/D15 balk (Fig. 78), levels 7 and 8 above the St. 9 sterile terra rossa level are occupation layers that predate the construction of both the Southwest Building (S17) and wall W29 to its north; both layers contain bones and fragments of unidentified but apparently early pottery. The builders of the lower two courses of wall W29 then dug into St. 7, 8, and 9 in order to set their wall on bedrock; St. 5 represents their backfill. It contains a mixture of Archaic and late Hellenistic wares, including an Eastern Sigillata A dish dating from the late second century B.C. to the beginning of the first century A.D. It also contains a bronze coin dating ca. 145-104 B.C., which suggests that wall W29 was a product of the late Hellenistic period, if not the early Imperial period. An Hellenistic date is to some extent corroborated by the fill to the north of wall W29 where the lowest course is buried in St. 5a fill that contained a fifth century lamp along with Archaic potsherds. The succeeding stratum, 4a, however, represents a backfill against W29 to support a floor leveled with the wall's top. St. 4a contains a vertically ribbed "Gnathian" sherd, not examined by Kenrick, that presumably places the floor and perhaps the wall in the Hellenistic period.

A limited *sondage* by the outer northeast corner of the F2 steps (Fig. 79) indicates that the lowest step rests on a buildup of at least two strata: D15, 2, 3 and 4. St. 3 consists of ca. 0.40 m. of reddish brown earth, slightly clay-like in texture and containing numerous broken bones and ash. Its top is leveled with the euthynteria (W29a) for the S10 southern colonnade. St. 4, of which only the upper few centimeters could be cleared, is harder and more clay-like. Its upper surface corresponds in level with the top of wall W29 and therefore with the St. 5 backfill left by the builders of wall W29 in C15/D15 to the east.

While too little of D15, 2, 4 was removed to yield any evidence for a date, the contents of St. 3 are important, since in addition to the bones and ash already mentioned, it brought to light several blown glass fragments not included by Oliver but dateable to the early Imperial period. While they could mean that the F2 steps and tank ought to date ca. A.D. 50, the greater likelihood seems to be that D15, 2, 3 represents a back-fill carried out at the time of the construction of the S10 Porticoed Chamber. In this regard it is noteworthy that its excavator found no trace of a foundation trench south of W29a to argue that its builders set the euthynteria into preexistent fill. Instead, St. 3 appears to post-date the erection of W29a. As already stated, wall W29—our hypothetical porch enclosure wall dated by the C15/D15, 1, 5 stratum fill to the Hellenistic period—must precede W29a that overrides its line. D15, 2, 4 beneath the fountain steps moreover seems to represent the continuation of C15/D15, 1, 5 and consequently may also be assigned, together with the F2 tank and steps, to the Hellenistic period.

If this interpretation of D15, 2, 3 errs to the extent that it belongs instead to the construction of the tank steps, it is worth recalling that the latest possible date for the Eastern Sigillata A dish reported above from C15/D15, 1, 5 is the early Imperial period. Future investigation of this area could succeed in elevating the date of both wall W29 and the F2 fountain to that period. Based, however, on the information presently available, a date late in the Hellenistic period seems preferable, thus making the F2 fountain complex contemporary with the W3 gateway and peribolos renovations.

CONTEXT AND DATE OF THE F4 CONDUIT

The drain stratigraphy has been discussed above in relation to wall T17.[42] A tan-brown stratum, C15/16, 1:4-2, 4, overlies the St. 5 fifth century layer and buries the conduit to within 0.10 m. of its cover slabs. St. 4 contained relatively abundant later Hellenistic material. After the drain fell into disuse, its side walls and cover slabs were pulled apart, which allowed its interior to fill up with St. 4 earth that had been used to bury partially the drain at the time of its construction. A late Hellenistic date for the conduit therefore seems secure.

COMMENTARY

Too little is known of the F2 fountain to permit much in the way of comparison with other fountains, since its sole reasonably well preserved feature is the waterproofed rectangular tank. Beyond that, one can conjecture that it used one or more marble lion's head water spouts on its still unexcavated east facade and that it may have been fronted by a porch, of which wall W29 is the only surviving part.

The best local comparative example of a fountain with a similarly proportioned tank enclosed by projecting wing walls is the Hellenistic period *Fountain with the Doric Colonnade*, located near the center of Cyrene's Sanctuary of Apollo directly west of the Roman Propylaeum.[43] Apart from its tank arrangement, the most

---

42. For a discussion of the F4 drain's stratigraphy (C15/16, 1:4-2) in relation to wall T17, see supra 127.

43. Stucchi, *Architettura* 141, figs. 116, 117, pl. I, no. 30. Goodchild, *Kyrene* fig. 13, no. 9 and fig. 56. Bacchielli (supra n. 15) fig. 5, pl. 1.

important aspect of this installation is the five Doric columns embedded in its tank's front and side walls and the six Doric columns (four free-standing; two half columns) that make up its prostyle porch. Its plan recalls the Roman period fountain near the southeast edge of the outer court at Eleusis, which Orlandos has argued represents a type usually associated with sanctuaries connected with shrines.[44] Since, however, the colonnade forming the south side of the S10 Porticoed Chamber cannot be directly tied to the F2 fountain, there is no proof that columns were a feature shared by all three fountains, nor is there any direct evidence that the Apollo Sanctuary fountain necessarily used lion's head spouts.[45]

Apart from roof drains, lion's head spouts are best attested regionally at Ptolemais where Kraeling found two sandstone examples used to deliver water to the frigidarium of the City Bath.[46] The *Fountain of the Nymph Kurana* in Cyrene's Apollo Sanctuary[47] used the mouth of the lion strangled by the nymph to feed water into a semicircular basin but otherwise shares little in common with the present example. Outside of the province lion's head spouts occur too frequently to require further comment, although the the Nymphaeum of Herodes Atticus at Olympia should be added to the examples already gathered by Kraeling,[48] since the Olympia spouts are indisputably associated with fountain basins.[49]

F1 Fountain and R3 Steps

A small rusticated fountain house (F1) was installed toward the center of the eastern end of the Middle Sanctuary in F11/12, 1 and E11/12, slope during the same period (Plan D; Figs. 2, 10, 80, 81; Pls. 85, 86). Flanked by flights of steps (R3) cut into the bedrock, the little fountain was erected on a shoulder of the bedrock slope where the limestone shelf abruptly drops nearly two m. (Fig. 2). The bulk of its remains consists of two short parallel walls of yellowish limestone. Its east wall (Fig. 81, left) is preserved to a height of three courses or ca. 1.30 m.; its length is 1.50 m., and its thickness 0.45 m. The west wall (Fig. 81, right) is four courses high or 2.20 m.; its length is 1.80 m. and its thickness 0.45 m. Blocks for a possible fifth course have turned up in fill from the immediate vicinity.

There are no traces of a front wall. The back of the installation is formed by the natural bedrock shoulder, which was dressed in antiquity to the present level of the top of the west wall. It is not clear how the upper parts of the rear and side walls were completed, but they may have risen several additional courses and then were roofed over to create a box-like compartment, framing the rocky shelf. Alternatively, the back wall may have been kept open and the complex left unroofed.

The builders of this little structure seem to have been anxious to preserve as much of the original rusticated appearance of its inner rocky shelf as possible. The most important interior features are two pits or basin-like natural crevices. The upper is a long, irregularly shaped depression (1.30 m. long, 0.45 m. wide, 0.50 m. deep) that takes up most of the rocky shelf across the rear at the level of the top of the second course of masonry. A second roughly similar crevice (1.00 by 0.45 by 0.40 m.) is located beneath the first at the level of the footings of the side walls. The two interconnect through a hole at the west side. The eastern edge of the upper pit has been worn by water spilling over its rock lip into the basin below, whose surface was coated with a pink waterproof plaster. Traces of plaster also appear on the hole linking the two pits as well as on the worn spillway. Both crevices contained debris when excavated, but it is impossible to say whether this was earthquake rubbish, implying that they remained open until the end of the sanctuary's active use, or was part of an earlier plugging-up with earth.

Traces of wear in the stone suggest that water entered the upper basin through a vertical crack in the southwest corner of the bedrock shoulder, but no evidence was recovered to indicate how the water was led to this point, nor is it clear how it would have been disposed of once it had filled the lower basin. With no traces of channeling in the bedrock, it has to be imagined that the upper basin was filled by a pipe run above ground that was dismantled before the final destruction, unless, as seems less likely, it was fed by a natural spring in the bedrock now dried up.

---

44. A. Orlandos, *ArchEph* (1916) 101. Mylonas, *Eleusis* 166, n. 22, figs. 3, 4, no. 3.
45. Two holes in the forward edge of the tank mark the places where some kind of spout originally introduced water into the shallow basin set between the two colonnades. These may have been lions' heads.

46. Kraeling, *Ptolemais* 162, 165, 193, pl. XLII, A. The frigidarium, formed by a large rectangular open court, had a sunken octagonal pool at its center in which was found the first spout. The second lion's head turned up in the south portico. According to their excavator, both were originally placed on the tops of the south and west walls of the court and were used to lead water into a channel in the southwest corner of the frigidarium and, in the case of one of the spouts, to feed the octagonal pool. Stylistically neither resembles Inv. 73-979.
47. Stucchi, *Architettura* 113, n. 11, 481-82, fig. 498, pl. I, no. 16.
48. Kraeling, *Ptolemais* 194, ns. 53, 54.
49. H. Shleif and H. Weber, *Olympische Forschungen* I (Berlin 1944) 72, fig. 14, pl. 36.

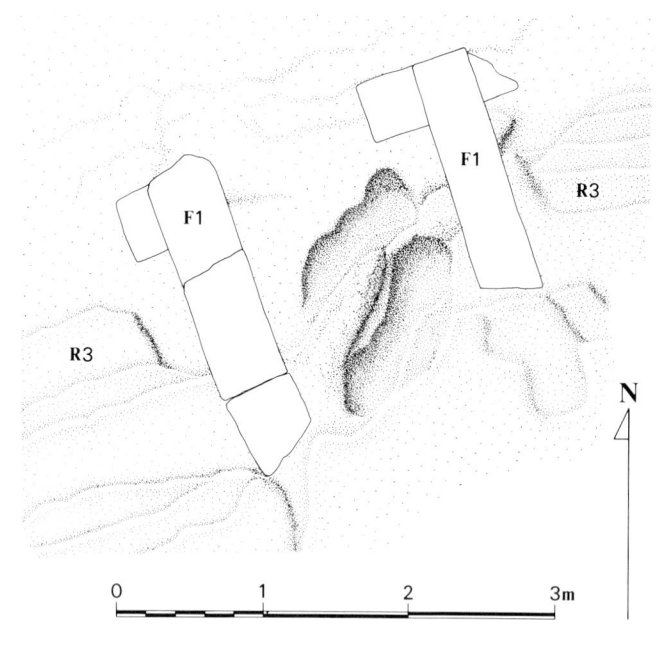

Figure 80: Plan of the F1 fountain. 1:50 scale.

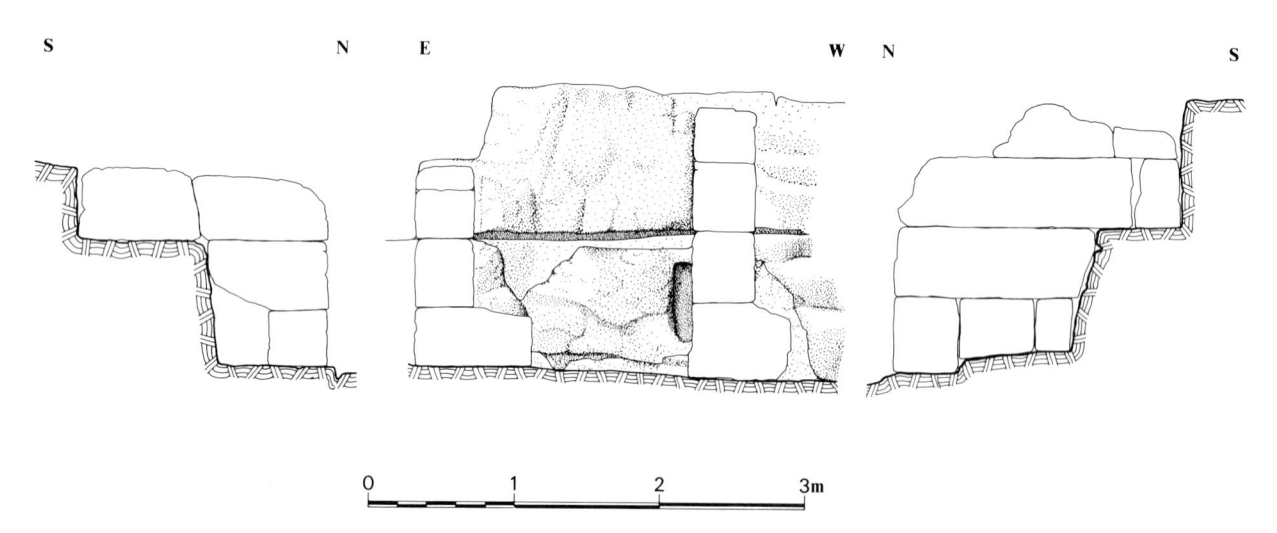

Figure 81: Elevation of the F1 fountain's walls, drawn from the east, north, and west. 1:50 scale.

The bedrock between the east wall of F1 and the nearby S7 Sacred Building was cut to form two steps (R3). Above these the rock is worn smooth by foot traffic. West of the fountain the natural pavement was cut into seven steps, and once again the bedrock in front of the fountain house and to its west was worn smooth. From this it is obvious that most of the rocky slope in this sector remained clear of soil through much of the active history of the sanctuary, with only thin patches of earth covering the natural pockets or depressions in the bedrock. The traffic pattern worn into the limestone pavement leads from the zone in front of the S7 Sacred House across the front of the F1 fountain house and up the stairs (R3) to the north facade of the early Imperial S8 Sacred House (Plan E).

CONTEXT AND DATE OF THE F1 FOUNTAIN AND R3 STEPS

Most of the fill in F11/12, 1 (Fig. 53) covering the bedrock to either side and in front of the F1 fountain consists of deep layers of St. 2 earthquake and St. 1 cultivation detritus. In contrast to the slope rising southeast of the F1 fountain that

THE HELLENISTIC, EARLY ROMAN SANCTUARY

Plate 85:   The F1 fountain house and S7 Sacred House from northwest.

Plate 86:   The F1 fountain house and R3 steps from northeast.

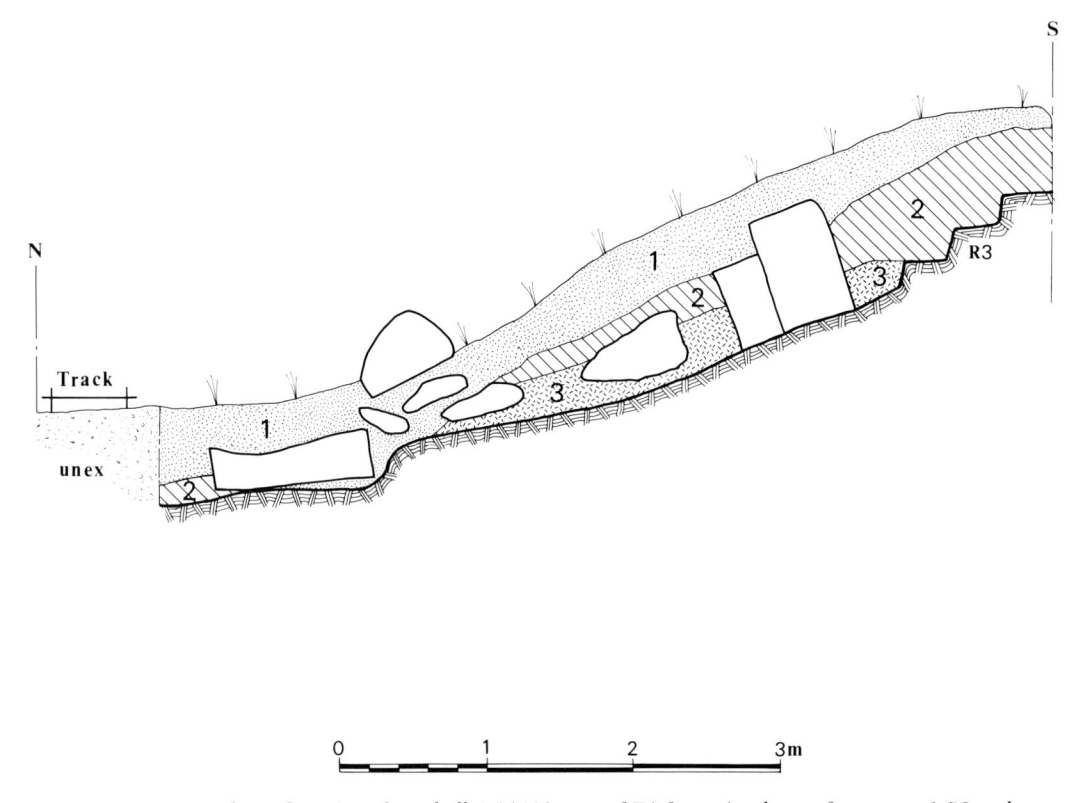

Figure 82: North-south section of east balk F11/12, east of F1 fountain, drawn from west. 1:50 scale.

is largely bare to bedrock, the slope below the eastern set of the R3 steps experienced a fair amount of F11/12 1, 3 soil buildup during the active use of the sanctuary, probably left to level off the natural breaks and sink holes that break up the limestone pavement at this level (Fig. 82). F11/12, 1, 3 consists of a reddish brown argillaceous fill, in places 0.30 m. thick, that ran up to the outer eastern face of the fountain house. A meter west of the fountain the same St. 3 fill is restricted to patches of soil simply covering the depressions in the bedrock. The same fill spread across the interior of the fountain house but contained no dateable artifacts. Elsewhere F11/12, 1, 3 contained a number of Hellenistic-Roman sculpture fragments, including a limestone hand holding a dove, and four Hellenistic bronze coins of which the latest dates to the second half of the second century. A close association between the St. 3 fill and the actual construction of the F1 fountain is impossible to establish. Nevertheless, at the very least the fill represents an occupation layer contemporary with at least some phase of the fountain's usage and, as such, provides the sole clue to its period, which should be post-Classical.

COMMENTARY

The impression generated by the F1 fountain is that it represented a rural fountain transposed into a sanctuary enviroment. While enigmatic to the extent that it cannot be closely dated, its essential function as a water source is beyond dispute. Like the architecturally more polished F2 fountain at the western end of the Upper Sanctuary and the nearby year-round spring Ain Bou Gadir,[50] it served as an important component in the general water supply system for the sanctuary grounds.

Taken in this sense its association with the resident cult has numerous precedents in the layout of other Demeter sanctuaries, beginning with Eleusis where several water sources are part of the resident myth.[51] In addition Pausanias refers often to water sources in association with other mainland Greek Demeter sanc-

---

50. Located 54 m. west of the Lower Sanctuary. *Final Reports* I, 36, fig. 39.

51. In the *Hymn. Hom. Cer.* 99 Demeter travels to Eleusis disguised as an old woman where she sits down at the *Parthenion* or "Virgin's Well" used by the local inhabitants for water. According to Kerenyi, the same well is called *Kallichoron* or "Well of the Beautiful Dances" on line 273, while in other versions of the story (Paus. 1.39.1) it reappears as the *Anthion* or "Well of the Flowers." Kerenyi, *Eleusis* 36-37, fig. 6. Mylonas, *Eleusis* 44, 45, 150, prefers to see the *Parthenion* and *Kallichoron* as separate wells, with the name *Kallichoron* eventually transferred to the former. In addition to these legendary associations and the various cisterns and Hadrianic aqueduct recorded at Eleusis, the outer court of the sanctuary was provided in the Roman period with the fountain house located east of the Greater Propylaea and next to the triumphal arch. See Mylonas, *Eleusis* 150-51, 165-66, 183-84, figs. 3, 4, no. 3. Kerenyi, *Eleusis* 71.

tuaries.[52] In the case of Asia Minor the best archaeologically recorded connection of water with Demeter's cult seems to be provided by Pergamon where a handsome fountain house was set up in the southeast corner of its sanctuary of Demeter. This was rebuilt around the same time as the Eleusinian version.[53] The Sicilian strain of Demeter's myth has its own quota of water references. The scene of the actual rape was placed either next to the Fountain of Cyane in the outskirts of Syracuse[54] or on the shores of Lake Pergusa near Enna.[55] The legend's association with Syracuse was reenacted in Diodorus' day by a rural festival in honor of Persephone in which sacrificial bulls were driven and apparently drowned in the waters of the Fountain of Cyane. The shrine to the water nymph and Persephone must have already existed by the banks of the tributary stream of the river Anapos by the begining of the fourth century B.C., if not considerably earlier.[56]

Elsewhere, from the Archaic period onwards, the Demeter Malophoros Sanctuary, built outside the defensive enceinte of Selinus, was supplied with water brought in from a spring located ca. 200 m. to its northwest by a stone conduit, which crossed the walled precinct to fill a small reservoir basin directly in front of the megaron.[57] The central placement of the basin argues that it played an important part in the practice of the cult. Other island sanctuaries corroborate the same centrality of water to the cult.[58]

---

52. The Sanctuary of Demeter, presumably the transplanted Temple of Demeter from Thoricus, was relocated in the southeast corner of the Athenian Agora immediately above the *Enneakrounos*. Paus. 1.14.1-4. H. Thompson, "Activities in the Athenian Agora: 1959," *Hesperia* 29 (1960) 334-43. R. Wycherley, *The Stones of Athens* (Princeton 1978) 85, 261. But see Travlos, *Pictorial Dictionary* 204 for the identification of a second, alternative *Enneakrounos*. Elsewhere, the Attic streams called the Rheitoi, which were consecrated to Demeter and Persephone, fed a salt-water lake near the Athens-Eleusis border; the lake's fish were reserved for the goddesses' priesthood. Paus. 1.38.1. The Karnasian grove near Oichalia in the Messenian plain contained a statue of Persephone, the Pure One, set next to a spring. Paus. 4.33.4. The Temple and Grove of Demeter in the Marsh was erected near a river outside the Marsh Gates of Megalopolis. Paus. 8.36.6. In Arcadia the Sanctuary of Eleusinian Demeter near Thaliades and the Sanctuary of Demeter at Onkion both rose by the banks of the river Ladon, in which Demeter washed away the stain of her rape by Poseidon disguised as a horse. Paus. 8.25.2-7. The incomplete (by Pausanias's day) sanctuary of Demeter and Kore at Skolos in Boeotia was erected by the banks of the river Asopos, Paus. 9.4.3, while the sanctuary of Mykallessian Demeter was constructed by the Euripos on the border of Boeotia and Euboia. Paus. 9.19.5. The oracular sanctuary of Demeter near Achaean Patrai was organized around the underground springhouse erected in front of her temple. Paus. 7.21.4-5: "There is a spring in front of Demeter's sanctuary with a dry stone wall on the temple side and a way down to the spring on the outer side. There is an infallible oracle here, not for all purposes but for the sick. They tie a mirror onto some thin kind of cord, and balance it so as not to dip it into the spring, but let the surface of the mirror just lightly touch the water. Then they pray to the goddesses and burn incense and look into the mirror, and it shows them the sick man either alive or dead. The water is as truthful as that" (trans. P. Levi, Penguin ed. [Middlesex 1971] Vol. 1, 283-84). See ibid. n. 107 for an interesting reference to the veneration of the head of St. Andrew once kept in the springhouse. Also see R. Flacelière, *Greek Oracles* (London 1965) 14 and M. Ninck, *Die Bedeutung des Wassers im Kult und Leben der Alten* (Leipzig 1921) 50. The sanctuary of Panachaian Demeter at Aigion was built by a spring. Paus. 7.24.2-3: "The beach where Aigion has all these sanctuaries gives a generous supply of water; it is delightful to see and drink from the spring" (Levi trans., ibid. Vol. 1, 292). The ruins of the sanctuary of Demeter and Kore at Potniai in Boeotia were associated in Pausanias's day with running water. Paus. 9.8.1. See Levi trans., ibid. Vol. 1, 324, n. 42 for a possible identification of this sanctuary with Classical ruins built into the modern springs near Tachi south of Thebes. The *Mysaeum* or sanctuary of Mysian Demeter near Pellene contained a sacred grove and springs. Paus. 7.27.9. M. Nilsson, *Griechische Feste* (Leipzig 1906) 327.

53. Bohtz, *Pergamon* 15-16, pls. 6, 3 and 33. Gruben, *Greek Temples* 490, fig. 151: "A holy fountain that, during imperial times under Antoninus Pius, had to submit to being given a more magnificent form, with a semicircular recess in which the water rushed down in three powerful jets."

54. Cic., *Verr.* 4.48. Ov., *Met.* 5.409 ff. Diod. Sic. 5.4. Pliny, *NH* 3.89. Ael., *VH* 2.63. Claud., *Rapt. Pros.* 2.61. *RE* 11, 2 (1922) 2234, *s.v.* Kyane (Ziegler).

55. Ov., *Met.* 5.385. *Fast.* 4.325. Claud., *Rapt. Pros.* 1.198. For an expansive discussion of the ancient sources see E. Freeman, *History of Sicily from the Earliest Times* I (Oxford 1891) appendix XI, 530-42.

56. Dionysios led a raid against the Carthaginians past the Temple of Cyane in 396 B.C. Diod. Sic. 14.72. Diodorus's legend places the origin of the ritual association of bull sacrifice with water in the time of Heracles, i.e., in prehistoric times. For its supposed connection with Punic religion see F. Movers, *Die Phoenizier* (Bonn 1856) 325 ff., against which E. Ciaceri, *Culti e miti della storia dell'antica Sicilia* III (Catania 1911) 465, n. 3. F. Cavallari believed that he had located the actual ruins of Cyane's shrine in a spot known locally as Cozzo di Scandurra, *NSc* 1887, 330 ff., but the identification was convincingly overturned by P. Orsi, who argued that the actual sanctuary building had been dismantled and its stones carried off for new buildings: *MonPiot* 22 (1916) 131-62, pls. XV, XVI. In Orsi's view, however, the sanctuary, with which he would associate the so-called Laganello head in the Syracuse Museum, was originally located near the fountain where the head was recovered early in the last century. If the association of head with sanctuary is to be accepted, Cyane's shrine ought to have originated rather early in the sixth century B.C. For her possible portrayal on later coins see D. White, "The Morris Coin," *Expedition* 28, 3 (1986) 3-21.

57. Gabrici, *Malophoros* 62-64, figs. 34-36, 77, 88.

58. Probably the most disputed water sources associated with Demeter's cult in Sicily are at Acragas, where the "rock sanctuary" beneath S. Biagio housed some kind of pre-Greek settlement, possibly even a sanctuary. This was built at the foot of the rocky scarp of the *Rupe Atenea* outside the later line of the Greek defensive walls. The site consisted of two grottos, whether natural or man-made being a matter of some debate. By the Archaic period the grottos came to be used to store terracotta figurines and busts of Demeter and Kore; they continued to be used in this manner until the Punic destruction of Acragas in 406 B.C. During the Timoleontic period, if not earlier, a narrow building was erected in front of the grottos to collect and

While the above examples make clear that water had an important place in the physical layouts of Demeter-Kore sanctuaries as well as their legends,[59] the actual uses to which water was put require some further explanation. Much of the water used in all sanctuaries (i.e., not just Demeter's) must have served for normal drinking and personal hygiene. In addition, some must have been used for preparing ritual meals and the subsequent washing up of the cooking and eating implements.[60] The hydraulic facilities discovered in several of the dining rooms in the Demeter Sanctuary on Acrocorinth are said to have been used for eating and washing,[61] and it seems equally probable that many of the water installations already listed in connection with mainland Greece, Sicily and elsewhere, including the Cyrene sanctuary where the dining facilities remain to be discovered,[62] were designed for similar non-ceremonial use.

On the other hand, water also had a direct part to play in ritual, a fact borne out particularly well by the evidence from Eleusis where there existed an official called the *Hydranos*. This person was responsible for purifying initiates by sprinkling them with water, a rite Mylonas has compared with Christian baptism,[63] citing the gloss in Hesychios which calls the *Hydranos* "purifier of the Eleusinians."[64] Clinton is unsure whether the passage refers to an actual priest,[65] and Pringsheim has suggested that the title of *Hydranos* could be assumed by anyone qualified to prepare initiates, in particular the members of the Eumolpids and the Kerykes.[66] A fourth century B.C. relief from Eleusis in the Athens National Museum may depict the Kore as *Hydranos* (who therefore could be a woman as well as a man), pouring water over the head of a mortal hero.[67] On the Lovatelli urn found near

---

distribute water. What still remains to be settled is whether the water, tapped from aquifers deep inside the hill, bypassed the grottos or not. And if it did not, how was it associated with the Archaic-Classical votives? In other words, was the site really a fountain sanctuary associated with Demeter during the Archaic-Classical period, or were the grottos used simply as storage areas that happened to be located close to a water source? For references to further discussion of what has considerable significance for the theoretical connection between pre-Greek water cults and Demeter, cf. supra 37, n. 27. The second area lies southeast of Acragas's colossal Temple of Zeus where a long portico building, associated with cisterns, water canals, and a large water tank filled at the time of its excavation with terracotta figurines and other votive objects, was erected in the second half of the fourth century B.C. The exact nature of the complex remains to be fully determined but seems at this juncture to have possessed a religious as well as practical character. The cult was chthonian and possibly devoted to Tyche, Artemis, Demeter, and Kore, while it has been argued that the tank was used for cathartic baths and ritual ablution. See E. De Miro, *MonAnt* 46 (1963) 81-198, esp. 189-95. P. Orlandini, *Princeton* 25. Elsewhere in Sicily, one of the niches at the back of the the cave associated with Demeter and Persephone at Enna contained a small spring. O. Rossbach, *Castrogiovanni, das alte Henna in Sizilien* (Leipzig 1912) 9. G. Zuntz, *Klearchos* 20 (1963) 120. D. White, *Hagne Thea, A Study of Sicilian Demeter* (Princeton University doctoral thesis, 1963) 109-16. At Morgantina the North Demeter Sanctuary by the city wall ca. 300 m. to the northwest of the Agora consisted of two domestic house complexes, separated by a street. The north house contained a small adyton-like chamber in its northwest corner equipped with a washing area, while directly to its east was a room containing a columnar-shaped altar. Its excavator has suggested that the washing area was used for ritual ablution connected with sacrifice. E. Sjöqvist, "Timoleonte e Morgantina," *Kokalos* 4 (1958) 8-9, figs. 1, 2. M. Bell, *Morgantina Studies* I: *The Terracottas* (Princeton 1981) 249-54, pl. 1, fig. d, for discussion and bibliography. Also see ibid. 98-103 for the cult of Demeter and Persephone at this site. The South Demeter Sanctuary at the same site, located ca. 100 m. to the southwest of Morgantina's theater, also contains an altar room, next to which was again an adyton-type chamber equipped with a lustral area "shaped quite like a modern shower stall." E. Sjöqvist, "Excavations at Morgantina 1959," *AJA* 64 (1960) 134. See also Bell, ibid. 254-56. Two additional house shrines, equipped with similar arrangements and dedicated to Demeter and Kore, have been identified in the same city but remain to be published in any detail. E. Stillwell, *Princeton* 594-95. When it is described more fully, the enigmatic Area VI Hellenistic sanctuary-bath structure may provide significant additional information for the role of water in Demeter's Sicilian cult. H. Allen, "Excavations at Morgantina (Serra Orlando) 1970-72," *AJA* 78 (1974) 370-82, esp. 372, 373, 381. Bell, ibid. 249. Finally, the discovery of yet another Demeter sanctuary may be in store in the region of S. Francesco. See *AR* 34 (1987-88) 136.

59. See also Nilsson (supra n. 52) 348, n. 3.

60. "And as he spake a certain Pharisee besought him to dine with him; and he went in, and sat down to meat. And when the Pharisee saw it, he marvelled that he had not first washed before dinner. And the Lord said unto him, Now do ye Pharisees make clean the outside of the cup and platter; but your inward part is full of ravening and wickedness. Ye fools, did not he that made that which is without make that which is within also?" *Ev. Luk.* 11.37-40.

61. N. Bookidis, *Hesperia* 38 (1969) 301-02, fig. 2. N. Bookidis and J. Fisher, *Hesperia* 41 (1972) 301, 306.

62. See supra 119, n. 4 for evidence of ritual dining stemming from the Hellenistic Lamp and Pottery Dump (S18).

63. Mylonas, *Eleusis* 236, n. 61. Kerenyi accepts the identification: *Eleusis* 61, n. 47. S. Angus, *The Mystery Religions* (reprint 1928 2nd. ed. New York 1975) 81 quotes Tertullian, *De Bapt* 5: "In certain religions ... it is by baptism (*per lavacrum*) that members are initiated ... in the Apollinarian and Eleusinian rites they are baptized, and they imagine that the result of this baptism is regeneration and the remission of the penalties of their sins."

64. Hsch. *s.v.* ὑδρανός (hydranos).

65. K. Clinton, "The Sacred Officials of the Eleusinian Mysteries," *TAPA* 64 (1974) 98.

66. G. Pringsheim, *Archaeologische Beitrage zur Geschichte des Eleusinischen Kult* (Munich 1905) 22, cited by Mylonas, *Eleusis* 236, n. 61.

67. Mylonas, *Eleusis* 194, n. 22, fig. 70. Kerenyi, *Eleusis* 61, fig. 14.

the Porta Maggiore in Rome, Heracles, made recognizable by his lion's skin, holds a piglet by its hind feet over an altar; a bearded priest purifies the altar by pouring water over its surface from a jug; two additional scenes on the urn provide further proof that the rites depicted on the urn are connected with Demeter's cult and specifically with purification.[68]

The use of a jug or pitcher in association with the act of purification recalls the popularity of hydria-bearing terracotta figurine types in many Demeter sanctuaries, including the Cyrene sanctuary.[69] Diehl has argued that the prevalence of painted Eleusinian scenes on fifth and fourth century hydriai stems in part from the use of actual hydriai in purification ritual.[70] While this cannot be corroborated by the number of fragments of hydriai found in the Cyrene sanctuary,[71] it has already been observed that the large number of its miniature hydriai suggests that the shape carried at least a symbolic ritual meaning for its dedicants[72] that in turn may well have been associated with purification.

Candidates for the Lesser Mysteries at Eleusis were normally expected to be ritually sprinkled with water to cleanse themselves of traces of defilement; on occasion the initiates were even required to bathe in the waters of the Ilissos,[73] which is interesting in light of the number of references elsewhere that exist to Demeter sanctuaries erected near the banks of rivers. By the third century B.C. the mystai, accompanied by the famous cry "Initiates into the sea!," purified themselves with sea water in the course of their procession to Eleusis in celebration of the great Feast of the Mystery in mid-September.[74]

The use of water for purification in a general sense has long been noted, along with fire, sunlight, and a host of less familiar cathartic agents.[75] Rohde has shown that to purify effectively the water should be taken from running springs, moving rivers and streams, or from the sea itself, since its lustral effectiveness lay in its ability to wash away evil and carry off pollution.[76]

Finally, apart from purification, water may have been used at Eleusis to invoke the concept of the earth's fruitfulness.[77] It was also associated with the rite of sacred marriage between hierophants.[78] The specifically oracular use of water developed for Demeter's cult near Patrai,[79] appears to have been rather narrowly restricted to that particular site. There is, in any case, no direct evidence that water ever played a similar role at Cyrene.[80]

Middle Sanctuary Steps

R1 STEPS

The steps which occupy rising ground between the S5 and S6 Sacred Houses came to light in E14/15, 1, D14/E14, 1, and D14/E14, 2 (Plan D; Figs. 6, 10, 12). Merged at a late stage in the sanctuary's development with the southern outer wall of the E14 Mound (S29),[81] their line extends for five m. in an east-west direction. Two courses of risers are preserved (Fig. 6), both of which rest on the sloping bedrock. The upper course consists of four blocks that range from ca. 0.80 to 1.15 m. in length, 0.60 m. in width, and 0.25 to 0.30 m. in height. Five blocks of similar dimensions make up the surviving lower course. The resulting treader width is ca. 0.30 m.

---

68. Kerenyi, *Eleusis* 54-59, figs. 12a-12d. Contra Kerenyi, Mylonas is inclined to believe that the composition reflects the goddess's Alexandrian cult rather than her Eleusinian.
69. To be published by Uhlenbrock. See now *Knossos* 68, 184, n. 5 and E. Diehl, *Die Hydria* (Mainz 1964) 189-93.
70. Diehl (supra n. 69) 187-88.
71. M. Moore, *Final Reports* III, 24-27. *Final Reports* II, 95.
72. *Final Reports* II, 95. Most of the miniature hydriai are Corinthian. A representative selection will be published by A. Kocybala.
73. Mylonas, *Eleusis* 241, ns. 88, 89. According to Demeter's Arcadian legend localized at Thelpusa cited supra n. 52, while searching for her daughter, the goddess changed into a mare in order to escape Poseidon, who then turned himself into a stallion to mate with her. After the enraged goddess had calmed down, she washed in the river Ladon to purify herself. Freese, *Demeter* 901. Farnell, *Demeter Cult* 50, 321, n. 41.

---

74. Kerenyi, *Eleusis* 60-61, n. 46. Diehl (supra n. 69) 187, n. 121.
75. L. Farnell, *Encyclopaedia of Religion and Ethics* (ed. J. Hastings, New York 1919) 482-88. Hom., *Il.* 6.228. *Od.* 2.261. Schol. Pind., *Ol.* 11.58. Eur., *IT* 1193. *OCD* (2nd ed. Oxford 1970) 1137. W. Burkert, *Greek Religion* (Cambridge 1985) 72, 73, 77-79.
76. E. Rohde, *Psyche* II (8th. ed. New York 1966) 588-90.
77. Diehl (supra n. 69) 188, n. 123.
78. Diehl (supra n. 69) 188, n. 126.
79. Supra n. 52 for the oracular cult near Patrai.
80. There is late inscriptional evidence for possible oracular activity connected with the sanctuary, but nothing to relate it to water. Infra 180, n. 37. See also Reynolds, site inscriptions forthcoming, cat. no. **16**.
81. *Final Reports* I, 96-99, fig. 103.

Plate 87: The R4 steps embedded in the squatter period W9 wall east of the S12 chamber, from northwest.

CONTEXT AND DATE OF R1 STEPS

The bulk of the steps were sealed under a deep layer of earthquake debris at the time of their recovery. Bedrock south of their line was covered with a thin D14/E14, 1, 3 fill associated with the steps' use but not necessarily contemporary with their construction. Its latest finds are local Hellenistic fine ware and Eastern Sigillata A sherds dated to the second or possibly first century B.C.

R3 STEPS

For the Middle Sanctuary steps associated with the small F1 fountain house (Plan D; Pl. 86), see supra **xx**.

R4 STEPS

The steps, embedded in the fabric of the squatter period W9 wall, are positioned directly east of the southeast corner of the S12 chamber and north of the northwest corner of the S6 Archaic Sacred House (Plan D; Pl. 87). Their clearance took place in E16, 2 (Fig. 12). Measuring ca. three m. east to west and, as preserved, consisting of only two risers, the R4 steps are all that survives of what may have once been a more extensive set of steps leading up the rock slope to the area of the Middle Sanctuary's southwest corner and its S11 chamber. The lower step consists of a single stretcher block, ca. 1.70 m. long, 0.30 m. high and projecting ca. 0.30 m. forward of the line of the step above. One or more blocks may have been removed from its original width in the process of erecting the post-A.D. 262 squatter wall (W9) that eventually covered the line of the steps. Whatever the case may have been, the second riser course was made up of two stretchers with a combined length of ca. three m.

CONTEXT AND DATE OF R4 STEPS

The rock slope north of the R4 steps was cleared of its earth covering at some time before the A.D. 262 earthquake, and no stratigraphy survives that can be associated with their construction. The latest E15, 1, 3 finds from the earth fill over bedrock immediately east of the steps consist of pottery dated to the second and possibly the first centuries B.C., together with a significant number of fragments of marble

Middle Sanctuary Access to Upper Sanctuary

R2 STEPS, G5 DOORWAY, AND S31 STRUCTURE

The steps here were part of a larger arrangement to accommodate passage from the approximate center of the Middle Sanctuary to the level of the Upper Sanctuary (Plan D; Figs. 4, 5, 6, 83, 84; Pl. 88). All three elements (G5, R2, and S31) were buried beneath structures that in time took their place at a higher level, i.e., the Colonnaded Vestibule (S15) and Late Structure (S23/S24) (Plan E), and therefore survive in only fragmentary condition. Their excavation occurred in D13 (Area 2), 2, D13 (Area 2) N. Ext., D14 balk, D14/E14, 1 (Fig. 12).

What survives of the R2 steps consists of a low platform topped with three flat blocks abutting the north face of the T1 pseudoisodomic peribolos wall at the point where the latter joins the T8 later Classical wall (Fig. 84). The platform measures overall ca. 2.60 m. east-west and 2.25 m. north-south. Its southwest corner carries a single slab that may be left over from the steps' superstucture. At its north end two courses of foundations extend slightly beyond the line of what is probably a final, upper foundation course (Fig. 5). This latter course projects ca. 0.20 m. beyond the line of the platform-proper and may itself have been the initial riser course, ca. 0.25 m. high, for the actual steps. On the other hand, the course set above it is cut with a projecting tongue that suggests that it was designed to key into additional blocks (no longer preserved) at its same level, which would rule out the course beneath it being a true step. In any case, the step risers leading to the G5 doorway in the T1 pseudoisodomic wall were, with the exception of the previously mentioned single slab in the southwest corner, entirely removed at the time of the construction of the S24 Late Structure that overrides their western face. The three surviving platform blocks, including the block with the projecting tongue, are here interpreted as simply the support for the missing stairs.

Their identification as steps rests on the fact that two orthostate blocks from the second course of vertical uprights of the pseudoisodomic wall (T1) have been cut down 0.35 m. (Fig. 83) with the clear intention of creating a 1.75 m. wide doorway (G5) through the T1 wall at a level 0.75 m. above the platform proper (Fig. 84). This leaves space for two additional risers ca. 0.25 m. high and 0.55 m. deep to bring the R2 steps to the level of the G5 door, which was itself eventually blocked up at the time of the construction of the S15 Colonnaded Vestibule. The level of the missing top step is indicated by a drafted margin across the face of the T1 bislabs.

The steps are restored (Plan D) as curving slightly to the north-northeast to comply with the present position of their north end. The deflection, however, may stem from the fact that they were shoved out of their original right-angled alignment with wall T1 in the course of later alterations.

Plate 88: The R2 steps and blocked-up G5 and G6 doorways leading from the Middle to the Upper Sanctuary, from north.

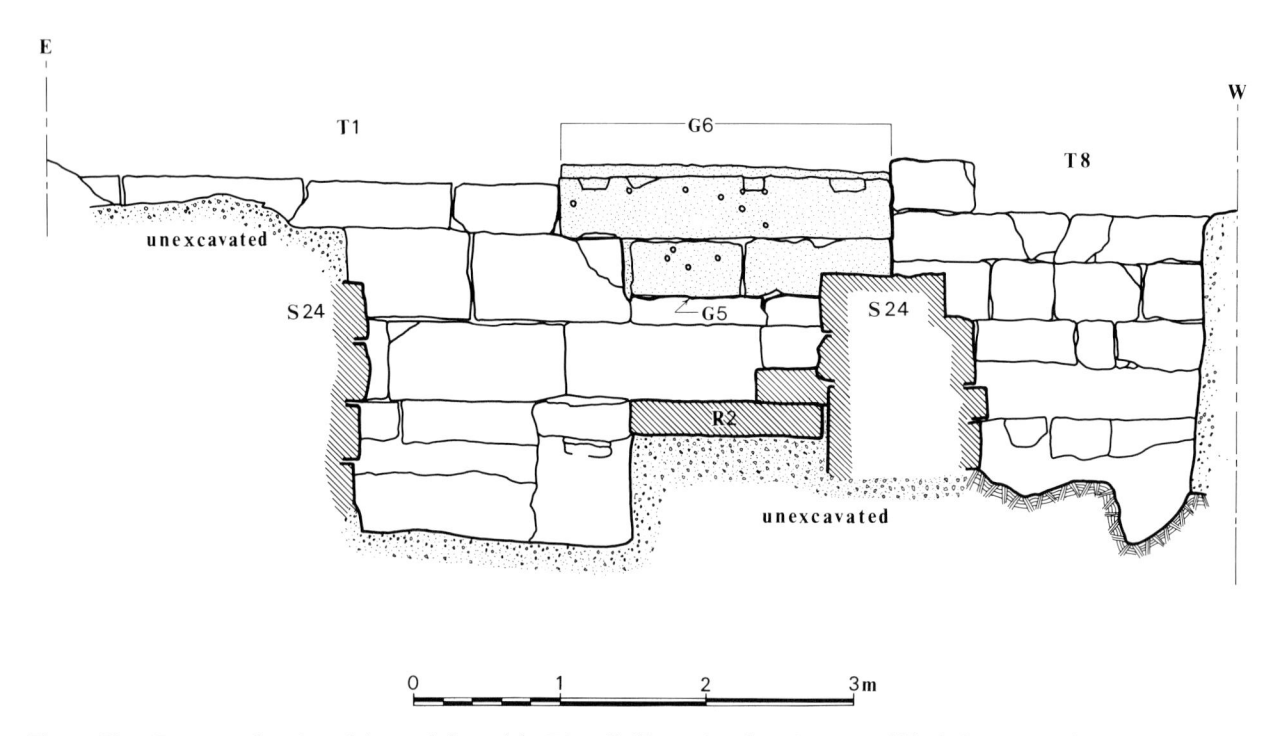

Figure 83: East-west elevation of the north face of the T8 wall, illustrating the R2 steps and blocked-up G5 and G6 doorways from the north. 1:50 scale.

The steps' platform is flanked by the remains of two sets of walls (W32 and W33) that are interpreted as belonging to the original Middle Sanctuary setting (S31) for an entrance to the Upper Sanctuary. The S31 entrance was superseded in time by the so-called Late Structure (S23/S24), which incorporated the heavy L-shaped W32 wall to the east into the basement of its eastern chamber (S24). The western unit (W33), which also formed a corner, was later submerged beneath the walls of S23.

Wall W32 is preserved to a height of three courses of large limestone headers and stretchers, averaging 1.20 to 1.30 m. long, 0.60 to 0.68 m. wide, and 0.22 to 0.40 m. high. It extends 2.45 m. north of wall T1 where it forms a right-angle corner that breaks off its return to the west after a distance of ca. 0.70 m. A fair amount of pushing and shoving has occurred since antiquity, with the result that wall W32 no longer forms a perfect right angle with either wall T1 or with what is taken to be its continuation west, i.e., wall W33, but enough congruency exists between the various parts to hypothesize the existence of a small rectangular enclosure (S31), constructed to box in the R2 steps leading to the G5 entrance to the Upper Sanctuary.

The upper, fourth course of W32, running north-south is partly built from reused material and seems clearly later than the remainder of the wall it overrides. It therefore seems to be an addition belonging to the time of the S24 east room of the Late Structure.

The northwest corner (W33) of the hypothetical S31 step entrance enclosure is preserved in two sets of blocks from the lowest courses of the west and north walls of the Late Structure's Room S23 (Fig. 60). They are distinguished from the walls that override them by their slightly different orientations which together form a proper right-angled corner aligned with the S31 enclosure's northeast corner (W32).

The block heights are ca. 0.30 to 0.32 m., their lengths vary between ca. 0.60 and 0.80 m. The end block of the north wall has a drafted margin that breaks off at its east end to indicate that the block was originally longer than it is today (Fig. 60).

CONTEXT AND DATE OF THE S31 STRUCTURE, R2 STEPS, AND G5 DOORWAY

The interior northwest corner of the S31 entrance enclosure is set on a thin bed of sterile terra rossa fill, while the exterior face of its north wall rises over a rubble layer covering the terra rossa, which once again yields nothing by which to date the structure.

The R2 steps rest on a light grey earth D13 (Area 2) 2, 2 fill mixed with marble chips and numerous small rubble stones that is ca. 0.70 m. deep. Moving north St. 2 is succeeded by a ca. 0.30 m. deep St. 3 burnt layer over the sterile St. 4 terra rossa and bedrock. Although recovered at a lower level than St. 2, the burnt stratum seems to be associated with the rubble foundations of the east wall of the Late Structure's S24 Room and must post-date St. 2. The St. 3 finds, however, are all pre-Hellenistic, and an alternative possibil-

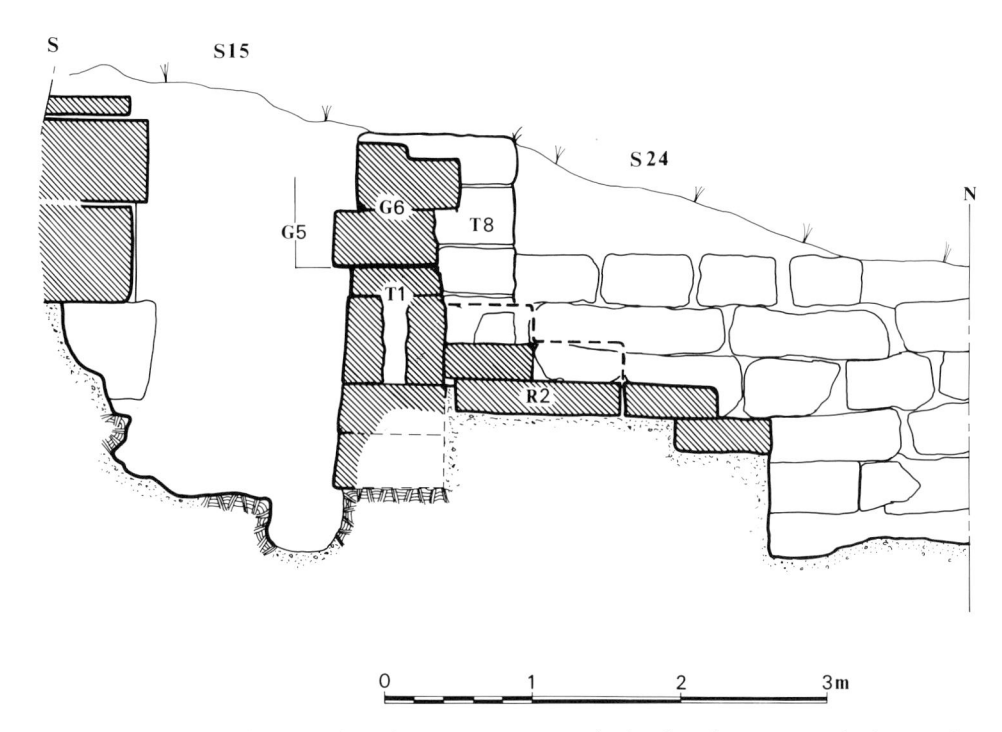

Figure 84: North-south section of the G5 and G6 doorways, restoring in broken line the R2 steps. The features drawn in fine line (wall T8 and S24 Late Structure) lie west of the section plane. 1:50 scale.

ity is that both the rubble footings and the fill survive from an otherwise largely obliterated Archaic occupation.

This leaves St. 2 as our significant layer, since it seems to be definitely associated with the construction of the R2 steps and adjacent W32 wall. Its latest dateable artifacts consist mainly of miscellaneous Hellenistic-Roman marble drapery fragments, fifth and fourth century terracotta figurines, a third century B.C. lamp, and a coin from the reign of Trajan. While the coin could date the entire complex to the next phase of the sanctuary's development, it was not excavated under the R2 steps but ca. 0.30 m. to their north in loose fill and may be intrusive. The remainder of the fill's reliably dateable finds are third century B.C. and earlier. I am inclined to place both steps and S31 enclosure, as well as the G5 doorway by association, into the Hellenistic period despite the difficulties raised by the coin, since this makes better sense in light of subsequent architectural developments in this area.

S7 Sacred House

The S7 Sacred House is the most completely preserved of all of the Middle Sanctuary independent shrine buildings (Plan D; Figs. 1, 10, 21, 85-92; Pls. 85, 89-92). Its excavation took place in the following areas: E10, balk, E10, bldg., F10, 1, and F11, 1 (Fig. 12). The house was erected less than a meter west of the restored line of the Hellenistic precinct's T9 east peribolos wall approximately halfway up the slope of the Middle Sanctuary. It faced down the hill, with its door located on the north. This, its main facade, is the only part of the house that apparently underwent significant renovation at a later time.[82]

A simple one-room structure measuring in its present state ca. 4.40 m. north to south by 4.35 m. east to west, the S7 Sacred House was essentially a 4.20 m. square in its original plan.[83] The interior was equipped with a stone bench across its back wall. Both the bench and at least parts of its interior wall surface were plastered and painted (Figs. 85, 88, 90; Pls. 91, 92). Late (post-A.D. 262) masonry blocking across the north face of the building largely obscures the original arrangement of its main facade. A fragmentary

---

82. The post A.D. 262 rebuilding of the S7a north wall will be discussed in the forthcoming study of the sanctuary's Imperial period architecture. See *Final Reports* I, fig. 121.

83. As preserved, the outline of the house has been pushed out of alignment. When first published in 1974 its north-south dimension was given as 5.05 m. Subsequent excavation of the northeast corner showed that what was initially taken to mark the corner was in fact part of a secondary filling in front of the building-proper. While the foundation stone drawn at the northeast corner (Fig. 85) has shifted east of its original position, the back wall's lower blocks survive intact. They measure 4.25 m. across, and this marks the structure's original and intended east-west width. See infra 158.

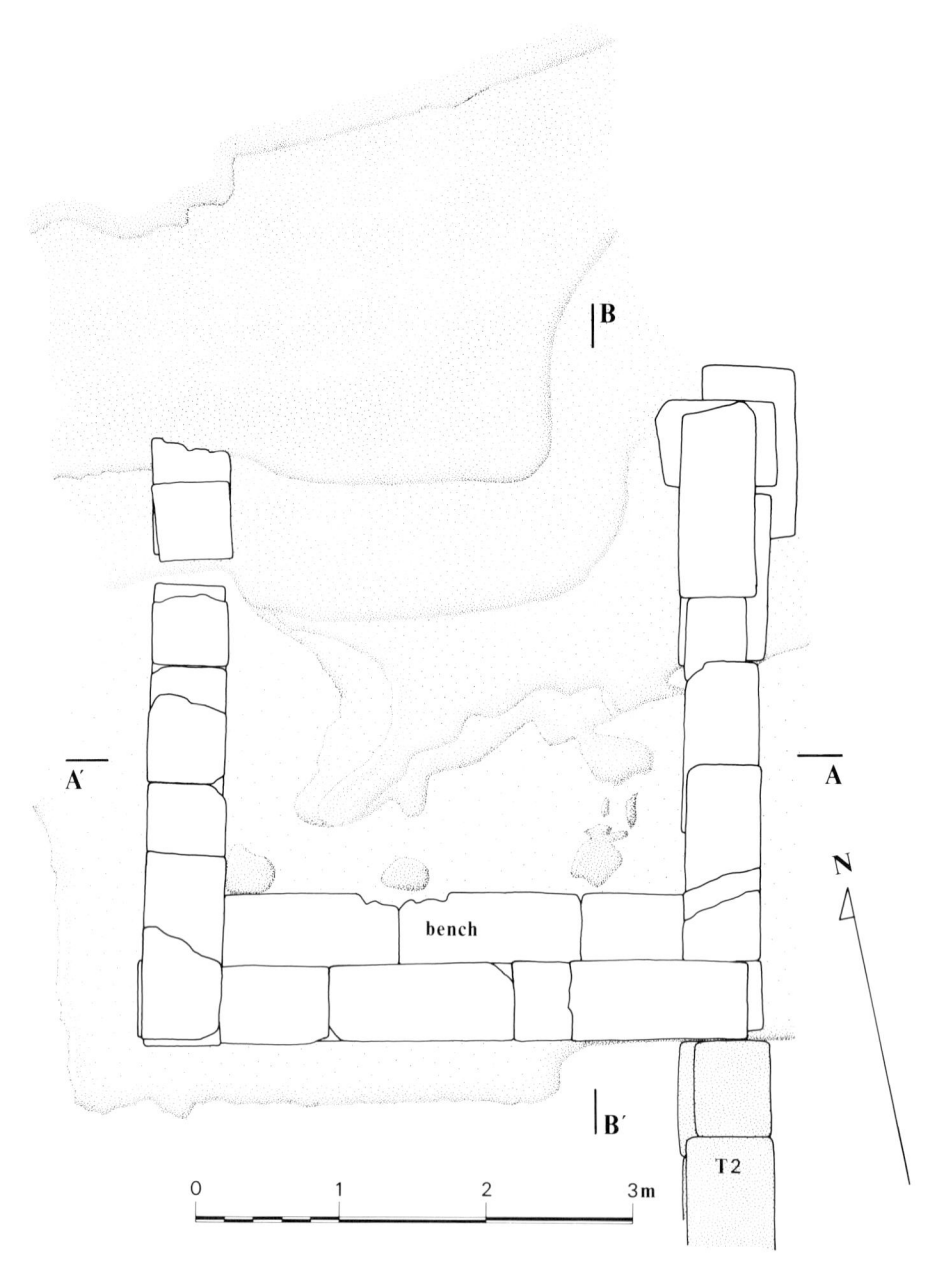

Figure 85: Plan of the S7 Sacred House. 1:50 scale.

moulded limestone column base in the earth fill directly behind the south wall might suggest some form of in-antis colonnaded facade if it had been found at the opposite end of the building, but its association presumably should be rejected because of its uphill location.[84] No traces of windows are preserved.

---

84. Arch. Cat. No. **F:5**. As a rule of thumb, architectural *frusta* from earthquake destruction layers are better left disassociated from structures that lie to their north (i.e., downhill) because of the steepness of the Middle Sanctuary slope.

WALL FOUNDATION TRENCH

The south wall and the rear half of the west wall were set in a low foundation trench cut into the natural limestone pavement (Figs. 10, 85, 86); the trench averages ca. 0.35/0.40 m. deep and 0.40/0.50 m. wide. Traces of similar trenching do not occur elsewhere around the house exterior. Its appearance in this spot must have to do with a natural crevice in the bedrock, which the builders chose to enlarge in order to provide their foundations with a better grip on the sloping limestone.

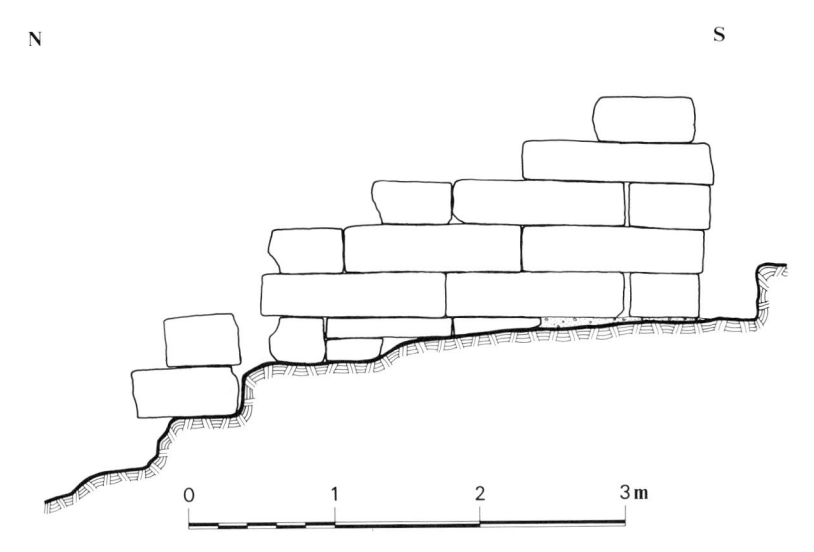

Figure 86: Elevation of S7's exterior west wall. 1:50 scale.

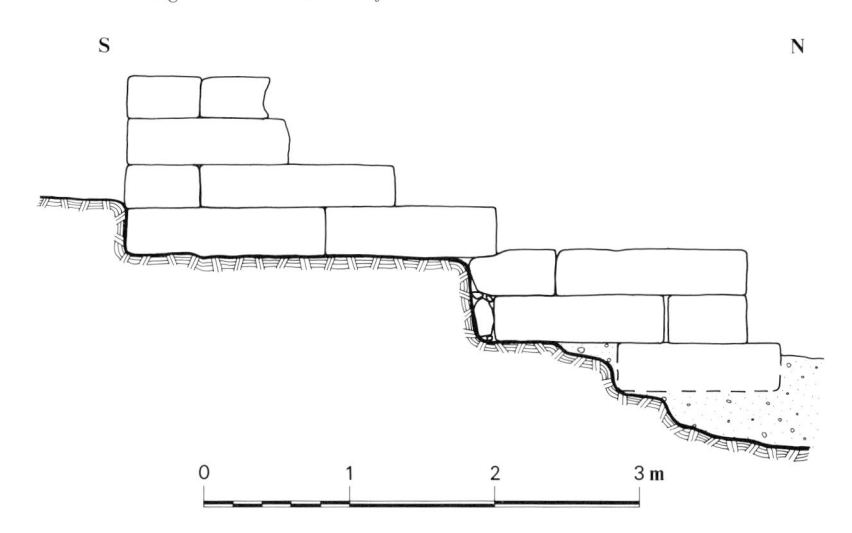

Figure 87: Elevation of S7's exterior east wall. 1:50 scale.

STONE

The surviving walls are built throughout from blocks of good-quality limestone, relatively free of shelly inclusions and capable of taking a sharp edge and precise masonry finish. When they were first cleared of their soil cover the blocks displayed an off-white color which forms a noticable contrast with the more yellowed surface of the adjacent Imperial T18 peribolos wall.

WEST WALL

Surviving to a maximum intact length of four m., the west wall rises to a height of five courses or 1.15 m. (Fig. 86). Much of the northern two-thirds use low foundations to even the superstructure over the sloping profile of the bedrock shelf, while the southern third rests on a thin bedding of soil. The northwest corner rises over an abrupt drop in the bedrock, leveled by the insertion of two standard-size courses; the upper stone probably was originally part of the short, broken block to its immediate south. The bulk of the wall blocks are laid out as stretchers, ca. 1.10/1.20 m. long, 0.32 m. high and 0.50 m. wide (block height-to-length ratio 1:3.6). In the southwest corner the first and third courses above bedrock bond with the rear, south wall.

The elegant use of L-shaped blocks to compensate for changes in bedrock levels observed earlier in the case of the S5 Sacred House[85] is here conspicuously absent.

---

85. See supra 87-88.

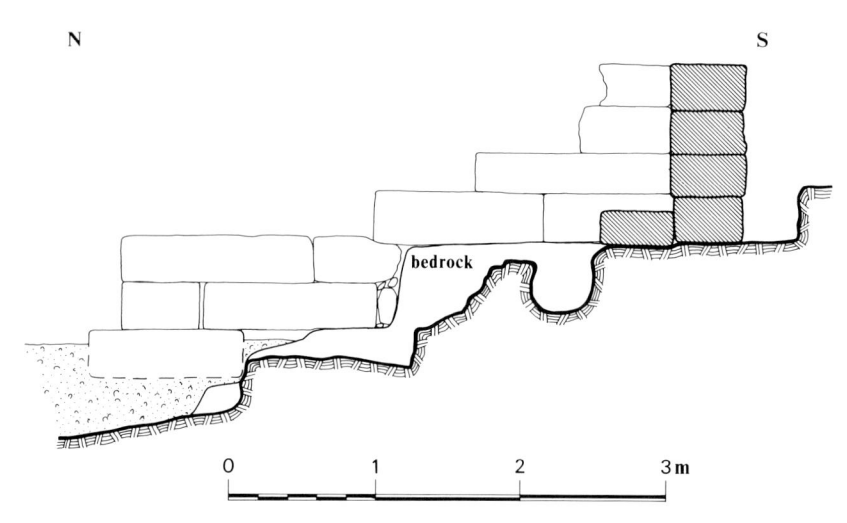

Figure 88: Elevation of interior east wall and cross-section of south wall of S7 Sacred House (see B-B' on Fig. 85). 1:50 scale.

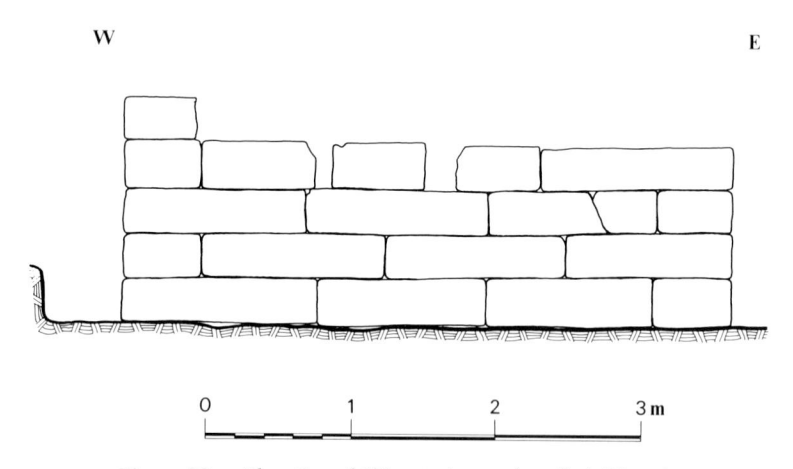

Figure 89: Elevation of S7's exterior south wall. 1:50 scale.

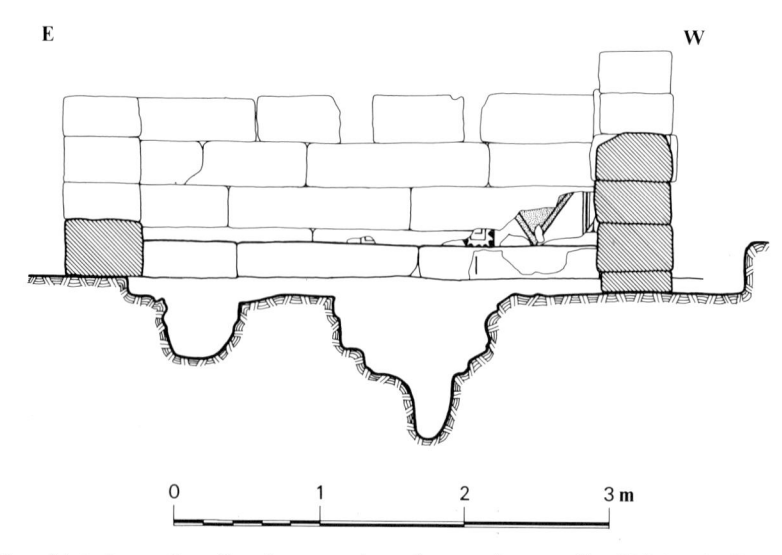

Figure 90: Elevation of interior south wall and cross-sections of east and west walls of S7 (see A-A' on Fig. 85). 1:50 scale.

THE HELLENISTIC, EARLY ROMAN SANCTUARY 155

Figure 91: Plan of S7 Sacred House with post-A.D. 262 blocking across its north facade; east-west section of blocking, drawn from north. 1:50 scale.

EAST WALL

The south corner preserves four stretcher courses, bringing the maximum height of the east wall above bedrock to ca. 1.50 m. (Figs. 87, 88). The dropoff in bedrock across the northern half of the building here required the insertion of three additional full-sized courses that rest on earth and the bedrock lip, in effect increasing the wall's overall preserved height to more than two m. The lowest block at the wall's north end,

Plate 92: Detail of inner southwest corner of S7 Sacred House, from northeast.

which has been pushed slightly to the east of its original position (Fig. 85), is ca. 0.05 m. wider than the blocks above and was originally not intended to be seen; it constitutes, in other words, the foundation of the building's northeast corner. Otherwise the block dimensions are approximately the same as those of the west wall.

In the southeast corner the second and fourth courses above bedrock bond into the rear, south wall.

SOUTH WALL

Measuring 4.25 m. in total length, the rear or south wall (Figs. 89, 90) survives to a maximum height of five courses or 1.50 m. above bedrock. Again, its elevation consists of a single file of mainly stretchers echoing the dimensions of the east and west walls with which it bonds. The lowest course is set directly on bedrock and, owing to the regularity of the bedrock shelf in this sector, required no leveling foundation course. The treatment of its painted interior face is described below under *Building Interior*.

NORTH WALL

As already stated, the original north wall was almost entirely replaced by a blocking of probable squatter period. By the time of the erection of the blocking wall the sacred house had fallen into ruin. At least two of the blocks used for the makeshift late wall were taken from S7's original north wall. Block "5b" (Fig. 91) was broken off from the ashlar "5a," set at the northeast corner to bond the east wall's second course above bedrock with the otherwise missing north wall. Block "17" may have been detached from the northwest corner. Other blocks seem to be fragmentary leftovers of ashlars that originally made up the missing upper portions of S7's east and west walls.

BUILDING INTERIOR

The bedrock pavement sheers off abruptly as one moves toward the front (north end) of the house (Figs. 1, 64; Pls. 91, 92), echoing the sloping interior of the S5 Sacred House. A thin layer of reddish clay containing occupation debris covered a lower layer of hard-packed stereo. Both strata followed the falling profile of the hillslope in a way that initially suggests that the forward half of the interior was left in a natural, rusticated condition and never possessed a permanent level floor. The bedrock to the rear was leveled off and a narrow bench set against the back wall, again recalling Sacred House S5. An irregular shelf of bedrock was left intact in front of the bench. Its forward edge was trimmed to form a ca. 0.10 m. high threshold-like lip that extended across the full width between the side walls. The lip's line, however, was interrupted by the natural crevices that indent the limestone shelf in the western half.

The shelf itself has a maximum depth of ca. 0.65 m. Three natural holes were sunk into its top surface (Pls. 91, 92). The western hole was plugged with sterile clay at the time of its excavation and appears to have been filled when the house was still in use. A second hole (0.37 by 0.22 m. by -0.22 m.) near the shelf's center was packed with earthquake debris to a depth of ca. 0.15 m., while the third hole in the southeast corner (0.44 by 0.46 by -0.41 m.) again contained earthquake debris to a depth of ca. 0.15 m. The earthquake debris makes it certain that both the central and eastern holes were kept partially open until the building was destroyed. Unfortunately nothing was found either inside or near the holes to explain their purpose.

It is debatable what kind of floor should be restored north of the rock shelf. A permanent stone pavement seems unlikely for two reasons. In the first place, no traces of flagging were recovered. Second and more tellingly, a lifesize male marble togate statue of Antonine date was excavated inside the house north of the shelf where it had presumably fallen during the final earthquake to damage the sanctuary.[86] At the time of its discovery the statue lay *below* the level of any floor that might be conceivably restored to the house's interior at the level of the rock shelf. The building therefore cannot have had a permanent floor at least immediately before the earthquake.

On the other hand, it is at least theoretically possible that the interior had a wooden floor built flush against the lip of the bedrock shelf. This would have left a crawl-space beneath its northern half, which, despite the lack of vestiges of decayed wooden planking, would help explain the otherwise peculiar sub-floor position of the fallen togate statue. Wood survives badly in Cyrene's soil, rain-soaked throughout the winter months and baked dry in summer and fall, except when it has been reduced to carbon or ash. The absence of wood ash could therefore simply mean that the floor never caught on fire. A wooden floor, moreover, could have been equipped with a trap door to the crawl-space across the building's northern half, if access was needed for either cultic or other more practical reasons. Alternatively, it should be borne in mind that the S7 house may never have had a floor of any kind and that it was the intention of its builders from the outset to expose its sloping bedrock interior in front of the bench and rock shelf to view while the building was in use.

PAINTED DECORATION

The bench at the back of the house rises ca. 0.22 m. above the rock shelf and is ca. 0.50 m. wide (Figs. 88, 90; Pls. 91, 92). It is made up of three limestone blocks, whose outer faces and tops are covered with a cream-colored plaster. A single extremely faint vertical line on the vertical face of the westernmost block is all that survives of whatever painted decoration originally covered the bench, but this is enough to show that at one time all of its outer face was probably divided up into separate painted registers.

The off-white plaster covering the south wall over the bench is ca. 0.025 m. thick. Starting at the southwest corner and moving east, the decoration today consists of three parallel vertical black lines of unequal thickness that evidently comprise a framing element. Next, the lower half of a geometric design (a tipped square, lozenge, hexagon, or chevron) follows in black line, with faded bluish black paint filling its center. Two sets of parallel black lines then form a badly preserved right-angle corner element, edged with triangular, tooth-shaped ornaments. A gap of roughly 0.90 m. next intervenes, followed by a small patch of plaster adhering to the wall just off the top of the bench. Its decoration again consists of parallel black lines forming a right-angled framing element, running right, with traces of red in-filling to its immediate left.

The corner of the west wall immediately above the bench repeats the triple-line vertical framing element, with bluish black in-filling to its right. In the corner formed by the rock shelf with the west wall at the foot of the bench three (?) rectangular panels ca. 0.15 m. high, separated by single black lines, survive in badly damaged condition, with some traces of red paint still adhering to their centers.

While it is of course possible that the painted decoration was added after the house had already been in existence for some time, there is no sign of earlier plaster coatings, and it seems more likely that the decor was approximately contemporary with the erection of the building.

---

86. The statue is Inv. 73-1255, Kane, sanctuary sculptures forthcoming, cat. no. **208**. See also White, *Final Reports* I, 107, fig. 112.

CONTEXT AND DATE OF THE S7 SACRED HOUSE

Four layers of E10, balk and E10, bldg. fill were excavated from the interior of the building. The brownish-black topsoil was succeeded by a brownish-grey St. 2 fill, with a dry, loose texture. Apart from numerous fallen wall blocks (stemming from the building's own superstructure as well as the nearby peribolos wall), its contents consisted of Hellenistic coins, lamps dating to the second century A.D., and corrugated plain ware sherds of second/third century A.D. date. This then gave way to brown, somewhat more moist St. 3 fill made up of additional fallen building blocks together with an unusually large amount of sculptural material dated from the Hellenistic Roman period to Antonine times,[87] early pottery, one corrugated sherd of the type attributable to the second/third century A.D., and a fourth century A.D. bronze coin.[88] The last-mentioned find is interesting, since it could be interpreted to show that the S7 Sacred House remained intact beyond the time of the A.D. 262 earthquake responsible for wrecking most of the remainder of the sanctuary and was in fact destroyed by the later earthquake of A.D. 365.[89] St. 3 also contained a fairly large number of terracotta roof tiles, including the site's type **D:2** pan tile (Fig. 99B).[90] A thin layer of largely sterile red St. 4 fill lies over the bedrock.

The foundation trench fill associated with the south wall and rear half of the west wall contained a selection of sixth, early fifth century pottery, including Attic Black Figure sherds not included in Moore's study. The trench behind the house also contained a late Hellenistic, early Roman marble statuette,[91] which suggests that the wall builders initially cleared the space reserved for the house's outer walls to bedrock. They then trimmed the rock surface to create their foundation trench and, once the wall was in place, backfilled with the earlier occupation fill strewn over the slope. For reasons unknown, the much later statuette got included with the earlier debris and now provides an approximate construction date for the building in the late Hellenistic period or slightly later.

The secondary blocking that closed off the front of the S7 Sacred House rested on and was mixed with a half-m.-thick F11, 1, 3 fill (Fig. 92) that may represent the continuation of the late St. 3 fill already noted inside the building. Here St. 3 produced fine wares dating to the later first century A.D., lamps of the second century A.D., and a corrugated red fabric sherd of the second/third centuries A.D., while inside the house the same stratum contained an early fourth century A.D. coin. It therefore seems likely that the bulk of the St. 3 debris resulted from the A.D. 262 earthquake and its A.D. 305-306 coin was mixed into its surface when its secondary blocking was erected across the house's front some time early in the fourth century. St. 1 and 2 must then be A.D. 365 earthquake fill that bury both the house and its secondary front wall for the last time. This seems to make better sense than interpreting each of the upper three strata as separate spills resulting from the later earthquake.

Commentary

PAINTED INTERIOR

The discovery of fragments of plain wall plaster from the S5 Sacred House[92] supports the rather obvious proposition that all of the site's independent house structures may have been at least intended to receive painted interiors, whether or not this was ever carried out. The S7 house is, however, the *only* structure to provide an example of such a decor. On the other hand, so little actually survives of the painted decoration from its bench and back wall surface that it is difficult to regain more than a vague impression of its original appearance.

What survives belongs entirely to the repertory of geometric decoration.[93] The colors, such as are left, are limited to black, bluish-black, and red. Either broad single straight lines of solid paint or a series of thin parallel lines seem to constitute framing elements that may have originally enclosed panels decorated with geometric motifs. While it is perhaps natural to assume that the panels were once part of a series of orthostates extended horizontally across the rear wall, the large V-shaped design incompletely preserved in the lower rear southwest corner immediately above the bench in theory could have been part of a vertical decorative band.

The likeliest types of geometric shape in use here are either a diamond-lozenge, a hexagon, or a square

---

87. These include Kane, sanctuary sculptures forthcoming, cat. nos. **45** (marble pig), **46** (marble statue base with animal's hooves), **4** (marble relief with horses' legs), **208** (marble male togate statue), **702** (limestone altar), **44** (limestone animal's head), **226** (marble portrait head of male Libyan).

88. T. Buttrey, *Final Reports* VI, cat. no. **791**, struck by Maximian, A.D. 305-06.

89. *Final Reports* I, 1, 93-103, 107-08, 118-19. White, *Summary* 27-28. Roques has argued that the A.D. 262 earthquake in fact never took place. D. Roques, *Synésios de Cyrène et la Cyrénaïque du Bas-Empire* (Paris 1987) 43-44, 96, 97, 209, 319. More will be said about this challenging idea as the site's sculptures, lamps, and post-Hellenistic architecture are published. In the meantime nothing has emerged from the studies by Kenrick, Oliver, and Warden of the site's fine ware pottery, glass, and other miscellaneous late finds to offset our belief that the sanctuary's active life was essentially over by the middle of the third century A.D. and that this cessation of activity was caused by an earthquake.

90. Inv. 73-1161 exemplifies the type, reconstructed infra 167, Fig. 99B; its maximum preserved dimensions are 0.038 by 0.24 by 0.07 m. No completely preserved specimen of a **D:2** pan tile has been recovered.

91. Inv. 73-1025, Kane, sanctuary sculptures forthcoming, cat. no. **141**.

92. Supra 86.

93. No traces of figural or otherwise representational painting were found here or anywhere else throughout the sanctuary.

tipped on one of its corners. Since the upper section of the present example is not preserved, the surviving "V" could also belong to a chain of horizontal chevrons, although it is not readily apparent how a row of large chevrons could have been combined at the left with what appears to be the lined, lower right-hand corner of a separate panel, edged with small triangular tooth or chevron patterns, set ca. 0.90 m. from the room's southwest corner.[94]

Although uncommon, diamonds or lozenges, hexagons, octagons, and squares do occasionally occur in later Hellenistic and Roman Imperial painted wall contexts, quite apart from their considerably more frequent appearance in mosaic, *opus sectile* flooring and stuccoed vaults. While I am not familiar with a linear chevron pattern used to decorate interior wall orthostates, a plastered altar decorated with a bed-moulding painted with a continuous chevron chain was recovered from House D, damaged in 88 B.C., in Insula 1 of the Stadium Quarter at Delos.[95] The upper third of a second century B.C. painted loculus slab from the Hadra cemetery at Alexandria is decorated with triangles set in squares.[96] A stuccoed wall face, decorated with raised mouldings and interlocking multicolored lozenge panels, has been excavated from a later Hellenistic context at Tel Anafa.[97]

Lozenges, hexagons, and squares do not seem to occur at Cyrene or elsewhere regionally on the walls of buildings and tombs. But in the case of Tripolitania a stuccoed wall from the Flavian period villa of Dar Buc Ammera at Zliten has a plaster frieze panel painted with a horizontal series of contiguous lozenges.[98] Outside of North Africa, House XXXIII at Priene, which belongs to the city's Roman occupation, is decorated with a series of interlocking octagon designs that are individually made up of elongated hexagons,[99] but here the motif appears to have been spread over the entire wall surface and was not divided into panels. Lozenge patterns are found on the surface of a tomb found in the Chersonesus, attributed to the fourth century A.D.[100] and on the wall of a vaulted chamber at Bordeaux.[101]

The best parallels, however, are provided by buildings from Thera, Pergamon, and Knossos. Beginning with Hellenistic-Roman Thera, the evidence stems from East Hall "S" and Room "M" from the so-called *Palace* and Room "C" from the *House East of the Temple of Apollo Pythios*.

Room "C" from the House East of the Apollo Temple[102] preserves traces of a painted rectangular panel, set above a low baseboard or plinth. The panel is decorated with a black lozenge, edged in red. The field surrounding the lozenge is further decorated with white right-angled triangles placed in alternatively orange and green backgrounds.

The wall of Room "M" from the "Palazzo"[103] is painted with a series of rectangular plain white plastered orthostates, separated by black lines and then further framed by thinner lines of red. Above these comes a row of vertically extended rectangular white-ground panels. The central pair is decorated with incomplete V-shaped elements, strikingly like the S7 design under discussion. In this instance the V-proper consists of a thick orange line, paralleled by a thin red line. The outer field is again decorated with right-angled triangles. If the panel (with floral center) preserved to the left of this pair provides an accurate indication of the original height of the Room "M" panels with V-shaped designs, the available space can only have accommodated tipped squares, and diamond-lozenges may accordingly be ruled out.

The north and west walls of East Hall "S"[104] from the "Palazzo" are decorated with a low baseboard or plinth over which is run a horizontal series of low rectangular panels. The center of every other panel is painted with a plain linear lozenge design. The intervening panels are treated as plain rectangles with ansated projections that perhaps explain the right-angle "corner" element to the left of the V-shape design on the rear wall of Sacred House S7. Solid grey, black, and orange are used for the lozenge and rectangle interiors, with red and black used for their linear outlines. Red and orange are used for the surrounding backgrounds.

---

94. See infra n. 104 for the possibility that the angle represents the ansated projection of an adjacent panel rather than its actual lower right-hand corner.

95. A. Plassart, *BCH* 40 (1916) 163. M. Bulard, *EAD* 9: *Description des revêtements peints à sujets religieux* (Paris 1926) 136, pl. XXVI, e.

96. B. Brown, *Ptolemaic Paintings and Mosaics and the Alexandrian Style* (Cambridge 1957) 37, pl. xxiii, 3.

97. S. Weinberg, "Tel Anafa: the Third Season," *Muse* 5 (1971) 10, pl. on back cover.

98. S. Aurigemma, *L'Italia in Africa. Tripolitania* I, Pt. 2: *Le pitture d'eta romana* (Rome 1962) 15-28, pl. 8. See ibid. 112-13, pls. 121 and 124 for fragmentary examples of painted wall decoration from Sabratha, consisting of lined panel frames and octogons. The latter originate from the Theater Baths.

99. *Priene* 317-18, fig. 363.

100. A. Barbet, "Peinture murale romaine à Bordeaux," *Peinture murale en Gaule*, BAR International Series 240 (1985) 110, fig. 10.22.

101. Dated to the second century A.D. See Barbet (supra n. 100) 95, fig. 10.6, 97-103.

102. F. Hiller von Gaertringen and P. Wilski, *Stadtgeschichte von Thera* III (Berlin 1904) 142, pl. 4.

103. Hiller von Gaertringen and Wilski (supra n. 102) 157, 163, 169, pl. 2.

104. Hiller von Gaertringen and Wilski (supra n. 102) 157, 163, fig. 147, pl. 2.

The excavator's original estimates for the dates of the Theran walls ranged from the second century B.C. to the Antonine period, with a preference for the latter. They do not appear to have been challenged by recent scholarship.[105] The rather striking similarity between the Cyrenean and Theran walls reminds one of the close political ties between Cyrene and Thera attested as late as the fourth century B.C.[106] There exists, however, no tangible proof that I am aware of that the political situation necessarily continued into the Hellenistic period, and the artistic similarities are probably little more than coincidental.

Room 2 in the Hellenistic Long Hall from the Asclepius Sanctuary at Pergamon provides a second useful parallel.[107] The orthostate level of its north and west walls is decorated with a series of painted stucco panels, ca. 0.70 by 1.20 m., decorated with mainly vertically run linear lozenges. The panels are set inside solid yellow-orange, red, and blue-green frames. A second century B.C. date has been assigned to the decor.

Finally, at Knossos the later second century A.D. residences known as the *Villa Dionysos* and the *House of the Diamond Frescoes* both contain rooms decorated with wall frescoes featuring large vertical diamond motifs.[108] In the case of the latter, the lozenge panels have been transferred from dado or orthostate level to provide the dominant decorative motif for the main body of the wall surface, a variation from the previously described systems that presumably signals their later date. Specifically, the wall here consists of a low dado or decorative base moulding of alternating panels imitating variegated marble. Above these are a series of large panels, approximately two-thirds the total height of the wall, set between thin, vertical "panels" that may be intended to suggest colored marble pilasters or columns. The large panels are decorated with either large solid red or marbled yellow diamonds over alternatively yellow and red backgrounds; the diamonds themselves are set off by blue borders.

HOUSE CONTENTS

A second interesting feature of the S7 Sacred House has to do with what it may have contained at the time of its destruction. It will be recalled that the bulk of the earth fill from the interior was associated with earthquake destruction.[109] Objects from earthquake strata across the steep Middle Sanctuary normally can be assumed to have slid downhill from whatever position they occupied immediately prior to the earthquake. In this case the walls of the house may have trapped or contained the heavier stone objects embedded in its strata 3 and 4, so that some of its sculptural finds may have been stored in its interior when the earthquake hit. On the other hand, it is equally possible that statues set up on the main Imperial period T18 east wall of the Middle Sanctuary could have been carried into the house by sliding earth.

The St. 3 earthquake layer contained, amongst other things, seven stone sculptures.[110] The two most important pieces were a lifesize marble head of an adult male Libyan and the previously mentioned lifesize headless togate statue. With the exception of the head and togate body, all the stone finds from the house were found badly broken and incomplete. This could mean that they were stored outside the house before the earthquake and were broken only when the earthquake struck. On the other hand, to complicate matters, it could also mean that they were being stored in the house as damaged discards.

The head of the Libyan male is largely intact, apart from a missing neck-tenon. It was discovered in the northeast corner of the house. The togate torso is complete except for its feet and missing base. It occupied approximately the center of the building, where it lay on its back in a line more or less perpendicular to the bench, with shoulders pointing up the slope.[111] In other words, the head was recovered down-slope and northeast of the torso's (missing) feet. If the house once had a wooden floor, the statue

---

105. Hiller von Gaertringen and Wilski (supra n. 102) 169-70.

106. The evidence is of course the Cyrenean fourth century "Stele of the Founders," which connects the grant of citizen-rights with a group of Therans. SEG 9, 3. S. Ferri, *AbhBerl* (1925) No. 5, 19-24. A. Ferrabino, *RivFil* 56 (1928) 222 ff. A. Graham, *JHS* 80 (1960) 94-111, esp. 100. A. Graham, *Colony and Mother-City in Ancient Greece* (Manchester 1964) 40 ff., 224 ff. Applebaum, *Jews and Greeks* 292-93, n. 194, assumes that personal ties would have endured as late as the post Jewish rebellion period. Given the depth of feeling that Synesius could apparently still feel in the late fourth century A.D. for a Dorian ancestry stretching back to Eurysthenes the Heraclid, it is probably not far-fetched to imagine that a few Cyreneans of every generation maintained loose ties with Thera. Synesius, *Epp.* 57 and 113. *Catastasis* 5.303A. A. Fitzgerald, *The Letters of Synesius of Cyrene* (Oxford 1930) 14. J. Bregman, *Synesius of Cyrene* (Berkeley 1982) 3, n. 4, 18, n. 4. S. Walker, *Cyrenaica in Antiquity*, eds. G. Barker, J. Lloyd, and J. Reynolds, *Society for Libyan Studies Occasional Papers* I: BAR International Series 236 (1985) 102-03. Roques (supra n. 89) 31.

107. O. Ziegenaus and G. De Luca, *Altertümer von Pergamon* XI, 2: *Das Asklepieion* (Berlin 1975) 36, pls. 20c, 111. I owe this reference to my former student, P. S. Bougia.

108. L. Sackett and J. Jones, *Archaeology* 32, 2 (1979) 18-27, figs. on pp. 19, 20. The authors say, ibid. 25, that lozenges set within rectangular panels have been found in England at Aldborough, Catterick, and at Lullingstone Villa. See also *AR* 19 (1972-73) 62-71; *AR* 20 (1973-74) 35; *AR* 24 (1976-77) 61.

109. See supra 159.

110. Listed supra n. 87.

111. See *Final Reports* I, 107, fig. 112.

might have been set up on the stuccoed bench, but this is largely conjecture. With the neck element joining the Libyan head to its body missing, it is impossible to determine with any certainty that the head goes with the togate statue. On stylistic grounds, however, the head has been assigned a Hadrianic-Antonine date, while the torso has been attributed to the Antonine period.

In the early years of this century Ghislanzoni found three standing draped female marble statues and a single togate male marble statue immediately north of S7.[112] It seems unlikely that such a small edifice was ever used to exhibit five large marble sculptures. But given all the statuary associated in one way or another with its interior, the S7 house, like the S5 Sacred House, may have been used to warehouse "decommissioned" honorific or votive dedications in the years immediately preceding the sanctuary's final abandonment. Because one cannot say how the structure was used before the fourth century A.D., apart from the all too enigmatic treatment of its floor and the rocky crawl-space across the northern half, comparison with temples, treasuries, etc. employed for exhibiting statues,[113] therefore seems pointless here.

RESTORATION OF THE S7 SACRED HOUSE

The restored elevations developed by James Thorn (Figs. 93-96) are based on the partially preserved east, west, and south walls, two cornice fragments found in surface strata north of the house, a pilaster capital also found north of the house in St. 2 earthquake debris, rooftiles found in the house's destruction level, analogies taken from other architectural *frusta* found throughout the site, and parallels with buildings elsewhere. While ideally one could wish for more physical evidence, the S7 Sacred House provides the most that the site has to offer before the Imperial period, and its tentative restoration provides us with our best opportunity for studying what is unquestionably the Archaic-Hellenistic sanctuary's most distinctive building type, namely the independent house. The following observations are heavily indebted to Thorn's written comments in addition to his drawings.

The measured width of the rear wall is 4.20 m., but as it survives the house plan (Fig. 85) is slightly out of square, since the top surviving course of its west wall toes in 0.14 m. by the time it reaches the northwest corner. While this could be the result of careless building, it is more likely that the wall blocks have been pressed out of alignment by earthquake pressure. The restored facade (Fig. 93) assumes that the latter is what has occurred. It therefore provides the building with a uniform width of 4.20 m. For purposes of calculating the elevation a simple grid was laid over the facade in which each unit of 1.05 m. equals three "feet," the latter calculated at 0.35 m. (i.e., 1.5 cm. less than the so-called Ptolemaic or Alexandrian foot used elsewhere at Cyrene and Ptolemais).[114] The north facade above the level of its stylobate is four units or twelve feet wide. The total building height from the bottom, third step of the crepidoma to pediment apex has been restored as six units or eighteen feet high. The complete width of the pediment is restored as five units or fifteen feet wide. The resulting facade above stylobate level to the base of the pediment is nearly (but not exactly) a four by four unit square. The pediment is one unit or three feet high, giving a ratio of pediment height-to-total height of 1:6. Its raking entablature has been restored as one foot high. Total pediment width and building height minus the crepidoma are again virtually the same, which contributes to the facade's overall squarish appearance. The ratio of total height to width is 6:5.

The three-stepped crepidoma across the front of the building is reconstructed from standard stretchers roughly one unit long. The top step is levelled with what is taken to be the missing ancient floor over the sump-like depression in the bedrock that occupies the forward half of the interior. The two restored elevations of the west wall (Figs. 95, 96) indicate how the bedrock steps down to accommodate the facade's projecting crepidoma. The offset lowest step block preserved at the northeast corner (Fig. 85) is duplicated at the opposite corner. Each of the side walls is fixed at four units or twelve feet long, which means that the building's plan is a square.

The ratio of side wall length-to-total height (as measured from the bottom of the restored projecting crepidoma) is 2:3.

The restored doorway (Fig. 93) integrates a fragmentary pilaster capital, one foot high (Fig. 97)[115] but is otherwise based on Gismondi's restoration of the door of the Cyrene Apollo Sanctuary's late fourth century

---

112. See *Final Reports* I, 11, 106, n. 74.
113. For other conventional settings of publically displayed sculptures during Imperial times see C. Vermeule, *Roman Imperial Art in Greece and Asia Minor* (Cambridge 1968) 2-3, 15-38.

114. For the use of the Alexandrian foot of 0.365 m. in Cyrenaican architecture during the late Hellenistic period see Stucchi, *Architettura* 94, n. 2, 117, n. 7.
115. Arch. Cat. No. **I:6** excavated north-northwest of the house in F12, 1, 2.

164   CYRENE FINAL REPORTS: VOLUME V

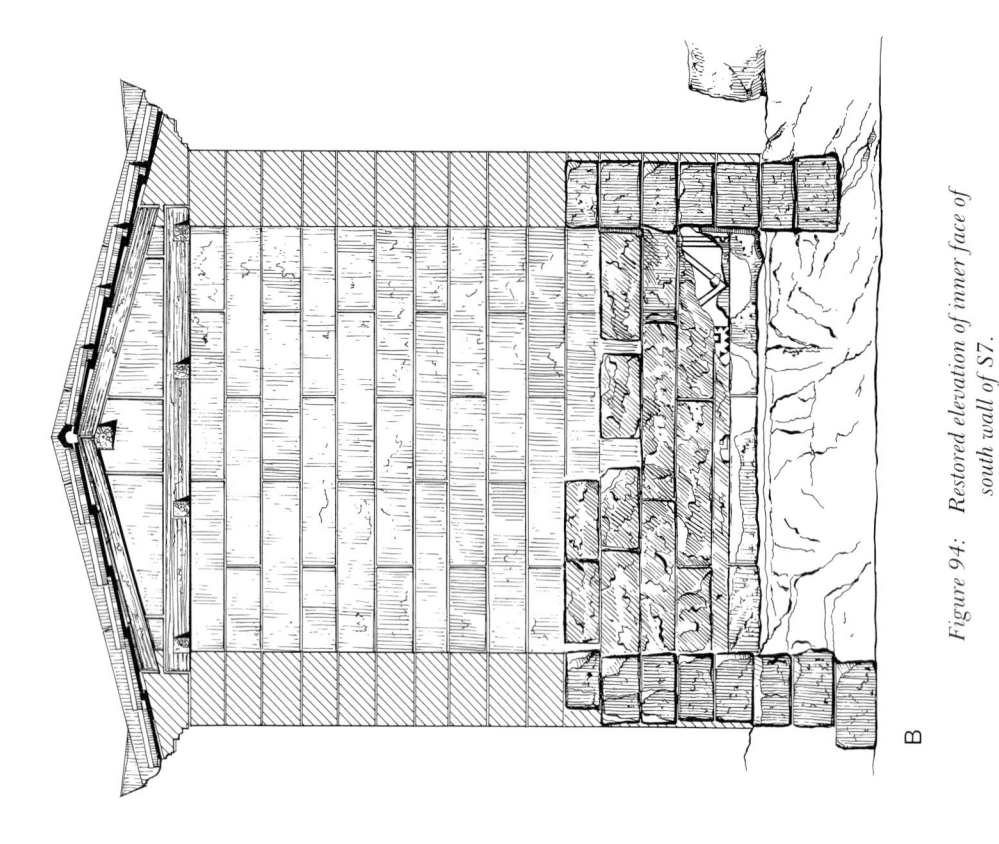

Figure 94: Restored elevation of inner face of south wall of S7.

Figure 93: North facade of S7 Sacred House, restored by J. Thorn.

THE HELLENISTIC, EARLY ROMAN SANCTUARY

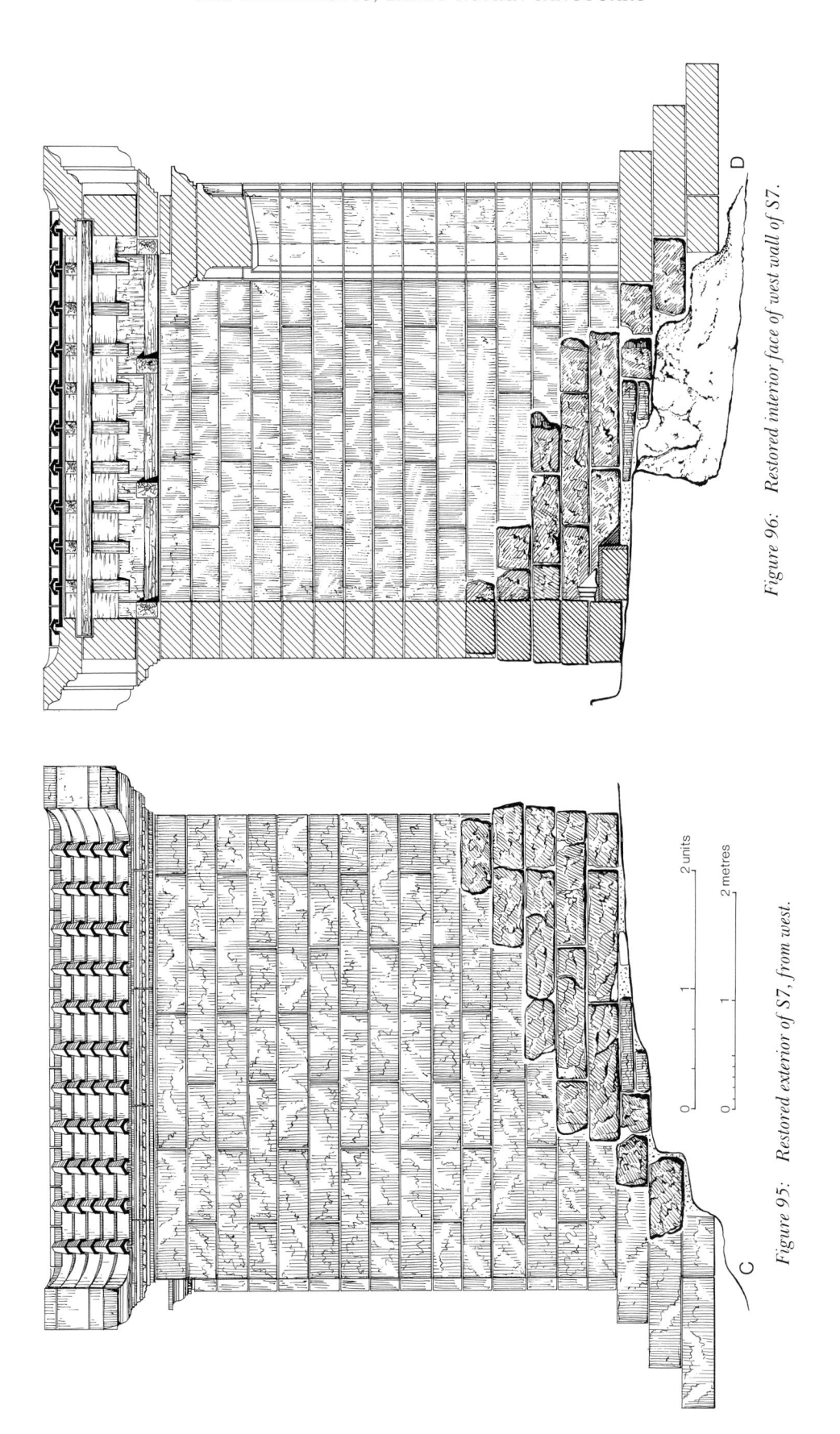

Figure 96:   Restored interior face of west wall of S7.

Figure 95:   Restored exterior of S7, from west.

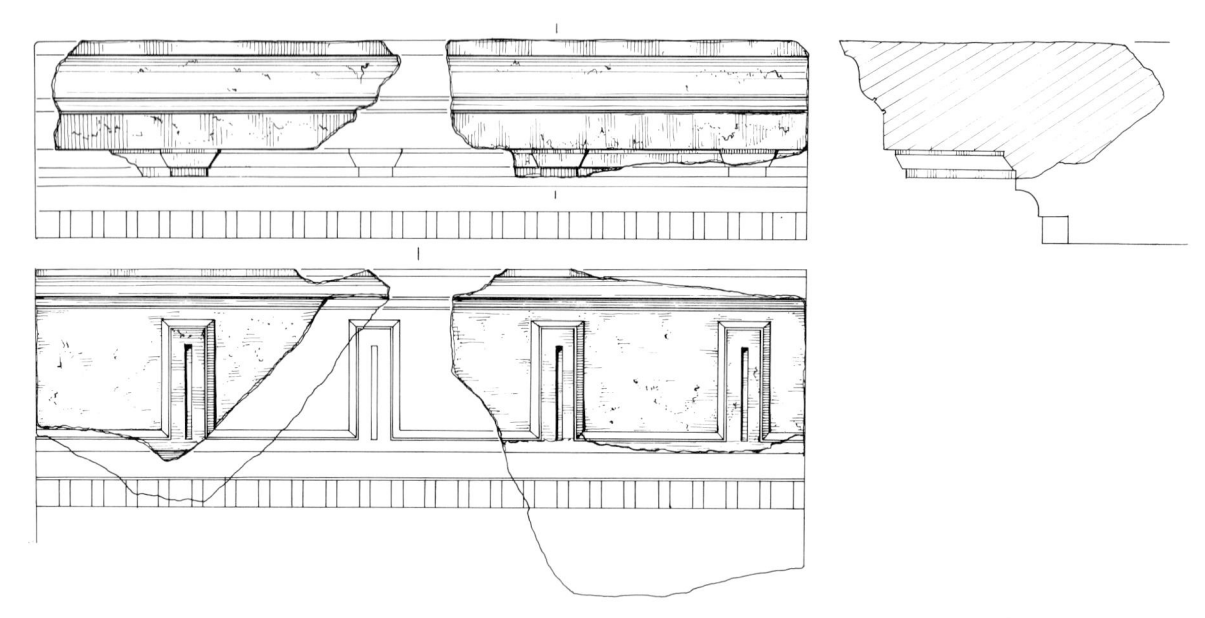

*Figure 97: Pilaster capital Arch. Cat. No. **I:6**, doorway of S7 Sacred House. 1:10 scale.*

B.C. *Strategheion*.[116] Its internal, jamb-to-jamb width is five feet, while its height from threshhold to bottom of lintel is ten feet.

The horizontal cornice has been restored from two limestone fragments found in surface stratum debris down the slope (Fig. 98).[117] Dentils appended beneath modillions have their parallels in more complete architectural mouldings belonging to later sanctuary structures whose publication is forthcoming as well as other Cyrenean structures. The desultorily carved modillions are spaced 17.5 cm. or half a foot apart. Gismondi's *Strategheion* supplies the basis for the remainder of the pediment restoration.

The drawing of the timber roof is entirely dependent on outside precedent, since nothing survives of S7's walls at cornice level to indicate the actual placement of beams. The models that have been used here are Gorham P. Stevens's familiar drawing of the North Portico of the Erechtheum and Gismondi's restoration of the Cyrene *Strategheion*.[118]

The roof tiles are based on type **D:2** pan tile fragments discovered in the house's own collapse fill.[119] They have an individual width of 0.35 m. (one foot) and a restored individual length of 0.525 m. (one and a half feet) (Fig. 99B). The modified Corinthian cover tile type (**C:2**) is well represented in debris elsewhere throughout the sanctuary (Fig. 99A). The estimated number of tiles needed to cover the roof is approximately 100 pan tiles and 110 cover tiles. No fragments of ridge tiles were found, which suggests that eleven cover tiles were used instead. There were also no antefixes or other forms of fictile revetment found that can be plausibly associated with this or any of the other small independent sanctuary buildings.

What then results is a single room structure, with a low pedimented roof and large doorway,[120] rising on a three-stepped crepidoma across its front. The cella unit inserted between crepidoma and pediment is treated as essentially a cube. The preserved cella width, the height of its preserved door jamb pilaster capital, the intervals of its preserved cornice modillions, and the preserved width of its pan tiles, taken together, suggest that a simple modular system, based on an ancient foot of 35 cm., may have been used to organize other features of both the plan and elevation.

---

116. I. Gismondi, "Il restauro dello Strategheion di Cirene," *QAL* 2 (1951) fig. 18. Stucchi, *Architettura* 98, fig. 87. In the relative simplicity of its fittings the Strategheion's door resembles some of the moulded door frames that survive in Cyrene's rock-cut tombs.
117. Arch. Cat. No. **J:23** (Inv. 78-734) from F10/G10, 1, 1 and Arch. Cat. No. **J:24** (Inv. 74-177) from F11, 1, 1. The fragments measure 0.92 by 0.25 by 0.20, and 0.24 by 0.16 by 0.08 m., respectively.
118. J. Paton and G. Stevens, *The Erechtheum* (Cambridge 1927) pl. XXIV. G. Stevens, *Restorations of Classical Buildings* (Princeton 1958) pl. XIV. Gismondi (supra n. 116) 18, fig. 15.

---

119 Supra n. 90. The flanged upper right-hand corner of the type **D:2** pan tile allows the tile to nest against the overlapping adjacent tile. For stone tile standards found at other Greek cities see J. Coulton, *Greek Architects at Work* (London 1977) 56, fig. 15.
120. Plain when compared with the ornate marble doorways inserted into the Agora's Temple of Apollo Archegetes and the so-called Second Apollonion. Stucchi, *Architettura* 48-51, figs. 34, 36, 38. Gismondi (supra n. 116) 13, figs. 8, 9. Also see supra Pl. 42 of the present volume.

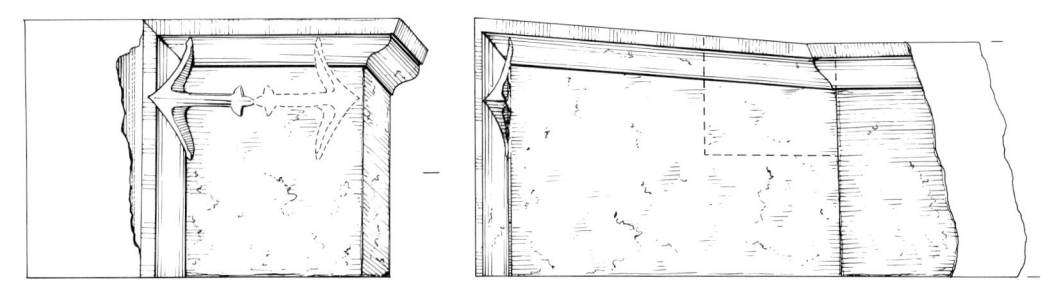

Figure 98: Horizontal cornice from S7 Sacred House, based on Arch. Cat. Nos. **J:23**, **J:24**. *1:10 scale.*

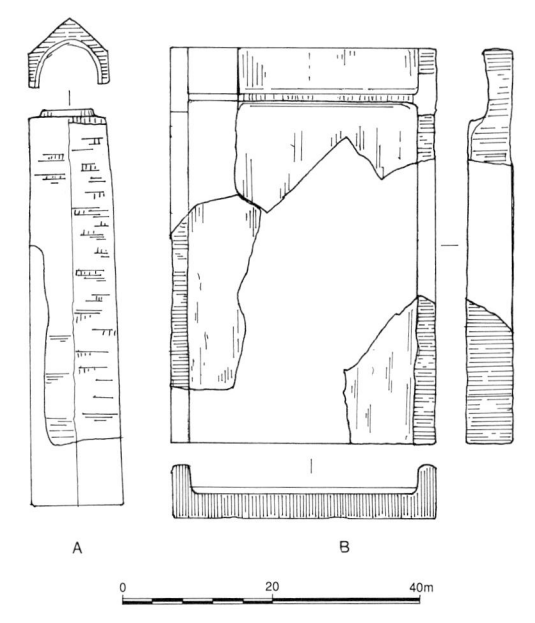

Figure 99: A: Type **C:2** *cover tile, used in restoration of the S7 roof. B: Type* **D:2** *pan tile of the type found in E10 balk, 3 and E10 bldg., 3 and used in restoration of the S7 roof. 1:10 scale.*

This foot nearly duplicates the regionally better documented Ptolemaic or Alexandrian foot of 36.5 cm.

COMPARATIVE STRUCTURES

Despite their ruinous condition the three Acrocorinth structures previously discussed[121] provide the closest analogies to the S7 building type from the repertory of Demeter sanctuaries outside of Magna Graecia and Sicily where examples are more abundant, if seldom better preserved.[122] Unquestionably, however, the closest parallel to S7 occurs on Thera where a remarkably preserved naiskos (Pl. 93; Figs.

100-102) is to be found a short distance off the modern road to Perissa between the modern villages of Megalochori and Emborio.[123] The little structure has survived to the present as a chapel dedicated to St. Nikolaos Marmarenios (or Marmarites in obvious reference to its marble superstructure), but an inscription found under an interior offering niche built into its rear wall indicates that the building was originally dedicated by Epilonchos and Kritarista to the Thea Basileia.[124] According to Kern "Basileia" is a variant for "Basile,"[125] whose specifically Athenian cult received a shrine near the Themistoclean wall between the Itonian and Halade Gates.[126] The cult title can be associated with a wide range of powerful goddesses, including Hera, Aphrodite, and the Magna Mater,[127] but her connection with Persephone is particularly strong. This emerges perhaps nowhere more clearly than in the texts of the gold leaves from Thurii, which repeatedly refer to the Kore as χθονίων βασίλεια or "Queen of them below."[128] A tie between Athenian Basile and the Kore may receive some confirmation from the amphiglyphon found in the district of New Phaleron and today in the Athens National Museum.[129] Its frequently discussed inscription labels its

---

121. Supra 102-103.
122. Supra 103-104.
123. See F. Hiller von Gaertringen, *Die Insel Thera in Alterum und Gegenwart* I (Berlin 1899) 306-08. *Blue Guide* (4th ed. London 1981) 635.
124. Hiller von Gaertringen (supra n. 123) 172, n. 183, 307. *IG* XII³, 416.
125. *Cf. RE* III, 1 (1897) 42-44, *s.v.* Basile and Basilein (O. Kern). The same equation was made by R. Wycherly, "Neileion," *BSA* 66 (1960) 60 but more recently has been rejected by H. Shapiro, "The Attic Deity Basile," *ZPE* 63 (1986) 135, n. 8. I owe the last reference to Keith DeVries.
126. Travlos, *Pictorial Dictionary* 332-34. Shapiro (supra n. 125) 134.
127. *RE* (supra n. 125)
128. *RE* (supra n. 125). Zuntz, *Persephone* 299-308.
129. O. Walter, "Die Reliefs aus dem Heiligtum der Echeliden in Neu-Phaleron," *ArchEph* (1937) 112-13. B. Ridgway, *Fifth Century Styles in Greek Sculpture* (Princeton 1981) 131, n. 2, 133, n. 12, 155-56, 200, fig. 98. N. Crosby, "A Basrelief from Phaleron," *AJA* 9 (1894) 202-05, pl. XII, was one of the first to explore the extent to which the subject of the relief may be related to the myth of Persphone.

Plate 93: The Shrine of St. Nikalaos Marmarenios or Marmaritis near the village of Emborio, Thera, dedicated in antiquity to the Thea Basileia. Photographed summer 1988; ground level has risen around its threshhold since Hiller von Gaertringen's day, and a concrete reinforcement has been added to the walls' footings.

Figure 100: Elevation of the principal facade of the naiskos of the Thea Basileia on Thera, drawn by W. Willberg in 1899. From F. Hiller von Gaertringen, Die Insel Thera *I (Berlin 1899), 306. 1:50 scale.*

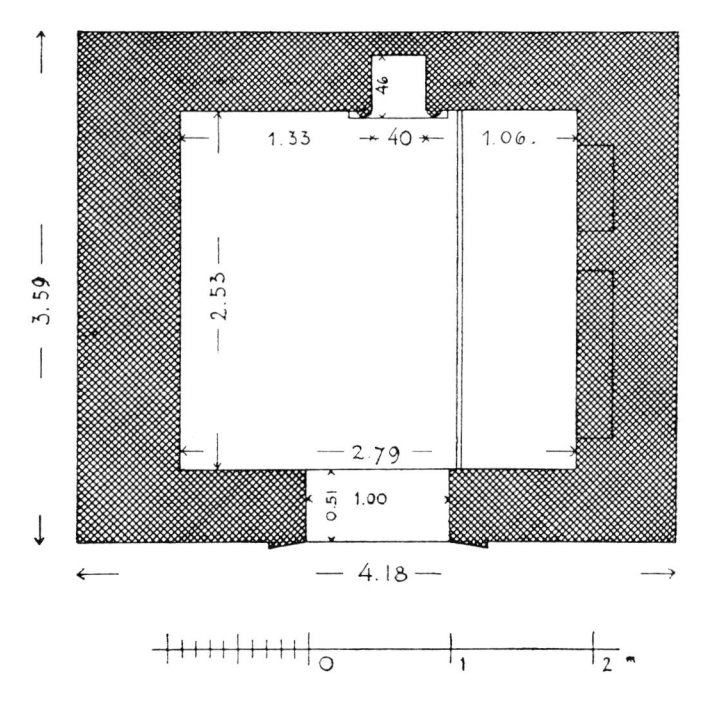

Figure 101: Plan of the naiskos of the Thea Basileia by Willberg. From Die Insel Thera I, *307. 1:50 scale.*

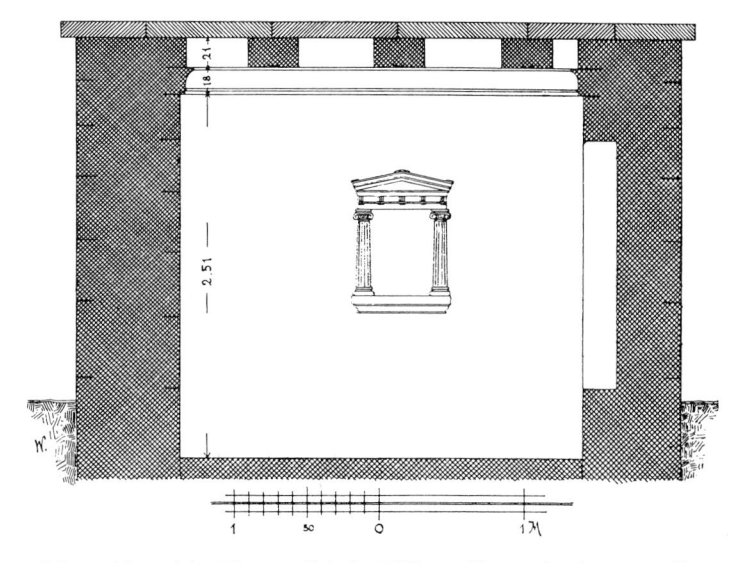

Figure 102: Cross-section of the naiskos of the Thea Basileia by Willberg, illustrating its rear wall. From Die Insel Thera I, *307. 1:50 scale.*

distressed heroine as either Basile or Iasile[130] in the act of being abducted by Echelos who drives a four-horse chariot led by Hermes Pseuchopompos. Whatever the identity of the female protagonist, the scene closely mimics the "raptus Proserpinae" illustrated elsewhere in a variety of media.[131] If not Persephone, the original occupant of the temple in the plain beneath the historical city of Thera must have been at least a female deity of a closely related chthonian type.

What, however, gives the Therean shrine set in the plain beneath the historical town of Thera a special piquancy is the fact that it virtually duplicates the width of the S7 building: Basileia Shrine 4.18 m.; S7 Building 4.20 m. Although originally built lower than S7, the Thera structure was less ground-hugging than it appears in contemporary photographs and in Wilberg's 1899 elevation. According to the latter, the ancient floor lay a full half meter below ground level by Hiller von Gaertringen's day. The present threshhold is evidently a post-antique insertion. Originally the structure almost certainly rose on a three-stepped crepis (now buried?). The lack of any uniform height to the surviving superstructure courses deprives us of any ready indication as to the course height of the crepis, but three foot-high steps of 0.35 m. (repeating the height of its fifth course above ground-level) would give the elevation an additional 1.05 m. to add to its height of 2.90 m. recorded by Wilberg. This would indicate a total height of ca. four m. for its above-ground superstructure measured to the bottom of the missing pediment. With a depth of 3.59, the structure is shallower than it is wide, but, like that of its Cyrenaean counterpart, the overall effect must have been remarkably cube-like. The near proximity of the Basileia (Persephone?) shrine to the town of ancient Thera overshadowing Perissa beach reminds us once again of the connection between the painted decoration across the bench and rear wall of the S7 building and that of the three rooms of the "palace," hall, and house on the nearby acropolis of Thera.

The Cyrene sanctuary independent house type, exemplified by the S7 house as well as its several Later Archaic predecessors, appears to resonate with two additional categories of monuments that lie outside temple architecture. The discussion of these has been reserved for the final, concluding chapter of this study.

S11 Storage Chamber

The upper southwest corner of the Middle Sanctuary is taken up with a small rectangular chamber, built into the corner formed by the Hellenistic T14 and T15 peribolos walls (Plan D; Figs. 9, 69; Pls. 36, 37). In its currently preserved state this attached room obviously did not function as a separately sited, independent entity, as did the previously described S1, S5, S6, and S7 Sacred Houses, and thus does not qualify as a "house." Instead S11 is best regarded as simply a storage chamber,[132] despite the fact that some of its latest contents suggest that it could have had more than a purely utilitarian function (i.e., it may have been used for ritual).

The room's excavation was carried out in D16/17, 1 (Fig. 12). The resulting plan measures externally ca. 4.50 m. east-west by ca. 3.80 m. north-south.[133] The interior has been left largely buried in undug fill sealed beneath the upper courses of the south wall T15) which were toppled forward by earthquake pressure.[134] The northeast corner of S11 has not been located with complete certainty, and its hypothetical east wall and entrance door remain to be brought to light.

NORTH AND EAST WALLS

As preserved, the S11 north wall consists of a foundation course made up of parallel stretchers, 0.28 m. high, set on bedrock. The three blocks making up the outer file are 0.45 m. thick and 1.00, 1.70, and 0.80 m. long respectively. Their north, vertical faces have been left with rough, unfinished surfaces. The inner set of stretchers is only partly exposed but appears to measure 0.60 m. in thickness. The foundations must return south at their west end, i.e., they form a right-angle against the inner face of the T14 wall. The overburden of the collapsed T15 wall prevented tracing the extent of the return, but what would have been the external northwest corner appears to have been cut away by wall T14, and therefore predates it. This constitutes the sole piece of constructional evidence for the existence of an other-

---

130. According to recent opinion a reading of an initial iota is to be preferred, but the issue of whether Iasile ever equalled Basile remains unsettled. Shapiro (supra n. 125) 136.

131. R. Lindner, "Der Raub der Persephone in der Antiken Kunst," *Beitrage zur Archaologie* 16 (1984) passim.

132. For an alternative explanation see infra 171.

133. I.e., including the thicknesses of the T14 and T15 walls.

---

134. Plans to reerect the T15 wall and excavate the chamber's interior could not be accomplished before the conclusion of work at Cyrene in 1981.

wise largely unrecorded pre-Hellenistic existence for S11.[135]

The outer, northern file of foundations supports two courses of stretchers. A single header block at the east end of the first course appears to mark the position of the otherwise largely missing east wall. The header has slid ca. 0.25 m. north of the chamber's north face as if pressed forward by the force of the earthquake. The header and the single stretcher making up the first course are ca. 0.40 m. high; the latter measures 1.70 m. long and is 0.45 m. thick. Its outer face has also been left slightly rough and its upper edge chamfered back. Of the second course only a single stretcher survives, 1.78 by 0.43 by 0.42 m.

A single block, 0.42 by 0.45 m., projecting from the balk south of the east end of the north wall and touching its corner, may be a second header belonging to the fourth course of the east wall, here dislodged from its original position.

No trace of an inner file of stretchers is preserved for the north wall's superstructure, and it is assumed that it was built to a single stretcher's thickness. The double width of the foundations may belong to the otherwise largely undocumented first stage of the building that may have preceded wall T14.

WEST AND SOUTH WALLS

As mentioned, the north wall foundations appear to form a right-angle return to the south against the inner face of wall T14. No trace of a superstructure rising above this foundation was recovered, but it should be borne in mind that most of the southwest interior of the S11 chamber is concealed beneath unexcavated soil and earthquake debris. On the basis of what is currently known, the west wall above the foundation level was provided by wall T14. The lack of any bond between the west end of S11's north wall and T14 has already been commented on. The absence of a proper bond may stem from the fact that S11 preceded T14 and eventually saw its original west wall replaced by T14, but we have no additional proof of that assumption.

The south wall is provided by wall T15.

ROOF

A significant quantity of roof tiles was recovered from levels associated with S11's collapse.[136] The strong presumption therefore is that S11 was not an open enclosure but was instead roofed.

---

135. But see infra 171-172 for the evidence of a possible earlier floor.
136. D16/17, 1, 3a and 3b.

CONTEXT, DATE, AND FUNCTION OF THE S11 STORAGE CHAMBER

The fill across the chamber interior (Fig. 69) consists of a layer of D16/17, 1, 1 topsoil mixed with the fallen stretcher blocks from the upper courses of wall T15. St. 2 is composed of dry, granular earth mixed with broken building stones and third century A.D. and earlier artifacts, and includes a heavy concentration of roof tiles that in this instance are to be associated with the largely unexcavated D16/17, A terrain south of wall T15 (Fig. 12). It is, in other words, the usual St. 2 mix of earthquake destruction material, and overrides the top surviving course of the north wall. As such it cannot be differentiated chronologically from the St. 3 layer beneath it on the basis of its contents, although the possibility exists that St. 2 here belongs to the later of the two earthquakes to strike the sanctuary occurring in A.D. 365.

St. 3a is a deep accumulation of densely packed reddish brown soil that engulfed the interior of S11 to the top of the fourth course of its west wall (T14). Lenses or localized layers of a harder, somewhat redder soil were separated by the excavator from the bulk of the stratum and designated St. 3b. No chronological differences emerged from their respective finds, and both 3a and 3b can be taken as variations of the single period fill, namely St. 3. Roof tiles are found throughout its lower levels, along with lamps dating to the third century A.D. Both inside the S11 walls and in the sloping ground to the north up to a point well beyond the Later Archaic T6 peribolos wall (Plan B) the lower St. 3 levels were saturated with a heavy concentration of terracotta figurines. Many more figurines were in fact found north of the actual chamber than inside it.[137] The same fill contained a significant quantity of locally made coarse ware miniature hydriai as well as miscellaneous Hellenistic and earlier coins.

While it is arguably possible that all of these items were borne into the chamber and then spread further down the slope by the earthquake, it seems more likely the bulk of at least the figurines, which tended to lie at the bottom of St. 3, was stored in S11 at the time of its A.D. 262 destruction. The room may therefore be tentatively identified on the basis of its St. 3a and b finds as a votive storeroom as far as its later usage goes. A total clearance of the interior will have to be undertaken to determine if S11 possessed a bench for votive display, in which event its original function is more likely to have been cultic than storage-related.

Two stratigraphically separate patches of soil (D16/17, 1, 5 and 6) were found in the lower northwest corner. St. 6 may be part of what was a trodden earth floor belonging to S11's original building phase when its west wall was independent of wall T14, if we are in fact justified in speaking of such a phase. St. 5, which partly overlies and therefore is later than

---

137. For obvious reasons it was possible to investigate the space north of S11, including D16/17, 2, more thoroughly than inside S11, and the resulting sample is therefore significantly more accurate. Nevertheless, the impression gained from the excavation of the northwest corner of S11's interior is that it contained fewer figurines than the ground directly to its north. To repeat the observation already made above, supra chap. 3, n. 150, J. Uhlenbrock's preliminary statistics indicate that the area produced 311 catalogued complete or semi-complete figurines and 888 uncatalogued heads. Of the catalogued examples, 82% date to the mid fifth century or later, while a full 95% of the heads post-date 450 B.C. On the other hand, only seven out of the total of 1,199 catalogued and uncatalogued terracottas are Hellenistic.

St. 6, represents a shallow backfill of the builders' trench cut at the time of the construction of wall T14 and used to level the floor of S11's hypothetical second phase. No finds were recovered from either, leaving us dependent on the chamber's structural relationship with wall T14 to provide an indication of its period.

As indicated above,[138] wall T14's construction belongs to the later second century B.C. While a foundation course for an independent west wall for S11 exists against the inner face of T14, no evidence was recovered to indicate that such a wall existed after the completion of T14, and the outer northwest corner of S11 shows signs of having been trimmed back to permit the erection of T14. The interior of S11 remained empty nearly to bedrock and its north wall stood intact to at least a meter's height until the A.D. 262 earthquake. This indicates that it was never fully dismantled and backfilled, and indeed the scatter of roof tiles found throughout the lower levels of its earthquake debris stratum seems to argue that it remained roofed until a late period. In other words, the erection of wall T14 did not terminate the existence of the S11 chamber; instead it seems likely that S11 used the former for its west wall and therefore began in the second half of the second century B.C. its existence in the form in which it presently survives.

S12 Chamber

The last semi-independent building element attributable to the sanctuary's Hellenistic period is a small rectangular chamber again attached to the Middle Sanctuary's main west T14 peribolos wall roughly half way up the slope (Plan D; Figs. 9, 70, 71, 103; Pls. 94, 95). Its clearance took place in E16/17 (Area 3), 1 and E16, 2. It measures externally 5.80 m. east to west and 3.70 m. north to south, while internally it measures 4.00 by a mere 2.70 m. Echoing the arrangement of the S11 Chamber just described, it makes use of the T14 peribolos wall for its west wall. Its W10 south wall (Fig. 103) was eventually integrated with a post-A.D. 262 earthquake period retaining wall (W9) which covered its south face and partially overlapped its original thickness. At the time of their excavation the north and east walls of S12 were preserved to only the tops of their lowest courses. No trace of a permanent floor was recovered, and it is possible that the room was never provided with more than a trampled earth floor. On the other hand, the north and east walls were stripped of most of their stones in later antiquity, and a stone pavement could have been removed at the same time.

SOUTH WALL: W10

The five courses of alternating header and stretcher masonry that survive (Fig. 103; Pl. 94) rise on foundations set on thin patches of reddish brown fill and the cracked limestone bedrock pavement. Roughly trimmed header stones ca. 0.30 m. high make up the foundation course, over which rise two additional more carefully trimmed, alternating header-stretcher courses, each ca. 0.50 m. high. Above this series rise two additional courses. The fourth course above bedrock is made up of stretchers, ca. 1.20 long and 0.30 m. high; the fifth consists of a series of headers ca. 0.50 m. long and 0.40 m. high.

The upper two are set back from the lower series by ca. 0.15 m. The rise and fall of bedrock across the room's interior is such that the third course is only 0.20 m. higher than the bedrock crown. Consequently, the setback separating the third from the fourth course above bedrock must mark the approximate level of S12's now missing floor pavement, if the room indeed ever possessed something more than trampled earth.

None of wall W10's courses bond with the T14 Hellenistic peribolos but instead are neatly butted against its inner face in a way that indicates the former can only have been added subsequent to the erection of T14. The top of the fifth course of W10 is leveled to its answering course of T14, but this appears to be coincidental, since all of the lower courses are not leveled.

NORTH WALL

Four flat stretcher foundation courses are preserved, resting directly on bedrock (Fig. 70). The individual blocks average 1.20/1.40 m. long, 0.80 m. wide and 0.30 m. high. The easternmost stretcher has been set into the trimmed-off bedrock, which rises to form the chamber's northeast corner at this level. As was the case with the south wall, the north wall abuts but does not bond with Wall T14.

EAST WALL

Three foundation headers are preserved in the southeast corner, measuring 0.55 by 0.30 by 1.10 m. A single stretcher, 1.35 m. long, lying across their inner faces, evidently survives from an otherwise lost second course.

---

138. Supra 124-125 for date of wall T14.

THE HELLENISTIC, EARLY ROMAN SANCTUARY

Plate 94: South wall (W10) of the S12 Chamber from north.

Plate 95: S12 Chamber from northeast. The later Archaic (?) wall W38 occupies right foreground.

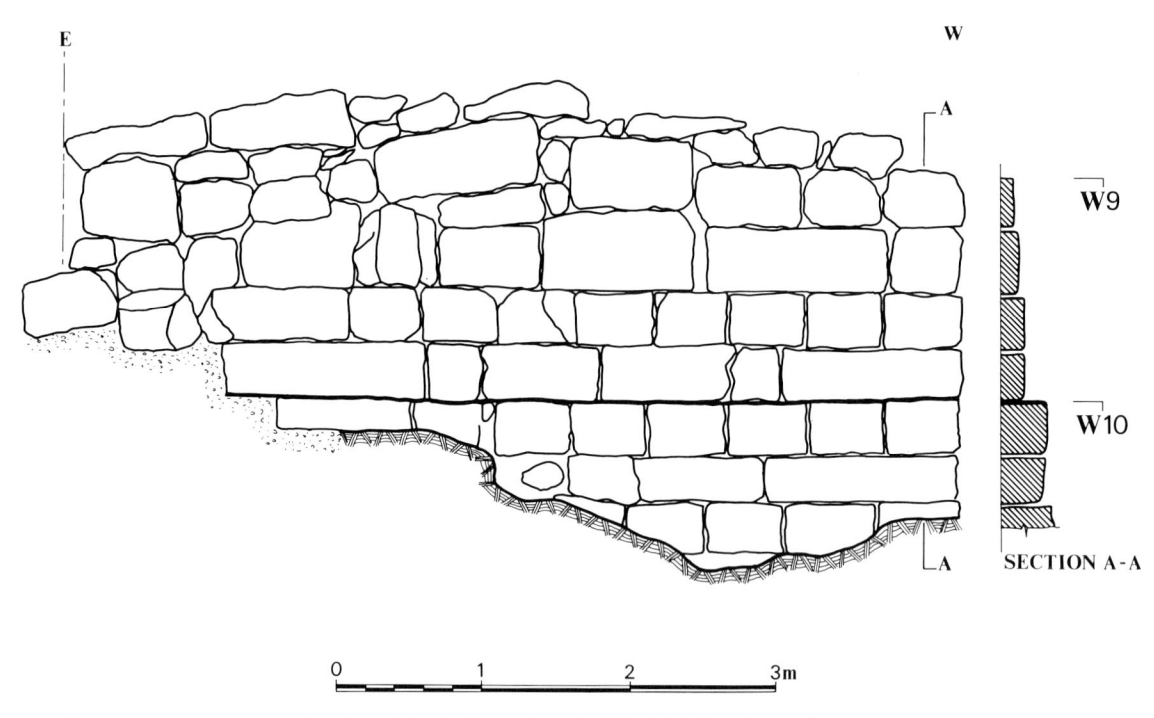

Figure 103: East-west elevation of the W10 south wall of the S12 Chamber and its squatter period W9 capping. 1:50 scale.

ROOF AND LATE MODIFICATIONS

The E16/17 (Area 3) 1, 1 fill that constitutes the only destruction layer to survive above S12's floor level contains a large number of broken pan and cover roof tiles. Some of these almost certainly were part of S12's roof, which, based on the tile evidence, appears to have stood intact until perhaps a relatively short time *before* the A.D. 262 earthquake. The north and east walls were removed before the earthquake, but the precise moment of their dismantlement cannot be fixed. The W9 late wall erected over the original W10 south wall is assigned to the post-earthquake period when S12 had clearly ceased its existence as a semi-independent chamber.

CONTEXT, DATE, AND FUNCTION OF THE S12 CHAMBER

Bedrock throughout the room's interior is marked by a series of sinkholes and natural crevices filled with a red argillaceous E16/17 (Area 3) 1, 3 fill (Fig. 71). A scattering of random terracotta figurine fragments across its top appears to stem from the St. 2 fill accumulated immediately above. St. 3 coins date to the later second, possibly early first century B.C.

E16/17 (Area 3) 1, 2 consists of a loose brown earth fill, distributed unevenly over the room's interior. Its thickest concentration was discovered in the southwest corner where, at a depth of over 0.60 m., its top was level with the setback of Wall W10's third course, which is taken to mark the missing floor surface. St. 2 appears to represent a stripped-back floor packing. It became progressively thinner as its excavation extended down the slope to the north. Some time *before* the A.D. 262 earthquake much of the layer must have been dug away to facilitate the removal of the north and east walls down to their lowest courses.

Its contents consisted once again of roof tile fragments, lamp fragments dating as late as the second century B.C., and masses of terracotta figurines. The figurines virtually saturated St. 2 inside a meter and a half's radius of the southwest corner, i.e., in the space where the fill survived to its greatest depth. In addition St. 2 contained 17 Ptolemaic bronze coins that once more depress the layer's date to as late as the second/first century B.C. No fallen building blocks or other obvious traces of destruction debris were found associated with this fill. It therefore provides a somewhat unusual instance of a stratum 2 layer *not* linked with the site's terminal earthquakes[139] but instead representing here the vestige of a votive dump used as the trampled earth floor for the room. With both E16/17 (Area 3) 1, 2 and 3 securely tied to the later second, possibly early first century B.C., the S12 chamber must once again belong to the same period as the general refurbishment of the peribolos system.

Since there are no traces of a votive bench in its interior, there is no reason to believe that S12 necessarily ever served to display, as opposed to storing, votives. In fact the primary reason for depositing the bulk of the terracottas figurines in its St. 2 floor packing may have been solely to provide a constructional backfill rather than warehousing unwanted

---

139. See White, *Final Reports* I, 103.

votes. In other words, its builders may have simply taken advantage of a convenient nearby source of fill which coincidentally happened to contain figurines and other discarded material.

The latest objects from St. 2 date to the second, possibly early first century B.C., which is the same period as the construction of Wall T14. The lack of a proper bond between the W10 and T14 walls means that the S12 Chamber must post-date, if even by only a fractional amount of time, the sanctuary's west wall against which it abuts. With its floor packing dated to essentially the same period as the west wall, it is unlikely that St. 2 could have accumulated gradually *after* S12's construction, which in turn casts some further doubt on the idea that the chamber was built primarily to store ex-votos, whatever its secondary usage might have been. If some form of actual ritual activity took place inside S12, no physical proof has survived to document its presence.

Commentary

Sanctuary storage houses like the epigraphically attested *tamieion* from the Delian *Thesmophorion*[140] and the Coan version excavated near Pyli[141] seem, as near as one can tell, to have been mainly used to house individual dedications that still retained either a religious efficacy or at least their intrinsic monetary value. To that extent they are best regarded as variant types of treasuries that can double as places for restricted votive display. While the original purpose of both the S11 and S12 Chambers is obscure at best, unlike the independent shrine houses (S1, S5, S6, and S7), neither seems to have been used for exhibiting objects.

Before, however, explaining them away as merely convenient dumping grounds for discarded votives (in this instance terracotta figurines), it is worth noting that in the context of a number of Sicilian sanctuaries[142] the argument has been mounted that a deposit of *ex-votos* (figurines, lamps, vases, loom weights, etc.) took on its own collective ritual identity when buried beneath either the floor of a sacred building or in the nearby earth.[143] In other words, a sanctuary offering experienced two separate stages in its life as a functioning votive. The first stage was when it was initially dedicated as an individual gift by the votary to the resident gods as part of a contractual agreement for services rendered or anticipated. The second stage occurred when the same object became a part of a mass of votives consigned to the ground associated with a building, in effect consecrating the very earth through the act of converting it into a *favissa*.[144] It is tempting to see something of the same process at work in the accumulation of figurines in and near the S11 and S12 Chambers beyond the more prosaic explanations offered above.

---

140. Supra 99, n. 106.
141. Supra 102, n. 126.
142. Supra 104.

---

143. P. Orlandini, "Diffusione del culto di Demetra e Kore in Sicilia," *Kokalos* 14-15 (1968-69) 335.

144. Aul. Gell., *NA* 2.10. This seems to be what in effect occurred in the case of the Demeter Malophoros sanctuary at Selinus. See B. Pace, *Arte e civilta della Sicilia antica* III (Milan 1935-1945) 474. Some of the minor Geloan sanctuaries consecrated to Demeter illustrate the same phenomenon. See also D. White, "Archaic Cyrene and the Cult of Demeter and Persephone," *Expedition* 17, 4 (1975) 11-12.

VI

Conclusion

> The 'Nordic' goddess and the Mediterranean one were unified throughout the myth of Kore's abduction by Aidoneus . . . even so, it (the myth) was never complete. The realm below could never really be without its queen, and she who returned to be with the Mother was the Maiden, the Daughter: this was τὰ τῆς Κόρης μυστήρια. No farmer prayed for corn to Persephone; no mourner thought of the dead as being with Kore.
>
> Zuntz, *Persephone* 77.

What the Wadi Bel Gadir sanctuary contributes is a detailed look at localized cultic activity spread over more than eight hundred years. The first six centuries of its architectural development that form the subject of this study reveal no abrupt or radical shifts in layout but instead display a gradual accumulation of separate parts—outer walls, terraces, gateways, steps and access doorways, "storage" rooms and other miscellaneous but all too frequently unidentifiable utilitarian structures, water works, and, above all, individual, independent shrine houses, whose collective appearance by the end of the period under review appears to be the consequence of practical requirements present from the outset. To a large extent the execution of the various separate parts exhibits a pervasive conservatism. In perhaps equal measure their final assembly betrays a form of topographical determinism in which the site, as opposed to any set of abstract religious/aesthetic theories, governs the cumulative architectural result.

The importance of setting has been repeatedly and I think rightly stressed. The sequestered extramural location overlooking a wild gorge undoubtedly satisfied a basic craving for isolation and privacy that has numerous precedents in other sanctuaries dedicated to these deities.[1] The close link with the surrounding agricultural region has been argued to be both physical through the mechanism of monumental stairs that led to a second architectural complex on the hilltop to the south[2] and economic based on revenues derived from the adjacent fields and grazing lands that in part may have been owned by the priesthood or were at least subject to their taxation.[3] The extent to which the sanctuary in its final form "faced" north in the direction of the walled city or south toward the grain fields and pasture lands stretching toward ancient Balagrae is, as has been stated elsewhere, not readily determined.[4] As far as actual building procedures are concerned, the selection, for whatever reasons,[5] of a steeply rising slope describing a nearly forty-five percent gradient demanded the use of a relatively sophisticated system of retaining walls and terraces that increased in complexity as the sanctuary gradually expanded out of its original nucleus.[6] What is interesting to note here is that, long after technical mastery had been gained over the setting, the later builders never attempted to replace the natural rise and fall of the landscape interior of the Middle Sanctuary with the flat "monumentalized" terraces surrounded by porticos familiar from Cos[7] and Lindos.[8] Instead, each independent building was left to the end with its own separate position and individual orientation across the interior's steep rocky ground in a way that is more reminiscent of the deployment of the various monuments along the rising, twisting Sacred Way at Delphi than, for example, the studied formality of the Demeter Sanctuary at Pergamon.

The response to the natural setting is exhibited in another way. Where construction took place at the level eventually developed into the Upper Sanctuary, the builders were dealing with essentially level ground (Figs. 1-9). Too little is known of the S2, S3, and S4 structures to be completely certain of their principal orientation, but all three appear to open to the south, i.e., up the slope to their rear. Otherwise a fairly clear-cut picture emerges across the remainder of the Upper Sanctuary in which the hypothetical gateway to

---

1. Vit., *De Arch.* 1.7.2: "Item Cereri extra urbem loco, quo nomine semper homines, nisi per sacrificium, necesse habeant adire; cum religione, caste sanctisque moribus is locus debet tueri." See *Final Reports* I, 48-53.
2. *Final Reports* I, 14-15, 46-47, 53, figs. 3, 17. White, *Suburban Expansion* 114-16.
3. White, *Suburban Expansion* 115-16. *Final Reports* I, 53.
4. White, *Suburban Expansion* 114-15.
5. For hillside settings see supra 37-38. Also *Final Reports* I, 31-53.
6. As the sanctuary grew, it moved downward to fill the lower levels of the wadi slope. Whether it also absorbed more of the higher terrain to its south in its later phases is less certain.
7. R. Herzog et al., *Kos, Ergebnisse der deutschen Ausgrabungen und Forschungen* (Berlin 1932). A. Lawrence, *Greek Architecture* (Baltimore 1957) 207, pl. 109. A. A. Boethius and J. Ward-Perkins, *Etruscan and Roman Architecture* (Baltimore 1970) 122.
8. E. Dyggve, *Lindos, fouilles et recherches* III: *Le sanctuaire d'Athena Lindia et l'architecture* (Berlin 1960). A. Tataki, *Lindos, the Acropolis and the Medieval Castle* (Athens 1980).

the east (Plan D, W3) gives access to an interior court (?) entered by a large doorway (G1). This in turn leads directly west to the the F2 fountain installation set at the opposite end of the precinct. In other words, the main axis of the largely flat Upper Sanctuary runs east-west, while the principal alignment of the steeply rising Middle Sanctuary is mainly south-to-north in the direction of the city towards which most of its components face.[9] In practical effect this opened the Middle Sanctuary buildings to observation from the city ramparts across the wadi,[10] a fact that should be borne in mind whenever one considers what sort of activities may have taken place inside the walls. By way of contrast, the Upper Sanctuary, even in its pre-Imperial phase, seems to look more toward the south and east in the directions of the principal access routes linking the sanctuary with Cyrene's suburbs and neighboring countryside.

In strictly regional terms the Pentapolis offers no close parallels to the overall plan of the Demeter and Persephone Sanctuary. In addition, the sanctuary's few elements that do echo other Cyrenean monuments, such as its Upper Sanctuary Propylaeum (S20) and Southwest Building (S17) (Plan E),[11] were not added until the Augustan period or later. Although the retaining wall system across the front of the Hellenistic Middle Sanctuary anticipates the Trajanic terracing that carries the northern edge of the Apollo Sanctuary's Roman Baths,[12] it is the later T20 post-A.D. 115 replacement (Pls. 1, 2)[13] that provides the best comparison with the Apollo Sanctuary's own great retaining wall. The urban Apollo Sanctuary housed a plurality of deities in a fairly wide assortment of temples, naiskoi, a treasury (if that is a proper title for the *Strategheion*),[14] monumental altars, fountains, and other sanctuary paraphernalia that are routinely encountered in the great mainland sanctuaries. Its monuments are mostly either distributed over the flat ground inside its irregularly shaped temenos or set on rising ground backed against the terraced embankments to their south.[15] The main emphasis rests on the centralized *Apollonium*, a fully peripteral temple of standard size, flanked by the smaller *Artemisium*, and coaxially aligned with a raised monumental altar. Taken together, temple, naiskos, and altar constitute a set-piece of conventional elements that is totally absent in the Wadi Bel Gadir sanctuary.

The Apollo Sanctuary's temples of Jason Magnus and Isis, its Strategheion, the stepped front of the Priests' Grotto, and other miscellaneous lesser structures compose a second major architectural grouping, placed against the sanctuary's southern flank under the shadow of the Acropolis Hill. They all share a more or less common alignment perpendicular to the embankments to their rear and a uniform northern orientation. These features again possess no direct parallels with the independently sited buildings spread *quamlibet* across the face of the Wadi Bel Gadir's Middle Sanctuary.

Elsewhere in Cyrene, the temenos arrangement surrounding the massive Zeus Temple in the northeast corner of the city still remains to be disclosed, but whatever is eventually uncovered is unlikely to offset the overwhelmingly dominant position of that great edifice, which obviously has no equivalent in the Demeter sanctuary. In terms of scale as well as plan the modest intramural Demeter Sanctuary occupying the northwest quarter of the Agora duplicates none of the features of its larger extramural counterpart.[16] The Byzantine Isis Sanctuary on the southwest slope of the Acropolis at Cyrene[17] is basically a collection of cult chambers sharing a common roof that bears no comparison with the Demeter sanctuary any more than does the more formal symmetry of the Asclepius Sanctuary at neighboring Balagrae where a conventional porticoed enclosure surrounds the temple erected against the precinct's rear wall.[18] Finally, the rural sanctuaries reported from the surrounding countryside such as the rupestrian sanctuary at Hagfa el Khasaliya[19] and the Sanctuary of the Goddesses at Budarag[20] presently add little to the discussion but may prove to have more in common with the Wadi Bel Gadir sanctuary than the intramural complexes just listed, if and when they can be more fully investigat-

---

9. The S6 Sacred House and S12 Chamber may have faced east. See infra **xx**.
10. *Final Reports* I, 48-53.
11. The S20 Propylaeum shares a good deal in common with the Apollo Sanctuary's Roman propylaeum. *Final Reports* I, s.v. 129. Stucchi, *Architettura* 271, fig. 269. The S17 Southwest Building's colonnade, now restored with fifteen columns instead of the sixteen given in *Final Reports* I, figs. 119-21, recalls the Agora's stoas although it is unlikely that the Southwest Building functioned merely as a stoa.
12. Stucchi, *Architettura* 581, pl. I, no. 29.
13. *Final Reports* I, 118.
14. The term used by Stucchi is "Donario," which he also applies to the Treasury of the Cyreneans erected at Delphi. *Architettura* 99.

---

15. Goodchild, *Kyrene* 120-21, fig. 13. Stucchi, *Architttetura* pl. I.
16. *Agora* II,1, 27-50.
17. Stucchi, *Architttetura* 441-42, figs. 449, 450.
18. Stucchi, *Architttetura* 262, fig. 258.
19. V. Purcaro, "Il santuario degli aratri di Hagfa el Khasaliya," *LA* 11-12 (1974-75) 287-94, figs. 1-5.
20. S. Ferri, "Il Santuario di Budrasc," *Notiziario archeologico della Libia* 3 (1922) 95-99, figs. 1-20. Stucchi, *Architettura* 109-10.

ed.[21] The remaining Pentapolis cities incidentally also fail to produce significant parallels.[22]

On balance, the sanctuary's architecture betrays its regional heritage more in finished details than in broad design features. For example, the careful handling of its pseudoisodomic bislab walls has an obvious counterpart in the "Second" Artemisium (whatever that structure's period) as well as a number of other city monuments.[23] Details of masonry finish or construction (meaning here rubble or polygonal stones combined with ashlars; ashlars with bevelled joints; ashlars with drafted margins and diagonally slashed faces; parallel herringbone rows of broad-toothed drove marks; rough picked surfaces) and the use of L-shaped blocks echo Agora and Apollo Sanctuary buildings as well as the nearby Apollonia defensive walls.[24] The block ratios listed in Appendix II show a preference for sturdy, squarish masonry units in the later Archaic and Classical periods and almost manneristically elongated blocks in the Hellenistic. This must reflect a broader tendency that remains to be documented elsewhere throughout the province. Few of the various architectural fragments scattered throughout the sanctuary belong to buildings before the time of Augustus, but, to anticipate the results of the forthcoming study of the Imperial architecture, the later column bases, capitals, pilasters, door frames, cornice mouldings, etc. all stylistically belong to the mainstream of Cyrenaican architecture. While a far cry from the complex use of ratios derived from irrational numbers that has been imputed by Bousquet and Stucchi to the Treasury of the Cyreneans at Delphi and the *Strategheion* at Cyrene itself,[25] the straightforward use of simple mathematical ratios expressed by units of three ancient feet in the plan and elevation of the S7 Sacred House has precedents in other local buildings too numerous to require individual citation.[26]

By describing it as "l'unica, misera eco cirenaica dei maestosi terrazzamenti dei ricchi santuari greci coevi"[27] Stucchi has put his finger on an important sanctuary trait, despite the fact that it is not so easy to say precisely where the nearest external parallels lie. Of all of the Demeter sanctuaries discussed above, Acrocorinth, Priene, Pergamum, and Cnidus perhaps come closest to Cyrene, although it is safe to say that none provides a matching blueprint; again one wishes more were known about the Cnidian version. Moreover, despite the fact that some of the terraced sanctuaries consecrated to other deities exhibit a certain communality of approach to sanctuary design with the present example, there is never enough to suggest a convincing direct link. In the final analysis, the Cyrene sanctuary deserves its own small but special niche within the larger framework of Greek sacred architecture.

As much as anything, the proof for this assertion depends on that elusive duality which seems to undergird its design and distribution of elements, absent, as far as one can tell, from all other Demeter sanctuaries. "No farmer prayed for corn to Persephone; no mourner thought of the dead as being with Kore." In its earliest phase the Middle Sanctuary grounds may have been divided by a north-south cross-wall into two parts. The eastern was larger than the western and may have differed from the latter in terms of wall construction.[28] During the later Archaic, early Classical phase the center of the eastern half was occupied by the S1 Sacred House (Plan B). The S5 Sacred House rose to its immediate west but on a slightly different axis. Both buildings opened down the hill to the north. The S6 Sacred House, added during the same period in the western half, is missing both its

---

21. Since I completed this text, E. Fabbricotti's discussion of the Budarag (or Budrasc) sanctuary, in which the latter is treated as a possible source for the important series of sculpted relief panels found in the course of building New Shahat during the later 1970s, has appeared. The relief series repeatedly depict, *inter alia*, Demeter and the Kore, and their associated rites, celebrated in privacy away from the city, are argued to have possessed a chthonian as well as a possibly oracular character. See "Divinita greche e divinita libie in relievi di eta ellenistica," *QAL* 12 (1987) 241-44, figs. 20-23.

22. It is sometimes overlooked that the Tocra sanctuary, familiar mainly because of its pottery, was consecrated to Demeter. Its architectural layout unfortunately remains an almost total mystery. *Tocra* I, 5-15.

23. Supra 59 ff.

24. Supra 106. See also *Final Reports* I, 14-16, for drafted margins and diagonal slashing on the walls of Applebaum's hilltop complex south of the sanctuary.

25. J. Bousquet, *Fouilles de Delphes* II, Pt. 1, fasc. 3 (1952) 77 ff. Stucchi, *Architettura* 99, n. 4. D. White, *ArtB* 59 (1977) 624.

---

26. But see Stucchi, *Architettura* 683 under "piede."

27. Stucchi, *Architettura* 108. While one might have wished that he was a little less obloquious in his overall assessment, a good deal of the excavation remained to be done at the time of his writing.

28. The western half seems to have used a combination of roughly dressed rubble or polygonal stones with squared masonry, while the eastern portion utilized a mixture of rubble with more carefully dressed plug-shaped polygonal stones. This theoretical division into two parts is further supported by a shift in the alignment of the early Archaic peribolos wall at the point where walls P8 and P9 meet (Plan A). Supra 20-24. Some minor, possibly meaningless differences have also been detected between the pseudoisodomic masonry of the eastern half of the later Archaic, early Classical T1 peribolos and its southwestern continuation, wall T6. Supra 50. The shift in wall alignment across the northern face of the Middle Sanctuary, however, continued to be observed until the end of the sanctuary's organized existence.

original eastern and northern walls, but if its imperial period S6a phase is any guide (Plan E), its main facade faced east. Assuming that the original spatial division into two unequal parts continued to retain some of its earlier validity into the later Archaic/Classical period, the eastern precinct contained two shrine houses, both facing north, while the slightly smaller western precinct ended up with a single house that looked to the larger unit to its east.

This dual arrangement persisted until Hellenistic/early Roman times when the two storage chambers (S11 and S12) were constructed along the western flank and the eastern precinct received the S7 Sacred House and F1 fountain house. Some degree of shift in the alignment of the north wall of the peribolos was retained to the end of the sanctuary's active life. *Where* and *why* it occurred along the wall after the early Archaic phase are hard to answer because the heavy Imperial period T20 curtain masks most of the retaining wall's inner face (Plan E; Pls. 1, 2). There was nothing in the tectonic structure of the sloping bedrock, so far as I know, to have prevented the ancient builders from running their wall in a straight line across the entire forward face of the sanctuary, if they had so wished. That they persisted instead in interrupting the line of their wall suggests that the old spatial division into two unequal halves was honored to the end.

Even if we are wrong to divide the Middle Sanctuary by restoring a north-south cross-wall, its basic duality can be inferred in other ways. In the first place, the site's inscriptions make clear that its grounds were explicitly consecrated to both the mother and daughter goddess and not just to Demeter, as was frequently the case in other parts of the Greek world.[29] Specific epigraphic texts associate the sanctuary with statues and *naoi* dedicated to Great Demeter, Parthenos (epithet of Kore?), and Kore.[30] In the opening years of the site's pre-World War I excavation Ghislanzoni reported an inscription to which he restored the names of Demeter and the Kore.[31] In the inscriptions recovered by The University Museum since 1969 Demeter is invoked six times[32] and the Kore four. Both deities are portrayed together on a marble relief and in a statuette group,[33] as well as separately on numerous other occasions where their differentiation is less clear-cut.

The agricultural aspect of the Cyrene cult bears out basically the same duality.[34] Apart from the numerous sanctuary votives in various media that depict plants and animals,[35] the goddesses' concern for nature's fertility is directly attested by their two locally recorded *epikleseis*. The first comes from a lead defixio recovered at Cyrene without specific provenience but apparently to be dated to the third century B.C. It names the mother goddess *Aglaokarpos* or "Bestower of Goodly Fruit."[36] The second is part of an inscribed Antonine-Severan statue base attached to a life-size marble statue of the Kore from the sanctuary.[37] The latter reads:

> Helvia Teimareta, having received an oracle in a dream, dedicated to Demeter and Kore a statue of Kore—the Kore who presides over the grain.[38]

Reynolds has observed that the retention of interest in the agricultural aspects of the Kore's role to such a relatively late period is one of the text's more interesting features.

Approaching the fertility aspect from another direction, Kane has identified the local divinity, Aristeus, son of the nymph Kurana, as the subject of a small Hellenistic-Roman marble relief found in surface fill from the area of the F2 fountain complex.[39] He is shown seated on a low, backless chair; a small quadruped, perhaps a cow or bull, rests in front of the god. In his Cyrenean guise Aristeus has pastoral-agricultural as well as chthonic interests that make his presence, otherwise not attested, especially appropriate here.[40]

What is pointedly missing in the texts is any reference to the actual name of Persephone, queen of the

---

29. Farnell, *Demeter Cult* 114, 116-17.
30. Supra 101. *Final Reports* I, 5, 14, 20, 22.
31. *Final Reports* I, 11, n. 56.
32. Seven times if a recently discovered dedication to Ceres, recovered by the Department of Antiquities after the completion of The University Museum's fieldwork, is included. See infra n. 65.
33. S. Kane, "The Sanctuary of Demeter and Persephone in Cyrene, Libya," *Archaeology* 32, 2 (1977) 58. S. Kane, "Sculpture Appendix," *LA* 13-14 (1976-77) 329-30, pl. XCVI, c. D. White, "Excavations in the Sanctuary of Demeter and Persephone at Cyrene. Fourth Preliminary Report," *AJA* 80 (1976) pl. 28, fig. 37. D. White et. al., *Expedition* 18, 2 (1976) 17-19, fig. 3. Also Kane, sanctuary sculptures forthcoming, cat. nos. **1, 90**.
34. Supra 44, n. 9.
35. *Final Reports* I, 29. *Final Reports* IV, editor's preface xxvii-xxviii.
36. *SEG* IX, nos. 105, 106. G. Pugliese Carratelli, "Supplemento Epigrafico Cirenaico," *ASAtene* XXIII-XXIV (1961-62) 324, no. 193, figs. 141, 142. J. Reynolds, "Cyrenaica 1962-72," *JHS-AR* (1972) 46-47, n. 208.
37. S. Kane and J. Reynolds, "The Kore who Looks after the Grain," *AJA* 89 (1985) 455-63, pls. 48-51. Reynolds, site inscriptions forthcoming, cat. no. **16**.
38. Kane and Reynolds (supra n. 37) 462. Reynolds, site inscriptions forthcoming, cat. no. **16**.
39. Kane, sanctuary sculptures forthcoming, cat. no. **6**.
40. Verq., *G.* 4.222. L. Vitali, "Una divinita della Cirenaica: Aristeo," *AfrIt* 2 (1928) 17-29, cited by Kane, sanctuary sculptures forthcoming. *RE* 2, 1 (1895) 851-59, *s.v.* Aristaios (Hiller von Gaertringen). Stucchi, *Architettura* 109, n. 3. Fabbricotti (supra n. 21) 238-40, ns. 91-102.

dead.[41] This conforms with practices recorded in many other Greek sites.[42] Despite the direct avoidance of her name, at least some facets of both the architecture and the votives seem filled with the immanency of that goddess's presence. The same third century B.C. defixio that recorded the *Aglaokarpos* also invokes the Kore as *Praxidike* or "She who Bestows Penalties."[43] A rather exceptional late Roman gold diadem worked in repoussé technique with a procession of seven deities found in earthquake debris in the area of the S1 Sacred House is unmistakably chthonian in terms of its decorative program; Warden has suggested that it originated as part of a deceased person's funerary regalia.[44] The Aristeus relief is not the only sanctuary stone relief that possesses funereal overtones, since eight similarly modest stone reliefs have been brought to light that appear to depict deceased heroized male horsemen. Kane believes that the riders refer to specific or real young men (as opposed to generic "youth"), since two that are named by inscription appear to have been granted posthumous honors by the city and then placed under the protection of Aristeus and Persephone.[45] A Hadrianic-Antonine portrait of an infant girl found in the S12 Chamber's earthquake debris has been identified as a memorial to a deceased child on the basis of its extreme youth as well as the indentations for a missing wreath in its hair.[46] The portrait attests the child's early initiation into the goddess's cult as well as her parents' longing to preserve the immortality of her soul in Persephone's safekeeping.[47] Over twenty statuette fragments of child portraits, mostly female, ranging in age from infants to adolescents have also been found, and at least some of these dedications must be at least prophylactic in intent when they are not posthumous-commemorative.[48] In either case, the children's futures were entrusted to Persephone, keeper of souls, rather than the Kore, the Corn-Maiden. In the sanctuary's important series of full-size statue heads and bodies, female subjects greatly outnumber the male, as one would normally expect in a sanctuary where the rites were so explicitly centered on women. While some must depict the resident goddesses, many portray mortal women (perhaps in their role as priestesses dressed to resemble the goddesses), men, and children. It is difficult to tell how many of these were actually alive or dead at the time of their statue's dedication. The sanctuary's various dedicatory inscriptions do little here to help resolve what is a particularly trying problem. Regrettably, at least for purposes of resolving this particular issue, the one inscribed statue base that survives attached to its original statue represents a goddess rather than a mortal.[49] Nevertheless, based on what is known of the aspirations for a life after death expressed by the cult's practitioners elsewhere, particularly Eleusis,[50] it seems likely that many of the site's Hellenistic and Roman period portraits refer to deceased persons, for whom a life of good works, grounded in the observances of the resident cult, would have led to an expectation of some form of existence beyond the grave. On the other hand, something of the same kind of eschatological requirement presumably underlies the dedication of statues of persons still living. The important point to grasp is that, whether one is dealing with portraits of the quick or the dead, it is to Persephone, queen of the dead, that they are directed even when Demeter and the Kore, *favete linguis*, happen to be named in the inscriptions.

This leads us to the Middle Sanctuary's four independent shrine houses. Strikingly little survives in an archaeological sense to explain their original purpose, but if we can assume that the restored S7 Sacred House (as well as its near counterpart, the well-preserved Temple of the Thea Basileia on Thera) reflects a generalized impression of the appearance of the remaining S1, S5, and S6 houses, it becomes apparent that the series resonates, *mutatis mutandis*, with three familiar categories of commemorative funerary art that perhaps help to shed additional light on their character.

The first is funeral stelai. Sometimes called *naiskoi stelai*,[51] gravestones framed with either pilasters or antae and crowned with pediments, are a familiar category of Classical grave marker. With antecedents going back to the late Archaic period,[52] the type

---

41. E. Rohde, *Psyche, the Cult of Souls and Belief in Immortality among the Greeks* (8th ed. New York 1966) 160. Zuntz, *Persephone* 78.
42. Farnell, *Demeter Cult* 118.
43. Supra n. 36.
44. P. Warden, "The Miscellaneous Small Finds," *Final Studies* IV, 14 cat. no. **39**.
45. Kane, sanctuary sculptures forthcoming, cat. nos. **7-14**.
46. Kane, sanctuary sculptures forthcoming, cat. no. **171**. D. White, "Two Girls from Cyrene," *OpRom* 9:2-4 (1973) 207-15, figs. 6-8.
47. The custom of initiating infants into the Eleusinian Mysteries to insure their future well-being in the event of premature death is well attested during the Imperial period. White (supra n. 46) 214, ns. 60-68.
48. Discussed more fully by Kane in her forthcoming study.

---

49. The Helvia Teimareta statue discussed supra 180, n. 37.
50. Farnell, *Mystery* 121. Farnell, *Demeter Cult* 192-93, 197. Rohde (supra n. 41) 218 ff. S. Angus, *The Mystery Religions* (reprint 2nd. ed. New York 1955) 139-40. W. Guthrie, *The Greeks and their Gods* (reprint Boston 1955) 284. Kerenyi, *Eleusis* 142.
51. C. Clairmont, *Gravestone and Epigram* (Mainz 1970) 46-47, pls. 6-16.
52. D. Kurtz and J. Boardman, *Greek Burial Customs* (Cornell 1971) 131-32.

Plate 97: Side/rear view of temple-tomb, Cyrene West Necropolis.

awaiting discovery in unexcavated ground or could even lie unidentified amongst the structures already brought to light. In theory Claudia Venusta's restored "naoi" could refer to any of the sanctuary's small houses. The most startling implication of their texts is unquestionably the fact that the sanctuary's houses were individually consecrated to single deities. It therefore remains at least hypothetically possible that the rites of Parthenos-Persephone, queen of the dead, were centered in the S6a Sacred House in the western sector, leaving the agriculture/fertility aspect of Demeter and the Kore's cult, along with the worship of the male god Dionysos, to be accommodated by the S1, S5a, and S7a houses over on the east.

The spatial distribution of the independent houses across the rocky ground of the Middle Sanctuary requires one final observation. Before the Imperial period when the Upper Sanctuary grounds received the large colonnaded Southwest Building across their western half (Plan E, S17) the sanctuary lacked any single, dominant monument—stoa, temple, mystery-hall or whatever. For an ancient visitor to experience the sanctuary in something approaching its entirety he or she was compelled to walk back and forth as well as up and down over a considerable amount of enclosed interior space. People circulating about, whether freely or in formal, ordered processions, was an important feature of Demeter ritual wherever it was practiced and nowhere more so than in Attica where the distances traveled could be measured in miles. It may recalled, for example, that on 13 and 14 Boedromion before the actual commencement of the Mysteries, the Athenian ephebes conducted the *hiera* from Eleusis to the Eleusinion at the foot of the Acropolis.[69] On the second day, Boedromion 16, the *mystai* flocked to the sea.[70] On 19 Boedromion, the day of the great pilgrimage or *Pompe*, the participants walked the fourteen miles from the Kerameikos to Eleusis with crowns of myrtle on their heads and bundles of leaves in their hands (*bakchoi*), carrying at the procession's head the statue of Iakchos-Diony-

---

69. Simon (supra n. 68) 25. Mylonas, *Eleusis* 245-46.
70. Mylonas, *Eleusis* 249.

sos.[71] Conceivably more germane to the celebration of the Cyrene cult for which there exists virtually no specific information, Mylonas has argued that the wanderings of the mother-goddess and her arrival at Eleusis may have been reenacted as part of the Eleusinian *dresmosune*, which would have involved some form of prescribed movement inside the sanctuary grounds.[72] The Attic rite of the Calathus, a festival separate from the Mysteries in which the basket of Demeter was drawn through the streets by carriage,[73] parallels Callimachus's poetical description of the Procession of the Calathus which stirred so much debate among earlier commentators on Cyrene's topography.[74] Enough has been said about that subject to deter bringing it up again here, but more than anything else what emerges from the Callimachean Hymn is that its rites involved the movement of the celebrants between either two separate, semi-independent sanctuaries or two temples.[75]

In terms of the local situation, beyond the fact that movement between the various Middle Sanctuary buildings could have been managed under the concealment of night or during daytime when its grounds were more open to direct observation from the city ramparts, there is simply no way of telling whether local ritual, conceivably modified by a lost Cyrenean tradition of the goddesses' myth,[76] ordered a predetermined, fixed itinerary, a kind of pagan "stations of the cross," or instead encouraged random free-access to its various parts. It is likely that both types of passage were permitted but varied according to the religious calendar: fixed processions occurring during set festivals, free-movement during open days. With the evolution of a more formally structured traffic pattern taking shape during the sanctuary's next phase on both its upper and lower levels, discussion of this matter has yet to be exhausted.

---

71. Simon (supra n. 68) 32. Mylonas, *Eleusis* 252-58.

72. G. Mylonas, *The Hymn to Demeter and her Sanctuary at Eleusis* (St. Louis 1942) 89.

73. Farnell, *Demeter Cult* 47.

74. *Final Reports* I, 13-14, 18, 47-48.

---

75. *Final Reports* I, 48, ns. 37-38.

76. For the possibility of a distinctively regional cult, see supra 44, n. 9, "Demeter Libyssa.".

Appendix I

Dates of Archaeological Contexts Organized by Area, Trench, Stratum, and Classes of Objects

The Appendix lists the earliest and latest examples representative of any given class of artifacts from each Area, Trench, and Stratum context. The following abbreviations are used in conjunction with "Artifact Type/Catalogue Number" entries to indicate artifact type, publisher, and place of publication; an asterisk designates artifacts that have not received a final Catalogue Number from their publisher at this time of writing, but whose dates have been communicated to the Series Editor for inclusion here.

EG G. Schaus, *Final Reports* II: *The East Greek, Island, and Laconian Pottery*
BF M. Moore, *Final Reports* III: *The Attic Black Figure and Attic Black Pattern Pottery*
FW P. Kenrick, *Final Reports* III: *Hellenistic and Roman Fine Wares*
IG S. Lowenstam, *Final Reports* III: *Scarabs, Incised Gems, and Engraved Finger Rings*
G   A. Oliver, *Final Reports* IV: *Glass*
MF P. Warden, *Final Reports* IV: *Miscellaneous Small Finds*
C   T. Buttrey, *Final Reports* VI: *The Coins*
RF I. McPhee, *Final Reports* VI: *The Attic Red Figure Pottery*
TC J. Uhlenbrock, *Final Reports*, forthcoming: *Terracotta Figurines and Plastic Vases*
S   S. Kane, *Final Reports*, forthcoming: *Stone Sculpture*
CP A. Kocybala, *Final Reports*, forthcoming: *Corinthian Pottery*
L   E. Fabbricotti, *Final Reports*, forthcoming: *Lamps*
I   J. Reynolds, *Libya Antiqua*, forthcoming: *Inscriptions*

In the case of certain classes of artifacts, the author uses a single catalogued entry to illustrate a group of similar artifacts. When an artifact occurring in a given context belongs to the larger class but has not itself been specifically catalogued, its generic catalogue number appears in parentheses. To illustrate this process from Kenrick's publication of the Hellenistic and Roman fine wares *Final Reports* III, his catalogue entry 70 from C10/11, A, 4 illustrates a ware dating from the late second to the end of the first century B.C. Where a comparable sherd occurs in another context, as for example C11, A, 3, it is referred to as (70).

The following abbreviations appear in connection with the dates:
A   Archaic
C   Classical
H   Hellenistic
R   Roman
n.d. No Date Assigned

All dates are before Christ, unless otherwise indicated.
All dates may be taken to be approximate, with the exception of Imperial regnal coins.

Area	Trench	Stratum	Artifact Type/Cat. No.	Date
C11	1	3b	EG/240	550-520
			Attic lamp	Late 6th to 480
C11	1	4	G/46	6th-1st
C11	2	2D	L/*	4th
		2NW	Attic black glaze	Pre-400
		5	CP/*	Late 6th, early 5th
C12/13	1	3	IG/15	6th
			MF/17	6th
			MF/132	Prob. A
		3/4	EG/521	590-550
		3/4	EG/557	540-520
C12/13	1	4	EG/310	600-550
			EG/525	590-550
			MF/190	Prob. late 7th-6th
			MF/13	Prob. A
			TC/*	550
			IG/29	610-500
C12/D12	G	3	MF/188	Prob. late 7th-6th
			MF/133	Prob. A
			TC/*	6th?
		4	Misc. Corinthian	Pre-500?
C13/D13	1	7	EG/303	600-575
			EG/566	540-520
			MF/189	Prob. late 7th-6th
			MF/195	Poss. 6th
C15/16	1:W4	4	C/75	490-475
			C/355	145-116
			TC/*	4th
			FW/(33)	2nd or 1st
			FW/(39-41)	2nd or 1st
			L/*	5th
			L/*	3rd-2nd
C15/16	1:W4	5	MF/21	Prob. late 7th- early 6th
C15/16	1:4-2	4	TC/*	H
			C/75	490-475
			C/266	222-145
			C/304	145-116
C15/16	1:4-2	5	EG/183	540-530
			TC/*	Mid 5th
			FW/(39-41)	2nd or 1st?
C15/16	1:4-2	6	TC/*	Early 5th
C14	1	4	BF/29	550-540
			Corinthian	pre-500
C15/D15	1	4a	"Gnathian"	H
		5	EG/243	550-500

APPENDIX I

Area	Trench	Stratum	Artifact Type/Cat. No.	Date
			L/*	5th
			C/484	145-104
			FW/(70)	Late 2nd-A.D. 10
D10	A	3	L/*	5th
			L/*	4th
			RF/52	450-425
			FW/1	Late 5th
			FW/8	4th/3rd
			TC/*	4th
			C/465	145-104
			C/594	104-96
D10/11	C	3a	C/155	Late 4th-308
			C/431	116-104
			S/222	A.D. 100
D10/11	C	6	IG/42	450-425
			RF/36	480-460
			L/*	5th
			TC/*	Early 5th
			C/682	116-96
D11/12	A	3	C/38	510-490
			C/123	Late 4th-308 B.C.
D11/12	1	3	MF/178	Prob. 6th
			MF/201	Prob. A
			C/36	510-490
			C/723	Late 2nd, early 1st
D11/E11	Balk	3	EG/481	600-575
			CP/*	575-550
			C/115	Late 4th-308
D12	1	4	TC/*	Mid 5th
D12	balk	3e	IG/44	400-350
			L/*	5th
			L/*	4th
		4	L/*	4th
			L/*	3rd
D13 (Area 2)	2	2	EG/236	600-575
			RF/16	380-350
			TC/*	?
			S/313	H-R
			S/546	H-R
			C/746	A.D. 98-117
			L/*	3rd
		3	TC/*	Late 5th-4th
	2, Ext. N	3	EG/286	575-525
D12/13	A	3	L/*	Late 7th
			EG/282	580-540

Area	Trench	Stratum	Artifact Type/Cat. No.	Date
			EG/249	540-520
			IG/23	625-600
			CP/*	595-570
			CP/*	575-500
			BF/207	Ca. 540
			BF/115	Late 6th
			TC/*	Late 6th
			TC/*	5th-4th
			C/41	510-490
			C/88	475-435
			S/185	Late H?
D12/13	A	4	MF/234	Late 7th, early 6th
			EG/289	600-575
			EG/374	580-560
			CP/*	595-570
			CP/*	575-500?
			TC/*	Late 6th
D12/13	B	4	CP/*	580-570
			CP/*	550-early 5th
			EG/289	600-575
			BF/163	Ca. 550
			BF/191	Early 5th
			IG/36	550-500
			TC/*	Mid 6th
			TC/*	Late 6th
			L/*	5th
			L/*	4th
			RF/93	Ca. 510
			MF/70	A
			MF/358	Prob. R
			FW/*	3rd
			C/40	510-490
			C/71	490-475
			C/655	116-96
D12/13	F	3	C/29	510-490
			C/76	490-475
			EG/110	575-525
			EG/182	560-530
			MF/87	7th-early 6th
			MF/256	6th-5th
			IG/28	700-650
			IG/1	6th
D12/13	F	4	IG/25	625-600
			TC/*	Late 6th
			EG/484	600-575

APPENDIX I

Area	Trench	Stratum	Artifact Type/Cat. No.	Date
			EG/30	590-540
			BF/153	590-580
			L/*	4th
			MF/71	A
		4/5	MF/54	A-C
D12/E12	D	3	L/*	5th
			L/*	4th
D12/E12	D	5	CP/*	595-570
			CP/*	575-550
			EG/325	600-580
			EG/183	540-520
			MF/4	6th
			MF/175	Prob. 6th
			IG/6	6th
			IG/8	6th
			RF/87	Ca. 410
			TC/*	Mid 6th
			TC/*	Late 6th
			FW/(41)	2nd or 1st
			S/174	Late 2nd, 3rd A.D.
D12/E12	1	6	CP/*	575-550
D13/E13	1	3	TC/*	Late 6th
			TC/*	450
			C/151	Late 4th-308
			S/150	Late 2nd-3rd A.D.
D13/E13	1	4	IG/18	6th
			EG/415	580-560
			EG/154	560-550
D14/E14	1	2	MF/185	Prob. A
			RF/61	490-480
			RF/66 B	430-410
			C/12	510-490
			C/756	A.D. 119-138
			L/*	5th
			FW/(88)	A.D. 200-250
			S/71	A?
			S/112	Later 2nd-early 3rd A.D.
			I/16	Later 2nd-early 3rd A.D.
D14/E14	1	3	CP/*	595-570
			CP/*	Late 6th
			L/*	5th
			FW/*	2nd-1st
D15/E15	1	3	CP/*	595-570
			CP/*	Late 6th
			TC/*	Mid 6th

Area	Trench	Stratum	Artifact Type/Cat. No.	Date
			TC/*	4th
			IG/5	6th
			G/53	550-late H
D15/16	1	3	CP/*	595-570
			CP/*	Late 6th
			TC/*	Early 6th
			TC/*	5th-4th
			MF/83	A
			MF/382	575-500
			EG/330	580-560
			EG/92	575-550
			IG/30	500
			C/4	510-490
			C/150	Late 4th-308
			C/472	145-104
			L/*	3rd A.D.
D16/17	1	2	L/*	5th
			L/*	A.D. 3rd
			C/652	116-96
			FW/(39)	2nd or 1st
D16/17	1	3	L/*	5th
			L/*	2nd A.D.
			MF/382	570-500
			IG/41	450
			RF/65	450-425
			C/310	145-116
			C/631	104-96
D16/17	1	4	CP/*	590-570?
			CP/*	550-500?
			TC/*	Early 5th
D16/17	2	3	C/244	222-145
			C/712	Late 2nd-early 1st
			C/805	A.D. 8th
			C/808	A.D. 1926
			TC/*	late 6th
			TC/*	4th-3rd
			L/*	5th
			L/*	2nd
D16/17	2	4	CP/*	525-500
			TC/*	Late 6th
			TC/*	Mid 4th
			EG/209	530-510
			L/*	6th
			L/*	3rd
			G/48	6th-1st

APPENDIX I

Area	Trench	Stratum	Artifact Type/Cat. No.	Date
			C/53	510-490
			C/172	300
			C/496	145-104
			C/808	A.D. 1926
E10	balk/bldg.	2	C/73-121	Late 4th
			C/73-46	Late H?
			S/365	H-R
			MF/40	R
			L/*	5th
			L/*	A.D. 2nd
			Corrugated ware	A.D. 2nd-3rd
E10	balk/bldg	3	BF/1	Early 6th
			BF/78	5th
			RF/22A	490-480
			TC/*	Mid 6th
			TC/*	Late 5th
			L/*	5th
			G/103	A.D. 75-100
			S/365	H-R
			S/226	A.D. 117-161
			C/791	A.D. 305-306
E10	foundation trench		EG/56	570-540
			Attic BF	A
			S/141	Late H/early R
E10	balk S	2/3	EG/293	600-570
			EG/57	570-540
			RF/21A	500-480
E10	balk S	3	G/2	525-500
			TC/*	Mid 6th
			TC/*	Late 5th
E10/11 (Area 1)	1	NE Pit	C/69-228	570-525
E10/11 (Area 1)	1	3	MF/467	7th
			EG/479	600
			EG/225	520-480
			CP/*	595-570
			CP/*	550-500
			BF/176	575-550
			BF/72	500-475
E10/11 (Area 1)	1	4	C/781	A.D. 150-52
			L/*	2nd A.D.
E10/11 (Area 1)	1	5	L/*	2nd A.D.
			C/87	490-475
E11	1	4	Misc. Corinthian	Pre-500?
			MF/110	Prob. A

Area	Trench	Stratum	Artifact Type/Cat. No.	Date
			TC/*	Early 5th
			TC/*	H
E11	3	3	EG/272	590-570
			EG/83	560-540
			BF/197	Early 5th
			G/3	525-500
			MF/231	A
			L/*	6th
			L/*	5th
			RF/87	Ca. 410
			RF/14	370-340
			C/219	277-261
E11	4	4	BF/283	Early 5th
E12	1	5	BF/173	575-550
			RF/47B-E	420-400
			RF/69	420-40
			L/*	3rd
			G/94	late 1st B.C.-mid 1st A.D.
			FW/*	2nd-1st
E12	1	6	MF/413	n.d.
E12/13	C	4	TC/*	Late 7th
			TC/*	550-525
			CP/*	595-570?
			CP/*	595-500
			L/*	5th
			L/*	4th
E12/13	E	3	MF/126	Prob. A
			MF/109	Prob. A
			C/21	510-490
E12/F12	balk	3	RF/56	425-375
			L/*	4th
			L/*	3rd A.D.
E13/F13	1	3	EG/216	550-530
			L/*	5th
			L/*	4th
			S/565	1st B.C.-1st A.D.
			S/110	A.D. 117-138
			FW/(64)	A.D. 50-100
E15	1	3	CP/*	n.d.
			MF/34	A
			EG/54	565-560
			FW/36	2nd or 1st
			C/359	145-116
E15	2	3	TC/*	Mid 5th
			TC/*	5th

APPENDIX I

Area	Trench	Stratum	Artifact Type/Cat. No.	Date
			C/6	510-490
			C/320	145-116
E15	2	4	C/70	490-475
			C/148	Late 4th-308
			G/52	550-1st
E16/17 (Area 3)	1	2	L/*	3rd
			L/*	2nd
			C/140	Late 4th-308
			C/560	104-96
E16/17 (Area 3)	1	2a	RF/113A	500-475
			FW/37	2nd or 1st
E16/17 (Area 3)	1	3	C/336	145-116
			C/685	Late 2nd, early 1st
F11	1	3	S/447	H-R
			S/628	H-R
			L/*	4th
			L/*	2nd A.D.
			FW/(56)	A.D. 30-80/90
			FW/(64)	A.D. 50-100
			Corrugated ware	2nd/3rd A.D.
F11/12	1	3	TC/*	Early 5th
			TC/*	Late 5th-4th
			S/355	H-R
			C/82	490-475
			C/132	Late 4th-308
			C/501	145-104
F14/G14	1	4	CP/*	late 6th-early 5th
			C/39	510-490
F14/G14	1	5	CP/*	late 6th
F14/G14	1	6	CP/*	late 6th-450
F16	1	3	TC/*	350
F16	1	3a	IG/26	625-600
			L/*	5th

Appendix II

Block Height-to-Length Ratios

Structure	Ratio
Later Archaic, Early Classical	
Wall T1	1:2.33
Wall T2	1:2.25
Wall T4	1:2
Wall T6	1:2.04
Wall T7	1:2.88
"Second Artemisium," lower bislabs	1:2.44
"Second Artemisium," upper bislabs	1:2.18
Ashlar Masonry Structure (S3)	1:2
S4 Building, main walls	1:1.8/ 1:2.2
S4 Building, late partition wall	1:2.9
S2 Building, east wall	1:1.94
S2 Building, west wall, lower course	1:1.65/ 1:2.5
S2 Building, west wall, upper course	1:2.22
Wall W30	1:2
S19, north wall	1:2
S1 Sacred House, late (?) south wall	1:3.28
S5 Sacred House, west wall	1:2.3
S5 Sacred House, south wall	1.2.03
S5 Sacred House, east wall	1:2.65
S6 Sacred House, south wall	1:2.6
S6 Sacred House, west wall	1:2.4

Structure	Ratio
Later Classical	
Southeast Peribolos, wall W2	1:2.08
Wall T8, top course	1:4
Wall W1	1:2.04
Hellenistic, Pre-Imperial Roman	
Wall T9	1:3.5
Wall T9a	1:3.8
Wall T13, lower courses	1:4.8
Wall T13, upper courses	1:4.5
Wall T14	1:3.5/1:4
Wall T15	1:4.4
Wall T17	1:1.5/ 1:2.40
G1 threshold	1:6.1
S31 entrance, wall W32	1:4.2
S31 entrance, wall W33	1:2.3
S7 Sacred House	1:3.6
S11 Storage Chamber, north wall	1:4.25
S12 Chamber, south wall (W10)	1:4
S12 Chamber, north wall	1:4.3
S12 Chamber, east wall	1:3.6

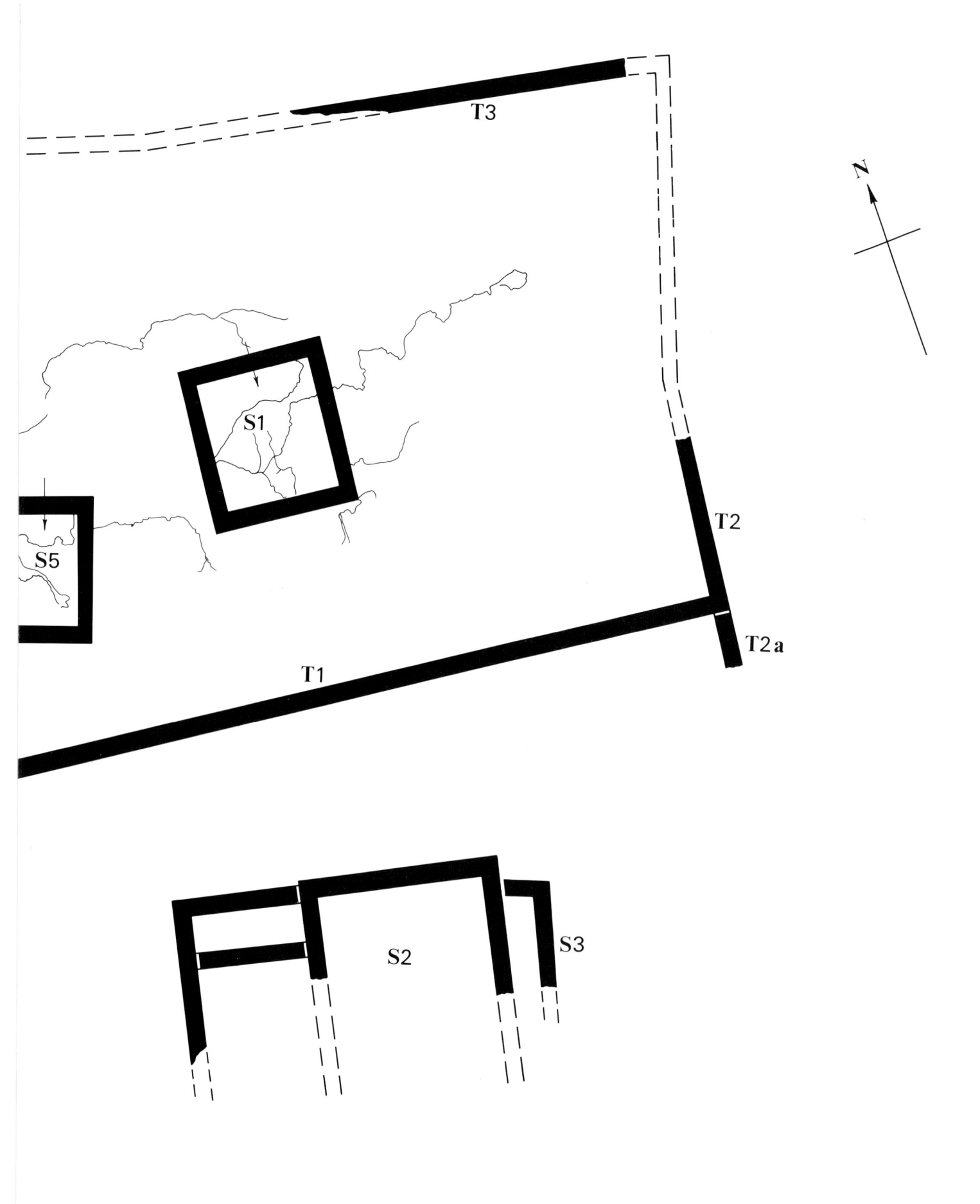

n of the later Archaic, early Classical period sanctuary.

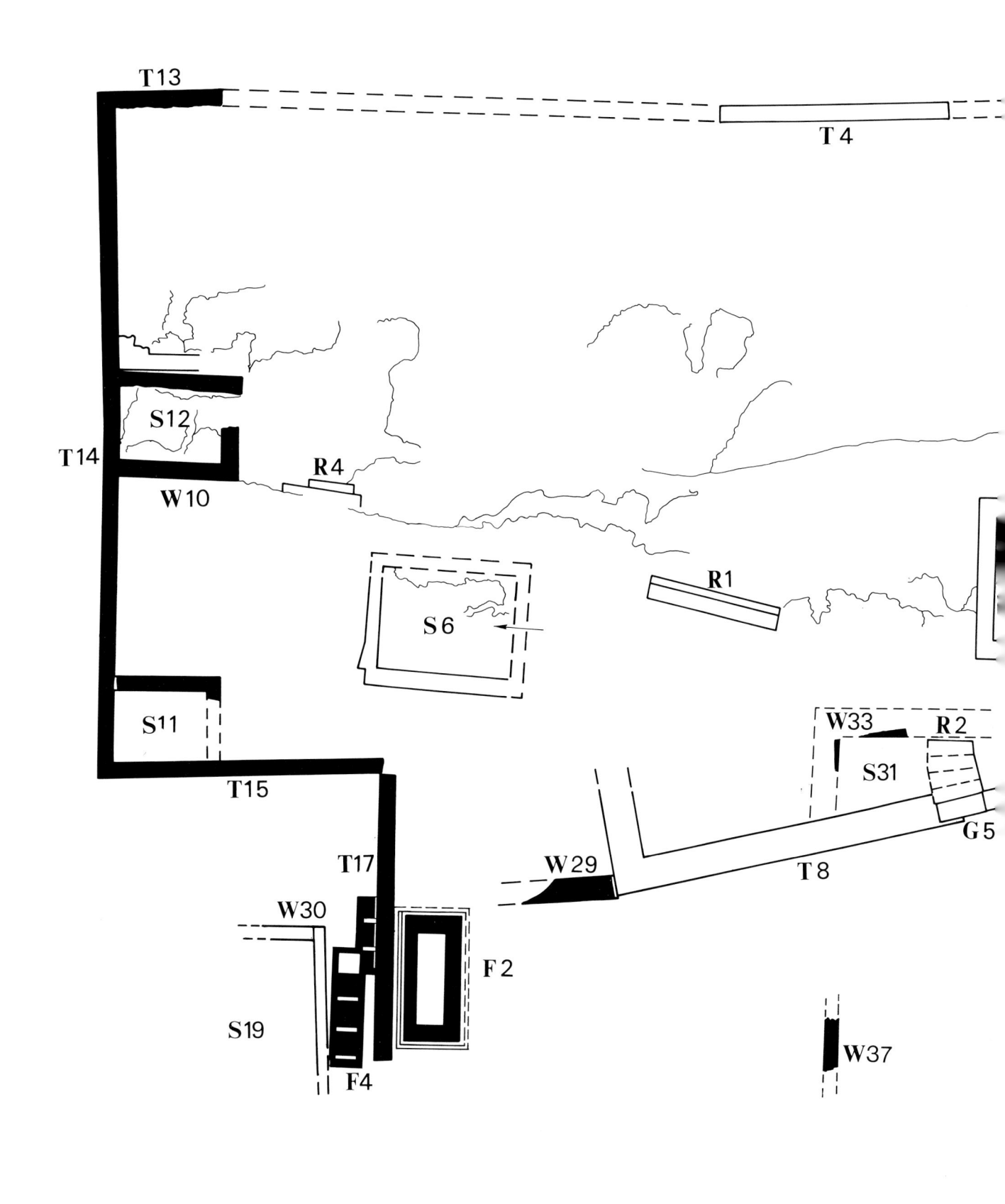

Plan D: Plan of the

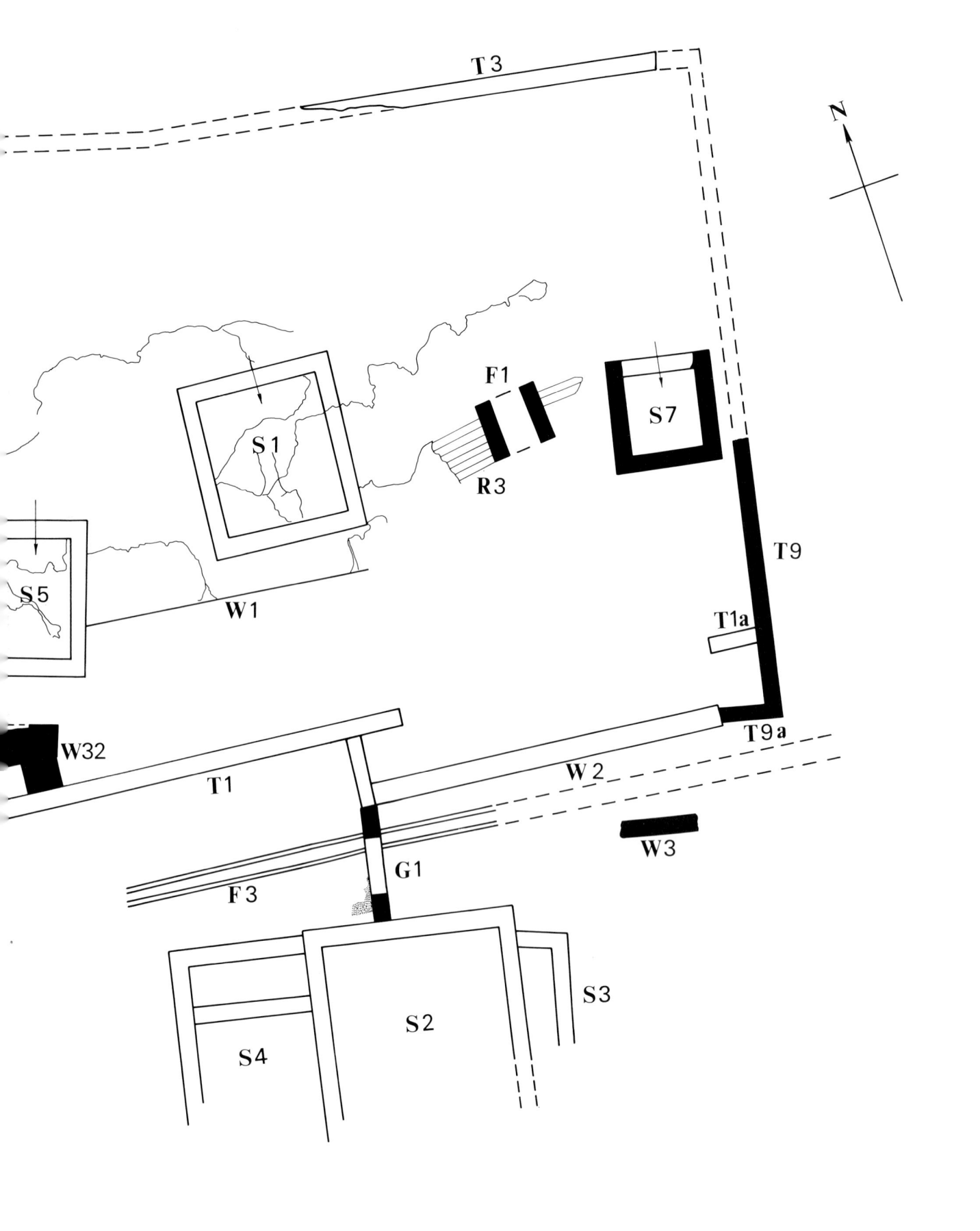

Hellenistic, pre-Imperial Roman period sanctuary.

Plan F: Evidential plan of sanctuary, showing lines of the major trans-site sections.

Masonry finish: 131

Modillion: 166

Monumental stairs: 177

Mortise: 49, 80

Mosaic: 103, 117, 121, 139, 161

Movement of people inside sanctuary grounds: 184-185

Orientation south of sacred buildings: 30, n. 13

Orthostate(s): 11, 57, 58, 59, n. 40, 60, 62, 70, 78, 82, 83, 94, 162

Pan tile: 166

Paint(ed): 151, 158, 159, 160, 162, 170

Painted interior, S7 Sacred House, comparisons with: 160–62

Periodization of the site: xiv

Perpend(s): 11, 44, 45, 46, 49, 53, 56, 58, n. 27, 59, n. 34, n. 40, 60, 62

Plaster(ed): 86, 141, 151, 159

Plug-shaped (as in masonry): 7, 9, 11, 18, 29, 41, 179, n. 28

Polygonal (as in masonry): 7, 9, 11, 18, 21, 24, 26, 29, 35, 39, n. 56, 41, 179, n. 28

Photo-rectified documentation of Middle Sanctuary wall: xv, 3

Pre-1916 excavations by the Italians: 6

Privacy of setting: 37, 177

Pry-hole: 4, 49, 80

Pseudoisodomic (as in masonry): 6, 11, 30, 35, 44, 45, 46, 47, 50, 55, 58, 59, n. 34, 60, 62, 71, 72, 74, 76, 78, 79, 81, 82, 83, 94, 98, 106, 109, 113, 114, 122, 149, 179, n. 28

Ptolemaic foot: 163, 167

Relationship of sanctuary to countryside to south: 37, 107, 177, 178

Rhea, Cretan mountain goddess rejected as precursor to Demeter: 37

Ritual dining: 119-20

Roof tile(s): 24, 41, 88, 102, 163, 166, 171, 172, 174

Rubble (as in masonry): 7, 9, 11, 21, 25, 26, 27, 30, 31, 33, 35, 38, 39, n. 56, 45, 50, 55, 58, 59, 62, n. 54, 63, 93, 132, 179

Sacred house, ancient terminology for: 98-101

Sacred House S6, its earliest floor: 15

Sanctuary,
  direction and orientation of its layout: 177-178
  foundation: 5
  hypothetical division into two parts: 24, 26, 35, 39, 57, 58, 179-180
  isolated setting: 37, 177
  movement of people inside its grounds: 184-185
  relationship to agricultural area to its south: 37, 107, 177, 178
  square meters covered by its grounds: 2

Sculpture (as in associated with sanctuary architecture): 6, 43, 91, 92, 93, 102, 103, 159, 162, 163, 181

Second Artemisium at Cyrene: 60-63
  block proportions, 63, 70-71

building periods: 60
late repairs and additions, 60, 62

Second colonization wave, ca. 580 B.C.: 36

Shell (as in fossilized, inclusions, micro-): 45, 74, 79, 130

Shrine house type, funereal associations of: 181-85

Silver coins, concentration of: 96

Sinkholes: 18, n. 11, 84, 115, 125, 174

Site stratigraphy: 3

Site sections: 3

Site terrain features, their symbolic value: 37-38

Site elevations: 3

Site survey: 4, n. 1

Site grid system: 4, n. 16

Slashed (as in obliquely or diagonally ... masonry): 126

Squared block (as in masonry): 7, 21, 24, 26, 30, 31, 35, 41

Stone, color or patination of: 73-74, 86, 109, 122, 123, 125, 130 153

Stone, quarry source: 74

Stone type: 130

Stone surface: 130-31

Stone surface, pecked or point-dressed: 74, 76, 78-79

Stone surface, diagonally/obliquely slashed or tooled: 131

Storage rooms in sanctuaries: 175, 177

Stucco: 86, 138, 161, 162, 163

Summary, contents of chapters: 1

Temene of Archaic sanctuaries: 38-39

Temene of later Classical and Hellenistic sanctuaries: 129

Temene, dual layouts: 39-41, 179-180.

Terra rossa, definition of: 14, n. 9

Thea Basileia, association with the Kore: 167-70

Thera, temple of the Thea Basileia, similarities between it and the S7 Sacred House: 167-70

Timber roof, Sacred House S7: 165, fig. 96, 166

Tooth-shaped painted design: 159

Triglyph: 62, 88

Votive dedications,
  earliest sanctuary: 5
  Hellenistic, early Roman sanctuary: 120-21
  later Archaic, early Classical sanctuary: 44, 102, 104
  later Classical Sanctuary: 107

Votives, display of: 105-106

Walls P2, P4 and P6, part of a single sacred edifice: 30

Water,
  appearance and uses of in Demeter sanctuaries: 144-47
  availability of: 37
  oracular use of: 145, n. 52

Women, importance to cult: 181

Wood floor: 93, 159

ARABIC SUMMARY

تركز هذه الدراسة على التطور المعماري لحرم ديميتر وبيرسيفوني المقدس الواقع خارج أسوار المدينة في قورينا (لوحه ١) بدءا من أساساته في أواخر القرن السابع ق . م حتى نهاية مرحلة ماقبل العصر الامبراطوري الروماني في عام ٣١ ق . م وإن أعمال التنقيب في الموقع سبق أن كانت موضوع تحليل مبدأي من قبل الكاتب بالاضافة الى أجزاء في ثلاثة مجلدات أخرى تتناول بالتفصيل أصنافا متنوعة من معثورات الحرم المقدس . وعليه يمكننا التوقع بأن القارىء قد أصبح على قدر من المعرفة بالحرم المقدس قبل أن يبدأ بقراءة الدراسة الحالية ، وسوف لا نحاول هنا أن نصف موقعها ، وظهورها العام ، وأعمال التنقيب مع أسباب التعرف عليها وبعض المسائل المبدأية الأخرى .

يمكن تعريف أي موقع أثري بأن تراكم زمني ومكاني معقد . والموقع الذي يستمر في الاستعمال لمدة ألف عام يمكن أن يتوقع منه أن يقدم شبكة معقدة من الاضمحلال ولعلها لا تعتبر عن نماذج نمو النظام الاجتماعي الذى أنتجها أكثر من عمارتها . والمراحل الأساسية لعمارة الحرم المقدس التي تناولها البحث هنا تظهر في ظلال الأحداث الرئيسية في تاريخ المدينة الأم بداية من التأسيس الاستيطاني في أوخر القرن السابع واستمرارا خلال توسعها اللامع والسريع إبان حكم الملوك الباتين ، وتصادمها المبكر مع السكان الليبيين الأصليين وصراعها مع مصر أثناء الاحتلال الفارسي . ويتبع هذا

تبلغ حوالي ١٩٠٠متر مربع . وبدلا من ذلك فإن ما شيد من جديد يظهر في مستوى الحمام المقدس الأعلى بشكل اساسي .

على أي حال سيتذكر قراء هذه السلسة للمجلدات الأربعة أن المراحل المبكرة هي التي اكتشفت فيها الغالبية العظمى من التقدمات النذرية والمعثورات الصغيرة في الحرم المقدس . ومن الناحية العدديه فإن العدد المكتشف في الموقع من المصابيح والفخار والمسكوكات ومعظم المعثورات المتنوعة الأخرى من العصر الروماني أقل بكثير من نماذج ماقبل العصر الروماني ومن نفس أنواع المعثورات . ولا يوجد ما يمثل الدمى الطينية والحجارة الكريحة المحزرة في المرحلة المتأخرة . والأستثناء الاساسي لهذا الوضع هو الزجاج ، والنقوش ، والمنحوتات الحجرية التي تتساوي في العدد في المرحلتين .

سبق هذه الدراسة نشر فخار شرق اليونان الأرخي والجزر ، واللاكوني ، الاتيكي الاسود ، والمزجج والهيلنيستي والروماني ، والجعران الأرخيه والكلاسيكية ، والأحجار الكريمة المحزرة ، وخواتم الأصابع المحفورة ، والزجاج ، والمعثورات الصغيرة المتنوعة ، وبقايا النباتات وسينشر الفخار الاتيكي الاحمر والمسكوكات في المجلد السادس . وماتبقى نشره هو الفخار الكورينثي ، الفخار الخشن والعادي ، والمصابيح ، الدمى الطينية ، نحت التماثيل الحجرية والنقوش . وسيكون نشر الفخار الخشن والعادي والمصابيح والنقوش خارج نطاق سلسلة تقارير قورينا النهائية .

- ٦ -

ويسرنى أيضا أن أسجل هنا الدعم والارشاد الذي تلقيناه من دائرة الآثار في قورينا برئاسة السيد بريك عطية طوال سنوات بعثتنا في ليبيا . ولهذا أود أن أعبر عن إمتناني واحترامي لكل مساعداته القيمة ، وبشكل خاص لأخلاصة الشجاع وصداقته خلال سنوات لم تكن سهلة دائما . ولقد ورد ذكر مساعداته الفنية في مقدمة المجلد الأول من هذه السلسة إلا أنها تستحق الذكر مرة أخرى ، لأنه بدون تعاونهم الفعال والأيجابي فأن العمل على القسم الخاص بالعمارة في هذا الموقع لم يكن بالامكان التقدم به . وان صالح ونيس أمين مكتبة دائرة الآثار ، وعبد الكريم الميار أمين مقتنيات المتحف ، ومحمد بوشريط سكرتير الدائرة ، وفضل الله عبد السلام ، مساعد مراقب الآثار وضابط اتصال البعثة ، وعبد الحميد عبد السعيد ، مدير الشئون الفنية في الدائرة ، يستحقوا جميعهم الثناء والشكر على أوجه الصداقة والمساعدة التي لا حصر لها . وفي الختام فقد حالفنا الحظ أن نعتمد على مواهب ثلاث من الشبان المساعدين المتحمسين في الدائرة الذين وافقوا على الانضمام الى البعثة الامريكية طوال موسمين كي يشرفوا ويسجلوا أعمال الحفر في عدد من القطاعات الأثرية الهامه . واحتفظ بالسجلات اليومية لأعمال الحفر كل من رمضان قويدر ، عبد القادر المزيني ، وأما فضل علي محمد (الذى يشغل في الوقت الحاضر منصب مراقب اثار قورينا) فقد قام بتدوين المعلومات الرئيسية لفهم عمارة الموقع .

رسمت من الشمال الى الجنوب . ووضع خط كل من مقاطع الموقع العرضية على خريطة الموقع بمقياس ١ : ٢٠٠ مثبت أو حجر بحجر (مخطط E) وسوف يشير مرجع هذا المخطط أن المقاطع التسعة من الشمال الى الجنوب رسمت بصورة متبادلة من الشرق (الاشكال ٢ ، ٤ ، ٦ ، ٨ ، ٩) والغرب (الأشكال ١ ، ٣ ، ٥ ، ٧) . ورسم المقطعان الشرقي - الغربي (الأشكال ١٠ ، ١١) من الشمال .

ألحقت المقاطع والارتفاعات برسومات إضافية تضمنت مخططات - المراحل الخمسة للموقع بمقياس ١ : ٢٠٠ (مخططات A - E) ومجموعات المخططات مفصلة لعناصر معمارية مفردة رسمت - إما بمقياس ١ : ٥٠ ، ١ : ٢٠ وأما الصورة الفوتوغرافية للارتفاع ومخطط الجدار الأمامي الهام للحرم المقدس الأوسط فقد عملت بمقياس ١ : ٢٠٠ (مخطط G) .

أخيرا إن منطقة الموقع ومخطط مربعاته المألوف الآن والذى ظهرفي كل من مجلدات السلسلة منذ المجلد الثاني يظهر من جديد في شكل معدل (شكل ١٢) كي يوضح شبكه المربعات في الموقع واحدا فوق الآخر أعلى رسم مركب للموقع من العصر الأرخي حتى الأسوار الهيلينيستية (بعبارة أخرى حذف أسوار ما بعد ٣١ ق . م .) فيما يخص شكل ١٢ يجب أن يفهم أنه ليست جميع أسواره بقيت مستعملة حتى نهاية العصر الهيلنيستي ، وبدلا من ذلك ، ان

ARABIC SUMMARY

أول العاملين اللازمين لتحديد الفترات الزمنية المعقدة للعمارة في الموقع هو ترتيب الطبقات الأثرية التي جرى شرحها مبدأيا في المجلد الأول من هذه السلسلة . وتقدم الفصول التالية مجموعة بمقياس ١ : ٢٠ من رسومات بيانية كي تساعد في توضيح النقاش في نص المحتويات الأثرية التي ارتبطت مع كل بناء مفرد .

ويخص العامل الثاني العلاقة المعمارية المتبادلة بين خصائص كل بناء منفصل وآخر والتي كثيرا ما تطرح أسئلة بالمستوى المناسب . وصورت هذه العلاقات من خلال مجموعات لرسوم الارتفاعات ، والتي الحقت بالصور الفوتوغرافية في بعض الأحيان . وقدم المزيد من المعلومات من خلال مجموعات تتكون من احدى عشر مقطعا عرضيا للموقع أعيد استنساخها بمقياس ١ : ٥٠ (الاشكال ١ - ١١) . ويسبب صغر قياسها فأن عرض الموقع لا يحاول أن يشير الى مستويات الطبقات وان القارىء الذي يرجع الى مقاطع الموقع العرضية يجب أن يحذر بأن العناصر المرسومة بالخط الأسود الثقيل توضح بقايا مبان قطعت بخط من المقطع الفعلي . وأن العناصر التي رسمت بخط باهت تشير إلى ما تبقى من عناصر معمارية رآها الرسام خلف مستوى كل مقطع مفترض ، وجرى إدخالها كي تقدم شكلا تقريبا أكثر لمنظر الموقع مع كل نقاط محطاته التسع . اثنان من مقاطع الموقع العرضية (الأشكال ١٠ ، ١١) يمتدان من الشرق الى الغرب ، بينما التسعة الباقية (الأشكال ١ - ٩)

- ٨ -

بإختصار اذن ، يمثل المجلد الحالي نشر الشكل المعماري للحرم المقدس لديميتر وبيرسيفوني وتوسعة الذى إمتد حوالي ٦٠٠ عام وغطى منطقة الحرم الأعلى والأوسط . وجاء هذا المجلد في الوسط ضمن سلسلة المجلدات كي يقدم فهما أكبر للمحتويات الأثرية التي وجدت ضمنها معظم المعثورات من الموقع بما في ذلك ما تم نشرة سابقا وما تبقى ينتظر النشر . وأن تقديم هذه الدراسة الآن بدلا من نهاية سلسلة المجلدات كما ذكر في البداية يقسم عمارة الحرم المقدس بشكل عشوائي الى مرحلتين .

وأعتقادنا أن الفوائد العملية للذين يرغبون في تتبع النتائج النهائيه للسلسلة المنشورة سوف تفوق المساوىء النظرية . يفهم من طول عمر الموقع المفترض أن مراحلة المعمارية قد بقيت فيما يمكن وصفه بحاله مكررة بالتحديد . وتغطي العمارة المتأخرة معظم الجدران التي شيدت قبل عام ٤٨٠ ق . م . وان بقاياها جديرة بأن تصور قطاعات مشوهة للمباني الأصلية التي كانت جزءا منها سابقا . والى جانب ذلك ، فإن المكونات المعمارية التي تعود الى ماقبل ٣١ ق . م والتي حافظت على وحدتها حتى نهاية استعمال الحرم المقدس ، مثل الحائط الغربى للحرم المقدس الأوسط ، والعديد من المنازل الدينية المستقلة والمختلفة ، قد دمرت تماما بزلزال منتصف القرن الثالث وزلزال منتصف القرن الرابع بعد الميلاد ، ولذلك فهي تعرف بشكل أفضل قليلا من المباني المعاصرة لها التي هدمت جزئيا في العصرين الكلاسيكي والهيلينستي وأن طول الزمن لم يتعامل مع هذا الموقع بلطف دائما .

- ٧ -

ب . كينرك ، التقارير النهائية ٣ : الفخار ....FW

الهيلينستي والروماني المزجج .

س ، لوينستام ، التقارير النهائية ٣ : الجعران ،................ IG

الأحجار الكريمة المخزرة ، وخواتم الأصابع المحفورة ..

أ ، أوليفر ، التقارير النهائية ٤ : الزجاج ....G

ب ، وردن ، التقارير النهائية ٤ : المعثورات الصغيرة المتنوعة ......MF

ت ، بترى ، التقارير النهائية ٤ : المسكوكات C

ى ، ماكفي ، التقارير النهائية ٤ : الفخار الأتيكى الأحمر ....RF

ج ، اولينبروك ، ينتظر النشر

الدمى الطينية والأواني البلاستيكيه ....TC

س ، كين ، ينتظر النشر ، نحت الحجارة ....S

أ و كوسيبالا ، ينتظر النشر ....CP

الفخار الكورنثي .

ى ، فابريكوتي ، ينتظر النشر ، الأسرجة L

ج ، رينولد ز ، ينتظر النشر ، النقوش I

حينما يوجد أي نوع من المعثورات سبق نشره نهائيا فأن إختصارة المناسب ورقم الكتالوج النهائي ضمنا في العمود الرابع للملحق ("نوع المعثور/ رقم الكتالوج ") للاشارة الى مكان نشرة ضمن السلسلة الحالية

- ١١ -

للدراسـات النهائيـة . وعلى سبيـل المثـال ، ("E.G./125") يشيـر الى ستامنوس لاكوني يورخه شاوس في ٥٢٥ - ٥٠٠ ق . م التقارير النهائية ٢ ، صفحة ٢٩ .

وفي حـالة المعـثـورات التي لم تنشـر بعد وتنتظر رقم الكتـالـوج النهـائي فإن نجمـة في مكان رقم الكتالوج تشيـر إلى أن التأريخ الموجود في الملحق قد أرسل إلي بانتظار عمليـة النشر في المستقبل . وعلى سبيـل المثـال ("TC/*") تشيـر الى دميـة طينيـة تنتظر رقم الكتـالـوج النهـائي في الدراسـة التـي سينشرها ج ، أو لينبروك للدمى الطينيه من الموقع .

وأخيـرا تقدم معلومات هامـة لمحتوى أثري لم يتم إدخالها في الدراسة النهـائية . واذا كـان تأريخـها يبـدو غيـر مـثـيـر للجـدل ، فـقد إدخالها تحت عنـوان وصفهـا القصيـر (مـثـال : سـراج) دون ذكـر مـرجع المؤلف رقـم الكتالوج .وفي العادة يرد وصفا أطول لمثل هذه المعثورات في النص الاساسي.

تضمن المعثورات في الملحق ١ عندما تقدم معلومات تأريخية ذات العلاقة فقط . وبعبـارة أخرى فقد حذف أى مـرجع الى المعثورات التي تحتل التأريخ المتوسط لأي نوع منها .

وعندما يدخل أكثر من معثورتين من أي دراسة ، فإن هذا يدل على تغيير رئيسي في الصنف ضمن الدراسة الفعليـة ، وعلى سبيـل المثال ، يمكن تضمين

قطعتي عملة فضية كي تدل على الانتشار الكامل لهذا النوع المعين من العملة ، بينما ادخال قطعة ثالثة يشير الى وجود قطعة برونزية من تاريخ متأخر .

وفي الختام يقدم الملحق ٢ قوائم نسب الارتفاع الى الطول لحجارة البناء التى وصفت في النص حينما توفرت تلك القياسات . ويستخدم الجدول طولين رئيسيين للكتله الحجرية التي يراها المشاهد في إرتفاع أي جدار (ارتفاع وعرض) ولا تأخذ في الأعتبار البعد الثالث (العرض) ، حيث أنه يفترض اذا كان لهذه الحسابات أي علاقة فإنها تكمن فيما اذا كان باستطاعة الناس رؤيتها وليس في صيغة غامضة ، ويمكن أن يدركها بناءوا الجدران فقط . ونظمت النتائج ضمن المراحل الزمنية العريضة لتطور الحرم المقدس التي إتبعت طوال هذه الدراسة . مثال على ذلك أوائل العصر الآرخي، أواخر العصر الآرخي ، أواخر / أو ائل العصر الكلاسيكي ، أواخر العصر الكلاسيكي ، هيلنييستي / قبل العصر الامبراطوري الروماني . وبينما يبدو أن هذه المعلومات تقدم بعض الأشارة الأضافية الى العصر فأننا نحذر القارىء من الأعتماد عليها بشكل كبير إذا جردت أو فصلت من عوامل أخرى .

بشيء من الثقة بوجود حرم مقدس أعلى ومتوسط (لوحه ٢) . وبينما هوية المباني الكلاسيكية من الحرم المقدس الأعلى ما تزال غير واضحة نوعا ما حتى العصر الهيلينستي ، فإن الدليل الممثل في المعثورات الأثرية لوجود ممارسة دينية على هذا المستوى جيد للغاية . ولا يحدث توسع الحرم المقدس الى الشمال نحو منحدر الوادي والى مستوى الحرم المقدس السفلي حتى العصر الأمبراطوري المبكر عندما يأخذ كل من مستويات الحرم المقدس الأعلى والسفلي المظاهر المعمارية لما سيبقى من خصائصها المعمارية قبل زلزال عام ٢٦٢ . وعلى سبيل المثال ، يعود المبنى الجنوبي الغربي المعمد من الحرم المقدس الأعلى (S17) ومدخل البوابه (S20) الى هذه المرحله ، مع مدخل الجسر (W14 / S28) الذي يربط الحرم المقدس السفلي مع السوق العام للمدينة (مخطط E) ويظهر أن معظم الكسر المعمارية من الحجر الكلي والرخام التى عثر عليها في الموقع مبعثرة في مستويات الزلزال على طول الحرم المقدس الأوسط يظهر أنها أصلا كانت ضمن أضافات الحرم المقدس الأعلى في العصر الأمبراطوري ، وهذه هي التي تشكل معظم المباني التي يمكن ترميمها في الحرم المقدس . والى جانب ذلك ، وبينما أن معظم الدليل المتبقي للنشاط المعماري حتى نهاية الهلينستي يتعلق بالحرم المقدس الأوسط ، ففي السنوات القليلة قبل دمار الحرم المقدس على أثر زلزال في القرنين الثالث والرابع من هذا العصر أضيف القليل من العمارة الجديدة على طول مساحته الداخلية التي

- ٥ -

ادخال المخطط لكل الجدران المعروفة قبل ٣١ ق . م الغرض منه ببساطة هو تسهيل مكان القارىء حيث يظهر محتويات طبقات أثرية منفصلة بالنسبة الى مبان أو عناصر معمارية مفترضة . ولمعرفة العصور التي تعود اليها المباني على القاريء أن يرجع الى مخططات E - A .

رتب الدليل التأريخي الذي جمع من المعثورات المتنوعة من الموقع أسفل ملحق ١ . ونظم الملحق بحيث يعرض طول العمر الزمني لكل نوع من المعثورات الذي يقدم دليلا له علاقة بتاريخ المحتوى الأثري المفرد وأشير اليه هنا حسب المنطقة ،المربع ، الطبقة أن المعلومات التأريخية الملخصة في الملحق جاءت من :

١- الدراسة النهائية للمعثورات التي إما سبق نشرها أو تصاحب هذه الدراسة.

٢- قوائم تأريخية أرسلت إلي بانتظار نشرها ضمن سلسلة تقارير قورينا النهائية.

يشار إلى كل دراسة نهائية بالاختصارات التالي :

ج ، شاوس ، التقارير النهائية ٢ : <u>فخار شرق</u>   EG ....

<u>اليونان ، الجزر واللاكوني</u> :

م . مور ، <u>التقارير النهائية</u> ٣ : <u>الفخار الأسود</u>   BF..............

<u>الأتيكي والفخار الأتيكي الأسود الملون</u> .

- ١٠ -

المجلد الخامس

ملخص

أتاح السيد جود تشايلد ، الذي كان يشغل منصب مراقب آثار شرق ليبيا في عام ١٩٦٧ للكاتب فرصة التنقيب في الحرم المقدس لديميتر وبيرسيفوني في قورينا . ولكن وفاته في العام التالى حرمت عملية التنقيب من فرصة التعاون مع أحسن من فسر الآثار الشاخصة من جيله ممن عملوا في ليبيا ، إلا أننا تعلمنا بعض الدروس من خلال مناقشاته الشخصيه المتكررة في المواقع الأثرية المفضلة لدية في المدن الخمس وكذلك في أوتيكا وقرطاجه حيث زارهما قبل وفاته المفاجئه ، وان تلك الدروس بقيت لتستفيد منها هذه الدراسة .

جاءت المساعدة في الكشف عن الجوانب المعقدة للحرم المقدس في معظم الأحيان من مصادر عديدة . وأنه ليسرنى أن أتمكن من تسجيل الشكر أخيرا لهذه المساهمات . ورد شكر أعضاء بعثة التنقيب الامريكيين في النسخة الانجليزية من هذا المجلد ولا حاجة لذكرها ثانية . وعلى أي حال قدمت جهات أخرى مساعدة هامة بصورة خاصة من البعثه الايطاليه برئاسة المرحوم ساندرو ستوكي ، الذي كان حتى وفاته العالم المختص بمواقع وعمارة المدن الخمس في شرق ليبيا . ولقد أثبت الدكتور كلاوديو فريجيريو ، المسؤول عن عمل بعثة الترميم الأيطالية المستمر في معبد زيوس في قورينا ، رغبته الطوعية ، في المشاركه في المعدات ، والخبرات والآراء ولن نذكر شيئا حول عواطفه وتشجيع صداقته .

- ١ -

تطور قورينا المضطرب المفهوم قليلا في القرن الخامس والذي ينتهي باغتيال آخر ملوكها ، وأن تجربتها الطويلة والمتقلبة مع الجمهوريين أدت الى فقدان حريتها إبان حكم البطالة واستيعابها بصورة نهائية من قبل الرومان في الوقت المناسب .

يتناول الفصل الثاني أقدم البقايا المسورة التي ترجع الى فترة الباتيين المبكرة (حوالي ٦٢٠ - ٥٠٠ ق . م .) .

ويناقش الفصل الثالث الحرم المقدس في الفترة الباتيه المتأخرة (حوالى ٥٠٠ - ٤٤٠ ق . م .) ويغطي الفصل الرابع العصر الجمهوري (حوالي ٤٤٠ - ٣٣٠ ق . م .) والفصل الخامس يتعرض الى تطور الحرم المقدس في العصرين الهيلينستي وبداية الروماني ٣٣٠ - ٣١ ق . م) ، ويشاراليه عادة بالفترة الهيلينيسية . وخلال هذه الفترات الأربعة يشهد الحرم المقدس تغيير داخلي دون أن يضحي بهويتة كحرم مقدس يقع على تل خارج أسوار المدينة ويضم منشآت دينية مستقلة متنوعة . وتضمنت التنازلات الرئيسية لموقعة المنحدر تنظيم سفح التل المنحدر إلى مجموعات من مناطق على هيئة مصاطب والتي مع الوقت تحددت بثلاث مناطق منفردة ومحددة ، الحرم المقدس الأعلى والأوسط والسفلي .

بقي من العمارة من أواخر العصر الباتي ما يكفي كي يجعلنا نتحدث